The United States
in World Affairs
1 9 7 0

The United States in World Affairs 1970

William P. Lineberry

Published for the COUNCIL ON FOREIGN RELATIONS

by SIMON AND SCHUSTER New York

The Council on Foreign Relations is a non-profit institution devoted to the study of political, economic, and strategic problems as related to American foreign policy. It takes no stand, expressed or implied, on American policy.

The authors of books published under the auspices of the Council are responsible for their statements of fact and expressions of opinion. The Council is responsible only for determining that they should be presented to the public.

For a partial list of Council publications see pages 357–359

FIRST PRINTING
SBN 671–21259–1
Library of Congress Catalog Card Number: 32–26065
Manufactured in the United States of America

PREFACE

With this volume covering events in 1970, the Council on Foreign Relations resumes publication, after a two-year hiatus, of its series entitled *The United States in World Affairs*. Like its predecessors, this volume surveys the development of American foreign policy in its global setting, striving toward a concise, descriptive analysis of one year's experience in the international life of the nation. It is designed less as a chronological account of the day-to-day efforts of American diplomacy than as one individual's view of the broad trends occupying the attention of the American public and its policy-makers and of the complex interplay of events at home and abroad that helped to shape them.

One of the founders of this series, Walter Lippmann, once said that the daily work of journalists amounts to little more than notes made by puzzled men. For this writer, the year 1970 seemed to offer more than its share of puzzling—even contradictory—phenomena. While the United States was moving consciously to lower its profile abroad and reorder its priorities at home, it nonetheless found time to involve itself in a short-lived invasion of the Communist sanctuaries in Cambodia, in a major initiative for peace in the Middle East, in substantial efforts to reform the United Nations and the international monetary system, overhaul its relations with Latin America, establish basic guidelines for its dealings with the black states of Africa, and to

5

pursue a broad range of complex negotiations and consultations with allies and adversaries alike. If a hesitant, world-weary America had really lost its way in the corridors of world power, as critics were inclined to suggest, the pace and drive of its diplomacy hardly seemed to confirm the judgment. In President Nixon's words, the world was entering a "new era," whose ultimate configuration, though momentarily unclear, would nonetheless differ markedly from the bipolar regime that had dominated the postwar period. In such a time of transition the crosscurrents stirred by shifting policies and changing relationships could only roil and muddy international waters never renowned for their sparkling clarity.

While President Nixon spoke repeatedly of a new era, however, the reader will see that the plan of this volume adheres more closely to the diplomatic patterns established in the past. After an examination of the internal constraints and broad policy formulations at work within America itself, the volume turns to an analysis of that staple center-piece in postwar diplomacy, the U.S.-Soviet relationship, and to the great issue of strategic arms limitation which occupied so many of the energies, hopes, and fears of both sides in 1970. Two other remnants of the past—both tied to and in some ways springing from the cold war era—are treated next: the conflict in the Middle East and the war in Indochina. The next three chapters of the book deal essentially with the Nixon Doctrine, its implementation in East Asia and its spreading ramifications in Latin America and Africa, where America's profile was clearly on the wane. The remaining chapters are given over to an examination of North Atlantic relations, of trade, monetary, and other economic affairs, and of America's role in the United Nations as it celebrated its 25th year of survival.

As a gesture to objectivity, the author has wherever possible allowed policy makers to state their views and policies in their own words, using for the most part such standard official sources as *The Department of State Bulletin* or the *Weekly Compilation of Presidential Documents*. The sources of all quotations and of other appropriate matter are indicated in the notes at the end of the volume, many of which cite the companion volume to this study, also published by the Council on Foreign Relations, *Documents on American Foreign Relations, 1970* (New York: Simon & Schuster, 1972). A chronology has also been appended, for readers interested in the dates of specific events, occasions, conferences, treaty signings, and the like.

The author is deeply grateful to the members and staff of the Council for their unfailing and generous assistance in the preparation of the manuscript. He is especially indebted to the research and editorial assistance of Elaine P. Adam, whose advice, experience, and patience proved invaluable; to Richard P. Stebbins, John C. Campbell, and David W. MacEachron, all of the Council staff, who undertook to read the manuscript in its entirety, offering many helpful suggestions for its improvement; to Helena Stalson, Helen Caruso, William Diebold, Jr., William Barnds, Andrew Pierre, James Chace, and George S. Franklin, Jr., also with the Council, for their assistance and comments with regard to various individual chapters; and to Donald Wasson, Janet M. Rigney, and other members of the Foreign Relations Library staff for their courteous and efficient support. The author is also indebted to those members of the Council's Committee on Studies who gave of their time and talents to review various portions of the manuscript—in particular to the Committee's Chairman, Grayson Kirk, and to William P. Bundy, Caryl P. Haskins, Carl Kaysen, Waldemar A. Nielsen, and Hamilton Fish Armstrong. Appreciation is also due to E. D. Weldon, our cartographer; to Grace Griffin, Production and Promotion Manager for the Council; and to Robert W. Valkenier for his help in the final stages of the editorial process. In gratefully acknowledging the assistance of these and many others, of course, the author reserves for himself ultimate responsibility for the book as a whole.

It would be improper to conclude without acknowledging a special debt for the generous guidance and comfort afforded this writer by Richard P. Stebbins, the author of this series for many years past and currently editor, with Alba Amoia, of the *Political Handbook and Atlas of the World* and its supplements, *The World This Year*. His graceful prose and high standards of scholarship have established a tradition for this series hard indeed to maintain, and readers will be pleased to know that a catch-up volume, covering the years 1968–69, is currently in process under his able direction.

W.P.L.

January 1972

CONTENTS

1 : "A New Approach . . . A New Era"

That the nation had undergone fundamental change in the decade since 1960 there could be no doubt. Americans had been on the move, heading out of their cities and into the suburbs, out of the hinterland and toward the coasts, shifting south and westward toward the sun and the last remaining open spaces, as the 1970 census revealed. They had edged past 204 million in total population and had very nearly doubled their gross national product. They drove more cars, owned more appliances, took more vacations than ever before in their history. And yet, by the end of the decade, they were clearly a troubled people, uncertain of their own future, divided over their role in the world. They had entered the 1960's on a brisk note of confidence. "Let every nation know," John F. Kennedy had told the world in his Inaugural Address, "whether it wishes us well or ill, that we shall pay any price, bear any burden, meet any hardship, support any friend, oppose any foe to assure the survival and the success of liberty." [1] The words contrasted sharply with President Richard M. Nixon's own appraisal of America's mission in his first State of the Union message delivered January 22, 1970. [2] "Neither the defense nor the development of other nations can be exclusively or primarily an American undertaking. . . . We shall be faithful to our treaty commitments, but we shall reduce our involvement and our presence in other nations' affairs."

13

Far more than its demographic profile or its accumulated store of wealth, America's mood had changed. The political rhetoric that had summoned a nation to hardship and sacrifice at the dawn of the 1960's had assumed, by 1970, a strangely hollow ring. To say that Americans had grown weary of the world and its endless round of crises might be to exaggerate. To say that they were tired of paying the price and bearing the burdens, bored by the shrilly-pitched ideological contest with Communism, disillusioned, even, by efforts to secure racial justice and eliminate poverty at home might be to overstate the case. And yet there was an element of truth in all of it. The 1960's had proved an exceptionally unsettling time—unsettling to old assumptions, uncongenial to old solutions. And Americans, as if responding to some ancient, instinctual drive, seemed once again to be turning inward for renewal.

Certainly the shift in America's attitude had found good and sufficient cause in the traumatic events of the 'sixties. That turbulent decade had seen three of the nation's ablest young leaders—President Kennedy, his brother Senator Robert F. Kennedy, and civil rights leader Martin Luther King, Jr.—shot down in an outburst of violence that had shocked the country to its core. It had seen the rise of a black nationalist movement and a youthful counterculture whose radical extremes sought, through their own disruptive acts of violence, the ultimate destruction of the Republic itself. And above all, perhaps, it had witnessed the tormenting spectacle of a nation seemingly at war with itself over a conflict halfway around the world in Vietnam —a conflict which, in taking over 44,000 American lives by the end of 1970 had dragged on to become the longest and surely one of the bitterest fought in the nation's history. For America and its people, it had become a telling sign of the times that 14 out of 16 places on the F.B.I.'s "most wanted" list of criminals were occupied by suspected "revolutionaries," most of them young, some of them black, and all of them allegedly committed to the revolutionary overthrow of the system they despised.

That the close of the decade had brought a troubled America to something of a crossroads was only too evident in the sudden outpouring of apocalyptic literature. No doubt every time of trouble casts up its prophets, but the year 1970 seemed peculiarly characterized by both the number of its prophetic voices and the contradictory nature of what they were saying. In the spring of the year political

scientist Andrew Hacker of Cornell University, seeing moral enerva-
tion and decay all around him, gloomily pronounced "the end of the
American era," in a book of the same title. ". . . [T]he American
temperament has passed the point where self-interest can subordinate
itself to citizenship," [3] wrote Hacker. "Contemporary Americans simply do not want—and will not accept—political leadership that makes
more than marginal demands on their emotions or energies." [4] America, Hacker concluded, was "about to join other nations of the world
which were once prepossessing and are now little more than plots
of bounded terrain." [5] It had "no more lessons to impart to others"
and had "ceased to be a model for people beyond our borders." [6]

This dismal diagnosis was shortly followed into print by what
could only be called its antithesis. In *Between Two Ages: America's
Role in the Technetronic Era,* another political scientist and former
member of the Department of State's Policy Planning Council—
Zbigniew Brzezinski—laid it down that, far from collapsing into moral
ruin, America was in fact leading the world into a revolutionary
new age, one "that is shaped culturally, psychologically, socially, and
economically by the impact of technology and electronics" (hence
the term "technetronic").[7] "In spite of its domestic tensions," Brzezinski wrote, "indeed, in some respects because of them, the United
States is the innovative and creative society of today . . . the focus
of global attention, emulation, envy, admiration, and animosity." [8]
That, said Brzezinski, was something the hot-eyed revolutionaries of
the New Left had failed to grasp, thereby making themselves "an
essentially negative and obsolescent force . . . more interesting as a
symptom of social change than for [their] programmatic message." [9]
"What makes America unique in our time is that confrontation with
the new is part of the daily American experience. For better or for
worse, the rest of the world learns what is in store for it by observing
what happens in the United States." [10]

The Brzezinski thesis was seconded late in the year by a French-
man, Jean-François Revel, who joined the fray with a book that won
wide attention in Europe. ". . . [T]here is a revolutionary America,
and an American revolution which is wholly new and which has
nothing to do with the revolutions of the nineteenth century," Revel
wrote. For this very reason, he maintained, Europeans did not understand, or chose to disregard, what was happening because they felt
they had lost their leading role in the creation of new precepts of civili-

zation.[11] Back across the Atlantic, the theme was being elaborated in still another way by Charles Reich, a professor of law at Yale University. America was indeed creating "new precepts of civilization," Mr. Reich contended in his controversial book, *The Greening of America,* but it was the youthful rebels and flower children denounced by Brzezinski as "negative and obsolescent" who were doing it. In their rejection of Vietnam, the military-industrial complex and all the glittering paraphernalia of the "technetronic" society, they were lifting mankind to a new level of political and social consciousness and paving the way for a saner, more loving future.[12]

What could one make of such a diversity of views and forecasts? It hardly seemed possible that Hacker, Brzezinski, *et al.* were writing about the same country. And yet taken together, they said a great deal indeed about the condition of America in 1970: a nation in profound transition, offering up enough movements, trends, and troubles, enough rays of light and foreshadowings of doom to feed a thousand theorists of its future. However pressing the demands of the outside world, America had once again become the focus of its own concern. And the sporadic thud of exploding bombs from New York to San Francisco (more than 1,600 in all over the course of the year) seemed at the time to underscore the urgency of its problems.

1 : Bipolar America?

The pattern was disturbing. On March 4, an explosion had ripped through a fashionable townhouse in the Greenwich Village section of New York, killing two young people and injuring several others seen fleeing the scene. Americans were subsequently shocked to learn that the townhouse was actually being used as an arsenal and bomb factory by youthful militants suspected of belonging to the extremist Weatherman faction of the radical Students for a Democratic Society. Shortly thereafter, New York City experienced one of the greatest bomb scares in its history when three blasts went off almost simultaneously at the offices of the IBM Corporation, Mobil Oil Company, and General Telephone and Electronics. An explanatory note, signed by a group calling itself "Revolutionary Force 9," charged that "All three [companies] profit not only from death in Vietnam but also from Amerikan [*sic*] imperialism in all of the Third World." [13]

Such were the oft-cited grievances of militant American youth, some of whom had shifted, in the course of one decade, from the tactics of passive resistance to an active strategy of urban terror. In the lexicon of young revolutionaries, in fact, 1970 had become the year of the urban guerrilla, a testament to the gathering cult of political violence at home.

The nation had been born in revolution. Was it about to die in one as well? Apparently not, for as one analysis of student protests indicated early in the year,[14] the overwhelming majority of young Americans were still committed to nonviolent tactics, while radical New Left groups had shown themselves a relatively minor factor in the protests that did take place. By late spring, moreover, with militants indicted or already on trial in New York, New Haven, Chicago, and Seattle (and on the run, apparently, elsewhere), the bombings tapered off. Even the "long, hot summer" of racial violence, looting, and burning which had become the nightmare of the 1960's had blessedly failed to materialize in 1970. But the underlying tensions were still there, tearing at the fabric of national unity, revealing, in the words of former Chief Justice Earl Warren, "a divisiveness in our society to a degree of intensity that has not been equaled in the past 100 years." [15] Above all there were the domestic agonies that sprang from America's involvement in Vietnam.

The nation had already seen thousands of its draft-age youth flee to Canada, ostensibly to avoid personal participation in that conflict. It had seen another 400 to 500 resisters seek asylum in Sweden—in a reversal of America's traditional role as a place of refuge for others. It had even grown accustomed to the antiwar demonstrations that had been taking place across the land for several years past. But for future historians looking back, 1970 might well be counted as the year when, for America as a whole, the Vietnam issue shifted from a politically frustrating venture, which it had long since become, to a nationally demoralizing one, freighted with scandalous revelations and raising fundamental questions about the kind of society America had become. First came charges, subsequently verified by the Army, that more than 100 South Vietnamese men, women, and children had been killed at Mylai village in 1968, in what could only be described as a massacre perpetrated by American troops. This was followed by the report of another Army inquiry, accusing 14 officers, including the Superintendent of the United States Military Academy at West Point, of involvement in the suppression of information about the mass killings. There were other charges: that American officers in Vietnam had been fraudulently awarded medals for valor based on acts of heroism invented by enlisted men under orders; that the chemical defoliants and herbicides employed by United States forces in South Vietnam had systematically destroyed wide swaths of that nation's productive land and food supply, causing untold damage to the very people Americans were presumably trying to save. And, of course, there were the widely publicized trials of those accused of the killings at Mylai, with their detailed revelations of the apparent barbarities that took place there.

As though all these developments were not tormenting enough for the nation's conscience, there was also the tragedy at Kent State University. The nation had witnessed numerous—even violent—demonstrations against the war before, but not until 1970 had Americans been killed in the course of such protests. Throughout the winter of 1969–70, President Nixon had been pressing forward with a program of troop reductions designed to deescalate America's involvement in the Vietnam conflict. But on April 30, he reversed himself for the moment, ordering American units into Cambodia in what seemed a sudden reescalation—even broadening—of the war. The effect on youthful protesters against the war was galvanic. Across the land, students mounted demonstrations and struck their classes. And then, on the campus of Kent State University in the rolling hills of northern Ohio, several days of disorder climaxed in a bloody confrontation between student protesters and Ohio National Guardsmen. When the firing had stopped, four students lay dead.

"A nation driven to use the weapons of war upon its youth is a nation on the edge of chaos." Such was the unanimous verdict of the President's Commission on Campus Unrest,[16] headed by former Governor William W. Scranton of Pennsylvania and established in the wake of the Kent State slayings. The Commission warned that "We are now in grave danger of losing what is common among us through growing intolerance of opposing views on issues and of diversity itself. . . . If this trend continues, if this crisis of understanding endures, the very survival of the nation will be threatened." In an extraordinary letter of protest to President Nixon,[17] Secretary of the Interior Walter J. Hickel expressed similar concern. Young Americans, he wrote, "believe they have no opportunity to communicate with government, regardless of Administration, other than through violent confrontation. . . . [W]e have an obligation as leaders to communicate with our youth and listen to their ideas and problems."

In part at least for his unsolicited advice, Secretary Hickel became on November 25 the first member of the Nixon Cabinet to be asked to resign. The President, for his part, received the Scranton Commission's report with coolly polite "personal thanks." In a letter to Scranton of December 10,[18] Nixon defended the right of youth to dissent, but denounced any group's "right to use physical coercion, disruption or violence to achieve its political end or social objectives." In a speech delivered at Kansas State University on September 16,[19] the President had already fixed the source of campus turmoil from his own point of view. Denouncing the "small bands of destructionists" who had "been allowed to impose their own rule of arbitrary force," Nixon declared that "it is time for the responsible university and college administrators, faculty and student leaders to stand up and be counted. Because we must remember," he continued, "only they can save higher education in America. It cannot be saved by government." In the President's view, "One of the greatest disservices that the disrupters have done in fact is . . . to reflect unfairly on those millions of students, like those in this room, who do go to college for an education, who do study, who do respect the rules, and who go on to make constructive contributions to peaceful change and progress in this country." Looking out over the smiling young faces before him, listening to their cheers, the President could hardly agree with the gloomy warnings laid down in the report of his own hand-picked commissioners or in the letter of his Interior Secretary. "The heart of America," he told his audience, "is sound."

And, indeed, if the remainder of the year were any indication, the President appeared to be right. The fall term found the nation's campuses in a surprisingly quiescent, almost sober, mood. And when, in the middle of November, United States forces carried out a quick series of bombing raids over North Vietnam, in concert with an unsuccessful attempt to rescue American prisoners of war by force, the universities barely seemed to stir. Even a hard-fought mid-term election campaign, in which Vice-President Spiro T. Agnew had denounced the President's opponents in Congress as "radiclibs," "pusillanimous pussyfooters," and "nattering nabobs of negativism," seemed unable to provoke the kind of passionate response that had almost come to be expected in American political life. Certainly, if America were undergoing a revolution—technetronic or otherwise—the voting results of the November 3 elections failed to reflect it. For while Democrats made marginal gains across the country as a whole, and while some of Mr. Nixon's staunchest supporters went down to defeat, so did such vocal opponents of his Vietnam policy as Senators Charles E. Goodell of New York and Albert Gore of Tennessee.

It was evident, in fact, that Mr. Nixon's own effort to wind down the war was having its effect on campus, and it was even possible that "the great silent majority" to which he so frequently appealed for support during the 1970 campaign—men and women frightened by the climate of violence, fearful of the rising incidence of crime and the growing use of drugs and narcotics among their children, angry at what they termed the "permissiveness" of the authorities—supported his views on these issues. For if 1970 had seen the rise of the urban guerrilla in America, it had also seen the rise of the "hardhat" and the "backlash." It was a year when presidential aide Daniel P. Moynihan, a social scientist known for his liberalism, confidentially advised a policy of "benign neglect" with respect to the nation's racial issue,[20] when American flag decals sprouted on car windows in apparent reaffirmation of the "lost" virtue of patriotism, and when a group of New York construction workers, wearing the hard hats of their trade, took it upon themselves to waylay a student-led protest against the Kent State killings, knocking about demonstrators and even a few innocent bystanders in the violent exercise of their wrath.

It was, of course, precisely this sort of polarization that Mr. Nixon had come to office vowing to dispel. The theme of his administration, he had told the nation after his election in 1968, would be to "Bring us together." Yet at times it appeared that his own domestic political strategy, with its emphasis on conservative Southern support, and even his own rhetoric (as when, shortly before the Kent State slayings, he referred to certain student dissidents as "bums"),[21] was accomplishing the opposite. In the tradition of his predecessors, the President was clearly seeking to carve out the "great middle ground" of American politics as his own. But if left and right were easily discernible in America in 1970, the great middle ground was exceedingly elusive by comparison. For much of the year the nation seemed headed in two conflicting—even opposite—directions, and it was undoubtedly Mr. Nixon's foremost problem to gather everyone back at stage center, where all could proceed, in unison, to advance.

2 : *Problems Old and New*

The President had gained his office in 1968 with a narrow 43.41 per cent of the popular vote; even so, he brought to his task a keenly developed political sensibility, sharply honed by years of hard work on the political hustings, and a long cultivated interest in foreign affairs. Confronted by a war that had been instrumental in driving his predecessor, Lyndon B. Johnson, from seeking reelection, and by a climate of growing domestic discord, his initial instinct was to call for a lowering of voices at home and a lowering of the nation's profile abroad. In place of the old "confrontation" politics of the cold war, he had foretold a new "era of negotiation," [22] and in many ways 1970 had unfolded as a test of that proposition—a year of negotiation designed to gauge the climate for conciliation abroad while responding to a deep-seated yearning for peace at home. On January 20, after a hiatus of two years, the United States Ambassador to Poland, Walter J. Stoessel, Jr., resumed talks in Warsaw with the Communist Chinese Ambassador Lei Yang. On April 16 and again on November 2, the second and third rounds of the Strategic Arms Limitation Talks (SALT) between the United States and the Soviet Union got under way in Vienna and Helsinki, respectively. On August 7 the efforts of Secretary of State William P. Rogers to spur both sides toward a negotiated settlement of the Arab-Israeli conflict bore fruit when a 90-day cease-fire and military standstill went into effect along the Suez Canal, and U.N. Special Representative Gunnar V. Jarring resumed his role as mediator—an agreement shakily extended for another 90 days on November 5. And throughout the year, week after week, negotiations aimed at stopping the bloodshed in Vietnam ground on in Paris with representatives of the Provisional Revolutionary Government of South Vietnam (the Vietcong) and the Democratic Republic of Vietnam (D.R.V.) on one side, and the United States and the Republic of Vietnam on the other. There were innumerable other talks under way as well—among the four allied powers of World War II over the perennial issue of Berlin, within the councils of the United Nations over such varied problems as the uses of the seabed and the need for improved peacekeeping machinery, among the Western allies over the purposes and direction of their various alliances.

"Jaw, jaw," as Sir Winston Churchill once said, is no doubt better than "war, war." And yet, for all the talking, 1970 did not speak decisively to the great issues that were troubling mankind in general or America in particular. As we shall see in later chapters, the renewed dialogue between Washington and Peking had barely begun before it was broken off on May 19—a token of Chinese displeasure with President Nixon's decision [23] to send American troops into Cambodia after the downfall there March 18 of Prince Norodom Sihanouk as head of state. The SALT negotiations, though conducted in a business-like atmosphere of cautious optimism, had failed to make the kind of headway that Secretary Rogers had privately judged essential as a measure of the genuineness of Soviet intentions. In a similar vein, the Rogers initiative for peace in the Middle East, when not threatened with destruction by the terrorist tactics of the Palestinian commandos, seemed for a time to be cast into grave doubt by Soviet and Egyptian violations of the standstill agreement along the Suez Canal. Even the Soviet-American cultural exchange agreement for 1970–71, signed in Washington on February 10,[24] was thrown awry late in the year when Moscow, retaliating for what it termed "provocations by Zionist thugs" against Soviet artists and officials in the United States, announced on December 11 the cancellation of scheduled visits by the Bolshoi Theater's opera and ballet companies.[25] And through it all, like some forlorn theme, ran the bitter deadlock in Paris. That the Vietnam war was winding down, that fewer and fewer Americans were being killed as the year progressed, that, indeed, there seemed at long last to be some faint glimmer of light at the end of that tunnel—such developments were far less a tribute to the seemingly irreconcilable course of the peace talks in Paris than to the Nixon administration's unilateral decision to reduce America's involvement in the conflict and "bring the boys home."

So if the world had entered a new era of expanded negotiation, its nations had yet to prove themselves altogether responsive to the sort of compromise solutions that successful negotiations normally entail. As a result, most of the old problems that had dogged the 'sixties—the tension in Soviet-American relations, the troubles within their respective alliances, the ever-spiraling race in strategic arms, the conflicts in the Middle East and in Vietnam—were still there, lapping unresolved at the shores of the 'seventies. And meanwhile, new problems and developments were crowding in upon the old. For example, 1970 saw a sudden resurgence of diplomacy in the heart of Europe as Chancellor Willy Brandt of the Federal Republic of Germany moved swiftly—and some feared recklessly—to normalize his country's relations with the Communist states to the East. It witnessed the rise to power in Chile of the Western Hemisphere's first freely elected Marxist President, Salvador Allende Gossens, who quickly set about establishing a "revolutionary" foreign and domestic program that was bound to cause discomfort—or worse—in Washington.

The year also saw a new tide of protectionist sentiment gathering strength in the United States as the nation, struggling to cope with the dual problems of inflation and rising unemployment, cast about for ways to ease its economic troubles—or at least to share them with the world. It was a year that brought new tremors of change in Eastern Europe, as the regime of Wladyslaw Gomulka in Poland fell in the wake of bloody rioting over food prices. It saw the death—and awaited the unknown consequences thereof—of two key figures on the world stage: President Charles de Gaulle, the father of modern French foreign policy, and Egyptian President Gamal Abdel Nasser, the leading architect of modern Arab nationalism. And it witnessed a growing concern, both within and without America, over that unwelcome byproduct of industrial affluence known as environmental pollution—a problem whose international dimension was underscored late in the year when Congress, in part at least out of concern to prevent further fouling of the earth's atmosphere, called a provisional halt to America's multibillion-dollar supersonic jet transport program.

Most disturbing of all, perhaps, 1970 was marked by a sudden upsurge in international terrorism—by a rash of political kidnappings and aircraft hijackings which were carried out, in most instances, by extremist political groups pursuing political ends. For centuries men had been struggling to institutionalize international violence, at least to the extent of establishing rules of war and even certain minimal procedural requirements for acts of aggression and conquest. But in 1970 a host of obscure, vaguely Marxist terrorist organizations, ranging from the Popular Front for the Liberation of Palestine and the Front for the Liberation of Quebec to the so-called "Tupamaros" of Uruguay, suddenly took it upon themselves to seize airliners loaded with passengers or to snatch diplomats and government officials off the streets and to hold them all as hostages to a list of political demands that usually included the freeing of fellow terrorists from prison. In 1970 alone, the German Ambassador to Guatemala, Count Karl-Maria von Spreti; an American police adviser in Uruguay, Dan Mitrione; Quebec Labor Minister Pierre Laporte; and former Argentine President Pedro Eugenio Aramburu were all murdered in such circumstances, while the assassination of Chile's army commander, Gen. René Schneider, in a bungled kidnapping attempt proved that rightists were not averse to such tactics either. As *The Economist* of London was moved to exclaim with exasperation: "If you are filled with rage because the twentieth century is as imperfect as the others, or because the injustice that hurts you most has not been removed from the world, or just because you cannot get other people to agree with you, you are entitled to grab the first person you see on the street and hold him at gunpoint in a cellar until the government buys you off." [26]

Yet for some observers, such acts of terrorism signified less a suddenly swelling tide of anarchy than a shift in the world generally away from the international polarization that had characterized the early cold war years and toward a new and portentous polarization within national societies themselves. Almost invariably, the demands of the kidnappers and hijackers were tied to some real or alleged grievance that, with the notable exception of the Palestinian hijackers, sprang from within rather than from without the countries in which they lived. "There is a new threat to the peace of the nations, indeed to the very fabric of society," Britain's newly elected Prime Minister Edward Heath told the United Nations on the occasion of its 25th anniversary in October 1970. "In the last few years there has been the growth of a cult of political violence, preached and practised not so much between States as within them. It is a sombre thought that in the 1970s civil war, rather than war between nations, will be the main danger." [27]

3 : In Search of a Policy

Of all these developments, President Nixon and his aides were only too painfully aware. "We could see that the whole pattern of international politics was changing," Mr. Nixon told the Congress in his first "State of the World" message, published on February 18.[28] "Our challenge was to understand that change, to define America's goals for the next period, and to set in motion policies to achieve them." On his first major trip outside the country after taking office (February 23–March 2, 1969), Mr. Nixon had touched base with his North Atlantic Treaty Organization (NATO) allies in Europe, doing more listening than talking in the course of it. Then from July 24–August 3, 1969, during a swing through the Pacific, the President had set forth an initial formulation of what was to become a central building block of his administration's foreign policy—the first vague outlines of what he would soon be calling "the Nixon Doctrine." At a news conference on the island of Guam on July 25,[29] the President spoke (for indirect attribution only) of America's traditional concern for developments in Asia and of the country's historic role as a Pacific power. But the time had come, the President added, to avoid the kind of policy that would make countries in Asia so dependent upon the United States that it would again be dragged into conflicts such as the one in Vietnam. America would keep its treaty commitments, the President emphasized, in a gesture of continuity to the era that was supposedly ending. It would continue to defend its allies from external attack. But the United States was also going to encourage, and had a right to expect, its Asian allies to take increased responsibility for their own security, and particularly so in those cases in which an internal threat was apparent.

Even in this initial formulation, it was clear that the Nixon Doctrine constituted a break with the past to the extent that it augured a new and lower posture for the United States—at least as far as Asia was concerned. Throughout most of the 'sixties, Washington had been concerned—indeed, almost obsessed—with the problem of actively countering those Communist-inspired "wars of national liberation," often civil in character, which former Premier Nikita S. Khrushchev had advertised as a key weapon in Soviet foreign policy. It was a concern that had led the nation into the quicksands of Vietnam, and it was one, apparently, that Mr. Nixon was determined to avoid. In a broad sense, this was a concession to the changed political realities, both domestic and foreign, pressing in upon him. But it was also very much in line with the strategic thinking of his chief adviser on national security affairs in the White House, Dr. Henry A. Kissinger.

A German-born professor of government at Harvard, and the

author of numerous books and articles on foreign affairs, Kissinger had been a foreign policy adviser to Governor Nelson A. Rockefeller of New York during the 1968 scramble for the Republican presidential nomination. He had frequently described himself after his appointment to the White House staff as a man who objectively set forth the options upon which presidential decisions were based—a sort of neutral clearing house of ideas for the President in the realm of foreign policy—but it was evident from the start that his own substantive thinking was strongly influencing Nixon's course. It was Kissinger's plan for a phased withdrawal of American troops from Vietnam,[30] prepared on behalf of the Rockefeller campaign, that became the core element in the President's own "Vietnamization" policy, which called upon Saigon gradually to assume more and more responsibility for South Vietnam's security. It was reportedly Kissinger's views on negotiating with the Russians that prompted the President to back away from his own campaign commitment to a policy of "military superiority" as the best guarantee of America's security and to enter instead, at a point of approximate nuclear parity, into the SALT talks with Moscow. And it was Kissinger's belief that the United States should begin yielding some of its far-flung defense responsibilities to its allies that eventually took root and flowered into the Nixon Doctrine itself.[31]

By 1970, at any rate, it was apparent that the various new lines of policy being spun out from the White House were ready for amalgamation into some sort of coherent framework. The result was the President's State of the World message. From its very first page, the President strove to make clear that the United States was altering its course in the world in an effort to come to grips with the realities of change. "This first annual report on U.S. foreign policy is more than a record of one year," Mr. Nixon declared. "It is this Administration's statement of a new approach to foreign policy, to match a new era of international relations." [32]

As solid evidence of this "new approach," the President promptly set forth the example of the Nixon Doctrine, which for the first time was officially spelled out in considerable detail. "Its central thesis," stated the President, "is that the United States will participate in the defense and development of allies and friends, but that America cannot—and will not—conceive *all* the plans, design *all* the programs, execute *all* the decisions and undertake *all* the defense of the free nations of the world." In refinement of this general (and in some ways none too novel) proposition, the President cautioned that "We have no intention of withdrawing from the world. . . . But a more balanced and realistic American role in the world is essential if American commitments are to be sustained over the long pull. In my State of the Union Address, I affirmed that 'to insist that other nations play a role is not a retreat from responsibility; it is a sharing of responsibility.' This is not a way for America to withdraw from its indispensable role in the world. It is a way—the only way—we can carry out our responsibilities."

It was apparent from the President's carefully worded qualifications that the Nixon Doctrine, whatever else it might be, was not meant to provide a screen behind which America could retreat headlong into isolation. And yet it was also apparent that the doctrine had been considerably broadened since its birth less than a year before in Guam. In his State of the World message the President sought to link the basic thrust of the doctrine to the broad concept of a new form of partnership with America's allies everywhere—one in which the allies would be expected to pull more weight and the United States, by implication, less. "Others now have the ability and responsibility to deal with local disputes which once might have required our intervention," he said. "Our contribution and success will depend not on the frequency of our involvement in the affairs of others, but on the stamina of our policies. This is the approach which will best encourage other nations to do their part, and will most genuinely enlist the support of the American people."

It was a theme that ran through the President's discussion of United States policy generally. In Europe, the President emphasized, "Genuine *partnership* must increasingly characterize our alliance. . . . We must change the pattern of American predominance, appropriate to the postwar era, to match the new circumstances of today." Mr. Nixon reiterated that the United States would maintain the level of its forces in Europe without cutbacks "at least through mid-1971." But he also affirmed that the problem of American troop levels would meanwhile be under review, and he called upon his allies for a "candid exchange of views" on Europe's real security needs in the years ahead. Taking note of West Germany's efforts to effect a *rapprochement* with its neighbors to the East, the President observed: "Since the problem of Germany remains the key to East-West problems in Europe, we would welcome such a normalization. Just as the postwar era has ended in Western Europe, it is our hope that a more satisfactory and enduring order will come into being in the center of the continent." That hope also seemed to reflect a new American resolve to encourage others to take the initiative, as long, of course, as those initiatives were compatible with Washington's over-all view.

And so it went with American policy elsewhere in the world. For Latin America, where Washington's role had been affected in the 1960's by the behavior of the Castro regime in Cuba and the demands of the Alliance for Progress, the President spoke of a "realistic approach" devoid of "grandiose spending programs that had no prospect of Congressional approval, or . . . promises that could not be fulfilled." United States aid would continue, the President said, with less restrictions than in the past; and America would even press for a system of tariff preferences for all developing countries. But, he cautioned, "We alone cannot assume the responsibility for the economic and social development of other nations. This is a process deeply rooted in each nation's history and evolution. Responsibility has to be shared for progress to be real."

The same applied to Asia and, with some modifications, to the Middle East and Africa. Everywhere the stress was on partnership, cooperation and mutual responsibilities. In Asia, Mr. Nixon said, "The responsibilities once borne by the United States at such great cost can now be shared." Specifically, he stressed, "Japan's partnership with us will be a key to the success of the Nixon Doctrine. . . ." Of the Middle Eastern countries, the President declared that "The day is past when the large powers can or should be expected either to determine their course or to solve their problems for them." If the Arab-Israeli conflict is to be resolved, "the United States cannot be expected to assume responsibility alone for developing the terms of peace or for guaranteeing them." Even in Africa the President seemed determined to cast America in the role of a friendly but disinterested—and even remote—well-wisher. "It is another lesson of the 1960's," he noted, ". . . that African defense against subversion, like African development, must be borne most directly by Africans rather than outsiders."

The message, then, was abundantly clear: the United States was preparing to lower its profile not only in Asia, where the Nixon Doctrine was born, but throughout the world generally. In a sense, it had all sprung from the President's pledge of "no more Vietnams." But it was also evident that Nixon, as an astute politician, had read the nation's mood and had simply concluded that America's foreign involvements would have to be trimmed for the sake of domestic priorities. As early as May 1969, opinion polls had revealed that only 9 per cent of the American public would favor a dispatch of United States troops to save Israel from being overrun by Soviet-aided Arabs. Only 26 per cent supported the use of American troops if West Berlin were invaded by outside Communist forces.[33] Such domestic considerations were reflected in Part III of the President's State of the World message, dealing with his administration's efforts to bring revised foreign policy objectives and defense spending into balance with each other and with over-all national priorities. As the President put it: ". . . for the first time, national security and domestic priorities were considered together. In fact, two strategies were rejected because they were not considered essential to our security and because they would have thwarted vital domestic programs."

The strategy that the administration ultimately decided upon represented, in the President's words, "a significant modification of the doctrine that characterized the 1960's. The stated basis of our conventional posture in the 1960's was the so-called '2½ war' principle. According to it, U.S. forces would be maintained for a three-month conventional forward defense of NATO, a defense of Korea or Southeast Asia against a full-scale Chinese attack, and a minor contingency—all simultaneously. These force levels were never reached.

"In the effort to harmonize doctrine and capability," the President continued, "we chose what is best described as the '1½ war' strategy. Under it we will maintain in peacetime general purpose forces adequate for simultaneously meeting a major Communist attack in either Europe or Asia, assisting allies against non-Chinese threats in Asia, and contending with a contingency elsewhere."

It should not go unnoticed that the immediate impact of this new strategy was a temporary reversal of the upward spiral in defense spending which had characterized much of the 1960's. As his Secretary of Defense, Nixon had appointed an old friend and one-time Chairman of the Republican National Committee, Melvin R. Laird. A former member of Congress from Wisconsin, well-versed in the intricacies of defense policy from his days on the House Armed Services Committee, and a man of considerable political skill, Laird had quickly become the most ardent advocate of the Nixon Doctrine in the entire administration. Without unduly ruffling feathers at the Pentagon, he had managed, by the end of 1970, to reduce over-all defense spending by 7 per cent, to cut the number of Defense Department employees by 661,000 (514,000 of whom were sevicemen), and to scale down the number of American troops stationed at home and around the world to a figure slightly in excess of 1 million, or about 30 per cent fewer than in the peak Vietnam year of 1968.[34]

The fact that the Nixon Doctrine fit hand-in-glove with such cutbacks did not, of course, obviate the problem of Communist intentions around the world—intentions which, as the events of 1970 would reveal, seemed hardly less threatening to American security than in the past. Of this problem, the President and his advisers were only too aware. And they chose to deal with the matter in two ways. On the one hand, the Nixon Doctrine itself provided that America's friends and allies, in the course of assuming greater responsibilities for their own defense, would be aided, where necessary, with greater infusions of American arms and equipment. Such aid would not apply, obviously, to the nation's richer allies in NATO or Japan, but it would serve to stiffen the military posture of nations like Thailand, South Korea and, of course, South Vietnam. Secretary Laird himself stressed the urgency of a vastly increased military assistance program for such countries as "the essential ingredient of our policy if we are to honor our obligations, support our allies, and yet reduce the likelihood of having to commit American ground combat units." [35]

On the other hand, it was also clear that the administration was banking heavily on a fruitful "era of negotiation" to bridge whatever security gap might develop between Soviet intent and American policy, and it was to that delicate task of diplomacy that the fourth and final part of the State of the World message was addressed. It could also be said, moreover, that the administration, in stating its case for negotiations, was uneasily aware of the weakness of this particular link in the logic of its policy. "Let us make no mistake about it," the President said, "leaders of the Communist nations are serious and determined. Because we do take them seriously, we will not underestimate the depth of ideological disagreement or the disparity between their interests and ours. Nor will we pretend that agreement is imminent by fostering the illusion that they have already given up their beliefs or are just about to do so in the process of negotiations."

Yet, from the President's point of view, there were clearly grounds for "cautious optimism." "If we have had to learn the limitations of our own power," he declared, "the lessons of the last two decades must have left their imprint on the leadership in the Kremlin—in the recognition that Marxist ideology is not the surest guide to the problems of a changing industrial society, the world-wide decline in the appeal of ideology and most of all in the foreign policy dilemmas repeatedly posed by the spread of Communism to states which refuse to endure permanent submission to Soviet authority—a development illustrated vividly by the Soviet schism with China." There was, moreover, the evidence of past agreement—the limited nuclear test ban treaty of August 5, 1963,[36] the treaty on non-proliferation of nuclear weapons (signed in July 1968 and in force March 5, 1970),[37] and even SALT, which had begun in a promising atmosphere in Helsinki on November 17, 1969.[38] Above all, there were the wearing, costly, and potentially disastrous consequences of continued hostility and the common interest both sides had in reaching agreement on such fundamental and mutual problems as arms control.

That negotiations would be long and arduous the President had no doubt. That there would be setbacks and disappointments, he also recognized. But the effort would have to be made, and not least of all, to justify a unilateral lowering of America's international profile. "Skeptical and estranged, many of our young people today look out on a world they never made," Nixon concluded. "They survey its conflicts with apprehension. Graduated into the impersonal routine of a bureaucratic, technological society, many of them see life as lonely conformity lacking the lift of a driving dream. Yet there is no greater idealism, no higher adventure than taking a realistic road for peace. It is an adventure realized not in the exhilaration of a single moment, but in the lasting rewards of patient, detailed and specific efforts—a step at a time."

4 : Advise and Consent

Taken as a whole—or even a step at a time—the President's message seemed to confirm a profound shift in American foreign policy. As Murrey Marder wrote in *The Washington Post,* "The Nixon Administration hopes to do in the 1970s what no President has accomplished since World War II: withdraw from the dream of an America preserving order throughout the world, and turn instead to the more modest goal of attempting to do only what American popular opinion, military power, and money can afford." [39] If that were true, the nation's foreign policy was in the process of coming into line with the dominant mood at home. But would it be equally in accord with the realities abroad? There were some critics who thought not, who judged the President's effort to be evasively ambiguous and contradictory. "Take the 'concept of partnership' . . . ," Professor Hans J. Morgenthau wrote.[40] "This concept . . . does not elucidate the issues of our relations with our allies, it rather evades them by glossing them over with an attractive phrase. If two partners see eye to eye on the issues concerning them there is no problem. If they don't, invocation of their partnership will not help them." In Professor Morgenthau's view, the President's message held only "a tenuous relation to the foreign policy actually pursued by the Nixon Administration. Such a document performs two major functions: it tells the American people what it is supposed to like hearing, and it presents the Administration's assumed modes of thought and action in a most favorable light. In these respects, it is very much like the prospectus or annual report of a corporation."

A similarly skeptical view of the enterprise was taken by Earl C. Ravenal, writing in *Foreign Affairs*.[41] "While pledging to honor all of our existing commitments," he claimed, "the President has placed them all in considerable doubt. While offering promise of avoiding involvement in future Asian conflicts, he has biased the nature of our participation." What was required of American policy, according to Ravenal, was not a ringing restatement of America's commitments or an effort to maintain them on the cheap, but their total redefinition, particularly insofar as the containment of China was concerned. This, Ravenal maintained, the Nixon Doctrine failed to do, and consequently it could not rule out the possible involvement of United States forces in another land war in Asia. In that respect the doctrine was no real improvement over the policy that led to Vietnam. "The basic question," he wrote, "is whether the Nixon Doctrine is an honest policy that will fully fund the worldwide and Asian commitments it proposes to maintain, or whether it conceals a drift toward nuclear defense or an acceptance of greater risk of local defeat."

From the administration's viewpoint, of course, there was virtue in a certain amount of vagueness, and even contradictions could serve to keep a potential aggressor guessing. Mr. Nixon was well aware of the trouble former Secretary of State Dean Acheson had brought on himself by prematurely declaring South Korea outside the American defense perimeter in Asia in 1950.[42] To avoid such pitfalls, the administration was deliberately stating its new foreign policy in less than precise terms. Yet it was one thing to keep the adversary guessing, quite another to play the same game with one's allies. With the handwriting already on the wall in Vietnam, what assurance had they that America would be by their side when and if the moment of truth should come? Even more to the point, how could they be sure that a recalcitrant American Congress would provide all the additional arms and military equipment that the Nixon Doctrine promised and presumed?

Already for several years, Congress had been chipping away at presidential requests for military assistance, and by the end of 1970 a full-scale investigation of the military assistance program, led by Democratic Senator William Proxmire of Wisconsin was in preparation. As *The New York Times* pointed out editorially, "The virtual monopoly of the executive branch for three decades in the determination of the foreign and defense policies of the United States received its first serious challenge in the 91st Congress." [43] In 1969, the Senate had overwhelmingly adopted a "national commitments" resolution [44] which warned the President, in effect, that henceforth he could not employ American forces in foreign conflicts, or even promise to do so, without the consent of Congress. Although it expressed only the "sense of the Senate" and lacked the force of law, that resolution was hailed by a member of the President's own party, Senator Jacob K. Javits of New York, as "a signal to the executive branch that it must adjust itself psychologically and procedurally to a new reality—the reality that the Senate will not again shrink from its responsibilities or yield its constitutional power with respect to national-security issues and the solemn undertaking of national commitments." [45]

The Senator's words had barely been published, however, before the President was announcing, on April 30, the dispatch of American troops into Cambodia.[46] Once again, congressional ire was roused. On May 4 the Senate Foreign Relations Committee complained that by acting "without the consent or knowledge of Congress Mr. Nixon was usurping the war-making powers delegated to the legislative branch." [47] It added that in the Committee's opinion the executive branch had been "conducting a constitutionally unauthorized, Presidential war in Indochina." The charge was promptly rejected by the White House, which contended that Mr. Nixon was relying upon his constitutional powers as Commander-in-Chief.

The Cambodia incursion nonetheless spurred two major congressional efforts to limit the President's freedom of action with regard to the war in Southeast Asia. One was the so-called Cooper-Church amendment to the foreign military sales bill.[48] Sponsored by Senators John Sherman Cooper, Republican of Kentucky, and Frank Church, Democrat of Idaho, it barred the President from spending any funds without congressional consent to "retain" American troops or military advisers in Cambodia after their scheduled withdrawal date of June 30, to provide air combat support to Cambodian forces, or to provide financial assistance to advisers or troops from other countries aiding Cambodia. After 34 days of intensive debate, the Senate passed the Cooper-Church amendment by a vote of 58 to 37 on June 30. The House, however, failed to go along, and not until late December was a heavily watered-down version of the amendment, restricting the use of foreign assistance funds, sent to the President for approval.[48a]

The other effort fared even less well. After prolonged debate characterized by strong opposition from the administration, the Senate on September 1 rejected, by a vote of 55 to 39, a so-called "amendment to end the war," which was attached to the military procurement authorization bill and sponsored by Republican Senator Mark O. Hatfield of Oregon and Democratic Senator George McGovern of South Dakota.[49] Had it succeeded, that measure would have required the administration to reduce United States troop levels in South Vietnam to 280,000 by April 30, 1971 and to withdraw all American forces by the end of 1971.

The defeat of the McGovern-Hatfield amendment by no means signaled an end to the President's troubles with Congress, however. The Senate, as a further indication of its displeasure over the Vietnam imbroglio, had already voted on June 24 to repeal the famous Tonkin Gulf resolution by which President Johnson had in 1964 gained congressional support for his Vietnam policy [50] (although the administration itself had not actively opposed repeal of this by now obsolete measure). In the meantime, moreover, a Senate Foreign Relations Subcommittee on United States Security Agreements and Commitments Abroad,[51] headed by Senator Stuart Symington, had discovered in the course of its investigations that the administration, without informing Congress, had been entering into understandings or commitments with a broad range of foreign countries, including a military contingency plan with Thailand, a presidential pledge of support for the Ethiopian government, and military aid for the Republic of Korea in return for that country's dispatch of troops to South Vietnam. On December 2, therefore, Republican Senator Clifford P. Case introduced legislation, first sponsored by Senate conservatives 16 years earlier, which would require the executive branch to transmit all international agreements to Congress within 60 days of their execution.[52] The aim was less to curb the President's agreement-making powers than to expose them systematically to congressional scrutiny. Later that same month, in a miniature replay of the Cooper-Church amendment debate, both the Senate and House voted out a supplemental foreign assistance authorization bill that further restricted the President from reintroducing ground combat troops or military advisers into Cambodia.[53]

Despite the President's own intentions as embodied in the Nixon Doctrine, it was evident that a nervous Congress remained dubious about the actual conduct of the nation's foreign policy. To be sure, the repeal of the Tonkin Gulf resolution was little more than a symbolic gesture. And even advocates of the Cooper-Church proposal had disavowed any intent to hurt the President, or to show doubt of his publicly pledged word on the withdrawal of American forces from Cambodian soil. Yet it was also apparent that the long years of trial and torment in Vietnam had put the Congress on guard against the President's foreign policy powers as never before since World War II. To the extent that the President's critics came from both political parties, the tradition of bipartisanship in American foreign policy was, in its way, being preserved. But the finger of congressional suspicion now moved freely from the White House to the Defense Department to the Department of State and back again. And it was clear that the Congress, no less than the mood of America itself, was demanding to have its say in that "new approach" to a "new era" of which Nixon spoke.

Inevitably, the most powerful voice in the exercise of this congressional function was that of Democratic Senator J. William Fulbright, Chairman of the influential Foreign Relations Committee. Even before Nixon came to office, the Senator from Arkansas had proved himself a foremost critic of American foreign policy, as his nationally televised duel with the then Secretary of State Dean Rusk during the

Vietnam hearings of 1967 made clear. The Senator's personal relations with Nixon's old friend and former law partner, Secretary Rogers, were judged better by observers in the Washington press corps, if only because Rogers had come to his task with the kind of fresh and open approach, which someone committed to past lines of policy could not afford. Even so, however, Senator Fulbright felt compelled to express his concern that Rogers was avoiding sufficient consultation with the Foreign Relations Committee, that foreign policy was primarily being conducted by White House officials like Henry Kissinger who were not available for questioning, and that, in fact, the Department of Defense was edging out the State Department in whatever influence remained between them in the conduct of the nation's international dealings.[54]

To some extent, the administration itself was aware of these problems. In his State of the World message, Mr. Nixon had discussed at length the government's foreign policy machinery, noting that "If we were to establish a new foreign policy for the era to come, we had to begin with a basic restructuring of the process by which policy is made. . . . At the outset, therefore, I directed that the National Security Council be reestablished as the principal forum for Presidential consideration of foreign policy issues." The President went on to describe the revised policy-making process as follows: "I assign an issue to an Interdepartmental Group—chaired by an Assistant Secretary of State—for intensive study, asking it to formulate the policy choices and to analyze the pros and cons of the different courses of action. This group's report is examined by an interagency Review Group of senior officials—chaired by the Assistant to the President for National Security Affairs—to insure that the issues, options, and views are presented fully and fairly. The paper is then presented to me and the full National Security Council." To handle crises or sudden emergencies, the President set up within the N.S.C. system a special senior panel known as the Washington Special Actions Group (WSAG), composed of the Assistant to the President for National Security Affairs, the Director of the Central Intelligence Agency, the Chairman of the Joint Chiefs of Staff, the Deputy Secretary of Defense, and the Under Secretary of State.

All of this was by way of saying that the White House rather than the State Department would become the central focus of the foreign policy process under Mr. Nixon—a none too surprising development given the President's own personal concern with the direction of such matters. But the system also implied an underlying lack of faith in the State Department's capacity to perform as the President's chief guide and counselor in the foreign policy field—a lack of faith shared in varying degrees of anger and frustration by Mr. Nixon's predecessors in office and reflected in Senator Fulbright's own grumblings on the subject. As Thomas P. Thornton, a member of the Department's Planning and Coordination Staff, observed: "Much of the decline in the Department's influence since World War II has been ascribed to the fact that we were not a resource-dispensing agency. Country teams and Interdepartmental Groups notwithstanding, the Department has been reduced to the role of one voice among many, often having less faith in its own product—diplomacy in the broadest sense—than in the resources of AID [the Agency for International Development] and Defense as the substance of international relations." [55]

With the encouragement of Secretary Rogers and the administration, therefore, the Department moved again to reform itself as 1970 got under way. In a speech before State Department and other employees on January 14,[56] William B. Macomber, Deputy Under Secretary of State for Administration, unveiled a wide-ranging plan designed to revitalize the nation's diplomatic service and restore the Department itself to a position of leadership in foreign policy. In addition to dropping the old Policy Planning Staff and replacing it with a Planning and Coordination Staff more closely tied to N.S.C. machinery, the plan stressed an over-all personnel system designed to develop specialists and management expertise among the Department's employees—a clear indication that the Department's long-festering argument over "generalists" versus "specialists" was being settled in favor of the latter. Most important, perhaps, the Deputy Under Secretary stressed that the reforms would come from within the Department itself, where, in fact, a strong movement for such changes was already under way among disgruntled personnel. "In the weeks immediately ahead," Mr. Macomber said, ". . . we will set up task forces to work on almost all the areas I will talk about today. . . . I invite everyone in the State Department to pass their [*sic*] thoughts along to the task forces or to my office."

The response was considerable. By July 20 the 13 task forces had submitted 468 recommendations to Secretary Rogers aimed, among other things, at strengthening the Department's capacity to carry out over-all coordination, direction, and supervision of American activities abroad.[57] Then on December 9 the task forces released a 600-page document entitled *Diplomacy for the Seventies*,[58] embodying a comprehensive list of reforms garnered from a year's study and investigation. This document urged a drastic overhaul of the Department's personnel policies designed to end the "persistent under-utilization of talent" that had led, in the report's view, to "growing dissatisfaction and high resignation rate" among young officers. The report noted that the Department's traditional reliance on "talented generalists" and its failure to recruit officers skilled in such specialized areas as agriculture, labor, development economics, finance, science, and the like had eroded the confidence of other Federal agencies in the Department's ability to provide foreign affairs leadership. It also urged measures to overcome the "strong pressures toward conformity" which had led to excessive caution in defending established policies and "dulled [the Department's] creative impulse."

What all of this meant in terms of the Department's future effectiveness, of course, remained to be seen, since it appeared that Henry Kissinger's special role would not be affected. But it was evident that the administration was moving on a broad front to reform not only the substance of American foreign policy but its machinery and techniques as well. Despite certain criticisms, moreover, it appeared that the President's "New Strategy for Peace" sat well enough with both Congress and the public, the main concern being that he would move neither far enough nor fast enough in lowering the profile to suit the nation's mood. As Senator Mike Mansfield, the Democratic majority leader, declared: "I honor and commend the President for bringing out this new policy, announcing, it, and sticking by it." [59]

. Yet the President himself was keenly aware that however much his new strategy suited the nation's mood, its real test would lie in its successful implementation abroad. And that was where the cruelest problems seemed to emerge. For if the United States was bent on lowering its profile in 1970, the Soviet Union appeared equally set on raising its own—in the Mediterranean Sea and the Indian Ocean, in the Middle East and South America, and even within the "socialist community" itself, where the Brezhnev Doctrine proclaiming a Soviet right to intervene by force in the affairs of other Communist states stood in marked contrast to the basic thrust of the Nixon Doctrine generally. In this regard, the President's dilemma was acute, for if Moscow interpreted his new policy initiatives as an invitation to Soviet expansion abroad, the danger of an eventual nuclear confrontation might be intensified rather than alleviated, with his strategy for peace devolving into a miscalculation for war.

· That such possibilities weighed heavily on the President's mind was apparent in the speech he delivered before the 25th anniversary session of the United Nations on October 23.[60] "The great central issue of our time—the question of whether the world as a whole is to live at peace—has not been resolved," Mr. Nixon said. "The issue of war and peace cannot be solved unless we in the United States and the Soviet Union demonstrate both the will and the capacity to put our relationship on a basis consistent with the aspirations of mankind." The President said he saw "no point in responding in kind to traditional cold war rhetoric." On the contrary, he said, "one of the paramount problems of our time is that we must transcend the old patterns of power politics in which nations sought to exploit every volatile situation for their own advantage, or to squeeze the maximum advantage for themselves out of every negotiation."

There was no hiding the fact, Mr. Nixon went on, that there were deep differences between the United States and the Soviet Union. But there were "four great factors that provide a basis for a common interest in working together to contain and to reduce those differences." The first was "a powerful common interest in avoiding nuclear confrontation." The second was "the opportunity to reduce the enormous cost of arms . . . to use our resources for building rather than destroying." The third lay in "the economic self-interest of each of us . . . to increase trade and contact between us." And the fourth was a common interest in meeting "the global challenge of economic and social development, one that would give our competition a creative direction."

"In the world today," the President told the assembled dignitaries, "we are at a crossroads. We can follow the old way, playing the traditional game of international relations, but at ever-increasing risk. Everyone will lose. No one will gain. Or we can take a new road.

"I invite the leaders of the Soviet Union to join us in taking that new road. . . ."

It was, in many ways, a presidential *cri de coeur* for Soviet cooperation and understanding at a time of fundamental change in America and the world. And it is to the Soviet response that our attention must now turn.

2 : "Where Are You Going, Russia?"

The question of our title was first posed more than a century ago by Nikolai Gogol, but from Washington's viewpoint it had lost none of its edge by 1970. There had no doubt been worse years in the cold war, when the search for an answer had almost become an obsession, when Washington seemed concerned by little else, and when numbers of Americans began to fear that the real issue facing the nation— namely, "Where are you going, America?"—had been obscured by the intense preoccupation with Kremlin policy. And yet, even in 1970, it was apparent that Gogol's question could not safely be set aside while America struggled introspectively to resolve its own problems or sort out its own future. Nothing guaranteed that an "era of negotiation" would stand any less in thrall of Soviet intentions than the "era of confrontation" that had purportedly come before it. Nor was there any evidence that Soviet intentions had themselves undergone significant change.

On the contrary, in July 1969, about the time when President Nixon was lowering America's Asian profile at Guam,[1] Soviet Foreign Minister Andrei A. Gromyko was setting forth what sounded like a new doctrine of Soviet globalism before a meeting of the Supreme Soviet in Moscow. "It is natural," he said, ". . . that the Soviet Union which, as a major world power, . . . [has] extensively developed international contacts, cannot look passively on at events which, although territorially remote, nevertheless have a bearing on our own security and the security of our friends. Our responsibility towards the Soviet people and our international duty make it incumbent upon us to ensure that the high prestige and the great power of the Soviet state effectively serve the cause of preserving and strengthening peace, of repelling the policy of worsening international tensions and of aggression, wherever that policy threatens peace." [2] By early 1970 the Russians were matching these somewhat sweeping words with deeds, dispatching Soviet pilots to man advanced MIG-21 fighters in the skies over Egypt and later providing Soviet crews to operate the technically sophisticated surface-to-air missiles installed along the west bank of the Suez Canal. They had already undertaken a major expansion of their strategic forces, drawing virtually abreast of the United States in strategic nuclear weapons capabilities and increasing their naval power to the point where they were challenging the supremacy of the American Sixth Fleet in the Mediterranean. By September, there were even signs—highly disturbing to Washington—that they might be laying preparations for the installation of a missile-carrying submarine base at Cienfuegos, Cuba.

It was as though the Kremlin had learned nothing from the harsh American experience of the 'sixties, or had chosen to interpret that experience in a manner wholly at odds with the American mood which had grown out of it. At a point in history when the cold war was said to be diminishing, when talk of *détente* was on the lips of Soviet and Western diplomats alike, what could be made of such behavior? Where, indeed, was Russia going, and how was it proposing to get there? One possible answer was that the Soviets were simply adhering to traditional expansionist policies, that they had tested resistance in Washington, found it lax, and were prepared to rush in wherever the opportunities arose. Another related possibility was that, unlike America's strategic planners, the Russians had yet to feel the pangs of overcommitment and therefore had no qualms about extending themselves, despite their own considerable share of internal troubles, in whatever quest for global influence they might wish to undertake. And still another may have been provided by Leonid I. Brezhnev, General Secretary of the Communist party, when he told his countrymen on June 12, 1970 that "the Soviet government has favourably received the statement of the United States President about his desire to go over 'from the era of confrontations to the era of negotiations.' However, we know that the only way to avoid mistakes in politics is to believe practical deeds and not verbal declarations, and we cannot but see that the peace-loving statements of the new U.S. Administration run counter to its aggressive actions, which are worsening the international situation." [3]

It was possible, in short, that the Kremlin had all along been acting defensively, out of those ancient insecurities and suspicions that had long characterized the policies of Russian czars and commissars alike. Such, at any rate, had become the broad contention of the so-called "revisionist" school of cold war historians in the United States,[4] whose influence had seemingly grown along with the nation's dilemma in Vietnam. But Western analysts had long been divided about the essential wellsprings of Soviet behavior, and their disagreements had been as much a product of the veil of secrecy surrounding the Kremlin's policy-making process as of any ideological cleavage within their ranks. However they may have chosen to read the inward motivations of Soviet policy in 1970, its outward cast was plain enough. If America was stepping back, Russia was stepping forward. If America was turning inward, Russia was looking increasingly beyond its borders, thinking more and more in global terms, and patiently pursuing policy goals that had yet to be deflected by the shifting tide of international events.

5 : Soviet Gains Abroad

On the surface, at least, that tide of events now seemed to be running distinctly in Moscow's favor. Soviet policy-makers could congratulate themselves that, at relatively minimal cost to the nation, they were chalking up a number of diplomatic gains in 1970. In Western Europe, they were engaging in a series of important negotiations with the Bonn government of Chancellor Willy Brandt, initially designed to culminate in a nonaggression pact but more broadly conceived in Moscow as a political device for sealing the post-World War II *status quo* in Central Europe and as a means of gaining access to West Germany's advanced technology and trade potential for the benefit of the Soviet economy. In the treaty, signed August 12 in Moscow,[5] the Russians gained both these objectives, although Bonn let it be known that final ratification of the agreement by the West German *Bundestag* was contingent upon a satisfactory outcome of the four-power talks under way on Berlin. Even so, however, Moscow had obtained Chancellor Brandt's signature to a document which affirmed existing territorial boundaries in the heart of Europe—"including," as stated in Article 3 of the treaty, "the Oder-Neisse line which forms the western frontier of the People's Republic of Poland and the frontier between the Federal Republic of Germany and the German Democratic Republic." These were long-sought Soviet goals which, in the absence of a formal peace treaty, tended to confirm the division of Germany into two states and to seal the *de facto* territorial consequences of World War II.

Nor were the Russians neglecting their ties with other Western European states. Ever since 1966, when President Charles de Gaulle was warmly received in Moscow on his first official state visit to the U.S.S.R., relations between France and the Soviet Union had been tending toward greater cooperation. It was Gaullist diplomacy, in fact, which had first made the notion of *détente* respectable in the West, and in 1970 the tradition of amity which it initiated gained added momentum, despite Moscow's unabashed elevation of West Germany to the forefront of its West European concerns. In June, Foreign Minister Gromyko flew to Paris for talks emphasizing the two countries' mutual concern over the conflicts in the Middle East and Indochina—about which the French and Russians shared closer views than on other East-West issues. At the same time, Gromyko took the opportunity to sound out French officials on their attitude toward stepped up investments in the U.S.S.R. Then in October, President Georges Pompidou spent a week touring the Soviet Union and discussing, in President Nikolai V. Podgorny's terms, the possibilities for mutually advantageous cooperation in developing the natural resources of Siberia—a project into which Japan had already been drawn. In a protocol signed by the two presidents at the conclusion of Pompidou's visit both governments pledged "immediate contact" should situations deemed a general threat to the peace arise, "with the object of concerting their positions on all aspects of those situations and on steps which would make it possible to cope with those situations." [6]

While strengthening their ties with France, the Soviets were also considerably expanding their trade and technical cooperation with such NATO members as Italy and Denmark. In July, they extended their friendship treaty with Finland—though it still had five years to run —for an additional 20 years. And in November, Gromyko was off on another of his jaunts during which he exchanged views with the leaders of Britain's new Conservative government in London and later, in an unprecedented step for a Soviet diplomat, visited Pope Paul VI at the Vatican. In an unusually long audience, the two men discussed such wide-ranging issues as the arms race, the Middle East crisis, the war in Vietnam, and that long-cherished goal of Soviet foreign policy, the convening of a European security conference.

It was in pursuit of this last mentioned goal, in fact, that much of the Soviet wooing of West European leaders seemed under way. Early in January the Soviet Foreign Ministry had once again dusted off this four-year-old proposal, designed, on the surface, to further those objectives being negotiated on a bilateral basis with Bonn—i.e., a sealing of the territorial *status quo* in Central Europe, a pledged renunciation of the use or threat of force, and an extension of trade, scientific, and technological relations "on an equal footing with the aim of developing co-operation among European states." [7] In Washington, however, the real objective was seen as a weakening of NATO and the U.S. position in Europe generally, which accounted for the Nixon administration's deep-seated reluctance to see such a conference convened.

While not specifically opposed to such a conference, therefore, the Western powers, led by Washington, had sought to tie its convening to a successful conclusion of Moscow's negotiations with Bonn and to the general issue of a mutual, balanced reduction of military forces in Europe by both NATO and the Warsaw Pact powers. With sentiment growing in Washington for a cutback of U.S. forces on the continent, the NATO Foreign Ministers at their spring session in Rome May 26–27, issued a declaration proposing that discussions of such mutual troop reductions begin forthwith.[8] Their counterparts in the Warsaw Pact, who met in Budapest June 21–22, responded by suggesting that the issue be incorporated into an expanded agenda for the European security conference, part of whose function would be the creation of a special body on European security that would undertake to study the matter.[9]

From Washington's viewpoint, however, that response seemed designed to stretch out negotiations on the troop issue past that point in time when the Nixon administration might have to decide, for economic and other reasons, to cut its troop strength in Europe unilaterally. For this reason, therefore, all the NATO members except France expressed coolness toward the Warsaw Pact suggestion at NATO's second ministerial conference in Brussels December 3–4, and for the time being the issue of a European security conference, together with the problem of balanced force reductions, was temporarily put on ice.[10] Nonetheless, Soviet diplomats could record some progress toward their goal during the year as a whole. Most West European leaders had, like Pompidou, already acceded to the usefulness of such a conference in principle, and its ultimate convening seemed only a matter of time.

Soviet diplomats could also record progress on another highly sensitive front during 1970—that of their border dispute and general ideological clash with the Communist regime in China. When the year opened, Sino-Soviet relations seemed at or near their lowest ebb in memory, with some Western commentators predicting the probability of war between the two Communist giants.[11] And in fact through the first half of 1970, such predictions seemed more and more plausible, even though talks aimed at resolving the border dispute had been under way since October 1969. In January the Soviet Foreign Ministry, alarmed by the prospect of Sino-American collusion, bitterly assailed Peking's decision to resume diplomatic discussions with U.S. representatives in Warsaw,[12] while the Soviet Defense Ministry, charging that Peking had launched itself upon an adventurous course of expansionism and world hegemony, issued a seemingly ominous warning against underestimating the Chinese military threat. By late April, around the time when the Kremlin was celebrating the 100th anniversary of Lenin's birth and Peking was launching its first artificial satellite into orbit around the earth, the mutual exchange of invective seemed to reach an all-time high, with Peking assailing Moscow as a "Hitler-type dictatorship" and Moscow attacking the private life of Party Chairman Mao Tse-tung.[13] In June, Premier Aleksei N. Kosygin reported on Soviet television that the seven-month-old Sino-Soviet border talks were getting nowhere because of Peking's "anti-Soviet course," [14] and it looked as though the issues dividing the two powers were, indeed, "irreconcilable."

But then the climate seemed to change perceptibly, as the last spasms of China's Great Proletarian Cultural Revolution began to fade and Peking gradually resumed its dealings with the outside world. Even when the Chinese had been attacking Moscow at their fiercest, the Russians had been careful to keep the door ajar to peaceful reconciliation,[15] and by July, Soviet patience appeared to be paying off. For more than three years the two powers had emphasized their mutual hostility by withholding ambassadors from each other's capital, but on July 1, Peking was suddenly reported to have agreed to accept a new Soviet envoy and to be ready to appoint an ambassador of its own to Moscow. On October 20, the new Soviet Ambassador, Vasily S. Tolstikov, head of the Leningrad party organization, took up his duties (the Chinese had already named their Deputy Foreign Minister, Liu Hsin-chuan, to Moscow), and relations seemed to have entered a new and conciliatory phase. Chinese attacks on the Soviet leadership, Western commentators noted, had virtually ceased, and as the 53rd anniversary of the Bolshevik revolution approached in November, Peking sent a warmer-than-usual message of congratulations to the Soviet people, expressing a desire to resolve outstanding differences and restore "friendly and good-neighborly" relations.[16] At the same time, Mikhail A. Suslov, theoretican and member of the Soviet Politburo, affirmed Moscow's own interest in restoring normal ties in the course of an anniversary speech delivered in the Kremlin.[17] On November 12, a Soviet trade delegation arrived in Peking in what seemed further evidence of a changing climate, and the Soviet regime routinely continued to back the seating of Peking in the United Nations as the annual battle over China's membership got under way during the General Assembly's 25th Regular Session.

It was almost as though the Marxist dialectic—thesis, antithesis, synthesis—were at work in Sino-Soviet affairs, for the year was ending on a note of cordiality almost as hardy as the note of vituperation on which it had begun. To be sure, the roots of Sino-Soviet hostility ran deep and strong (as Suslov himself had intimated in his speech), the border conflict appeared no nearer to solution than before, and the armed might now conspicuously in evidence along both sides of the Sino-Soviet frontier hardly spoke in favor of "friendly and good-neighborly" accord. If state relations had improved, in short, it remained clear that ideological relations had not. Yet while moving to secure their position in the West, the Soviets had also managed to gain at least some respite from their troubles in the East—a not inconsiderable achievement for a nation traditionally obsessed with its geographic security. They had thereby strengthened their hand for a more active pursuit of those global ambitions to which Gromyko had alluded.

Good fortune, of course, had played its role. The coming to power of Social Democrat Brandt in West Germany in October 1969, the reorientation of Chinese policy in the wake of the Cultural Revolution—these events had laid the groundwork for much of what the Kremlin could count as progress toward its goals. Yet, unquestionably, Soviet officials were also playing their hand shrewdly. The election of Salvador Allende as Chile's first Marxist president, for example, seemed to confirm the wisdom of what the Russians had been preaching all along with respect to Latin America—that the peaceful road to power was best for that region as a whole. Indeed, the friendlier attitude of leftist-nationalist regimes in Peru and Bolivia tended to underscore the virtues of such an approach. And after years of patient work on the Asian subcontinent, the Soviets found themselves, for the moment at least in the unusual position of being able to supply arms to both India and Pakistan without arousing the usual recriminations from either.

In short, some long-standing Soviet policies were beginning to bear fruit, and nowhere were the gains more evident than in the Middle East, where Soviet diplomats—and soldiers—were consolidating their patron-client relationship with a number of Arab states and solidifying a Russian foothold in an area that had long been considered a preserve of the West. From Syria and Iraq to Egypt, Yemen, Southern Yemen, Libya, and the Sudan, Soviet arms and diplomacy had become the mainstay of Arab governments in their confrontation with Israel. In Egypt, particularly, Soviet influence had grown to the point where defense against Israeli air power was almost wholly in Russian hands, though Egyptians were being trained as fast as possible to assume the technologically complex burden themselves. If Russia was indeed in search of warm-water ports to facilitate the expansion of its naval power, it had found a partial fulfillment of its quest on the southern shores of the Mediterranean, in the Red Sea, and on the Gulf of Aden.

By virtue of the unstable nature of the Arab regimes with which they were dealing, the Soviet position, of course, remained precarious. But for all intents and purposes, they had successfully mounted a challenge to NATO's southern flank, were in a position of considerable influence over the Suez Canal once that waterway was cleared of wreckage from the 1967 war and reopened, and were well on the way to gaining enough of a foothold in the Arab world to pose a potential threat to the continued flow of Arab oil to Europe and Japan. In a negative sense, they had succeeded in further reducing Western influence in an area that abuts their own backyard.

It was this last achievement—the whittling away of Western influence—which prompted some observers to speculate that a key aim of Soviet policy in general had become the isolation of its foremost adversary, the United States, and the gradual erosion of America's position in the world.[18] And, in fact, if the Russians were showing a conciliatory face to their immediate neighbors in Western Europe and China in 1970, if they were showing patience and solicitude toward their third-world clients, they had nonetheless turned a stony and hostile countenance toward the United States, despite the latter's own self-imposed stirrings toward an isolation that might suit Soviet designs. In June, a 5,000-word editorial published in *Pravda* pointedly confined its standard criticisms of "imperialist" nations to the United States, for the first time singling out West Germany for praise.[19] The implication was that, from the Soviet viewpoint, Washington now stood alone as the key source of international tensions.

It was a theme to which Soviet commentators adhered throughout the year, even while speaking hopefully of progress toward strategic arms limitation. To Washington's charge that Moscow had deliberately violated the spirit of the Middle East cease-fire and standstill agreement by moving SAM-3 missiles into the standstill zone, the Soviets replied indignantly that they were not an official party to the agreement, that the Egyptians who were a party had denied such allegations, and that the United States was itself deliberately trying to sabotage the cease-fire it had sponsored. To Washington's warning against the building of a missile-carrying submarine base in Cuba—a move which would have constituted a violation of the 1962 Kennedy-Khrushchev agreement banning strategic weapons from the island—the Soviets responded with an equally sharp denial and the countercharge that Washington was seeking, for domestic political reasons, to stir up new tensions. These were exchanges of the purest cold war vintage and gave emphasis to Brezhnev's contention in June that American-Soviet differences were "really deep" [20] and to President Podgorny's view that relations between the two powers were "in a kind of frozen state." [21]

Nor were relations proceeding any more smoothly on that non-diplomatic, people-to-people basis in which President Dwight D. Eisenhower had once held stock. In March, for example, the National Aeronautics and Space Administration reported that 27 different efforts to engage Soviet scientists in more fruitful discussions and cooperation on space projects had got nowhere. In April, American industrialist

Henry Ford II announced his own interest in building a large truck manufacturing complex on the Soviet Union's Khama River, but the plan was later scotched when Ford, citing public criticism of the project by Secretary Laird, turned it down.[22] A further strain in U.S.-Soviet relations came as the result of attacks on Soviet diplomats and installations in New York by members of the so-called Jewish Defense League—a militant American group protesting Soviet policies toward Russian Jews and Israel. These attacks stirred sharp notes of Soviet protest and what appeared to be retaliatory acts against American journalists in the Soviet Union.

Some comforting notes were sounded toward the end of the year. On December 12, Moscow and Washington quietly concluded a mid-Atlantic fishing pact and also signed an accord on joint atomic research, providing for mutual cooperation in the peaceful uses of atomic energy. On October 28, moreover, the two powers had signed a space-docking agreement, calling for the development of mutually compatible rendezvous and docking systems in outer space and proving that, with patience and perseverence, cooperation in this area was in fact possible after all. On the whole, however, Soviet-American relations remained under a cloud of mutual mistrust and apprehension as the year ended, and neither side seemed particularly optimistic about chances for dramatic improvement in the months ahead.

6 : *Internal Constraints*

There had always been times when the Soviet method of policy-making seemed to offer distinct advantages—no recalcitrant legislature to deal with, no demonstrating students, no harsh questioning and criticism by the press—and certainly the gains of 1970 appeared to speak in favor of that view. And yet it had also long been apparent that Moscow's policies could be no less responsive to' internal conditions than those being made in Washington—that, indeed, much of Soviet foreign policy sprang directly from domestic considerations. Viewed from this perspective, much of what we have termed Soviet "successes" in 1970 can be seen in a different light. The wooing of Western Europe, for example, could be viewed as a concerted Soviet effort to close the yawning technological gap with the West; the steps toward reconciliation with China, an effort to clamp down the lid on the

Kremlin's most explosive foreign problem while the Russians, no less than the Chinese themselves, sorted out their own internal difficulties; even the hostile posture toward the United States, a result of internal power bargaining designed to placate, for the moment, the demands of Russia's own military-industrial complex. In such circumstances, nothing by way of Russia's foreign ambitions precluded an eventual softening in the Soviet attitude toward Washington, particularly while the United States remained the font of world technological progress and was inclined, itself, toward an accommodation of differences.

· It was precisely with reference to this point that the Soviet nuclear physicist, Andrei Sakharov, had published his own "convergence theory" in the West in 1969. In 1970, Professor Sakharov returned once more to his theme, and his remarks, published in an "open letter" [23] to the Kremlin's top leadership, served to illuminate the constraints at work within Soviet society itself. "Comparing our economy with that of the U.S.," Sakharov wrote, "we see that ours lags not only in quantitative but also—saddest of all—in qualitative respects. We surpass America in the mining of coal, but we lag behind in oil drilling, lag very much behind in gas drilling and in the production of electric power, hopelessly lag behind in chemistry and infinitely lag behind in computer technology. . . . We simply live in another epoch. . . ." The cure for this deplorable record, Sakharov maintained, lay in the liquidation of "the bureaucratic, dogmatic, hypocritical style" that prevailed in Soviet life and the institution of a program of democratization keyed to freedom of information and an end to political censorship and persecution.

If the Kremlin leaders were shaken in any way by this audacious challenge from one of the nation's foremost physicists (Dr. Sakharov had been called "the father of the Soviet H-bomb"), they gave no indication of it. Indeed, they hardly needed reminding that the nation faced major economic difficulties. By mid-July the party's Central Committee was announcing that the 24th Party Congress, set by party statutes for sometime in 1970, would have to be postponed until March 1971, and the reason apparently stemmed from unresolved economic problems and the inability of Soviet planners to agree on the Five-Year Plan for the period 1971–75, which the 24th Congress would be asked to approve. Only a decade earlier, Premier Khrushchev had confidently boasted that the Soviet gross national product would overtake that of the United States by 1970. But if the decade of the 'sixties had been a period of rapid growth for America, it had been a time of limited growth and mounting economic troubles for the U.S.S.R. The reforms that had been introduced at the time of the eighth Five-Year Plan in 1965—designed to bring about a limited decentralization of the economy and make more use of material incentives—had, by the admission of their own author, the Soviet economist Y. G. Liberman, proved a failure.[24] Inflation and inefficiency were still problems. Technological innovation still lagged.

To be sure, the industrial growth rate had rebounded from its downward stumble in 1969, averaging 8.3 per cent for 1970 as a whole. But most of the long-range goals originally set by the eighth Five-Year Plan were not achieved, and statistics showed an increasing trend toward reliance on the importation from the West of machinery and equipment needed for further industrial expansion. In 1965, for example, the Soviet Union had bought $510 million worth of such imports from major non-Communist nations. By 1970 the figure had risen to $1.1 billion.[25]

It would seem obvious that Moscow was seeking, in part at least, to resolve some of these internal troubles by strengthening its economic ties to Western Europe. At home, however, it was clearly rejecting the unsolicited advice of Dr. Sakharov. Far from increased democratization, in fact, the Soviet state seemed to be moving toward renewed centralization and even some aspects of re-Stalinization. In an unpublished speech to party leaders in December 1969, Brezhnev himself had deplored the country's sluggish economic performance, stressing the need for tighter state control, austerity, and greater work discipline.[26] Early in 1970 the price of vodka was almost doubled by state decree, putting teeth into the complaints against drunkenness and absenteeism being made by party organs. At the same time, there were new indications that the official Soviet view of the late Joseph V. Stalin, the dictator so long in disgrace for his harsh and ruthless policies, was once again being revised. In April came reports that critics of his methods were being jailed, and on June 25 a fatherly-looking bust of the late dictator unceremoniously appeared atop his grave behind the Lenin mausoleum on Moscow's Red Square.

That some of Stalin's methods were indeed returning to fashion seemed apparent in the tough treatment meted out to that small band of Soviet dissidents whose protests were increasingly being heard in the West, if not within the Soviet Union itself. For the Kremlin leadership, in fact, it may have seemed particularly galling that, in the centennial year of Vladimir Ilyich Lenin's birth, much of the protest taking place was being made in the name of a return to "Leninist norms" and against any retreat to Stalin's fearful legacy. Such was the case with the aging Soviet General, Pyotr Grigorenko, who had championed the cause of the Crimean Tartars (victimized during the years of Stalin's rule) and the principles of "pure Leninism," to which he continually exhorted Soviet authorities to return and for which he had been confined to a state mental asylum.

Top scientists like Sakharov presented the regime with a more delicate problem, and the eminent physicist was left free to pursue his criticism of official policies, even gathering some of his fellow intellectuals into a Committee for Human Rights (from which anyone belonging to "a political party" was pointedly banned). But the authorities did not go lightly with other dissident voices. The youthful historian, Andrei Amalrik, who had answered the title of his own book, *Will the Soviet Union Survive Until 1984?* [27] by predicting its disintegration into war and chaos, received a three-year sentence to a labor camp after his arrest in May. Even the famous Russian writer, Aleksandr Solzhenitsyn, whose anti-Stalinist novels had gained him the Nobel Prize for Literature in 1970, was under sharp attack from the Soviet press and refused to travel to Stockholm to collect his award out of fear that Soviet authorities would not allow his return to Russia.

Within the Kremlin itself, on the other hand, the continuing system of collegial rule appeared to belie Stalin's legacy of monolithic control. For a time in the spring, after Brezhnev had made three major televised speeches to the nation in the course of a week, rumors swept the West of an impending shakeup at the top, with Brezhnev emerging, like Khrushchev and Stalin before him, as the undisputed leader of the nation. In fact, there were various indications that Brezhnev, if not in absolute control, had taken his place as first among equals. There was, first of all, his solo appearance at Soviet Army maneuvers in March—without the usual retinue of Politburo colleagues. Brezhnev, it was speculated, was drawing key support from Russia's increasingly influential armed forces. And then came word of the publication, at first in Bulgaria and later in the U.S.S.R. itself, of his collected speeches and writings—a tribute unknown within the collective leadership since the time of Khrushchev's ouster. Yet the "impending shakeup" never occurred. On July 15, the newly elected Supreme Soviet reappointed Kosygin and Podgorny to their posts, keeping the collective leadership intact, and if any struggle over policies and power had taken place it appeared to have been deferred until the 24th Party Congress in 1971.

˒ Nonetheless, and despite the apparent gains abroad, it remained a widespread view in the West that the Soviet leadership faced grave internal problems. As one analyst of Soviet affairs put it, "The predominant motive [of Politburo members] seems to be a desire to avoid all change and reform in the hope that no crisis will spring up and that the contradictions within their society and economy will go away." [28] Ironically, Soviet leaders had long been predicting the inevitable collapse of capitalism in the West, and in 1970 they watched the revolutionary tremors that were shaking America in particular with fascinated satisfaction. In a speech to the Young Communist League on May 26, Brezhnev had hailed the "turbulent upsurge" of American youth as "a significant sign of the sharpening of the general crisis of capitalism." [29] Yet there was also evidence that the Kremlin itself faced an upsurge of disaffection among its own youth and that many of the country's nationality groups continued in a state of discontent more portentous than any comparable problem in America.

In October, two Lithuanian nationalists seized a Soviet airliner in mid-flight, killed the stewardess and seriously wounded the pilot and co-pilot, forced the plane to Turkey, where they sought (and received) political asylum. A month later another Lithuanian, this time a sailor aboard a Soviet trawler fishing off the coast of Massachusetts, threw himself onto the deck of a U.S. Coast Guard cutter in a desperate— and unsuccessful—bid for political asylum in America. (When the Coast Guard returned the protesting sailor to Soviet custody, President Nixon suspended the three officers who bore responsibility for the decision and initiated an investigation of the affair.)

Pressures for greater autonomy among that half of the Soviet population that was non-Russian had been building for many years past, but in 1970 the authorities seemed to fear most the rising Zionist sentiment among Soviet Jews, many of whom, in turn, felt menaced by the combination of traditional Russian anti-Semitism and a sharpening official campaign against Israel and Zionism generally. In March, six prominent Soviet Jews publicly disputed official denials of anti-Semitism and claimed that thousands of Jewish citizens would leave the Soviet Union for Israel, if only permitted to go. In June, the authorities, in an apparent effort to quash any "freedom-to-emigrate" movement, arrested 20 people in Leningrad—eight of them Jews— and accused them of plotting to hijack their way out of the country. When two of the accused—both Jews—were sentenced to death in December for their role in the "plot," the world-wide outcry was so great that a higher court was moved to commute the sentences. But the general severity of the punishments came as a warning to Soviet minorities everywhere of the draconian means the state could employ to deal with any "nationalities" problem.

7 : Events in Eastern Europe

It should not have surprised the Kremlin leadership that after 53 years of Soviet power, the issue of nationalities remained as vexing as ever. For years Moscow itself had been plucking the chords of nationalist sentiment among nations in tutelage to the Western powers, and it seemed a foregone conclusion that if the Arabs of the Middle East or the Latins of Cuba so richly deserved their "independence and free- dom," then the Latvians, Estonians, Tartars, and other minorities of the Soviet Union might soon be questioning their own status as well. The dilemma had already confronted Soviet leaders on several occasions in Eastern Europe, and they had responded to it as toughly and dogmatically there as in the trial of the Leningrad Jews at home. The invasion of Czechoslovakia in August 1968 and the enunciation of the Brezhnev Doctrine, in effect asserting the Soviet right to inter- vene in the internal affairs of its Communist allies, spelled out in unmistakable terms the Kremlin's own determination to deal ruthlessly with nationalist and reformist sentiments wherever they threatened disruptions within its sphere of influence.

Certainly, the Brezhnev Doctrine itself had lost none of its gloss in 1970. If anything, it acquired an added sheen, for in May Brezhnev and Kosygin flew to Prague, ostensibly to celebrate Czechoslovakia's 25th anniversary of liberation from Fascist rule by signing a 20-year friendship treaty on May 6, but actually to seal the legitimacy of the Soviet invasion of 1968. The treaty formally reiterated the key theme of the Brezhnev Doctrine by declaring "that support for, and the consolidation and protection of, the socialist gains achieved at the cost of the heroic efforts and selfless labour of each people, are the common internationalist duty of socialist countries," and it committed both parties to "undertake the necessary measures to defend the socialist gains of the peoples and the security and independence of both countries." [30] In his speech hailing the occasion, Brezhnev himself could paradoxically observe that "the treaty signed by us today is based on the complete equality, sovereignty and independence of each of the two sides and includes the principles of fraternal mutual assistance, all-round co-operation and mutual support—principles which are in fact peculiar to the countries of socialism." [31] Precisely how "peculiar" those principles were had not been left to the imagination. Though he made no explicit reference to the events of 1968, and though he failed to mention the 80,000 Russian troops permanently stationed on Czechoslovak soil, the implications of Brezhnev's remarks —and of the treaty itself—were clear to one and all. The Brezhnev Doctrine had not been idle chatter. It was no *ex post facto* device to explain away the sudden occupation of one "friendly" state by another. It was a living, breathing instrument of Soviet power and as such a warning to the maverick regimes of Nicolae Ceauşescu in Rumania, and to nationalist forces elsewhere in Eastern Europe, of the limits of Soviet tolerance.

Within Czechoslovakia itself, meanwhile, the last vestiges of the "Prague spring" which had so stirred Soviet wrath were playing themselves out. Party membership, which stood at 1.6 million when the then First Secretary Alexander Dubček launched his series of liberal reforms, had by the end of 1970 dropped to 880,000—the result both of an extensive purge and of the refusal of many Czechoslovaks to renew membership after the events of August 1968. Dubček himself was gradually being reduced to the status of a "non-person." In January 1970, during the party shakeup which saw Oldřich Černík replaced as Premier by the more conservative Lubomir Štrougal, Dubček's resignation from the Central Committee was formally "accepted." By March 21, Dubček had been suspended from the party itself, while his former close aide, Josef Smrkovský, was expelled. On June 26, Dubček was successively removed from his post as Ambassador to Turkey and, finally, formally expelled from the party like Smrkovský and thousands of their sympathizers before him. By year's end, he was reportedly awaiting a job as clerk with the state forestry agency in Bratislava.[32]

The vast purge which had come in the wake of the Soviet invasion had literally shattered the political, economic, and cultural life of the nation. Under an article of the Labor Code adopted in 1970, any enterprise was empowered to dismiss anyone whose record suggested that he had acted against "the socialist society." As *The New York Times* reported,[33] "Leading economists are working as bookkeepers, scientists are in manual jobs, professors are working as postal clerks and diplomats as minor clerks." Due to the absence of "reliable" teachers, the Education Ministry was even forced to suspend the teaching of almost all courses in Marxism, despite their role as a staple in both university and high school curricula. The state was also moving, under pressure from the Kremlin, to reverse the trend toward greater regional autonomy for Slovakia, while other reforms of the Dubček period had long since been halted and reversed.

In one respect, at least, the bitter winter that had followed Prague's spring was less withering than might have been expected: No one implicated in the Dubček reforms had yet been shot, and few had been jailed on political charges. Nor, it was generally believed, would such actions be taken so long as Gustáv Husák, Dubček's successor as Party First Secretary and a man who had himself been the victim of a political trial in Stalin's day, remained in power. But Husák was under pressure from rightists within the party who apparently yearned for an even harder line, with some of his colleagues on the Central Committee openly accusing him of being insufficiently pro-Soviet. Nonetheless, for the time being, the Soviets continued to back Husák, perhaps out of an uneasy awareness that, whatever else a harder line might accomplish, it would not solve those critical economic problems which the Dubček reforms had been designed, in part, to overcome. On the contrary, with Czechoslovakia's intellectual and scientific elite being systematically removed from public life, economic prospects seemed as grim—or grimmer—than ever as the country's negative growth rate in 1970 made clear.

Here, in fact, was another grave dilemma faced by Soviet policy-makers in Eastern Europe. On the surface, the Brezhnev Doctrine seemed stronger than ever, yet the internal challenge to Communist statecraft remained fraught with potential explosiveness. After 25 years of Soviet domination, the countries of Eastern Europe, like the Soviet Union itself, lagged strikingly behind their counterparts on the Western half of the continent in almost every respect in which comparison was possible, and the problems that had been nagging at the internal fabric of Soviet society—the economic difficulties, the growing technological gap *vis-à-vis* the West, the pressure of intellectual and nationalist forces, and the monopolization of power by an older generation—all of these had been and were being reflected on a miniature scale among the Kremlin's Communist neighbors. In that sense, what may well have been the most significant event within the Soviet orbit in 1970—the sudden downfall of the Gomulka government in Poland—came as a timely reminder to the Kremlin itself of the bewildering speed with which change, no matter how stoutly resisted, can come about even under a Communist regime.

The problems facing Poland in 1970 were not altogether different from those facing Czechoslovakia or the Soviet Union itself. Inflation, combined in Poland's case with an exceptionally poor grain harvest, had compounded underlying economic weaknesses to bring the nation as a whole to the brink of financial crisis. As one of Gomulka's ousted colleagues had pointed out, the rate of growth of Polish national income was slowing significantly despite increased employment and capital investment since 1955. And despite efforts to modernize industry and improve productivity, production costs were going up instead of down.[34] Faced with the prospect of having to import some 4.4 million tons of grain from the West at an unplanned-for cost of $300 million—a sum which Poland lacked in foreign exchange—the nation's economists urged a sharp rise in consumer prices as the only way of resolving their problems.

On December 13, Polish newspapers duly published an edict of the Council of Ministers announcing price increases on food, fuel, and clothing, supposedly softened by a decrease in the price of some major appliances. In the week that followed, rioting, vociferously led by disgruntled workers and housewives, broke out in the northern Polish cities of Gdansk and Gdynia, spreading gradually to big cities elsewhere. On December 17, Polish Premier Józef Cyrankiewicz reported in a televised address to the nation that 20 persons had been killed in the disorders and that the police had been ordered to shoot demonstrators if necessary. In fact, Western reporters and many Poles themselves placed the toll far higher. One Swedish journalist in Gdansk at the height of the rioting reported four days of heavy fighting, including the use of tanks by government forces, that destroyed the center of the city. "What happened in Gdansk," he wrote, "was a revolution —and a successful one."[35] About 3,000 shipyard workers marched on Communist party headquarters, routed the local leaders (who flew a white flag from the top floor and filed out with their hands raised in surrender), and set fire to the building. When police and military reinforcements moved in, he reported, a "bloodbath" began. Riot police opened fire on demonstrators, including women and children. All told, by this account, more than 300 were killed in Gdansk alone.

That the rioting had been more serious than official reports indicated seemed confirmed when, on December 20, party chief Wladyslaw Gomulka and four other members of the Politburo, including the Chairman of the Council of Ministers, Marshal Marian Spychalski, resigned their posts. On December 23, Premier Cyrankiewicz also resigned (replacing Spychalski as President) and was succeeded by Piotr Jaroszewicz, an alternate member of the Politburo. For Gomulka, who had come to power in 1956 after similar riots in Poznán took at least 53 lives, events had come full circle, and few Poles appeared to regret the downfall of the ailing leader, once a symbol of Polish resistance to Stalinism. His successor, Edward Gierek, immediately promised to take a new look at the nation's price and wage policies. But if Gomulka's resignation had served to restore order, Gierek's ascension had hardly dispelled the nation's basic economic dilemma. He would have to find ways of appeasing worker discontent without further undermining the already decrepit state of Poland's economic health. At the same time, in apparent recognition of the Catholic Church's continuing hold on the Polish people, Premier Jaroszewicz, in a conciliatory gesture, asserted he would try to normalize relations with the Church. (Pope Paul's scheduled visit to Warsaw had to be temporarily postponed when the riots broke out.)

Moscow seemed fully aware that the new Polish leadership faced difficult problems. Despite the unpleasant example set by the ouster of a Communist leader in the wake of riots by workers, Soviet leaders were quick to congratulate Gierek on his promotion and expressed confidence in his ability "to overcome the difficulties that have arisen in the life of the country." [36] At the same time the Kremlin moved to reexamine price hikes scheduled, under the 1971 budget, to take effect within the U.S.S.R. itself. That the Soviet state was no more immune to worker disaffection had been demonstrated in 1962, when rioting over increased prices had swept Novocherkassk and other Soviet cities. Even the economic *wunderkind* of the Eastern bloc, the German Democratic Republic of Walter Ulbricht, had shown its vulnerability to such upheavals. From the Soviet viewpoint the proven fragility of the Gomulka regime and its unsuccessful efforts to patch over deep-seated problems might logically have pointed up the need for fundamental reform and a reordering of priorities within Soviet bloc states generally. Yet resistance to reform and an outright fear of change seemed to be a hallmark of the carefully indoctrinated bureaucracies of most of these nations, and the continued risk of sudden upheavals seemed for the moment preferable to serious efforts aimed at reordering the system.

For years, of course, Yugoslavia had offered an alternative model of development, largely free from Soviet interference and design, and in recent years Rumania, too, had struck out—though far less boldly—on a semi-independent course of its own. Less well known, but perhaps no less significant, were Hungary's efforts to tread a delicate line between the obvious implications of the Brezhnev Doctrine and a degree of internal flexibility at home.

By 1970, these efforts were becoming apparent in various ways. While strictly toeing Moscow's line in matters of foreign policy, the regime of János Kádár was moving cautiously toward a controlled "revisionism" that allowed greater political choice, cultural expression, and economic independence to the population without entailing major political risks for the regime itself. In January, for example, the government announced an easing of travel restrictions to the West which made Hungarian regulations among the most liberal in the Soviet bloc. In April, it moved to transfer some local functions out of party hands and establish them in regularized state agencies. At the same time, it announced that voting lists for upcoming parliamentary and local elections would continue to contain only approved candidates—but it provided for a choice among them. Culturally, safety valves were being provided through a free-wheeling toleration for satire aimed at the regime (but *not* the Russians), while pro-Guevara elements among young people in particular were even allowed an occasional platform in the party press. Most notably, far-reaching economic reforms begun in 1968 and emphasizing decentralization and limited democratization had pushed Hungary farther along the road to a consumer society than any other East European nation. The result seemed to be a relatively content population, a secure regime, and the absence of rival, bickering factions within the party itself.

By contrast with Hungary, Rumania had taken an opposite tack, applying a hard, almost Stalinist, line at home while acting in open defiance of Moscow's wishes abroad. It had openly resisted Soviet efforts in the Council for Mutual Economic Assistance (Comecon) to integrate Eastern Europe's economies. It had sharply limited its participation in Warsaw Pact activities, most notably refusing to take part in the Soviet-led invasion of Czechoslovakia in 1968. It had openly courted the Western powers for economic support, maintained a cordial, non-polemical attitude toward Peking, preserved relations with Israel in the wake of Moscow's tough anti-Israeli campaign, and in general proved itself an irritant to Soviet plans and policies across the board. Yet by the end of 1970, it seemed probable that Rumanian leaders were having second thoughts about their defiant course, that they were beginning to feel more trapped and isolated than independent and secure in their efforts to carve out a special place for themselves in Eastern Europe.

In part this was due to the fact that their "opening to the West" had not proved as profitable as Rumanian leaders had hoped, particularly as far as the United States was concerned. They expressed considerable disappointment over President Nixon's failure to follow up his 1969 visit to their country with measures designed to aid them.[37] And, although Party Secretary and Chief of State Ceauşescu was warmly received and heartily praised by Nixon during his own official visit to Washington October 26–27, 1970,[38] he again failed to gain those substantial economic concessions—including, in particular, his nation's quest for most-favored-nation treatment which both Poland and Yugoslavia already enjoyed.

In the meantime, Rumania was paying heavily for its "go-it-alone" course. Already among the poorest countries in Eastern Europe, it was supporting one of the highest rates of investment in the area (at the cost of increased private consumption) and confronted a growing volume of external debts. When the worst floods in the nation's history struck in May, both Washington and Peking were quick to supply emergency aid in the amount of about $400,000 each, while the Russians ultimately provided a delayed grant of only $50,000—an obvious token of their displeasure with Ceauşescu's heretical tendencies. What the Rumanians feared and had to avoid was the kind of self-imposed isolation that had beset Albania, a nation which felt constrained to issue trade feelers to such countries as Greece and to establish diplomatic ties with Switzerland, in an effort to ease its almost total dependence on Peking. Yet, somewhat like the Albanians before them, the Rumanians found themselves by the end of November with begging cup in hand, negotiating a long-term, interest-free loan from the Communist Chinese themselves—the first of its kind granted by Peking to a Warsaw Pact nation.

Despite the difficulties of his position, however, Ceauşescu continued to fly the banner of defiance through most of 1970. In April, he was again attacking the Brezhnev Doctrine of limited sovereignty and reminding Soviet leaders, in a speech in Moscow honoring the centennial of Lenin's birth, of his country's independent outlook and interests. In May, his ministers refused to participate in Comecon plans to establish a Moscow-based International Investment Bank, designed, among other things, to facilitate Soviet economic expansion through the use of funds obtained from capitalist sources.[39] Nor was Rumania represented when the Bank began operations on January 1, 1971. Even the biggest Warsaw Pact maneuvers in its history, held in East Germany October 12–17, failed to draw more than 20 or 30 Rumanian staff officers. Ceauşescu, in fact, could honorably hail the signing on July 7, after a two-year delay, of a 20-year friendship treaty between his country and the U.S.S.R. as an encouraging sign of improved relations. For while neither country claimed to have made any important concessions in the document, the Soviets nonetheless appeared to accede to Rumania's independent line as long as the U.S.S.R. itself was not endangered by it, and the Brezhnev Doctrine language so apparent in the Soviet-Czech treaty of a few weeks before was notably absent. Ceauşescu himself took note of the occasion by calling upon Communists everywhere to engage in a world-wide debate designed to update Marxism-Leninism, and particularly those aspects of the doctrine governing "fraternal" relations among socialist states.[40]

If Rumania still felt the constraints of Soviet hegemony in Eastern Europe, Yugoslavia was in a more enviable position. Linked by a new trade treaty to the European Economic Community (E.E.C.), enjoying most-favored-nation treatment by the United States, Yugoslavia had long defied the Kremlin's dictates both at home and abroad, and continued to travel its independent course with apparent success in 1970. But problems were clearly developing on the not-too-distant horizon. Like many of its Eastern European neighbors, Yugoslavia was also suffering from inflationary pressures, a chronic deficit in its balance of payments, overindebtedness (around $3 billion), and lagging efficiency, even though its economy had been organized along far more liberal lines. At 77, the country's aging President, Marshal Josip Broz Tito, was still a shrewd and vigorous statesman whose forceful personality provided the key source of unity in a diverse and multinational state. But given the nation's mounting economic difficulties and its tradition of regional antagonisms, what was to hold it together once Tito was gone? Would the Russians move to divide and conquer, playing one nationality off against another (much as they held a lever of persuasion on Rumania through the 2 million people of Hungarian extraction living there)?

These were problems that worried Tito himself. On October 4, therefore, the Yugoslav party Presidium moved to endorse a sweeping reorganization plan, drawn up earlier by Tito himself and designed to ease the national transition after his death. Under the plan Tito would become Chairman of a Presidential Council, composed of representatives of the country's six federated republics, with the presidency rotating among them on a yearly basis after Tito's death or retirement. From the viewpoint of the Yugoslav dissident, Milovan Djilas, the plan simply confirmed a trend that was evident throughout Eastern Europe ". . . [O]ne does not have to be a sage," he wrote, "to perceive that within Yugoslavia the disintegration of the Marxist-Leninist ideology has been under way for some time. And today it is undeniable that such disintegration—in contrast to the ferment within the Czechoslovak party before the Soviet intervention —develops primarily along nationalistic rather than democratic lines. . . . Because of this, the proposed reorganization of the apex of the government—a 'collective' presidency instead of a president— will aggravate, rather than lessen, the inefficiency of the administration and the bickering of the already dissociated [regional] chiefs." [41]

Not all Yugoslavs were so pessimistic as Djilas, but to help resolve their more immediate problems, many were counting on an increased flow of capital investment and trade from the United States. In that regard, President Nixon's two-day visit September 30–October 1, 1970 (the first such to Yugoslavia by an American head of state) provided an opportunity to strengthen economic ties. The United States did, in fact, move to expedite trade and technical cooperation as a result of the Nixon-Tito talks.[42] But in his characteristically independent way, President Tito also took the occasion to warn bluntly that the superpowers alone should not decide the world's fate and to urge a widening of diplomatic processes to give greater voice to smaller nations on important international issues. "In the same way as a 'larger' peace cannot rest for long on 'smaller' wars," Tito told Nixon, "so international cooperation cannot be promoted on the basis of anyone's monopoly or on the negation of the legitimate interests of other countries and peoples. In the absence of peace and progress for the small and underdeveloped, there can be no stable peace nor durable progress for the large and developed either." [43]

8 : The Nixon-Kissinger Approach

From the American viewpoint, Nixon's personal call on Tito was clearly designed to bolster Yugoslav independence at a time of mounting Soviet influence in the Mediterranean and increased Soviet pressure on East Europe, generally. There was, moreover, the added factor of Tito's close personal ties to President Nasser at a time when the United States was seeking Arab cooperation in its effort to secure and extend a 90-day cease-fire and standstill in the Middle East conflict. Similar tactical considerations had motivated Nixon's state visit to Rumania a year earlier and his cordial reception of Ceauşescu in Washington at the time of the U.N.'s 25th anniversary celebration in October 1970.[44] Ceauşescu was not only being honored for his quasi-defiance of Moscow; he was also being utilized because of his unusual rapport with Peking in the context of Washington's own low-keyed efforts to improve relations with that capital. It was no doubt in pursuit of these considerations that the State Department authorized, in 1970, the sale of advanced U.S. oil refinery equipment to Rumania, while turning down a similar request from Communist Poland.[45]
• It would be wrong, however, to conclude that the Nixon administration had merely picked up the threads of former President Lyndon B. Johnson's policy of "building bridges" to Moscow's East European allies, with the aim of undermining Moscow's control. For one thing, the limitations of that policy had been made evident by the Soviet invasion of Czechoslovakia in 1968. For another, it was obvious that Washington itself was not rushing to shower Rumania with such prized rewards as most-favored-nation treatment. More so than his predecessor, Nixon was attempting to deal with the Soviet Union as the recognized leader of the East European bloc, relegating such countries as Yugoslavia and Rumania to shorter-term, tactical consideration in the process. As the President put it in his State of the World message to Congress: "It is not the intention of the United States to undermine the legitimate security interests of the Soviet Union" in Eastern Europe. "By the same token," he added, "the

United States views the countries of Eastern Europe as sovereign, not as parts of a monolith. And we can accept no doctrine that abridges their right to seek reciprocal improvement of relations with us or others." [46]

The President's trip to Yugoslavia clearly sought to further a "reciprocal improvement of relations," but it was also part of a larger package that carried him to Italy (September 27–28), the Vatican (September 28), and on a tour of U.S. Sixth Fleet and NATO installations in the Mediterranean (September 29–30). [47] The trip had in fact been hastily arranged in the wake of a serious conflict between Palestinian commandos and the armed forces in Jordan and the subsequent abortive invasion of that country by Soviet-equipped troops from Syria. Tactically, therefore, its aim was clearly to "show the flag" at a time when Soviet activities in the eastern Mediterranean and the Middle East were causing deep concern in Washington. As Secretary Rogers had indicated in his October 9 press conference, these activities had raised "very serious questions . . . about their [Soviet] intentions," [48] and the President's nine-day journey (including a windup stop in Ireland) was meant above all to remind the Russians of American power in the Mediterranean region and of U.S. determination to use it should the need arise. It was in that spirit that the President told Pope Paul VI, "Tonight after I leave the Vatican, I will be flying to sea and there I shall see the mightiest military force which exists in the world on any ocean." [49] Such words clearly seemed calculated to impress others than officials of the Roman Catholic Church.

Did the Russians get the President's message? The tone of irritation with which the Soviet press commented on the President's trip indicated that they had. Nor could Moscow have been pleased by President Tito's decision to skip the funeral of his good friend, President Nasser (whose sudden death on September 28 had momentarily cast doubt on the Yugoslav leg of Nixon's journey), and proceed instead with arrangements to receive President Nixon. But the untimely passing of a key protagonist in the Middle East drama did have the effect of silencing the guns of the Sixth Fleet as its elements passed in presidential review, and to that extent Nixon's efforts were probably robbed of their fullest impact. With the world's eyes concentrated on a tumultuous state funeral in Cairo, there was relatively little attention left for a sabre-rattling exercise under way in Mediterranean waters.

That the President nonetheless made a practice of keeping his own eye on the Soviet adversary, whatever the crisis at hand, had been evident for some time. Only five months earlier, on April 30, the President had also directed a stern message to the Russians—and also seen its impact blunted by the course of events. In his televised address to the nation announcing the joint U.S.-South Vietnamese strikes into the Cambodian sanctuaries long used by Vietcong and North Vietnamese troops, Nixon had warned in a clear allusion to Moscow that "It is not our power but our will and character that is being tested tonight. . . . If we fail to meet this challenge, all other nations will be on notice that despite its overwhelming power the United States, when a real crisis comes, will be found wanting." [50] White House spokesmen had emphasized to newsmen that the President was gravely concerned by the reported presence of Soviet pilots in the U.A.R. and that he was therefore doubly anxious to signal the Kremlin of his own determination to act boldly, even if in another part of the world.[51] In the upshot, however, a wracking series of protest demonstrations across the United States climaxing in the death of four students at Kent State University,[52] substantially robbed the President's warning of its intended force, and far from being chastised, Moscow, as shall be seen in Chapter 4, was emboldened to even greater commitments of men and materiel into the troubled Middle East.

٭ However disturbed by the hand of fate, both the President's trip to the Mediterranean and his earlier handling of the invasion of Cambodia said a great deal about his approach to dealing with the Kremlin. The President apparently believed, for one thing, that he could not show weakness in one part of the world without encouraging the Soviets to test that evidence of weakness elsewhere— the so-called "linkage" theory by which Moscow was presumed to connect disparate events or problems into a patterned whole (and under which the administration would, in its turn, seek to resolve one problem—e.g., the calling of a European security conference—by linking it to the solution of another—e.g., Berlin). Nixon also felt that deliberate unpredictability could, on occasion, prove a virtue in dealing with Moscow—a means, in fact, of encouraging caution on the part of the Soviets, since they could never be sure of his response to any of their own moves. Finally, the President seemed to believe that a series of step-by-step, or escalating, responses to Communist actions was less effective than one bold and sudden move, since the former gave the adversary time to adapt while the latter took him by surprise and kept him off balance.[53]

٠ How all of these theories meshed with the President's over-all policy toward the Soviet Union, with its emphasis on the search for conciliation and mutual understanding, was hard to say. In his 1964 book, *A World Restored,* Kissinger had argued somewhat dialectically that the key aim of American foreign policy could not be "total security"—impossible to achieve in any case without total conquest— but only the kind of "relative security" that grows out of a broad international agreement over "permissible aims and methods." Within that framework, Kissinger said, lay a stable world order whose foundation "is the *relative* stability—and therefore the *relative* instability—of its members." [54] It was possible that the President's occasional reliance on unpredictability and his penchant for the bold and sudden move fit this pattern of relative instability and thus meshed with his over-all approach to dealing with the Russians on a realistic basis. But it was also possible that the President had momentarily veered from the broad understanding on "permissible goals and methods" which his own preoccupation with Soviet "intentions" seemed to stress.

٠ Whatever the case, the President faced graver problems in his handling of Moscow than the possible internal contradictions of his own policy. At a time when the Kremlin leadership was uncovering its global ambitions, the administration in Washington was beginning to cut back on overseas involvements, to define its interests around the world more narrowly, and to encourage what the then Under Secretary of State, Elliot L. Richardson, had termed "the development of spheres of restraint." [55] The accustomed style in U.S.-Soviet relations—the old pattern of irresistible force, on the one hand, meeting immovable object on the other—was undergoing a process of transformation, and the administration clearly felt trapped between its desire to adjust to the mood at home and its continuing will to resist Soviet expansionary efforts abroad.

That the President himself was keenly aware of the predicament was evident in his speech to the nation on Cambodia. Recalling those decisions which had led to American victory in two world wars, which had brought the Korean war to a conclusion, and which had removed Soviet nuclear weapons from Cuba and the Western hemisphere, the President said: "But between those decisions and this [Cambodian] decision there is a difference that is very fundamental. In those decisions, the American people were not assailed by counsels of doubt and defeat from some of the most widely known opinion leaders of the Nation. . . . I would rather be a one-term President and do what I believe is right than to be a two-term President at the cost of seeing America become a second-rate power and to see this Nation accept the first defeat in its proud 190-year history." [56] The President, in short, was making it clear that his will to resist—even, in his view, his duty to do so—would prevail over "all political considerations" of a domestic nature.

· But again the question arose as to whether the Russians were listening. For however much the President's exercise in unpredictability may have shaken his own constituency or members of the Congress, it failed apparently to dissuade the Soviets from the goals they had set upon in the Middle East and elsewhere. On May 4, Premier Kosygin held an unusual press conference in Moscow specifically to denounce the Cambodian incursion and to warn that "President Nixon's practical steps in the field of foreign policy are fundamentally at variance with those declarations and assurances which he repeatedly made both before assuming the presidency and when he was already in the White House." [57] By early October, the Soviet Premier was underscoring his attitude by forgoing a visit to the 25th anniversary celebration of the United Nations because of what he termed an officially inspired anti-Soviet campaign in the United States.[58] And by mid-October, *The New York Times* was reporting that U.S.-Soviet relations appeared seriously strained for the first time since Nixon had assumed the presidency, after Secretary Rogers and Foreign Minister Gromyko had met in a tense atmosphere and failed to resolve such troublesome questions as continuing violations of the Middle East standstill agreement, the presence of Soviet submarine tenders and other such facilities in Cuban waters, and renewed disruptions of traffic in and out of West Berlin by Soviet bloc authorities.[59] By the time Gromyko met with Nixon on October 22, the question of the submarines and of access to West Berlin appeared to have been cleared up, with the Russians blaming uninformed East German guards for disruption of the traffic to West Berlin. But the problem of the Middle East remained deadlocked, further discussion of the Soviet presence in Cuban waters was avoided, and it remained conspicuously evident from the Soviet viewpoint that Nixon's era of negotiations remained little more than a variant on the era of confrontation that supposedly came before it and to all intents and purposes continued in effect.

3 : SALT and Sufficiency:
Which Way the Arms Race?

Despite the evident and continuing tensions in U.S.-Soviet relations, there remained a glimmer of hope carefully nurtured by each side. After a delay of three years, the Strategic Arms Limitation Talks (SALT) had finally begun in Helsinki on November 17, 1969. President Nixon had described them as "one of the most momentous negotiations ever entrusted to an American delegation," [1] and the initial meeting gave promise of substantive progress to come. The atmosphere had been cordial and businesslike—in marked contrast to the usual flurry of propaganda that had characterized earlier efforts in the field.

For almost 25 years the United States and the U.S.S.R. had warily circled each other over the issues posed by their open-ended—and increasingly expensive—race for nuclear superiority, but their fear of each other had invariably outweighed their fear of mutual annihilation, and despite limited agreements on nuclear weapon tests and nonproliferation, progress toward a general arms control agreement had been repeatedly frustrated. SALT itself provided an example of the kind of problems involved. The talks had first been proposed to Premier Kosygin by President Johnson in January 1967.[2] But it was not until July 1968 that President Johnson was able to announce that the two powers had agreed to proceed with discussions.[3] Then came the August 1968 invasion of Czechoslovakia, and the actual start of the talks was delayed another 15 months.

68

. There had been other obstacles in prior years as well: the mutual suspicions (and jealously guarded prerogatives) of each side's military-industrial complex, the chronic inability to agree on methods of inspection and verification, and so on. Yet there were also scattered indications, beginning around 1962–63, that the two powers were moving toward a better understanding, based on a series of limited and narrowly defined agreements that augured well for the future. In August 1963, in the wake of the Cuban missile crisis, a direct communications link known as the "hot line" was established between Washington and Moscow.[4] That same year the two powers signed a treaty prohibiting nuclear testing in the atmosphere, in outer space, and under water,[5] which opened the way to other areas of agreement. On July 1, 1968, Washington and Moscow signed another pact prohibiting the spread of nuclear weapons to other states—the so-called Treaty on the Nonproliferation of Nuclear Weapons,[6] which President Johnson hailed "as the most important international agreement since the beginning of the nuclear age." [7] (The treaty entered into force March 5, 1970, following the deposit of 48 ratifications not including, however, such key countries as Japan, India, Brazil or Israel.)[8] The two sides were also making progress toward another treaty banning the use of the seabed (beyond a 12-mile coastal zone) for military purposes, and on September 1, 1970 presented to the Conference of the Committee on Disarmament (C.C.D.) at Geneva a revised joint draft which took into consideration the views and suggestions of various nonnuclear coastal countries.[9] On December 7, the United Nations General Assembly commended the draft treaty by a vote of 104 to 2, with 2 abstentions,[10] and another significant milestone on the road to arms control had been passed.

In the meantime, a report by U.N. Secretary General U Thant [11] had given impetus to the issue of arms control with respect to chemical and biological weapons, and on November 25, 1969 President Nixon had moved unilaterally [12] to renounce biological warfare and the development, procurement, or stockpiling of biological weapons, to reaffirm the long-standing policy that the United States would never be the first to use lethal chemicals in any conflict, to extend that policy to cover incapacitating chemicals, and to submit the Geneva Protocol of 1925 [13]—prohibiting the use of most chemical and biological weapons—to the Senate for ratification. In addition, on February 14, 1970, the administration announced it would "confine its military programs for toxins, . . . to research for defensive purposes only," and would order "the destruction of all existing toxin weapons and of all existing stocks of toxins. . . ." [14] (Despite these unilateral steps, however, the budget for fiscal year 1971 authorized as much spending for research on chemical and biological warfare as the preceding budget had done. By the end of 1970, it was also evident that the United States had neither destroyed its stockpiles of these weapons nor dismantled its facilities for their production. And Congress had yet to take any action toward ratifying the Geneva Protocol, in part because of continuing disagreement over the legal use of certain gases, such as tear gas, under the convention.)

9 : The Prospects for SALT

Against this background of limited but steady progress, the prospects for some sort of treaty that would clamp a lid on the strategic arms race seemed brighter—and more within the realm of possibility—than usual. Economically, there were compelling reasons for both sides to seek quantitative as well as qualitative limits on these costly weapons programs. Americans were growing increasingly concerned about neglected domestic priorities in the face of administration requests for such technologically advanced specimens of nuclear weaponry as the Safeguard antiballistic missile (A.B.M.), designed to intercept incoming enemy missiles, and the multiple, independently targetable reentry vehicle (MIRV), which could carry a cluster of nuclear warheads to different enemy targets on one missile. The Russians, for their part, faced a general technology gap with the West in large measure because of a desire to concentrate their expertise and resources on similar devices. There was, moreover, an apparent appreciation by both sides that the likelihood of either one attaining a decisive advantage was growing more and more remote, that the loss of two or more major cities in any all-out nuclear exchange would be unavoidable no matter how sophisticated the defensive system or how powerful the offensive "first-strike" capability. And there was, finally, the overhanging fear that continued and intensified competition, particularly with regard to the new defensive technology of A.B.M.'s, could only widen the gulf of suspicion and uncertainty that already separated the two powers.

Because the issues involved in strategic arms limitation were so complex, however, and the problems of verification so difficult, the Nixon administration decided upon a flexible approach to SALT. As the President described the process in his State of the World message: [15] "We first laid out preliminary models of possible strategic arms limitation agreements. We compared these both with each other and with the situation most likely to prevail in the absence of an agreement. This process greatly improved our understanding of the types of agreements we should consider and pointed up some of the fundamental issues." The President then directed the formation of a Verification Panel to examine the enforcement and inspection problems involved in each strategic weapons system, first in isolation and then in combinations of them. "In the process," the President continued, "we established a comprehensive inventory of the possibilities of a wide range of limitations. . . . We were not tied to a single position; instead we had building blocks for several different positions depending on our decisions and what might prove negotiable." [16]

SALT's first round in Helsinki seemed, in the President's view, to confirm "the validity of our approach. The discussions," Nixon said, "were serious and businesslike. The Soviet representatives demonstrated considerable preparation. They also seemed to welcome the 'building block' approach. We were able to develop an agreed work program for further discussions without acrimony and in full awareness of the likely nature of such discussions." [17] By the time round two got under way in Vienna on April 16, 1970 the two sides were in a position to move to more specific proposals. On July 24, the head of the American delegation, Gerard C. Smith, Director of the U.S. Arms Control and Disarmament Agency (ACDA), reportedly presented his Soviet counterpart, Deputy Minister of Foreign Affairs Vladimir S. Semenov, with a package proposal designed to limit the number of strategic missile launchers—land, sea, and air—on each side to 2,000. Quickly dubbed the "Vienna Plan," the proposal was also said to call for a special limit on the deployment of giant Soviet SS-9 missiles and for a hold-down on A.B.M. systems, either by confining A.B.M. emplacement to Washington and Moscow or by placing some sort of numerical limit on launch facilities (preferably below 100, and none at all, if possible).

On the whole, the American proposal seemed a modest and limited starting point. It sought to freeze or reduce the number of arms without imposing restrictions on the continued qualitative improvement of weapons. It did not, for example, seek to ban MIRV's or to place limits on the kind of intermediate-range weapons deployed by both sides in Europe (an aspect of arms limitation which Washington preferred to leave for NATO-Warsaw Pact discussion). Technically speaking, since the Soviet Union was believed to possess more than 1,400 intercontinental ballistic missiles (I.C.B.M.'s) and the United States more than 1,000 (plus some 650 Polaris and Poseidon submarine-launched missiles), the plan did not even call for a major rollback on existing arsenals, although the long-range U.S. bomber fleet of some 550 aircraft might have to be reduced in size. For all its modesty, however, the Vienna Plan would still have represented a major breakthrough in the field of arms control, if adopted. And initially, at least, the Soviet reaction seemed favorable.[18]

The remainder of the second round (until its adjournment on August 14) was largely given over to a detailed discussion of what the U.S. delegation termed its "outline" proposal. When round three opened in Helsinki on November 2, the Americans were eagerly awaiting a Soviet response or counterproposal. Again the mood was cordial, the opening statements of each side optimistic in tone. But the hoped-for Soviet response was not forthcoming. Instead, the Russian delegation continued to probe for details about the American proposals of July. There were indications that both sides were finding the "specifics" hard to swallow. The Russians were said to be insisting that any comprehensive agreement on limiting offensive weapons include the hundreds of U.S. fighter-bombers based in Europe and aboard aircraft carriers in the Mediterranean. The U.S. was maintaining that only long-range bombers, I.C.B.M.'s, and submarine-based missiles could be classed as strategic offensive weapons. They wanted fighter-bombers classed as the "tactical" equivalents of Soviet intermediate-range missiles and discussed separately as part of an over-all force reduction in Europe. The Russians also indicated a willingness to place a limit on defensive antiballistic missiles alone. They had already deployed some 64 A.B.M. launchers around Moscow and apparently favored limiting this aspect of the arms race to a similar system around Washington. The United States, however, in a reversal of its 1968 position, was said to be insisting that any curb on defensive missiles be accompanied by a limitation on offensive systems as well.

When round three ended on December 18, the tone of optimism

that had previously characterized the official statements of both sides seemed less in evidence. Semenov simply described the sessions as "useful." Smith said merely that "during the past seven weeks both delegations have continued to set forth their views." [19] Instead of a quick and dramatic agreement, long and difficult negotiations seemed in store. SALT was proving fully as complex as the systems it sought to control.

10 : Meanwhile, Back at the Pentagon . . .

When SALT was about to get under way in November 1969, Secretary Rogers had observed that one key objective of the meetings would be to reduce the risk of an outbreak of nuclear war by opening a dialogue about strategic issues.[20] And indeed it could be supposed that, even if SALT failed of agreement after many rounds of negotiation, the dialogue in itself would prove valuable as an educational process, gauging intentions, transmitting warnings, exchanging advice and exhortations, and in general alerting both sides to the full range of the dangers they faced. Yet the very existence of an on-going dialogue also posed certain dangers in its own right. As one American prophet had written when the talks were just beginning "each side is going to blame the other for any delays or failures that may occur; each side is going to become hypersensitive to the possibility that the other side is secretly exploiting delay to achieve strategic advantage; and each side may come to believe that it must therefore build, or threaten, a new strategic weapon system in order to bring the other side to its senses, to show vigilance and to avoid inferiority. . . . The SALT talks could accelerate the arms race by encouraging these lines of thought in both countries." [21]

In fact, through much of 1970, that is precisely what seemed to be happening. As early as January 30, President Nixon was telling a news conference [22] that he had decided to go ahead with the second phase of A.B.M. development, despite the reported inclination of the Johnson administration to halt both A.B.M. and MIRV deployment pending an agreement with the Russians. On February 10, the U.S.S.R. was alleged to be deploying some 75 SS-11 I.C.B.M.'s in two areas previously used only for medium-range missile installations. By the 20th of that month, Secretary Laird was warning the Senate Armed

Services and Appropriations committees that, at its then current rate of build-up, Soviet missile deployment could place the United States in a strategically inferior position by the mid-1970's. While urging a go-ahead with A.B.M., the Secretary also warned that the United States must be ready to rush ahead with plans for a new long-range bomber (the B-1) and other weapons improvements to keep abreast.[23] Moscow chose to answer Laird through an article in *Pravda,* which denied Soviet efforts to achieve nuclear superiority while attacking Laird's "belligerent speeches" and "militaristic calls" for an expanded arms race. Such talk, the article said "cannot but give rise to very serious doubts as to the sincerity of the intentions of the United States in respect to talks with the Soviet Union on limiting the strategic arms race." [24]

This apparent war of nerves nonetheless continued—indeed, it appeared to gain momentum—even after the second round of SALT began April 16. On April 20, for example, Laird was again alleging a nuclear weapons build-up by Moscow, this time charging that while the United States was reducing its own nuclear stockpile by 40 per cent the Soviets had been quadrupling the total megatonnage at their disposal. A week later, President Nixon joined in with a sharp warning to Republicans in Congress that the United States had already fallen into second place in nuclear megatonnage, in the number of land-based missiles, and in A.B.M.'s, adding that it could be second in submarine-launched missiles by 1974. Such warnings gained teeth when the U.S. Air Force, despite a rising volume of congressional protest, announced on June 19 the deployment of the first Minuteman III MIRV's at Minot Air Force Base, North Dakota—the same day, ironically, on which SALT negotiators had held their longest session to date.

On July 9, Laird was back with a charge that Moscow was continuing to deploy its own I.C.B.M.'s at an intensive rate in an apparent effort to increase dramatically its nuclear "first-strike" force, while on July 23, Kissinger joined the fray by claiming that a go-ahead on A.B.M. deployment was in fact essential precisely in order to ensure progress in SALT—presumably as a means of goading the Soviets into an agreement. Again defying congressional pleas, the United States on August 3 jumped another hurdle in MIRV deployment by successfully launching under water a massive Poseidon missile, slated for installation in 31 nuclear-powered submarines, while a Soviet trawler lay three miles off the launch site, busying itself with the collection of ejected debris. Since Poseidon was capable of carrying ten independently targetable reentry vehicles, each armed with a nuclear warhead, its deployment had the effect of considerably expanding America's own nuclear strike force.

It was by now quite evident that, however calm and dignified the proceedings in Vienna and Helsinki, the background pressures in Washington and Moscow were building—if not along hysterical lines— at least along more pessimistic ones. Whether either or both capitals were seeking to steal a march on the other, whether they were maneuvering to create pressures for a quick agreement at SALT, or whether they were simply reacting out of age-old habit while the talks dragged on could not be said with authority. But the results of what they were doing while their negotiators were talking added up to a considerable deterioration in the basis for any workable strategic arms limitation agreement. Between November 1969, when round one of SALT opened, and December 1970, when round three closed, the United States had begun deployment of MIRV warheads on Minuteman III land-based rockets, had begun substituting MIRV Poseidon missiles on its nuclear submarines, and had moved into the second stage of its Safeguard A.B.M. system. The Soviet Union had allegedly moved ahead to the installation of hard-site silos for its huge SS-9 missile, had deployed additional SS-11 missiles, had tested a multiple reentry vehicle (not, however, an independently targetable one), and had continued to build its fleet of Polaris-type nuclear submarines to 30 (13 operational and 17 in construction), compared to 41 for the United States. Both sides had at the same time continued an extensive research and development program designed to improve the accuracy of their offensive weapons, the reliability of their defensive ones, and to apply the fruits of advancing technology, generally, to their strategic arsenals.

The seemingly frantic pace of such activity might have led casual observers to think that even the slightest edge in nuclear weaponry could prove decisive to either side. Yet, even as the third round of SALT was getting under way in Helsinki on November 2, the Stockholm International Peace Research Institute, a Swedish group whose influential Chairman was political economist Gunnar Myrdal, issued a report [25] which found that both sides possessed nuclear stockpiles vast enough to obliterate every person in the world with an equivalent of fifteen tons of TNT. "The balance of terror," said the report, "is not delicate: quite substantial changes in the numbers of warheads on one side or the other would not effectively alter the power balance. There is consequently a wide range of possible agreements on numbers on either side which would leave both sides with a second-strike capability. . . ." The report also claimed that, despite Washington's statements to the contrary, the United States still enjoyed nuclear superiority in strategic weapons over the U.S.S.R. "Even if the whole Minuteman force were wiped out at a stroke—which is not now technically credible," the report said, "there would remain huge United States and allied nuclear forces capable of delivering tens of thousands of warheads [on the Soviet Union]." Specifically, the report had in mind the 7,000-plus U.S. nuclear weapons stationed in Europe and aboard aircraft carriers, which U.S. negotiators had designated as "tactical" and therefore outside the purview of "strategic" arms limitation. Yet, from the American viewpoint, the Myrdal report itself seemed lacking in several respects. It failed, for example, to take into consideration the vast dispersal of population and industry which makes the Soviet Union, in contrast to the United States, such a difficult target. In blithely dismissing the possible development of a "first-strike" capability by either side (i.e., the capability to knock out all retaliatory nuclear forces in one blow), it also dismissed a concern of overriding importance to both sides. The possibility of a major technological breakthrough in that area continued to haunt each and was hardly viewed as fanciful by either.

In other ways, too, the United States saw itself as having more at stake in strategic arms limitation than the Soviet Union. As François Duchêne, Director of the Institute for Strategic Studies in London, observed, "For a generation, the United States has had pretensions to nuclear 'superiority,' just as she has enjoyed untrammelled freedom of the oceans, and has exploited both for political advantage. Now, SALT tends to ratify the parity of deterrence between the super-Powers at a time when the reach of the Soviet Navy is extending into the Mediterranean, the Indian, and even the Atlantic and Caribbean regions. The two trends together underline the decline of the almost unchallenged freedom of strategic movement of the United States during the cold-war period and the end of the equally exaggerated isolation of the Soviet Union in her Eurasian heartland. Accordingly, SALT, which can be seen by one wing of Western opinion as a step to *détente,* could also be seen by the opposite wing of Soviet opinion as a step towards cancelling the advantages the U.S. has gained from her strategic superiority." [26]

Another analyst, the French expert on Communist affairs, Michel Tatu, observed that the shadow of Communist China was also present as a sort of silent partner in the SALT discussions. In a policy study for the Atlantic Institute,[27] Tatu maintained that the Russians were using the Chinese threat "not in order to buy a rapprochement with the West at the 'cost of concessions,' but to convince the West that they [the Russians] deserve concessions by virtue of their special position." By "shutting their eyes to the Chinese factor," Tatu claimed, both Washington and Moscow could probably agree on a limitation of their own strategic capabilities at a level of parity. But the looming threat of China's growing nuclear potential would inevitably have a destabilizing effect on any agreement reached—could, indeed, even foreclose the possibility of agreement in the first place. Already, he noted, China's progress in strategic weaponry had forced the Americans and Russians alike to step up their own nuclear programs. "It is partly in order to outface China that the Soviet Union has developed its military potential in the last few years, deploying its fleet in distant waters and particularly the Indian Ocean, to the alarm of the Western Powers also."

That the Soviets had indeed been beefing up their military posture —and that Washington in particular had grown alarmed—was only too evident in the repeated warnings of Laird and other U.S. officials. Admiral Thomas H. Moorer, who had succeeded General Earl G. Wheeler as Chairman of the Joint Chiefs of Staff on July 2, put it bluntly in a speech in December. "In the past decade," he said, "the strategic balance between the United States and the Soviet Union has changed from one of United States superiority to one of nuclear parity. The favorable strategic equations of the 1960's which helped us emerge with the winning position from the Cuban crisis are now only of historical significance." [28] Even more alarming for Washington, in some ways, was the Soviet naval build-up, which, far more than any accumulation of I.C.B.M.'s, lent substantive credence to the Soviet quest for global power status.

As part of the festivities attending the centennial anniversary of Lenin's birth in April, the U.S.S.R. had dispatched more than 150 ships of its fleet on a globe-circling tour—an oceanic demonstration designed, no less than Nixon's Mediterranean tour, to impress the world with one power's massive naval might. Between 1960 and 1970,

Moscow had increased the number of its nuclear-powered submarines from an estimated three to 70; it had raised the number of missile-firing surface ships from little more than ten to an estimated 170. At the end of 1970, it had approximately 41 warships deployed in the Mediterranean (compared with 35 to 40 vessels in the U.S. Sixth Fleet, whose over-all firepower remained superior); it had a cruiser, three destroyers, five submarines, and various support ships on permanent station in the Indian Ocean; and, according to Vice-Admiral Hyman G. Rickover of the U.S. Navy, the Russians had at least 13 advanced, nuclear-powered submarines, each capable of launching from under water 16 nuclear missiles with a range of over 1,000 miles, and were building additional such vessels at the rate of 12 a year (five to ten a year according to the Institute for Strategic Studies).[29] Such an array of warships seemed hardly calculated to protect the Soviet Union's meager trade lines; on the contrary, most Western analysts judged it essentially offensive in nature and purpose.[30]

• By contrast, the United States was paring its own defense budget to what Secretary Laird, in a statement before Senate hearings on February 20, had called "a rock bottom." [31] That statement had requested total defense spending for the fiscal year ending June 30, 1971 of $71.8 billion, more than $5 billion below the amount spent for fiscal year 1970 and the lowest level of defense spending, as a percentage of either the gross national product or total Federal spending, in 20 years. Most of the projected savings were directly traceable to scheduled cutbacks of U.S. forces in Vietnam (all told, civilian and military manpower would be reduced, under the budget proposal, by 311,000 bringing the total number of personnel on active duty in the nation's armed services below three million). As for strategic forces and new programs, the Secretary stressed that his fiscal 1971 spending estimates reflected "a transition budget." "It is designed to preserve the basic capabilities we currently have while retaining key options until a clearer picture of the future strategic environment emerges. This should come from our own continuing review and from such other factors as SALT and the changing threat." [32] The Secretary did stress, however, that the U.S.S.R. "is not making similar reductions in its defense budget. In fact, the Soviet Union is pulling abreast of us in many major areas of military strength and ahead of us in others. . . . It is clear that the Soviet Union is embarked on an ambitious program to achieve a global military capability." [33]

11 : Congress Takes a Hand

Under the Kissinger formula, of course, strategic parity could be seen as more constructive, in the final analysis, of a stable world order than the old reliance on "nuclear superiority" had been. And in his State of the World message, President Nixon had described his own administration's strategic goal as one of nuclear "sufficiency." [34] Nonetheless, Secretary Laird, in a statement on the defense budget,[35] proposed additional funding for engineering development of the advanced B-1 long-range bomber; he asked initial procurement of a short-range attack missile and continued development of a subsonic cruise armed decoy; he wanted continued development of Minuteman III and Minuteman force modernization, conversion of six nuclear submarines to Poseidon configuration, development of a new submarine incorporating an Undersea Long-range Missile System (ULMS), continued engineering development of the Airborne Warning Control System (AWACS), development and deployment of a new satellite strategic surveillance system, development of a third nuclear-powered aircraft carrier, and continued deployment through phase two of Safeguard.

What thus seemed "sufficient" from the administration's viewpoint began to look "excessive" to certain members of Congress. As noted above,[36] a generalized discontent with American foreign policy had been festering in Congress for several years, and it was the fate of the Defense Department that its budget requests offered the most inviting target of reprisal for a body whose most effective means of policy persuasion lay in its power to control the Federal purse. That the kind of broad congressional exhortation embodied in the "national commitments" resolution of 1969 [37] had done little to sway administration policy-makers was evident in the President's decision to invade Cambodia on April 30.[38] In its concern to call a halt to MIRV and A.B.M. deployment before they added new complications to the tasks facing SALT, the Senate on April 9 by a vote of 72 to 6, had passed a resolution calling upon both the U.S. and the U.S.S.R. urgently to pursue limitations on offensive and defensive strategic weapons alike and requesting the President to propose an immediate suspension of further deployment of such weapons by both parties.[39] At his news conference on March 21, the President termed the thrust of this resolution "irrelevant to what we are going to do." Negotiating a freeze on offensive and defensive weapons "is what SALT is all about," Nixon said. "It takes two, however, to make a deal." [40]

This observation was equally applicable to the President's relations with Congress, however. No sooner had the President announced his own intention of going ahead with A.B.M. deployment than Senator Mansfield and Senator Fulbright were aligning themselves against him on this issue. Senator Edward M. Kennedy observed that the administration's own proposed spending cuts were almost exclusively tied to the fruits of Vietnamization and suggested that cuts in other areas would also be possible without endangering the national security.[41] In May, a bipartisan group of Senators announced their own plans to scrutinize and cut Pentagon spending with an eye to a reordering of "the relative priorities between military, security, and domestic needs," generally.[42] The critics wanted Laird's "rock bottom" budget slashed an extra $5.2 billion, and they grew increasingly skeptical of administration warnings about Soviet intentions as the year wore on. In October, Senator Fulbright publicly charged that all the uproar about an alleged Soviet submarine base in Cuba was aimed at "hoodwinking the American people." Pentagon officials who had briefed the Senate Foreign Relations Committee, he said, not only had no evidence that such a base was under construction but did not even try to convince the panel that it was.[43] In December, a Senate Foreign Relations subcommittee went on record to warn that America's own long-standing policy of ringing the Soviet Union and Communist China with tactical nuclear weapons could eventually provoke an international crisis, should either of those powers seek to "break out of the nuclear ring" by deploying their own nuclear weapons overseas.[44]

Such congressional sniping inevitably had its effect—on the defense budget where it counted most. To be sure, congressional critics failed to halt deployment of MIRV's, expansion of A.B.M.'s, or to slash the over-all budget by $5.2 billion, as they had sought. But the Department of Defense Appropriation Act, as signed by President Nixon on January 11, 1971,[45] did reflect their cumulative discontent by whittling roughly $2 billion from Secretary Laird's "rock-bottom" figure. It also managed to deny the Navy funds for a third nuclear carrier, chopped funds for the B-1 bomber in half, and reduced spending for research and development by $400,000. Congressional critics also succeeded in forcing a compromise in A.B.M. deployment, cutting the administration's funding for the expansion of this program to a little over $1 billion and limiting the number of new sites to two.

On the whole, the administration found itself sorely distressed by this outcome, as did its supporters in Congress. Secretary Laird declared that the cuts would "increase the risks to our national security,"[46] while Senator Barry Goldwater was moved to protest that left-wing elements were engaged in a systematic effort to weaken the U.S. defense posture.[47] Representative L. Mendel Rivers, Chairman of the House Armed Services Committee, averred that the United States was on the "brink of disaster," its future hanging "by a thread" because of the cutbacks.[48]

And indeed, before the year was out, administration sources were warning that the downward trend in defense budgets, sustained for the first two years of Nixon's term, would have to be reversed in the national interest. The Penatgon itself was apparently counting on a $5 billion increase in its spending plans for fiscal year 1972, although the White House was said to have pared this amount to $1 billion.[49] Secretary Laird did not forecast a specific figure, but he was reported to be thinking of a defense budget somewhere in the vicinity of $74.5 billion to $77 billion. Nor did these figures appear to exclude the possibility of some sort of arms limitation agreement through SALT. As one Pentagon official said, "If you control only a piece of the arms race, it's like squeezing a pillow. You're going to have a bulge somewhere else."[50]

In short, the administration was of the view that, no matter what the outcome of SALT, the defense budget would probably rise again in the years immediately ahead. Given the effects of inflation and certain automatic pay increases for armed forces personnel, the Pentagon could argue that, somewhat like Alice, its budget would have to run twice as fast merely to stay in the same place. For example, the President's Commission on an All-Volunteer Armed Force, headed by former Secretary of Defense Thomas S. Gates, issued a report [51] on its findings on February 21 proposing the establishment of an all-volunteer army, with conscription replaced by a standby draft to be used in the event of national emergencies. The net cost of this professionalizing of the armed services was estimated at $2.7 billion in additional pay and allowances, each of which would rise by as much as 50 per cent. Although the administration backed the essential thrust of the Gates report and committed itself to the volunteer army concept, Secretary Laird warned that, in part for budgetary reasons, the changeover would not be possible by July 1, 1971, as recommended by the Commission, but would have to be delayed at least until July 1, 1973. In the meantime, of course, the draft would continue in effect with a new Director of Selective Service, Dr. Curtis W. Tarr, a former university president, succeeding General Lewis B. Hershey, who resigned the post on February 17.

That large—perhaps growing—numbers of Congressmen would nonetheless stand in opposition to any rise in defense spending already seemed clear from the outcome of the budgetary battle for fiscal 1971. Moreover, the Pentagon's case for future increases was hardly helped by revelations of inefficiency—or worse—that were coming to light in the conduct of Defense Department operations. In the spring, Congress had been scandalized by reports that Army intelligence agents, operating under a Defense Department intelligence budget of $2.9 billion, had been amassing dossiers on the activities of private citizens, government officials, and such reformist organizations as the American Civil Liberties Union and the National Association for the Advancement of Colored People. According to one former Army intelligence officer, the program of domestic surveillance got under way in 1965 and mushroomed after the ghetto riots in Detroit and elsewhere in 1967. "Today," he charged, "the Army maintains files on the membership, ideology, programs and practices of virtually every activist political group in the country." [52] Although the Nixon administration promptly ordered a halt to such operations, the damage, from the budgetary viewpoint, had already been done. Subsequent revelations about massive cost overruns on the new Air Force C-5A jet transport —cost overruns which had brought the Pentagon and the Lockheed Aircraft Corporation to the point of legal action in the courts—also served to deepen congressional suspicions that defense spending had yet to hit the "rock bottom" figure of which Secretary Laird boasted.

For Congress no less than for the administration, however, it would be the quality of Soviet-American relations that would in the end prove decisive in the struggle over America's security needs and the means of financing them. The President had argued broadly for "sufficiency," and on that point, at least, both Republicans and Democrats, hawks and doves, even revisionists and cold warriors seemed in agreement. In its broad outline, the American defense posture remained very much geared to "where Russia was going," and Gogol's century-old question would no doubt continue to shape its profile— low or high—in the years that lay ahead.

4 : The Middle East Tinderbox

In his book, *The War Business,* George Thayer had pointed out that an armed conflict breaks out somewhere in the world on an average of once every five months.[1] Most, after a time, are settled in one way or another. But two—one in the Middle East and one in Southeast Asia—had been dragging on at inordinate length by 1970, laying waste ancient lands and peoples, hammering at the world's nervous system, and threatening to involve the great powers in a confrontation they devoutly hoped to avoid. Of these, the Arab-Israeli conflict was the older and, in President Nixon's words, the "more dangerous, more dangerous because it involves—and this is not the case in Vietnam—a collision of the super powers." On the first day in July, the President spelled out the stakes in the area this way: "The Mideast is important. We all know that 80 percent of Europe's oil and 90 percent of Japan's oil comes from the Mideast. We know that the Mideast, . . . is the gateway to Africa, it's the gateway to the Mediterranean, it's the hinge of NATO, and it is also the gateway through the Suez Canal down into the Indian Ocean." [2]

Left unsaid, but no less in the forefront of the President's thinking, was what former Under Secretary of State George W. Ball had recently called "the quantum jump in Soviet adventurism" in the region.[3] With its endemic instabilities and its location at the spiritual and geographic crossroads of three continents, the Middle East had for centuries served as a chessboard for great power ambitions. It is said that

Russia's Peter the Great (who ruled from 1682 to 1725) had advised his successors "to approach as near as possible to Constantinople and India . . . [and] penetrate as far as the Persian Gulf." What the Czars failed to do in more than 200 years of trying, Soviet leaders had accomplished in little more than a decade and a half since the mid-1950's. They had skirted around the Northern Tier alliance (the Central Treaty Organization or CENTO, linking Turkey, Iran, Pakistan, and Britain), formed to contain them and had implanted themselves in the heart of the Arab world. By 1970, they had placed an estimated 3,500 military advisers in the United Arab Republic alone. They were the sole suppliers of arms to Syria, Iraq, and the People's Democratic Republic of Yemen as well as to Egypt, and they were developing, in competition with Communist China, a patron-client relationship with Southern Yemen. They had established naval facilities in the Egyptian ports of Alexandria and Port Said, at Latakia and Tarus in Syria, at Hudaydah in Yemen, and at the former British base of Aden south of the Red Sea in Southern Yemen.

More than anything else, the Arab-Israeli conflict had paved the way for these gains. Only two decades before, Moscow could count few friends in the area outside the fledgling state of Israel, whose right to an independent existence it had energetically supported in the United Nations. Sometime early in the 1950's, however, Soviet policy had begun reversing gears. By 1954, the Russians were backing Arab complaints against Israel before the U.N. In 1955, they concluded an arms deal with Egypt, the region's most populous state, and secured at last the client they had been angling for. Both the combined Anglo-French-Israeli assault on Egypt in 1956 and the so-called Six-day War of 1967 had served to quicken the dependence of a badly battered U.A.R. on Soviet support. After the conflict in 1967, in particular, the Russians moved swiftly to rearm Egypt, Syria, and Iraq, supplying an estimated $3 billion in military and economic aid to these countries and endorsing Arab demands as their own before the United Nations and the world.

But it was not until 1970 that the extent of Moscow's investment in the area—and the lengths to which it was willing to go to protect its newly won stakes—became clear. Toward the end of February, following a desperate plea for help from Nasser, the Soviets began shipping some of their most advanced and sophisticated antiaircraft missiles—the redoubtable SAM-3's, capable of fending off the kind of low-altitude attacks in which the Israeli Air Force specialized—into Egypt. Accompanying these weapons were an estimated 1,500 Soviet military personnel, whose job it would be to man them.

Were the Russians thus committing their own troops to the Middle East conflict in a manner reminiscent of America's own gradual involvement in Vietnam? More and more, it began to seem so. On April 28, the Israeli government reported that Soviet pilots had been flying defensive missions over Cairo, Alexandria, and other key missile installations since the 18th of that month. By this time also, according to United States sources, the number of Soviet troops and technicians committed to the U.A.R. had risen to an estimated 10,000.[4] In fact, the Russians were believed to have already sustained a number of casualties in the fighting—on the Golan Heights of Syria in 1967 and subsequently within Egypt itself as the result of heavy Israeli air attacks. During Israeli raids on Egyptian SAM-2 sites in 1969 alone, Russian casualties reportedly totaled 12 advisers killed and 29 wounded.[5] What made the build-up of 1970 so ominous, however, was that Soviet combat personnel—as distinct from mere "military advisers"—were now directly manning missiles and planes in the U.A.R., engaging and perhaps even downing Israeli aircraft in the process.

Coming as it did on top of the Soviet naval build-up in the Mediterranean, the massive arms deliveries to the Arab states, and the thousands of military advisers already on hand, this sudden commitment of Soviet combat personnel to one of the most volatile conflicts of the postwar era appeared to confirm the darkest fears of the Nixon administration. As the President put it in his State of the World message,[6] "One of the lessons of 1967 was that the local events and forces have a momentum of their own, and that conscious and serious effort is required for the major powers to resist being caught up in them." Noting the rise of Soviet activity in the area, the President went on to warn that "This has consequences that reach far beyond the Arab-Israeli question. The United States has long-standing obligations and relationships with a number of nations in the Middle East and its policy is to help them enhance their own integrity and freedom. . . . But the United States would view any effort by the Soviet Union to seek predominance in the Middle East as a matter of grave concern."

For almost 25 years, Washington had been struggling to contain

Soviet power within the rough limits set by World War II. That was the meaning of the Truman Doctrine of 1947, designed to block Soviet penetration of Greece and Turkey; it was also the meaning of such defensive alliances as NATO and CENTO (to the latter of which the U.S. was closely tied by its "observer" status). To be sure, the primary arena of Soviet-American competition had always been Europe, where the stakes, from the point of view of both powers, were highest. But the oil-rich Middle East was a strategically important zone of contention as well. Lying athwart the Southwest perimeter of the Soviet Union, the region was of obvious concern to Russia, whose large Muslim population and common border with Turkey, Iran, and Afghanistan made the U.S.S.R. something of a Middle Eastern power in its own right. Nor could Moscow be unaware of the growing strategic significance of the Suez Canal to its burgeoning Navy. Closed (as had been the case since 1967), it made the Red Sea the farthest point on earth from the U.S.S.R. by water. Open, that waterway provided the Soviet fleet with direct access via the Red Sea to the Persian Gulf and the Indian Ocean.

Though geographically more distant, the United States was nonetheless also intimately tied to the area, mainly through its interests in those two seemingly unmixable quantities—oil and Israel. At a profit of more than $1 billion a year, American companies pumped and sold 50 per cent of the Mideast's oil (mostly to Western Europe and Japan, thereby serving to ease the chronic deficit in the U.S. balance of payments). At a less material, but no less compelling level, the United States recognized a tradition of friendship and aid for Israel dating back to that nation's founding. When the Jewish state was established in 1948, Washington had been the first capital to grant diplomatic recognition. In the 20-odd years that followed, it had provided the young democracy with at least $1 billion in government aid, while the American Jewish community contributed another $1 billion. Following the Six-day War, the United States emerged as Israel's key outside supplier of modern arms. And increasingly the United States had assumed the role of Israel's prime defender before the U.N. and other international forums, even though no formal defense treaty tied the two states together, no American troops were stationed on Israeli soil, and despite occasional U.S. condemnation of Israeli retaliatory raids on its Arab neighbors in the U.N. Security Council.

Such a dichotomy of interests—Israel on the one hand and Arabian oil on the other—had long blurred the lines of an effective U.S. policy in the Middle East and had prompted some prominent Americans, such as former Secretary of State Dean Acheson, to regret U.S. support for Israel's founding as a policy error, the deleterious implications of which should have been avoided in the first place.[7] Yet as President Nixon never tired of pointing out, the area had long been rife with more conflicts than met the eye of the average headline reader, both before and after Israel's birth as a nation.[8] The Arab monarchs who controlled most of the region's oil seemed no more disturbed by Israel's preemption of Palestine than by the intrigues carried on against them by such radical Arab states as Egypt, Syria, and Iraq. Even the Russians who backed these nominally socialist regimes were wary lest they be outflanked on the left by the still more radical Palestinian commandos, who showed occasional signs of capturing the Arab imagination much as Nasser had done before them. Amidst this welter of conflicting attitudes and interests, any great power was advised to move gingerly and with caution. And, indeed, even in the rush of their deepening involvement in Egypt, the Soviets seemed bent, for the time being, on bucking up that country's defenses rather than moving it toward any immediate offensive capability that might serve to prod events beyond Moscow's control.

With an eye toward its remaining friends in Lebanon, Jordan, Saudi Arabia, and the oil sheikdoms of the Persian Gulf, and given its general desire for good relations with all the countries in the area, the United States could tread no less delicately in its support for Israel. Indeed, during its first year in office the Nixon administration talked a great deal about a new, "even-handed" approach to the area's conflicts, although the main lines of its policy followed rather closely those of the Johnson administration before it. It supported, for example, U.N. Security Council Resolution 242 of November 22, 1967,[9] which called for Israeli withdrawal from territories occupied in the Six-day War, the acknowledgment by all states in the region of "their right to live in peace within secure and recognized borders," guaranteed freedom of navigation through the area's international waterways, a just settlement of the Palestinian refugee problem, and guarantees for "the territorial inviolability and political independence of every State in the area, through measures including the establishment of demilitarized zones." Until such agreements could be worked out with the assistance of U Thant's Special Representative, Ambassador Gunnar V. Jarring of Sweden, the administration proposed to try to maintain a balance of arms in the area that would help insure Israel's security against any renewed Arab attack. At the same time it took a position against substantial Israeli territorial gains at Arab expense, while seeking, both within the framework of the United Nations and on the basis of bilateral talks, to dissuade the Soviets from further activities in the region that could lead to a possible great power confrontation. President Nixon summed up the U.S. attitude on January 30, 1970, when he said "We are neither pro-Arab nor pro-Israel. We are pro-peace." [10]

12 : War Fever on the Rise

Yet as 1970 opened, peace seemed to hang by the slenderest of threads in the troubled Middle East. The efforts of mediator Jarring had long since foundered on the rocks of Arab-Israeli intransigence, and he had temporarily returned to his official post as Sweden's Ambassador to the U.S.S.R. Then in April of 1969, the United States, the Soviet Union, Britain, and France had taken up the problem [11] and, with the subsequent narrowing of the discussion to a bilateral, U.S.-Soviet basis, some progress on the main lines of a possible agreement was evident. But the discussions then proceeded to bog down in the face of seemingly insurmountable Soviet-American differences. On January 12, 1970, the State Department made public a Soviet note which rejected the American proposals of the preceding October 28 as "one-sided" and "pro-Israeli" and blamed Israel for the "sharply deteriorated" situation in the area.[12] State Department officials, who had publicly labeled the Soviet note a "retreat" from Moscow's earlier positions, expressed their own doubts about the further value of continuing the bilateral talks, though the Big-Four discussions went on. As it was, they noted, the American proposals, set forth publicly in a speech by Secretary Rogers on December 9, 1969,[13] had come under attack by the Israelis and by many Americans for being "pro-Arab," in that they called on Israel to withdraw from all Egyptian territory captured in the war. The Soviets, for their part, wanted the meetings to continue, but it was clear they also wanted further concessions from the United States and Israel that would benefit their Arab clients.

On three previous occasions when diplomacy had faltered in the Middle East, Arabs and Israelis had taken it upon themselves to resolve their differences in the classic resort to arms. Was another such showdown in the offing? Certainly the rising intensity of military actions in the area pointed in that direction. On April 23, 1969, President Nasser had declared the U.N.-sponsored cease-fire of June 1967 null and void and had begun a much publicized "war of attrition" against Israeli forces occupying the Bar Lev line on the east bank of the Suez Canal. As the fighting gradually escalated along this front, Israel responded with a series of deep penetration raids that saw American-supplied Phantom jets ranging far and wide over the Nile Valley, striking with apparent impunity at the very heart of the Egyptian state. At the same time, Egyptian artillery, antiaircraft, and radar installations on the west bank of the Suez Canal were subjected to an almost daily pounding from the air, forcing the evacuation of at least 600,000 civilians from the region's communities and reducing its already barren landscape to pock-marked, almost lunar configuration.

The motives of President Nasser in launching an attempted war of attrition had been clear at the start: frustrated by Israel's refusal to withdraw from occupied territories and by the apparent lack of progress toward a settlement under Jarring's auspices, the Egyptian leader seemed determined to make Israel pay in blood and fire for each day its troops continued to stand upon Arab soil. The Israelis, for their part, rejoined the battle with the aim of keeping Cairo on the defensive, blasting the Canal's west bank to prevent any build-up of Egyptian forces that could lead to a cross-Canal operation, and staging deep penetration raids to expose both the hollowness of Nasser's war-of-attrition claims and the severe vulnerability of the U.A.R. itself to Israeli air power. By early 1970, there could be little doubt that the Israeli raids, which reached repeatedly to the outskirts of Cairo, were having their intended psychological effect. On January 24, Israeli Defense Minister Moshe Dayan could claim with considerable justification that "all of Egypt is the field of battle, the theater of our operations," [14] and could rest assured that Israel was, indeed, wearing down the adversary's offensive capability and bringing home the truth, as he put it, to the Egyptian people. On February 8, Nasser himself virtually conceded as much by admitting the fact of Israeli air superiority before his nation on television. Once again Egyptians could ruefully reflect that events their leader had set in motion were redounding against them and threatening the very stability of the governing regime.

But Nasser had yet to exhaust the full range of military options available to him, however risky they might prove to be. In January, he embarked on a secret mission to Moscow, there to plead in person for the additional arms needed to ward off further Israeli attacks, including a request for the highly advanced SAM-3 missiles. In an apparent last-ditch effort to prevent the deployment of these reputedly formidable weapons beyond Soviet frontiers, Premier Kosygin addressed an urgent note to President Nixon on January 21, deploring the worsening situation in the Middle East and warning that Israel's deep penetration raids must be called off.[15] In his response of February 4, the President argued that tensions in the area could best be reduced by a return to the cease-fire which Nasser had broken, by multilateral efforts to curb the delivery of additional arms, and by a more positive reception of past U.S. proposals designed to restore peace.[16] At this time the United States was itself in the process of considering an Israeli request for an additional 25 Phantom and 100 Skyhawk jets, with regard to which Nixon, on January 30, had promised a decision within 30 days.[17] As it turned out, the 30 days passed without any U.S. decision being made. But by the end of February, Soviet hardware had already begun to flow into Egypt.

With that development, it was the Israelis who began to grow increasingly worried, the Egyptians who appeared increasingly confident. Though launched in response to Nasser's war of attrition, Israel's deep penetration raids had begun to cost the latter heavily in terms of world public opinion and perhaps even of U.S. support. This seemed particularly the case after two incidents involving the destruction of civilian installations near Cairo. In the first, on February 12, Israeli jets demolished a nonmilitary metal processing plant, killing 80 civilian workers and prompting a rebuke from the United States,[18] which had been privately critical of the deep penetration raids from the start. In the second, on April 8, Egyptian sources reported the bombing of an elementary school, with 30 children and one teacher killed and 46 wounded. Israel denied a role in this incident, but again the United States expressed its shock. By now, moreover, incensed Egyptians were openly blaming Washington itself for such mishaps, claiming that without American support and equipment such raids would never have been possible in the first place.

For once, it seemed, the Egyptians had a compelling argument, for Washington had already found it exceedingly difficult, if not positively embarrassing, to accede to any Israeli request for more aircraft while the jets it had already supplied showed such utter mastery of Egyptian air space. Secretary Rogers had intimated as much during his news conference of March 23, in which a decision on Israel's long-standing bid for additional jets was politely but indefinitely postponed.[19] While promising "close and careful scrutiny" of stepped-up Soviet activities and a "continuous review and evaluation" of the military balance, the Secretary nonetheless declared that "In our judgment, Israel's air capacity is sufficient to meet its needs for the time being." He warned that any Soviet steps taken to upset the balance would prompt a reconsideration of this "interim decision," but he hoped "that our restraint will afford fresh opportunities for all concerned—in and outside the area—to diminish hostilities and enhance the prospects for peace." To that end he promised renewed and energetic efforts to move the parties involved toward a negotiated settlement.

From Israel's viewpoint, Washington's "decision not to decide" came as a sharp disappointment. Confronted by Soviet missiles on the ground, Soviet pilots in the sky, and American disapproval of their tactics, they had little choice but to call off their deep penetration raids in mid-April and concentrate their fire along a 15-mile-wide belt stretching down the west bank of the Canal and the Red Sea, an area which Dayan was determined to keep clear of SAM-2 and SAM-3 missiles even if it meant direct clashes with Russian pilots.[20] Yet the area remained as much a powder keg as ever, with some of the fiercest fighting since the Six-day War still to come. The aerial dogfights which had swirled over much of Egypt in March, and which at one point had seen nine Egyptian MIG-21's bite the dust in a period of three days, now gave way to sharp clashes on the ground. On April 30, in the biggest engagement since the 1967 war, a battalion of Egyptian troops crossed into Sinai to attack Israeli positions along the Bar Lev line, and during one ten-day period at the end of May and early June, Israeli jets were reported to have dropped more bombs on Egyptian positions along the west bank than had been employed by all the combatants in the 1967 conflict. It was estimated that between the time when Israel halted its deep penetration raids on April 18 and the American-sponsored cease-fire went into effect on

August 7 some 10,000 Egyptian troops lost their lives in the hail of fire and steel that rained down upon them in the Suez and Red Sea regions.

Nor was all quiet along Israel's front with Jordan, Syria, and Lebanon. Two major clashes involving tanks and planes had already occurred between Israeli and Syrian forces in February and March, and on June 16 Israeli troops struck once again along the road to Damascus, their target an army camp and bridge near the Syrian capital, which were shelled in retaliation for what the Israelis claimed had been 49 cease-fire violations by the Syrians in the previous 30 days.

"Spring-offensive" time had also arrived for the Palestinian commandos, whose highly publicized if largely unsuccessful raids on Israeli border settlements appeared to cause less trouble for the government in Jerusalem than for the governments of Jordan and Lebanon, from whose territory the varied commando organizations chose to spring their attacks. Under pressure from these organizations, the Lebanese government had on November 3, 1969 reluctantly yielded control of the Arkoub region bordering Israel to Palestinian forces, which shortly initiated a series of rocket attacks and forays against Israeli settlements to the south. On May 12, 1970, in the largest such operation since the 1948 war, Israeli tanks and armored columns crossed into the region in force and for 32 hours did battle with commando units, at the same time studiously seeking to shun any direct engagement with Lebanese Army elements. Nonetheless, taking note of their sudden vulnerability, the Lebanese promptly moved to speed the expansion of their own armed forces, while the raid itself was duly condemned in the Security Council on May 19. The vote was 11 to 0, with the United States and three other nations abstaining because the resolution failed to condemn commando activities on the part of the Arabs.[21] Apparently unsatisfied with these achievements, however, one of the more radical commando groups, the so-called Popular Front for the Liberation of Palestine (P.F.L.P.), proceeded on May 22 to ambush an Israeli school bus near the Lebanese border, firing bazookas at point-blank range and killing 12 of those aboard—mostly children— in what by now had become a new Lebanese front in an old but apparently expanding conflict.

13 : Cease-fire: The Rogers Plan

By the time the third anniversary of the 1967 war rolled around on June 5, both sides appeared to be soberly girding for the decisive battle that each believed lay ahead. For the 2.5 million Israelis, surrounded in a hostile sea of 90 million Arabs, any war of attrition was a problem of serious concern, no matter how great the toll exacted from the enemy in retaliation. Nor could the Arabs, and particularly the Egyptians, take that toll lightly as it reached seemingly higher and higher proportions, straining already impoverished economies and deepening the wounds of dissension within Arab society itself. Yet for all the apparent alarm in world capitals over these outward signs of deterioration, the Arab-Israeli conflict remained a strange and in many ways subdued sort of drama. Despite blackouts, sand-bagged bunkers, and other air-raid precautions, Cairenes and the great mass of Egypt's 33 million people seemed to go about their business with an equanimity as timeless as the pyramids at Giza. In Israel, trade and tourism boomed, and even the newly occupied Arab communities on Jordan's West Bank appeared to have settled into a comfortable if fatalistic routine. Such attitudes could be seen as a harbinger of peace in the area, even as the armies carried on their sporadic warfare. And, in fact, a peace of sorts was slowly emerging on the Mideast horizon.

At his news conference of March 23,[22] Secretary Rogers had promised a fresh attempt at peace efforts and, true to his word, he met with Soviet Ambassador to Washington Anatoly P. Dobrynin two days later, in a resumption of the direct U.S.-U.S.S.R. dialogue that had more or less been in abeyance since the first of the year. Though Dobrynin reportedly voiced little interest in the kind of arms embargo which Washington had been pressing for, he was said to indicate that Moscow had obtained Nasser's agreement to a new initiative for peace in exchange for new missiles and aircraft that the Russians were supplying. On April 8, Assistant Secretary of State for Near Eastern and South Asian Affairs, Joseph J. Sisco, embarked on a tour of Mideast capitals to sound out prospects on the spot, his first stop being Cairo. An energetic man with long experience as a negotiator, Sisco was officially received with respect and cordiality in the U.A.R., Lebanon, Saudi Arabia, and Israel. (His planned visit to Jordan was called off at the last minute, after Palestinian mobs set fire to the United States Information Service center and stormed the U.S. Embassy compound in Amman, in noisy protest against his mission.) Yet on his return to the United States 17 days later, he could report little by way of concrete progress. "The clouds of suspicion and distrust still hang heavily over the area," the Assistant Secretary said, "and there remain fundamental differences between the parties." [23]

But Sisco's efforts were far from over. In Washington, he met with Dobrynin, amidst indications from Cairo that new American initiatives for peace would not be unwelcome. But again rising concern over the continuing Soviet arms build-up in the U.A.R. began to overshadow these efforts. On April 28, the Israelis had reported that Soviet pilots were now flying defensive missions over the Nile Valley, and Israeli Foreign Minister Abba Eban, alarmed by what he termed an almost revolutionary change in the military situation, was shortly imploring Washington to reconsider Israel's request for more aircraft, in line with Secretary Rogers' promise of March 23. During May, authoritative sources in NATO echoed Eban's assessment by reporting that the balance of power in the Middle East, long heavily in Israel's favor, was steadily shifting toward the Arab states, while military analysts in Washington warned that the Soviet build-up in Egypt seemed aimed at challenging and destroying Israel's Air Force.[24] In Eban's view, the Soviets were seeking nothing less than domination of the air space over the Suez Canal, which he speculated the Russians wanted to reopen under their own auspices.[25] Whatever the case, by the end of May, 73 U.S. Senators had signed a letter to President Nixon urging him to accede to Israel's request, followed early in June by a similar plea from 85 members of the House of Representatives.[26]

The problem facing Secretary Rogers was now exquisitely acute. If he adhered to his promise to accede to the Israeli request for jets, the prospects for a new peace initiative (also promised), would be shattered by a hardening of the Arab stance against the United States. On the other hand, it was conceivable that neither Cairo nor Moscow was as interested in peace as both were in gaining a strategic advantage over Israel, and were shrewdly playing their cards with that end in view. As Assistant Secretary Sisco posed the issue in a subsequent speech: ". . . the big question mark is: Do the Russians really want the kind of stable peace that the United States is talking about, or do they see sufficient advantage in the turmoil, which, if it can be controlled, works in support of the objectives of the Soviet Union in the area and to our corresponding disadvantage? This is really the big question mark. This is what the U.S.-U.S.S.R. talks have been all about." [27] On April 29, the President had ordered the State Department to undertake a thorough review of all the political and military aspects of the situation,[28] and on May 1, the U.S. Ambassador to Moscow, Jacob D. Beam, called on Soviet officials in a direct effort to clarify Soviet intentions. Though Beam failed to gain the kind of assurances Washington sought, warnings and inquiries continued throughout the Sisco-Dobrynin colloquy, with the United States making it clear that its response to the Israeli arms request would be keyed to a sober assessment of Dobrynin's explanations.

These explanations must have proved sufficiently convincing, for in June, Rogers opted for a try at peace-making, and once again the Israelis were disappointed in their quest for aircraft.[29] The decision itself was preceded by a flurry of highly secret diplomatic activity, beginning with a hint from the U.A.R. on June 17 that it would carefully study any new U.S. peace proposal and would even welcome a visit from Rogers.[30] Two days later, the United States officially presented to Israel, Jordan, and the U.A.R. Secretary Rogers' plan for a 90-day cease-fire, tied to a resumption of negotiations under Jarring's auspices.[31] On the 20th, a Saturday, Rogers called in Dobrynin, apparently to discuss the proposals with him; and at his press conference of June 25,[32] the Secretary of State unveiled the essential thrust of his initiative. The object, he said, "is to encourage the parties to stop shooting and start talking under the auspices of Ambassador Jarring in accordance with the resolutions of the Security Council," adding that "to disclose at this time the details of the political initiative or to discuss publicly military assistance to Israel" would be inappropriate, "because of the sensitive nature of the discussions now underway." (But he was said earlier to have given Israel private assurances that the planes they sought would be theirs should the 90-day truce fail to materialize.) ". . . [W]e very seriously and profoundly hope," Rogers went on, "that this initiative, taken together in collaboration with others, will result in the beginning of discussions which might lead to a peaceful solution of this problem that has plagued the Middle East for 20 years."

The immediate response of both Egypt and Israel to the proposals seemed to make that hope something of a trifle, indeed. On the very day that Rogers announced his initiative, it was rebuffed by Nasser who demanded Israeli withdrawal from the Golan Heights even before evacuation from Sinai (a hardening of Egypt's position), and told a cheering crowd in Benghazi, Libya that his own forces were preparing to cross the Suez Canal and deal the Israelis a crushing blow.[33] Other militant Arab governments and guerrilla groups were equally scornful, with the Syrians calling it "a bloody, malicious declaration against the Arab world's future." [34] Jordan, on the other hand, which still considered that the 1967 cease-fire continued in effect, maintained a discreet if nervous silence. Israel, too, said nothing initially, but in a major speech before the Knesset on June 29, Premier Golda Meir categorically rejected the concept of a temporary or conditional cease-fire and reiterated "the absolutely vital nature" of her country's request for additional jets from the U.S.[35] She saw no "substantial possibility" for peace at this time, she said, and Israel would therefore proceed with present policies and methods, which stressed an almost daily pounding of Egyptian positions across the Canal and along the Red Sea.

Yet American officials refused to be dismayed. "It will be a while before we hear [anything positive]," Sisco commented on June 30, "because there is a general recognition in the area that the U.S. initiative is an important new opportunity. . . . We tend to be optimists. . . ." [36] And, in fact, it seemed evident that the initial reaction of the belligerents themselves was more reflexive than substantive—the product of many years of carefully cultivated intransigence and suspicion, not to mention the possible preliminary posturing involved should negotiations actually come about. But it was also clear that both sides were burdened by genuine doubts that a cease-fire would be in their respective interests, even one limited to 90 days. For almost three months, the Israelis had been waging an increasingly desperate and costly struggle to maintain air superiority over the Suez Canal zone. In the process, they had begun losing more and more aircraft to their targets, the Soviet-supplied antiaircraft batteries, including SAM-2's, whose successful installation might eventually provide a covering umbrella for an Egyptian invasion of Sinai. The Israelis were therefore reluctant to enter into any temporary cease-fire that might allow the enemy to gain by stealth what Jerusalem had been expending blood and aircraft to prevent.

For Egypt and Jordan there were other kinds of problems. In the heated, emotional atmosphere of the Mideast dispute, the slightest indication of compromise or accommodation unloosed angry tremors of shock and indignation from militant Arab nationalists everywhere, and in particular from their Palestinian contingents. King Hussein of Jordan had already come near to being dethroned by Palestinian commandos convinced that he was too "soft on Israel." Nor was Nasser any less immune to the anti-Israeli passions of his own country-men—passions he had himself masterfully roused to a pitch of high fury in the past. To renounce a war of attrition in favor of a return to a cease-fire could prove a risky step for any Arab leader concerned with preserving his own patriotic image—to keep his head, in the jargon of Middle Eastern politics—and particularly so if the resultant negotiations failed to redeem the lost territories and, with them, Arab pride.

Yet it was also true that both sides seemed as weary of the conflict as they were wrought up by it. And certainly their respective patrons were frightened by its demonstrated tendency to run wildly out of control. On June 29, therefore, President Nasser once again flew to the Soviet Union for what were described as decisive talks—talks which would determine whether Egypt's future course would lie in the direction of a cease-fire and renewed negotiations or mounting escalation and trial by combat. For more than two weeks, the Egyptian leader remained closeted with Soviet officials, while indications grew that a course toward peace was beginning to emerge. On July 17, in a joint communiqué issued at the conclusion of the talks, Soviet and Egyptian leaders repeated their demands for Israeli withdrawal from occupied territories and for a just settlement of the Palestinian refugee problem, but called for a political settlement within the framework of the U.N.[37] The communiqué made no mention of stepped up military action or of increased Soviet military aid. Under Soviet pressure, it seemed, the Egyptians were opting to give the Rogers initiative a chance.

From this point until the cease-fire went into effect on August 7, events moved steadily, though not without difficulty, toward an end to the fighting and a resumption of negotiations. On July 23, Nasser announced his agreement to a 90-day cease-fire, warning that it con-stituted "a last chance" for peace and that the Arabs would not "yield one inch" of territory in the negotiations that lay ahead. Jordan followed on the 26th, despite sharp opposition from most of the commando groups that maintained their headquarters in the Hashemite Kingdom and despite U.S. warnings that Jordanian authorities would be responsible for barring commando attacks once the truce went into effect. Both Iraq and Syria had predictably rejected the initiative, but they were, along with other Arab critics of the plan, verbally chastized for their opposition by Moscow, which had already communicated its own support for the proposal to Washington.[38]

Perhaps because they had learned to distrust the durability of cease-fires arranged by outside powers in the past, the Israelis proved more difficult to persuade. While avoiding outright rejection of the U.S. proposal in her speech of June 29, Premier Meir had charged that Nasser could agree to a truce only because he needed a lull, mainly to install SAM-3 missiles along the Canal, and thus "to prevent our air force from silencing the Egyptian artillery aimed at our positions, and enabling Egypt to make an attempt to cross the Canal." [39] On the day Nasser had acceded to the proposal, Foreign Minister Eban had voiced similar fears, and the hard-lining Gahal party had threatened to quit the Israeli Cabinet should Mrs. Meir's government agree to even a limited formulation of the proposal.

In a letter to Premier Meir on July 27, President Nixon was reported to have attempted to dispel these Israeli fears and to offer assurances of continued American support. Although the letter was not made public, the President seemed to give the gist of its contents during his news conference of July 30. After noting the concern being expressed by Israeli officials over a possible military build-up by the U.A.R. during the cease-fire, the President said, "We and others have attempted to assure them that that would not be the case. If there's a cease-fire, a natural proposition connected with that, a condition with that, is that there will be a military standstill during that period. . . . I believe that Israel can agree to the cease-fire and can agree to negotiations without fear that by her negotiations her position may be compromised or jeopardized in that period." [40] Apparently reassured by these remarks, the Israeli Cabinet, by a vote of 17 to 6 (with Gahal in opposition), agreed on July 31 to accept the U.S. initiative. That same day, President Nixon expressed his own gratification that "all three governments to whom we addressed our initiative have responded positively and accepted the U.S. proposal." Then he reiterated the point that "It is an integral part of our cease-fire proposal that neither

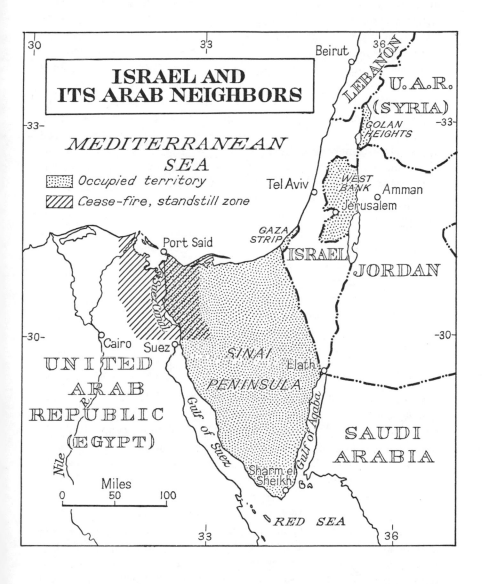

ISRAEL AND ITS ARAB NEIGHBORS

MEDITERRANEAN SEA

Occupied territory

Cease-fire, standstill zone

Beirut

LEBANON

U.A.R. (SYRIA)

GOLAN HEIGHTS

Tel Aviv

WEST BANK

Amman

Jerusalem

GAZA STRIP

ISRAEL

JORDAN

Port Said

Cairo

Suez

SINAI PENINSULA

Elath

Gulf of Suez

Gulf of Aqaba

UNITED ARAB REPUBLIC (EGYPT)

Nile

SAUDI ARABIA

Sharm el Sheikh

Miles
0   50   100

RED SEA

side is to use the cease-fire period to improve its military position in the area of the cease-fire lines. All would have to refrain from emplacing new missiles or other installations and from undertaking a military buildup of any kind in such an area." [41]

At 6:00 P.M. on August 7, New York time (1:00 A.M., August 8, Cairo time), the 90-day cease-fire and standstill agreement went into effect. By mutual consent, Israel and Egypt had agreed to police each other's adherence to the standstill provision, which strictly ruled out any military build-up or offensive actions within a 32-mile-wide zone on either side of the Suez Canal. The policing was to be accomplished by aerial reconnaissance by each belligerent on its own side of the Canal and would be assisted by the U.N. Truce Supervision Organization, headed by Maj. Gen. Ensio Siilasvuo of Finland following the retirement after seven years of Lt. Gen. Odd Bull at midnight July 31. The zone was believed sufficient to assure Israel against the kind of missile build-up it feared along the Canal, and it was reliably reported that the U.S.S.R. had given its own "categorical commitment" to abide by the military *status quo* in the standstill area. [42]

At the same time, U Thant announced the reactivation of the Jarring mission, making public a letter from the Swedish mediator setting forth the terms and conditions of the Rogers initiative. [43] These terms revealed that Egypt, Jordan, and Israel had agreed to appoint representatives to discussions under Jarring's auspices and that "the purpose of the aforementioned discussions is to reach agreement on the establishment of a just and lasting peace between them based on (1) mutual acknowledgment by the United Arab Republic, Jordan, and Israel of each other's sovereignty, territorial integrity and political independence, and (2) Israeli withdrawal from territories occupied in the 1967 conflict, both in accordance with resolution 242." From Washington's viewpoint, Arab and Israeli acceptance of these carefully worded terms represented something of a diplomatic breakthrough in itself. U.S. officials pointed out that for the first time President Nasser and King Hussein had committed themselves to a "just and lasting peace" and an acknowledgment of Israel's "sovereignty, territorial integrity and political independence." Similarly, Israel made its first clear-cut commitment to withdraw from territories occupied in the Six-day War. [44] These were gratifying steps toward a long-sought settlement of the Mideast conflict and seemed to augur favorably for the success of the admittedly grueling negotiations that lay ahead.

As Secretary Rogers hoped, the shooting had finally stopped and the talking was at last due to begin.

14 : The Saboteurs of Peace

Duplicity and deceit can hardly be called new elements in the ancient art of diplomacy, yet there was good reason to hope in 1970 that the worst of such practices were behind mankind. In an age of thermo-nuclear peril, the solemn words of statesmen assume a significance beyond the ken of older times, when a false word could be put to right on the field of battle and war itself was viewed as little more than diplomacy carried to its most treacherous extent. The Nixon administration's anxious preoccupation with Soviet "intentions," the U.S.S.R's constant concern that American deeds match American words could both be traced to such elemental understandings of diplomacy's changing mode. Yet, if the strategic prize were great enough and the risks small enough, who could say whether one more broken pledge, one more agreement quickly scrapped, would shatter progress toward a climate of trust that had yet to be instilled?

In the case of the Middle East, the arduously arranged cease-fire had hardly begun before it was being violated. In the words of Defense Minister Dayan, "On the night the cease-fire went into effect, the agreement was violated by the Egyptians, who advanced Egyptian and Soviet missile bases toward the Suez Canal front." [45] Nor did this appear to represent some sort of last-minute snag. The violations continued, as did the attacks on Israeli settlements by Palestinian commandos operating out of Jordan. The Israelis themselves broke the truce on August 14 by attacking Jordanian Army posts from the air, in announced retaliation for King Hussein's failure to keep the Palestinians in leash. At a news conference on August 17, Foreign Minister Eban charged that Egypt and the Soviet Union were "mocking" their acceptance of the cease-fire provisions through continued deployment of weapons within the standstill zone and setting up "a psychological attitude calling basic confidence into question. What," he asked, "are signed commitments worth?" [46]

Their worst fears having been realized, the Israelis now appeared determined to stall the start of their talks with Jarring until redress was made—a position which brought them into conflict with the

peace-makers in Washington. On the day before Eban's news conference, Secretary Laird had denied any Soviet or Egyptian violations
of the cease-fire subsequent to the first uncertain hours it went into
effect. "I think the important thing for us now is to move forward
towards negotiations and not debate what went on 12 hours before
[the cease-fire began] or 12 hours afterward," Laird said.[47] In fact U.S.
officials were reportedly highly irritated with the Israelis for making
such charges public. On August 18, Sisco informed the Israeli Ambassador to the U.S., Itzhak Rabin, that evidence of Egyptian violations was not conclusive enough to delay peace negotiations, and
urged prompt resumption of the Jarring talks.[48] The Israeli Foreign
Ministry complied on the 20th and announced its readiness to begin
negotiating, but it was evident that relations between Washington and
Jerusalem were by now under considerable strain. As Eban had put it:
"On the one hand our adversaries endanger our security; on the
other, our friends impugn our accuracy and sincerity." [49] From the
Israeli viewpoint, it appeared that Washington was less irked with
Soviet and Egyptian violations of the cease-fire than it was with
Israel for having pointed them out.

It was not long, however, before Washington was echoing Israel's
complaints, though it continued to press for resumption of the Jarring
talks. For their part, Moscow and Cairo heatedly denied the allegations, charging in turn that Israel itself had violated the agreement
by building military roads and other fortifications in the standstill area.
On August 28, Brezhnev called for an "honest observance" of the
cease-fire by all sides, but by then such remarks were only an affront
to the Israelis, and Eban, who had had one meeting with Jarring in
New York, was called home for consultations. On September 6, in
the face of continuing Egyptian violations, the Israeli Cabinet decided
to withdraw from further discussion until new missiles installed
along the Canal were removed.

This time there were no recriminations from Washington. Only
three days earlier, the State Department had itself announced that the
latest evidence confirmed continuing Egyptian violations of the cease-
fire agreement.[50] As Assistant Secretary Sisco was to remark later
in the year, the evidence was "categoric and incontrovertible.

"There are several types of violations.

"First, in a number of instances where no positions existed at the
time of the cease-fire, weeks later positions had been constructed—
new positions.

"Second, in a number of instances positions had been partially begun at the time of the cease-fire. Weeks later these positions had been completed.

"Third, there were a number of positions already constructed at the time of the cease-fire in which there were no missiles or no missile-related equipment. Yet weeks later missiles were in these positions, both SAM-2's and SAM-3's, and many of them in an operational capacity.

"And fourth, positions and missiles were moved more closely to the Suez Canal itself." [51]

Sisco added that there had also been Israeli violations of the cease-fire, mostly consisting of reconnaissance flights conducted over the Egyptian side of the Canal instead of the Israeli side, where the agreement had confined them. But he denied that any violations had had a decisive effect on the military balance, although they had "placed Israel at a greater disadvantage militarily." As a consequence, by September, the United States began shipments of arms to Israel in line with the administration's earlier pledge to Premier Meir.

In the wake of these disappointing developments, the United States turned its main efforts to prolonging the cease-fire past its November 5 expiration date and to achieving a rollback of the Soviet missiles, which Israel now demanded as a precondition to resuming the talks. On October 5, Egyptian Foreign Minister Mahmoud Riad categorically barred the latter, refusing even to discuss the issue of a rollback, and three days later the Soviet Foreign Ministry angrily branded the U.S.-Israeli charges as "a deliberate fraud . . . another far-fetched excuse for wrecking by Tel Aviv of the contact Gunnar Jarring had just established with both sides." At the same time, Moscow appeared to deny that it had agreed to anything more than a general cease-fire, which it claimed to be respecting, stating that "the Soviet Union did not take part in drafting any terms of cease-fire in the Suez Canal Zone. These terms were put forward by the American side." [52]

Washington had better luck with its efforts to extend the cease-fire beyond November 5, although the terms of the extension were not those favored by U.S. officials. On October 29, the U.S. representative to the U.N., Charles W. Yost, submitted a draft resolution on the matter to the General Assembly, but it was shortly withdrawn for lack of sufficient support.[53] Instead, the General Assembly on November 4 adopted an Egyptian-backed version calling for extension of the cease-fire for three additional months, but calling as well for the unconditional resumption of the Jarring mission and in other ways favoring Arab demands. Since neither the U.S. nor Israel were inclined to agree to a resumption of the talks until a missile rollback had been achieved, the United States joined fifteen other nations in voting against the resolution, which was adopted with 57 nations in favor and 39 abstaining.[54]

On November 5, the guns along the Suez Canal remained quiet as the U.A.R. proclaimed a three-month extension of the truce, which Israel thenceforth professed to regard as a nonbinding, day-to-day arrangement. Both sides were now openly reinforcing their positions in the forbidden standstill zone, and despite the thrust of the General Assembly's resolution, resumption of the Jarring talks seemed as remote as ever. Assistant Secretary Sisco described the situation as "fluid and evolving," but he drew encouragement from the fact that neither side had taken up arms again. "The role of the United States will be to encourage both sides to move toward positions in any negotiation which will meet the legitimate concerns of both sides," Sisco said. "Our national interest goes beyond any one state in the area, and it is up to us to try to help move the parties." [55] In the weeks that followed, the cease-fire held, and the United States once again began urging Israel to resume discussions with Jarring despite continued Egyptian refusal to roll back the missiles. On November 18, President Nixon asked Congress for a supplemental appropriation of $500 million for credit assistance to Jerusalem,[56] at which point Israeli insistence on a complete rollback also appeared to soften, and in December Jerusalem signaled its willingness to meet with Jarring once again. At year's end, despite the blows it had received, the Rogers initiative was still alive. As President Nixon had observed on August 29, "we have made some progress. Because, after all, there is a cease-fire. People aren't being killed now. And as long as that goes on, it looks better than it was." [57]

15 : The Palestinian Equation

The cease-fire had indeed survived not only the cheating and recalcitrance of the parties involved, but a deliberate—and almost successful—attempt at sabotage by the Palestinian commandos. In this respect, President Nixon's remarks, cited above, had been somewhat premature, for within a few days of their utterance people were again being killed in the Middle East as Palestinian commandos rose to fight the Jordanian Army following an attempted assassination of King Hussein. That most Palestinian guerrillas had openly and bitterly opposed the Rogers initiative—indeed, they had opposed any sort of compromise that would leave Israel in existence—was known from the start. Unknown was what the commandos would do should the initiative gain acceptance. This was one of the many problems worrying the U.S. and was commented upon by Sisco at the conclusion of his Mideast trip in April. "I return reinforced in the belief," he said, "that there can be no peace unless it takes account of the legitimate concerns of all in the area who are touched in their daily lives by the Palestine problem. . . . While the Palestinians themselves speak with many voices, the United States is keenly aware of their sense of frustration and is as dedicated to the just solution of their problems foreseen in the November 1967 Security Council resolution as it is to all other parts of that resolution." [58]

In the twenty-odd years since they had fled from Israel, the Palestinian refugees had swollen in number to an estimated 1.4 million, of whom 40 per cent had failed to find new homes or jobs and had been settled into various "temporary" refugee camps in Jordan, Lebanon, Syria, and the Gaza Strip. As temporary wards of the international community, most of them had subsisted on a dole administered by the U.N. Relief and Works Agency for Palestine Refugees in the Near East (UNRWA), an agency chronically short of funds almost from its start in 1948 but particularly hard-pressed since the 1967 war, which created a new flood of refugees. In its annual report issued in October of 1970, Commissioner-General Laurence V. Michelmore warned that UNRWA faced a deficit of $6 million in its $47 million budget for 1971, and called on U.N. members to provide funds or face a disruption of its services. (A General Assembly resolution in support of these sentiments was duly passed on December 8).[59] Michelmore cited, in particular, the "persisting effects of the 1967 hostilities" and the growing impact of "the policies and activities of the various *fedayeen* movements on the situation in some host countries and on the attitudes of the refugees in all of them." [60]

And, indeed, after the 1967 war a new breed of Palestinian seemed to have emerged, younger in age, more radical in spirit, and contemptuous of the conventional tactics which had done nothing to "liberate" the former homeland. These younger Palestinians drew inspiration from the guerrilla techniques of the national liberation fronts in Algeria and Vietnam and from the Cuban-style revolutionaries of Latin America. They determined to make the tactics of the guerrilla and the terrorist their tactic, and their objective was nothing less than the complete obliteration of the Jewish state.[61]

By 1970, the *fedayeen* (meaning "those who sacrifice themselves" in Arabic) had organized themselves into a dozen or more commando groups claiming a total membership of 26,000 to 36,000, of whom as many as 20,000 belonged to the so-called Palestine Liberation Army, the military arm of the Palestine Liberation Organization (P.L.O.), which in turn served as a coordinating body for ten commando groups. Most of these groups were organized around the particular personalities of their leaders, but two distinct ideological strands were apparent in the movement as a whole. One, more moderate, was personified by *al-Fatah* and led by Yasir Arafat, who also doubled as Chairman of the P.L.O. *Al-Fatah* was the largest of the commando organizations and held the destruction of Israel as its main purpose. Another, smaller branch, adhered to the revolutionary Marxist leanings of Dr. George Habash's Popular Front for the Liberation of Palestine (P.F.L.P.). It sought not only the destruction of Israel but the overthrow of "reactionary" Arab governments in league with "imperialists" and of more moderate Arab regimes as well. Unlike *al-Fatah* and the P.L.O. (from which it was excluded), the P.F.L.P. drew much of its support from Peking.

It was the P.F.L.P. and one of its offshoots, the self-styled General Command of the Popular Front, which specialized in such purely terrorist acts as the attack on the Israeli school bus, aircraft hijackings, and assaults on the planes and offices of El Al, the Israeli airline. For example, the General Command claimed credit for the explosion on February 21 of a Swiss airliner bound for Tel Aviv that killed all 47 aboard, including a high Israeli official. Such tactics were bluntly designed to focus international attention on the plight of the Palestinians, and to the extent that they aroused shock and indignation on a worldwide basis, it must be said that they succeeded. But the tactics also aroused misgivings and opposition within the commando movement and among Arabs in general, exacerbating long-standing frictions between Arab moderates and radicals and intensifying the discomfort of the Jordanian and Lebanese governments, which together played host to the great majority of Palestinian refugees.

The inability of Jordan in particular to control the activities of the various commando groups operating there gave rise to serious questions about the effectiveness of King Hussein's rule and even about its durability, as the Palestinian movement drifted more and more toward radical extremes. On June 9, the 34-year-old monarch was ambushed while driving to Amman from his summer palace, apparently by Palestinian commandos bent on carrying out a key element of the P.F.L.P. program. Although the King escaped unharmed, widespread fighting immediately broke out between the commandos and Jordanian Army units in Amman, raged across the city for five days, and claimed an estimated 200 dead and 500 wounded, according to the Palestinian Red Cross. During the fighting, the commandos virtually seized control of Amman, holding 60 Westerners (including a number of Americans) as hostages in the city's two leading hotels, and fatally shooting Major Robert P. Perry, the U.S. military attaché. Although it was *al-Fatah* that claimed responsibility for Perry's death (and later attributed it to an accident), it was the P.F.L.P. that called most of the shots in the fighting and used the Western hostages to wring concessions from Hussein. As Habash himself put it when the hostages were finally freed on June 12: "Believe me—and I am not joking—we were determined to blow up the hotels with the hostages in them if we had been smashed [by the Jordanian Army] in our [refugee] camps." [62]

What the guerrillas wanted—and what Hussein finally granted in an effort to restore peace—was the dismissal of certain Jordanian officials hostile to the commando cause and an end to anti-commando harassment at the government level. It was thus apparent that Hussein's own position had been further weakened, that the successful P.F.L.P. tactics had drawn the commando movement as a whole further to the left (the P.F.L.P. was now included in the Central Committee of the P.L.O.), and that the commandos now represented as much a threat—if not more—to moderate Arab governments as they did to Israel. (Lebanon moved to enforce a law forbidding the commandos to carry arms in towns and villages after Palestinians and their sympathizers, shouting "Death to Hussein!", had burned the Jordanian Embassy to the ground in protest over the fighting.) All in all, the rising tide of commando militancy was a source of concern to ruling Arab and Israeli governments alike. The Israelis had reason to fear any take-over by extremist elements in Jordan and possibly even in Lebanon; and Nasser himself could only foresee that once such Arab regimes as Hussein's were out of the way, his own could easily come under Palestinian attack. Only Syria and Iraq, with their own leftist brands of Baathist rule, chose to egg the commandos on. But the last act of the Palestinian drama had yet to unfold. If for the moment the commandos were riding high, events would soon reveal that they were also riding for a fall.

When the Rogers initiative was launched on June 25,[63] it was quickly denounced by every Arab government except Jordan, but none of the verbal attacks was as scathing—or as sincere—as those of the commandos, who saw any move toward a negotiated peace as the beginning of the end of their own liberate-Palestine movement. It was hardly surprising, therefore, that leading commando organizations threatened to use force, if necessary, to thwart any implementation of the U.S. proposals.[64] What was surprising was the timing of one group's sabotage efforts in September—around the time when wholesale violations of the standstill provision had already laid the peace initiative low. The means were spectacular: a series of airplane hijackings ostensibly designed to free seven convicted Palestinian terrorists from jails in West Germany, Switzerland, and Britain, where they were being held for previous hijackings or terrorist acts, and additionally to gain the release of more than 2,000 captured commandos imprisoned in Israel. But the underlying aim of these exploits was to remind the world of the Palestinian factor in the Mideast equation, to demonstrate that even a small band of determined Palestinians could stand as an effective roadblock to a peace they did not want.

Once again, it was the P.F.L.P. that led the way. On September 6, four jets bound for New York with more than 600 people aboard were hijacked over Europe in a coordinated assault by the P.F.L.P. One of the aircraft, a Pan American 747 with 171 aboard, eventually set down at Cairo airport, where it was promptly blown up by the guerrillas minutes after the passengers and crew had fled. In a second incident, an El Al jet flying from Amsterdam landed safely in London after two hijackers had been overpowered by the guards and passengers. The remaining two jets were diverted to an old and little used airstrip 40 miles northeast of Amman in the Jordanian desert. Three days later, a BOAC jet carrying 117 people was hijacked over Lebanon and joined the other two in Jordan. With 300 terrified men, women, and children as hostages, the P.F.L.P. commandos proceeded to bargain for the release of their jailed comrades with a three-member liaison group from the International Committee of the Red Cross, representing the United States, Britain, Switzerland and West Germany. For nearly a week, the hostages alternately shivered and sweltered in the cold of the desert night and the blazing heat of the day while the commandos expounded their demands before newsmen and quarreled among themselves over the terms for release of the passengers. Then on September 12, they trucked their weary and shaken captives into Amman, released all but 40 who remained as hostages, and blew up the abandoned airliners.

The hijackings unloosed a chain of dramatic developments. Around the world, airlines immediately began instituting new and stricter security precautions. At the United Nations, the normally soft-spoken U Thant denounced the P.F.L.P. actions as "savage and inhuman," and on September 9, the Security Council unanimously called for the immediate release of all hijacked passengers and crews.[65] Two days later, President Nixon announced among other safeguards the placing of specially trained guards on all U.S. domestic and overseas flights to cope with "the menace of piracy," and called on the international community to adopt a convention "providing for the extradition or punishment of hijackers" and "to take joint action to suspend airline services with those countries which refuse to punish or extradite hijackers involved in international blackmail."[66] Meanwhile Israeli security forces rounded up more than 450 Arab residents of the West Bank and the Gaza Strip in an apparent bid to remind the P.F.L.P. that hostage-taking was a game that more than one could play. (Most were released within a few days.) And even the most militant Arab governments, together with the more moderate commando groups, began pleading with the hijackers to free their prisoners unharmed.

But it was in Jordan itself that events moved swiftly toward a bloody *dénouement*. For months Hussein had vacillated in the face of increasingly bold commando provocations, but the spectacle of international extortion being played out on a makeshift runway near his own capital proved more than even he could bear. Following another unsuccessful attempt on his life on September 1, the Jordanian Army moved ruthlessly to slap all the commando organizations back in line, and once again Jordan was plunged into civil war. This time the fighting lasted several weeks, and this time it was the King's fierce

Bedouin troops who gained the upper hand. The commandos, who had boasted on more than one occasion that Hussein ruled only at their sufferance, were routed from Amman and surrounded in their strongholds in the north, near the Syrian border. As the tide of battle moved against them, they issued increasingly desperate calls for aid from fellow Arabs and decried the indiscriminate massacre of thousands of Palestinians whom they claimed the vengeful Army was slaughtering without compunction. The Arab leaders who had feared Hussein's ouster now began to fear that the commandos would be destroyed, leaving the Arab cause without that symbol of Palestinian resistance on which it thrived. On September 19, President Nasser, Colonel Muammar al-Qaddhafi, Chairman of Libya's Revolutionary Council, and Major-General Jafar Muhammad al-Nimeri, President of Sudan's Revolutionary Council issued an urgent appeal for an immediate cease-fire (though two previous appeals by Hussein himself had been disregarded). Then on the following day, Jordanian authorities reported that armored troops and heavy artillery had crossed the border from Syria into Jordan for the second day. There were even rumors (later proved false) that the 12,000 Iraqi troops stationed in northern Jordan since the Six-day War were moving to aid the hard-pressed guerrillas.

This seeming expansion of the conflict appeared to alarm not only Jordan and its neighbors, including Israel, but the great powers as well. On September 18, *Tass,* the Soviet news agency, had warned the United States and Britain, as well as Syria and Iraq, not to interfere in Jordanian problems.[67] In the meantime, the United States had already been moving to strengthen the capabilities of the Sixth Fleet in the Eastern Mediterranean, and, as subsequently revealed, had consulted with Israel on September 21 about the possibility of joint intervention should Hussein prove unable to halt the Syrian advance.[68] According to the arrangement, Israel would send its own forces against Syrian armor while the Sixth Fleet and other U.S. airborne units (on alert from West Germany) would protect Israel's flanks from outside attack. Additionally, the United States privately communicated its own warnings to the U.S.S.R. against any Soviet-supported Syrian onslaught and otherwise made it clear that Hussein's ouster by Moscow-linked forces would be strongly opposed.

As it developed, Hussein's own Air Force and armored units proved more than capable of defending themselves, and Syrian tanks began beating their retreat on September 23. That same day, a conference of Arab leaders, which had been meeting in Cairo on and off since September 6, announced an agreement between Hussein and four captured commando leaders that amounted to a virtual capitulation by the Palestinians. Although this accord was promptly repudiated by the P.L.O. Central Committee, it was apparent that the commandos were finished without Syrian help. (The Iraqis, as it turned out, failed to lift a finger for the commando cause.) On September 27, Hussein, Arafat and the heads of eight other Arab governments signed a fourteen-point pact in Cairo calling for an immediate cease-fire and the mutual withdrawal of army and guerrilla units from Amman. A three-man committee, headed by the then Premier Bahi Ladgham of Tunisia, was appointed to superintend the restoration of order in the Jordanian capital and oversee the nation's civilian-military affairs. On the same day, as well, Hussein himself named Ahmad Tuqan, a Palestinian, as head of a new government (the second that month) consisting of seven civilians and six Army officers. The next day, all the remaining hostages held by the commandos were released, their ordeal, like Jordan's, having at last come to an end.

All told, the fighting this time had killed an estimated 1,500 and wounded an additional 5,000. Most of these were commandos, and it was apparent that their movement had suffered a considerable setback. The P.F.L.P. and its offshoot, the General Command, were badly mauled, in particular, and leaders like Habash and Nayef Hawatmi, were either in hiding or on the run, with dead-or-alive rewards of $14,000 each on their heads. By October 10, Arafat was boasting that his guerrillas were stronger than ever, and three days later, an accord worked out by the Ladgham committee did seem to restore to the commandos the freedom they enjoyed before the fighting broke out, with their right to publish a paper and operate a radio station remaining unimpaired. The government even yielded on its demand that Palestinian militia groups be disarmed.[69] But throughout the remainder of the year, the Jordanian Army continued to press its newly won advantage, cleaning out whatever commando strongholds remained in the north, and by December 15 had succeeded in forcing a promise from the P.L.O. Central Committee that its militiamen (as distinct from commando regulars) would in fact give up their arms. Shaken and short of weapons, the P.L.O. itself had meanwhile called for a purge of incompetent guerrilla leaders.[70]

As for Hussein: though he had gained the enmity of many Arabs by his tough and telling crackdown on the Palestinians, he had personally emerged stronger at home than in many months, and the world could only marvel at his skill in avoiding assassination and holding tenaciously to the Hashemite throne. On October 28, he appointed his third new cabinet in six weeks, headed by a loyal Jordanian, Wasfi at-Tal (the fifth Prime Minister in 1970), and consisting of other members known for their open hostility to the commando cause and to Syria. After the shattering events of September, reports that the King had been dickering with the Soviets over an arms deal—widespread earlier in the year—were heard no more. It appeared, instead, that the Jordanian monarchy had additional cause for comfort in a close relationship with the United States which, in the confirmed belief that Hussein still merited support, soon proffered an additional $30 million in military assistance credits (with another $5 million in such credits slated for Lebanon as well).[71] That, in addition to the humanitarian aid that began flowing from the United States to Jordan in September,[72] put a firmer seal on the two countries' uneasy relations and seemed to parallel an easing in U.S.-Israeli tensions stemming from their close cooperation in planning against the Syrian threat.

Even so, the repercussions—and casualties—from Jordan's second civil war in four months were far from over. By mid-October, both Syria and Iraq were on the brink of governmental crises over the varied but controversial performance of their respective forces in the Jordanian affair. In Iraq, Air Marshal Hardan Abdul Ghaffar al-Takriti, a Deputy Prime Minister of the ruling Revolutionary Command Council, headed by President and Prime Minister Ahmad Hassan al-Bakr, was stripped of all his posts on October 15 and given a ceremonial post in the Foreign Ministry, reportedly because he advocated intervention on the side of the commandos in Jordan's civil war. Shortly thereafter, Jordan announced that the 12,000 Iraqi troops stationed there since 1967 were being pulled out, their withdrawal to be completed by October 22.[73] (By year's end, however, only a partial withdrawal had taken place.)

In Syria, meanwhile, similar frictions between the military and civilian wings of the Baathist party were reported to be undermining the leadership of President-Premier Nureddin al-Atassi, who was said to have resigned his dual posts on October 16 and been placed under house arrest. After a month of intraparty haggling, a new leadership was announced on November 16, with former Defense Minister Lt. Gen. Hafez al-Assad emerging as the "strong man" and Premier and Ahmed al-Khatib as Acting Head of State. The changes in both Iraq and Syria appeared to signal a shift away from extremism and toward a closer relationship with the U.A.R., from which the radical Baathists in general had grown estranged.

In Lebanon, by contrast, Hussein's victory appeared to ease rapidly building frictions within the government over commando activities on its soil. After the setbacks suffered by their comrades in September, half of the 3,000 guerrillas on Mount Hermon moved back into Syria, and Lebanese authorities could once again safely turn their attention to purely domestic matters, in line with their long tradition of avoiding involvement in the region's conflicts. On September 23, in a calm and cordial atmosphere, former Minister of Economy Suleiman Franjieh was inaugurated for a six-year term as Lebanon's fifth President, succeeding Charles Helou. On October 5, Saeb Salam was designated Premier, replacing Rashid Karami.

All of these repercussions seemed as nothing, however, compared to the death of President Nasser, who in a sense was the greatest casualty of all stemming from Jordan's internal strife. A man who had spent the better part of his working life in an effort to forge Arab unity, who had suffered two humiliating military defeats at the hands of the Israelis, who had talked convincingly of the need to lift his impoverished, near-feudal country into the modern era, and who had settled on increasing dependence on the Soviet Union as a way out of his problems, Nasser devoted most of 1970 to exhaustive bargaining with the Russians over Egypt's defense problems and to equally exhaustive bargaining with the Americans over the terms of peace. In failing health, he had summoned Hussein and Arafat to Cairo on September 26 to negotiate the terms of the cease-fire in Jordan in a final effort that had ended in success. On September 28, shortly after bidding farewell to the Emir of Kuwait, Sabah al-Salim al Sabah (who had participated with other members of the fourteen-nation Arab League in arranging the truce), he fell dead of a heart attack at the age of 52.

With his death, the Arab world lost its most prominent leader, and its grief seemed inconsolable. At his burial on October 1, a frenzied crowd of millions stormed around the funeral procession in Cairo, scattering dignitaries and overwhelming onlookers in the hysteria of their sorrow. Statesmen from around the world had come to pay him homage—Secretary Richardson representing the United States, Prime Minister Kosygin from the U.S.S.R., Foreign Secretary Sir Alec Douglas-Home of Britain—and even many Israelis seemed to regret the passing of a leader who had first impressed the world as a radical and dangerous quantity but who had come to be regarded as a comparatively moderate advocate of Arab aspirations. From his quarters aboard the *U.S.S. Saratoga* in the Mediterranean, President Nixon observed that "The world has lost an outstanding leader who tirelessly and devotedly served the causes of his countrymen and the Arab world." Later, in Naples, his thoughts, like those of others, turned to Egypt's future. "We are, of course, waiting to see," the President said. "We want good relations with all countries in this area. We would like to have good relations with the U.A.R." [74]

In the U.A.R. itself, meanwhile, Nasser's lieutenants were moving swiftly to maintain continuity and to allay the possibility of a sudden coup. After conferring at length with Kosygin, they agreed to continue efforts toward a political settlement of the Arab-Israeli conflict and privately assured the United States of their determination to continue Nasser's policies in this regard. [75] On October 5, a group of Nasser's most intimate associates decided upon Vice-President Anwar al-Sadat, the interim ruler, as the next President and on October 15, his election for a six-year term was ratified by more than 90 per cent of the votes in a nationwide popular referendum. A deeply religious · bitterly anti-Israeli man who had been appointed Vice-President as recently as 1969, the reputedly impulsive Sadat was at first viewed as a little known stopgap who would serve only until an expected power struggle within Egypt's ruling party, the Arab Socialist Union, had thrown up a more effective leader. As is so frequently the case, however, the relatively unknown Sadat rose to the demands of his new office, filling the shoes of his predecessor in a manner few thought possible. On October 21, he designated Dr. Mahmud Fawzi as Premier, and almost instinctively the two men moved to ease those domestic problems which had so pressed upon Egypt in the wake of the Arab-Israeli conflict. At home, there was a relaxation of censorship and political persecution, with a broad amnesty going into effect for hundreds of political prisoners jailed by Nasser's police. On October 31, the new government ordered price cuts of 10 to 15 per cent on a wide range of foods and consumer goods. At the same time, parliament moved to encourage renewed foreign investment, a development that cheered Western governments fearful of a sharp turn to the left by the new regime. On December 28, in further evidence of his moderate approach, President Sadat ordered Premier Fawzi to begin returning property confiscated from Egyptians over the preceding ten years to its rightful owners.

Abroad, the new regime continued the quest for Arab unity which had been Nasser's greatest dream. On November 9, following several day of talks with Presidents al-Qaddhafi of Libya and al-Nimeri of the Sudan, Sadat announced an agreement to work toward a federation of the three countries stemming from the tripartite alliance already in effect among them. (On November 27, the new Syrian government announced that it was joining this alliance to pool resources for the struggle against Israel.) The regime had already taken various steps to placate and reassure the West, and it was hardly surprising that it should move even more emphatically to reassure its prime patron, the Soviet Union. In a speech of November 12 marking his election as Chairman of the Arab Socialist Union, Sadat emphasized that Soviet-Egyptian friendship was stronger than ever, revealed that Moscow had promised to increase its support of the U.A.R. in the wake of Nasser's death, and referred explicitly to Soviet defense facilities in Egypt.[76] It thus appeared that Egypt's new President, no less than his predecessor, was prepared to go the route heavily dependent on Soviet economic and military aid—so long as the door to the West remained slightly ajar.

16 : The Northern Tier and the Persian Gulf

With Nasser's death, the Soviet Union had lost its single most important and valued friend in the Middle East. But it had not lost Egypt as its foremost client in the area; it retained a strong position in the Arab world and continued making inroads of sorts even in those Northern Tier states—Turkey and Iran—that were closely allied to the United States. The strategic importance of Turkey, in particular, had been rising in tandem with Soviet penetration of the Eastern Mediterranean, since it was through Turkish-dominated waters that much of the Soviet fleet gained access to the area. The importance of Iran in the troubled Persian Gulf region was also rising as Britain moved toward that day in 1971 when it would remove the last of its forces from the area.

Warmer relations had been developing between the U.S.S.R. and Turkey ever since 1964, when Moscow had shown solidarity with the Turkish side in the latter's dispute with Greece over Cyprus. Through most of 1970, the Cyprus issue remained relatively quiet, although the island's aging President, Archbishop Makarios (with whom Moscow had also managed to stay on good terms), was the intended victim of a foiled assassination attempt, reportedly stemming from right-wing Greek elements. Negotiations on the local level between Glavcos Clerides, the leader of the numerically dominant Greek community, and Rauf Denktash, speaking for the Turkish minority, continued into their third year, without real progress but without a breakdown either. Meanwhile, on June 9, the U.N. Security Council, which had been working to assure peace between the two communities, voted unanimously to extend the mandate of the eight-nation U.N. Peace-keeping Force in Cyprus (UNFICYP) until December 15, shortly before which it was extended for another six months.[77]

With the Cyprus issue muted and Soviet-Turkish relations continuing on an even keel, the main source of tension along the Northern Tier appeared to stem from Turkey's own internal troubles and the impact they were having on U.S.-Turkish relations. On June 16, some 75,000 Turkish students and workers, many wielding clubs, attempted to storm the richer, European sectors of Istanbul in an angry demonstration marked by anti-American overtones. That demonstration was quelled only by the intervention of the Turkish Army and Air Force, whose patience with the ruling government of Premier Süleyman Demirel appeared on occasion to be running thin. Though fundamentally friendly to the United States, Demirel himself was making concessions to the rising tide of Turkish nationalism which saw improved relations with the U.S.S.R. as an effective counterbalance to too great a dependence on the United States, whose position among neighboring Arab states, in any case, remained a weak one and whose performance on the Cyprus issue was still a source of pique among Turks.

In the light of such developments, it was hardly surprising that CENTO was by 1970 afflicted with a growing sense of malaise and uselessness. At the annual meeting of its Council of Ministers, held in Washington May 14–15,[78] President Nixon had sent a special message reaffirming U.S. support for the organization and hailing the "mutual friendship and mutual respect" on which it was based.[79] But the President also observed that "Much has changed during the 15 years of CENTO's existence," and although he seemed to be referring in the main to the measures for economic cooperation which had increasingly become CENTO's life-blood, few of the Ministers present could have doubted that the military side of the alliance was undergoing a de-emphasis far more profound than anything under way in NATO. Early in October, in fact, the United States found it necessary to seek an explanation from Turkey as to why it was allowing Soviet trucks, some of them hauling jeeps and possibly other military supplies, to cross Turkish territory en route to Syria and Iraq at a time of continuing crisis in the Middle East. Although the Turks denied that their territory was being used as a conduit for Soviet military aid to the Arabs, they did formalize the trucking arrangement by signing an accord on the matter on October 21 with the Soviet Union which, in effect, guaranteed the Russians a direct land route to two key Arab clients.[80]

Nor were the Soviets neglecting relations at the other end of the Northern Tier with Iran, where President Podgorny had paid a state visit in March and where he returned in October to celebrate the opening of a 630-mile natural gas pipeline from the Qum fields to the U.S.S.R. As with Turkey, Soviet economic aid to Iran had been rising. (The United States, meanwhile, continued to supply Iran with large military credits and more Phantom jets than Israel was getting.) Like Turkey, moreover, Iran was concentrating on internal development while gradually readjusting its foreign policy stance, with an eye to Britain's forthcoming withdrawal from the Persian Gulf. Not that the Iranian ruler, Muhammad Reza Shah Pahlavi, was preparing to concede Soviet hegemony over the Gulf when the British pullout became complete. On the contrary, that seemed an ambition to which Iran itself aspired. But the Shah did apparently believe that the friendlier the giant to the north, the easier his time in coping with the assorted radical Arab regimes and petty Arab rivalries that threatened the Gulf's stability.

It was primarily with the revolutionary Iraq and Southern Yemen governments in mind that Iran had increased its defense budget by 50 per cent early in the year. Already these governments were said to be supporting leftist guerrilla movements broadly aimed at toppling the seven tiny Trucial States, protected by the U.K. and ruled by autocratic sheik dynasties, as well as other states of the Persian Gulf littoral, including Muscat and Oman, Qatar, Bahrain, and Kuwait, to the last of which Iraq laid special claims. Nor did the Iraqis make any pretense about their contempt for these feudal and backward states, whose deprived masses had yet to know the peculiar joys of Baath-style socialism. By mid-July, no less than four separate guerrilla groups, under the unified banner of a so-called Popular Front for the Liberation of the Occupied Arab Gulf, were proclaiming a revolt against the aging and despotic Sultan Said bin-Taymur, who had ruled Muscat and Oman like a fief since 1932. Before the guerrillas could fully test their strength, however, the old Sultan was ousted in a palace coup on July 23 by his son, Qabus bin-Said, who promptly proclaimed a new deal for the country's half million people, called for political reforms, and changed the Sultanate's name to Oman in what was described as an effort to promote national unity. Like King Faysal of Saudi Arabia before him, the new Sultan then proceeded to lend support to the two-year old Federation of Arab Amirates, composed of Bahrain, Qatar, and the seven Trucial States and designed to bring a measure of unity and stability to the area in the wake of Britain's planned withdrawal.

For its part, Iran had already gone to considerable lengths to win the confidence and respect of the normally distrustful rulers of the Federation. For years the Iranians had been irritating the small Arab sheikdoms on the Gulf by laying claim to the British protectorate of Bahrain, an island fifteen miles off the coast of Saudi Arabia. But on several occasions during 1968 and 1969, the Shah had indicated that Iran would accept the results of a referendum on the island's future after British withdrawal, provided the U.N. supervised it. With the permission of Britain, Iran, and Bahrain, U Thant appointed Vittorio Winspeare Guicciardi as his Personal Representative in March 1970 to sound out the people of Bahrain about their future status. In a report of April 30,[81] Guicciardi concluded that "the overwhelming majority" of Bahrainians wanted full independence and sovereignty within the "Arab nation." On May 11, the Security Council unanimously endorsed the report,[82] and the *Majlis* (the Iranian parliament) voted 184 to 4 to go along. Following this amicable settlement of the age-old dispute, other rulers of the region began traveling to Tehran, where they were warmly received by the Shah, the Prime Minister, Amir Abbas Hoveida, and other aides.

In any contest that pitted traditional regimes against revolutionary ones in the Persian Gulf area, it was doubtful that the bonds of Arab brotherhood—fragile as they had elsewhere proved to be—would draw the rulers of the small sheikdoms to the side of Arab revolutionaries whose distaste for monarchies had already been fully revealed. Indeed, these rulers might well prefer Iran's help in coping with any "liberation" movements aimed against them. Not surprisingly, therefore, none of them had shown interest in an Iraqi proposal, set forth on July 18, for a regional defense alliance specifically aimed at excluding Iran.[83] Even Saudi Arabia's King Faysal had indicated his willingness to cooperate with the Shah, as long as Iran was prepared to respect Arab rights in the Gulf. Saudi Arabia had, after all, seen its own support of royalist forces in Yemen go steadily down the drain as Soviet-supported republicans in that country gradually gained the upper hand in the bitter seven-year civil war. In April, surviving royalist forces closed shop at Saudi behest, and in the following months the Saudis were sending food assistance to the republican regime, while the latter, under the moderate leadership of Premier Abdul Rahman al-Iryani, was placing former royalists in important governmental posts as a gesture of reconciliation.

If time were, indeed, running out for the sheiks and kings of the region, as many seemed to believe, the monarchs themselves seemed bent on making it run out as slowly as possible. In the final analysis, whether the radical Arabs outmaneuvered—or even outlasted—the traditional regimes appeared to make relatively little difference. The crux of the region's problems probably lodged as much with the competing intentions and ambitions of the great powers as with the petty rivalries at work among the Persian Gulf states themselves. The impact of Britain's withdrawal from the Gulf could not be fully measured until it was completed. And Soviet policy, as elsewhere in the area, very much remained to be fathomed.

5 : Indochina: The War Spills Over

The German historian Golo Mann once wrote that "Great wars usually finish up as something completely different from what they were at the beginning, and people forget how and why the conflict began." [1] In that sense, Vietnam could more than qualify as a "great war." In its long and seemingly endless course, the conflict had gone through a multiplicity of phases—from scattered guerrilla attacks to major pitched battles, from the strategic hamlet concept to the policy of search and destroy, from intensive allied bombing of the North to Vietnamization in the South—and involved by 1969 more than half a million soldiers from the United States alone. And in Washington the official rationale for American involvement seemed to shift in rhythm with the tide of events. What had begun as an effort to block the thrust of Communist expansionism in Asia, to meet the challenge of "wars of national liberation" and to keep the Southeast Asian "dominoes" from falling, had by 1970 become an urgent effort to salvage a non-Communist South Vietnam and withdraw.

In early 1965, when the United States decided to commit massive numbers of troops to the conflict, the situation had indeed looked grim to official Washington. The Khrushchevian doctrine on the importance of wars of national liberation still rang in policy-makers' ears. Chinese Defense Minister Lin Piao would shortly make his famous statement outlining a world-wide guerrilla war in which the impoverished countryside (the poor nations) would gradually but inevitably surround and strangle the rich cities (the "imperialist" powers).² Indonesia was moving steadily closer to an axis with Peking, and South Vietnam itself seemed doomed to a quick collapse as the Communist insurgency spread from village to village and encroached upon the cities. "The East is Red," went a popular Chinese song of the time, and there were those in Washington who fearfully agreed it might soon be so.

By the time Richard Nixon took office in 1969, however, the situation had changed sharply. China had been engulfed in its Cultural Revolution, quarreling all the more vociferously with Moscow in its wake. Indonesia had done an about face, not only breaking with Peking but slaughtering or interning most of its own Communists in the process, while South Vietnam had drawn significantly back from the precipice of defeat that had nearly swallowed it. Even the "cold war" had begun to assume less savage and desperate contours. At the same time, however, the Vietnam war dragged on, with well over 500,000 U.S. troops committed to the struggle, some 31,000 Americans already killed in the course of it, and Hanoi showing no signs of calling it quits. Under such circumstances, and with antiwar sentiment rampant at home, Nixon faced a fateful decision as to the course of his own policies toward the conflict. He could pursue the winner-take-all strategy of his predecessor, but he risked inheriting that same public clamor against the war that had played a role in driving Lyndon Johnson from office. He could withdraw abruptly, as many critics of the war urged, and proclaim the country's initial objectives achieved, *i.e.,* the aggressor punished, the dominoes stayed, etc. But his key advisers maintained that those original objectives were now beside the point. "The commitment of five hundred thousand Americans has settled the issue of the importance of Vietnam," Kissinger had written in *Foreign Affairs.*³ "However fashionable it is to ridicule the terms 'credibility' or 'prestige,' they are not empty phrases; other nations can gear their actions to ours only if they can count on our steadiness."

In short, if withdrawal were to come, it should not be at the price of an American defeat—of a subverted South Vietnam run from Hanoi. It should only come gradually, over a period of time that would, in the President's judgment, allow the government of South Vietnam to prepare adequately for its own defense and security. It was a conclusion the Johnson administration had come to in its own last months in power, and the Nixon administration dubbed it "Vietnamization"—a policy of gradually turning the brunt of the fighting over to South Vietnamese forces while steadily scaling down American involvement in the conflict. The President had unveiled the broad outlines of this policy at Guam in July 1969,[4] and in a speech on November 3 of that year he stated that the rate of American withdrawal would be conditioned by (1) "the progress which can be, or might be, made in the Paris talks"; (2) "the level of enemy activity"; and (3) "the progress of the training program of the South Victnamese forces." [5]

Under this flexible and open-ended timetable, American combat forces in South Vietnam had already been reduced by more than 60,000 men as 1970 got under way. U.S. air operations had been curtailed by 20 per cent, and the number of weekly casualties had dropped sharply from the prevailing highs of previous years. Although no progress could be reported from the Paris talks, the level of enemy activity had clearly been reduced and the training of South Vietnamese forces appeared to be proceeding according to schedule. Most important from the President's viewpoint, perhaps, was the palpable easing of tensions over the war within the United States itself. In a televised interview towards the end of 1969, Secretary Rogers could state with apparent confidence that he thought "the President has made a fine start; the war has been deescalated, he has support in this nation, he has support in the international community. And I think that the program has prospects of success, and I think most impartial observers who go to Viet-Nam now come back with that conclusion." [6]

17 : Inside South Vietnam

Not surprisingly, given the bitter divisions already stirred by this war at home, there were those who disagreed with Rogers' assessment. On February 1, the Senate Foreign Relations Committee released a report [7] suggesting that administration policy rested "on far more ambiguous, confusing, and contradictory evidence than pronouncements from Washington and Saigon indicate. The success of present American policy appears to depend on three factors:

"1. The progressive Vietnamization of the military effort.

"2. The stability and cohesiveness of the Thieu Government.

"3. The expectation that the enemy can and will do nothing to inhibit Vietnamization or disrupt the Thieu Government's stability."

The report indicated that a failure to realize any one of the three factors could thwart the over-all success of the administration's policy. If Vietnamization failed, the report said, "the United States cannot withdraw and still claim to have achieved its stated objectives." If, on the other hand, North Vietnam were to launch a massive attack at any point in the course of the American withdrawal, "the United States would be faced with the agonizing prospect of either halting —or even reversing—the process of withdrawal, on the one hand, or being forced, on the other hand, to effect an accelerated, complete withdrawal which would be interpreted at home, and probably abroad, as a military and political defeat." With everything depending on Saigon and Hanoi, in the Committee's view, the United States had now made itself hostage to both sides.

The President had sought to allay some of this criticism at his news conference on January 30.[8] His first aim, he said, was a negotiated peace, even though the North Vietnamese were "just as recalcitrant in their position as they have been and just as stubborn." But regardless of the outcome of the peace talks, "the policy of Vietnamization was irreversible," and should Hanoi step up the fighting as the U.S. withdrew, the President said, "we will react accordingly and we have the means to do so which I will not hesitate to use." As Nixon saw it, by "irreversibly" shifting to South Vietnam "the primary responsibility" for its own defense, the United States was, if anything, being freed from its hostage role. And to discourage Hanoi against any temptation to step up the fighting, he indicated that American air and naval power would be on hand to aid the South Vietnamese "for a longer time than support in terms of ground forces."

Statistically, the actual course of the war did seem to favor the President's more optimistic view. Figures indicated that the rate of enemy infiltration for 1969 was down 100,000 to 110,000 compared with 250,000 in 1968. As 1970 began, over-all enemy troop strength in South Vietnam and in the nearby Cambodian sanctuaries was estimated at 240,000 or down 50,000 from the previous year.[9] At the same time, President Nguyen Van Thieu claimed that 97 per cent of the country's rural population had been brought under the relative control of the South Vietnamese government. Even if that figure was exaggerated, it was at least evident that major cities like Saigon, Hué, and Danang were increasingly secure from enemy attack.[10] The so-called pacification efforts of the Thieu government had long inspired conflicting reports as to their success, but it was clear that most roads were now open and safe and that many refugees from the fighting were returning to their homes. Thieu, himself, meanwhile, had consolidated his position of power and looked stronger than at any time since taking office in 1967. With the non-Communist opposition apparently in disarray, he seemed to have overcome earlier uncertainties about the Nixon administration's policies, the Paris talks, and the battlefield prospects.

As for North Vietnam and its Vietcong allies, though unyielding at the bargaining table, they did show signs of easing up their efforts in the war itself. In the first two months of 1970, enemy infiltration dropped again by about 40 per cent below previous levels.[11] There had traditionally been a lull in the fighting prior to any Communist offensive in February, but this time the offensive never came. To be sure, the Communists stepped up offensive operations in Laos, perhaps as a way of reminding Washington that Vietnamization alone was no cure-all for the broader conflicts of the area. But in South Vietnam itself both sides seemed bent on avoiding major battles, with the Communists refraining from large-scale assaults and the U.S. holding back on search and destroy operations. From Washington's viewpoint, the enemy seemed to be settling back into the kind of small-unit guerrilla tactics which had long been its forte, economizing forces and preparing for a protracted conflict of the type outlined by North Vietnam's Defense Minister and master strategist, General Vo Nguyen Giap. The aim would be to keep the fighting subdued enough to encourage a U.S. pullout but sharp enough to disrupt pacification and outlast the Thieu regime.

Somewhat surrealistically, then, the war seemed to be circling back to its starting point of a decade or so before. During a visit to Vietnam in February, Secretary Laird said he foresaw three phases in the Vietnamization process: (1) the South Vietnamese would assume full battle responsibility; (2) they would take over air and logistical support; and (3) the U.S. presence would be cut back essentially to advisers.[12] That was what the American role had been when the whole thing began.

The hope in Washington, of course, was that this time the South Vietnamese would be able to hold their own. But while the Thieu government had ruled for almost three years, and though the United

States continued to prod it discreetly toward a more progressive outlook, there were few observers who doubted that the regime faced serious problems in shouldering the obligations that Washington was now handing over to it. Not least among these was the problem of paying for the war. Even with emergency doses of aid from Washington, prices in South Vietnam had climbed 32 per cent in 1969, and inflation continued to harry the government throughout the first half of 1970. In an interview in June with the French newspaper, *Le Monde,* President Thieu estimated that it would take at least four or five years before South Vietnam's economic and military situation could be stabilized.[13] Meanwhile, the apparent inability of the regime to root out corruption and inefficiency had again become evident in January when, partly in response to American pressure, President Thieu shifted three commanding generals and replaced four province chiefs.

In March, the Saigon Senate approved a major land reform bill, already passed by the House, which would turn 60 per cent of the rice land over to the farmers who till it, but its implementation in succeeding months was slow. There was also evidence that the government was moving to repress political opposition in a manner reminiscent of the last years of the dictatorial Ngo Dinh Diem regime. In March Tran Ngoc Chau, a congressional deputy and leading opponent of President Thieu in the 1967 elections, was sentenced to ten years at hard labor by a specially convened military court, in what was widely viewed as an arbitrary and vindictive display of presidential power. His conviction was overturned by Saigon's Supreme Court two months later, but Chau continued to languish in jail. Militant Buddhists, protesting the war and the government's policies, once again found themselves in confrontation with Saigonese troops, and shortly after the government moved to close all schools and universities in face of mounting unrest in May, two more Buddhists, a monk and a nun, publicly burned themselves to death. At best the regime seemed to enjoy only the passive acceptance of South Vietnam's long-silent majority. Of its outright popularity, none boasted.

In North Vietnam, by contrast, morale reportedly continued to run high, despite internal economic strains and the uncertainties flowing in the wake of President Ho Chi Minh's death on September 3, 1969. Signs of a possible struggle over his succession between Party First Secretary Le Duan and the leading pro-Peking ideologist, Truong Chinh, appeared to fade as Duan increasingly emerged as the central figure in the regime. On the 40th anniversary of the founding of the Vietnam Workers' (Communist) Party in February, Duan struck the keynote with an appeal for greater economic productivity at home and a warning that "Our people must be prepared to fight many years more and fight until the enemy gives up his aggressive design, brings home all his troops, and respects the sovereignty of our people and the territorial integrity of our country." [14] With the apparent support of the new President, Ton Duc Thang, and of Prime Minister Pham Van Dong, he also called for a policy of benevolent neutrality toward the Sino-Soviet dispute, urged greater flexibility in economic planning and management, and called for the admission of new and younger members into the party hierarchy in a general effort to strengthen the nation's capacity to fight a "protracted war."

Given a continuing flow of aid from the U.S.S.R. and Communist China, moreover, North Vietnam's 20 million people seemed fully capable of carrying on just such a protracted conflict as determinedly as they had in the past. If they had reduced for the time being their infiltration into South Vietnam, they were stepping it up in Laos and Cambodia, and they still supported an estimated 175,000 to 200,000 of their own troops outside their frontiers. In addition, more than 300,000 armed regulars were being held ready for combat within North Vietnam itself, including the five elite "steel" divisions which had carried the victory banners after General Giap routed the French Army in 1954 at Dienbienphu. Finally, it was also apparent that despite certain gains, the government of President Thieu had yet to crack the infrastructure of the National Liberation Front (N.L.F.), the political mainspring behind the Provisional Revolutionary Government (P.R.G.) of South Vietnam, whose cadre of 50,000 or more agents continued to include many non-Communist nationalists but whose political subservience to Hanoi remained probable.

Despite this background of continuing problems in the South and persisting determination in the North, President Nixon nonetheless felt sufficiently encouraged to announce further U.S. troop cuts on April 20.[15] Progress in training and equipping South Vietnamese forces had "substantially exceeded our original expectations last June," the President reported, and "very significant advances" had "also been made in pacification." Although the enemy had stepped up activity in Laos and Cambodia, and although he could report no progress from Paris, the President went on to say that there had been "an overall decline in enemy force levels in South Vietnam since December," and that during the first three months of 1970, "the number of Americans killed in action had dropped to the lowest first quarter level in 5 years. . . . In June [1969] we announced withdrawal of 25,000 American troops; [16] in September another 35,000 [17] and then in December 50,000 more.[18] These withdrawals have now been completed and as of April 15, a total of 115,500 men have returned home from Vietnam.

"We have now reached a point where we can confidently move from a period of 'cut and try' to a longer-range program for the replacement of Americans by South Vietnamese troops.

"I am, therefore, tonight announcing plans for the withdrawal of an additional 150,000 American troops to be completed during the spring of next year [1971]. This will bring a total reduction of 265,000 men in our Armed Forces in Vietnam below the level that existed when we took office 15 months ago."

The American public could note with satisfaction that the President's withdrawal timetable was proceeding without interruption or reversal. At that rate, all but some 50,000 American troops would be out of Vietnam by the time presidential elections rolled around in November 1972. But the President also felt compelled to warn again against any stepped-up military effort by the Communists—and this time his warning specifically encompassed enemy action in Cambodia and Laos, as well as Vietnam. "I again remind the leaders of North Vietnam," Nixon said, "that while we are taking these risks for peace, they will be taking grave risks should they attempt to use the occasion to jeopardize the security of our remaining forces in Vietnam by increased military action in Vietnam, in Cambodia, or in Laos.

"I repeat what I said Novemebr 3d and December 15th. If I conclude that increased enemy action jeopardizes our remaining forces in Vietnam, I shall not hesitate to take strong and effective measures to deal with that situation."

Ten days later, President Nixon would find occasion to prove true to his word.

18 : The Cambodia Coup

Alone among the nations of Indochina, the tiny Kingdom of Cambodia had escaped direct involvement in the war and revolution that howled along its borders with Laos and Vietnam. Leaning now to the West, now to the East, it had wound its delicate way through the region's conflicts under the diplomatically nimble leadership of Head of State Prince Norodom Sihanouk, whose ability to defend his country's precarious neutrality had almost become legendary by 1970. But for Sihanouk, no less than for his warring neighbors, events were coming to a head. For if the Cambodian leader had succeeded in preserving his country's formal neutrality, he had failed in keeping it free from foreign incursions. More and more, he had found himself siding with Moscow, Peking, and Hanoi, availing himself of their aid while lashing out at the policies of the United States and its allies in Southeast Asia. And more and more, North Vietnamese and Vietcong forces had been using the Cambodian eastern provinces as a convenient place of sanctuary from which to plan and launch strikes against South Vietnam. By early 1970, an estimated 40,000 Communist troops were strung out in the jungles along Cambodia's eastern frontier, and even the Communist Central Office for South Vietnam (C.O.S.V.N.) was reported by allied intelligence to be holed up near the Cambodian town of Memot in the so-called Fishhook region about 50 miles north of Saigon. It was largely from Cambodian sanctuaries that Communist forces had geared for the Tet offensive in 1968. It was there that they regrouped and resupplied whole divisions, treated many of their wounded, indoctrinated new recruits, and even maintained their families. And it was there that American and South Vietnamese forces, operating under the doctrine of "hot pursuit," frequently chased them, thereby drawing Cambodia itself increasingly into the vortex of the fighting.

For many Cambodians such flagrant deployment of alien troops on their soil only served to mock Sihanouk's long-stated quest for genuine neutrality, and organized protests soon spread from the eastern provinces to the site of the North Vietnamese and N.L.F. embassies in Phnom Penh. There were even indications that Sihanouk himself was growing perturbed by the extent of Communist activity within his country's borders. In February, he paid an unusual if backhanded tribute to the United States, declaring publicly that "American imperialism" not only assured Cambodia's independence and territorial integrity but also was "an essential condition of the 'respect,' of the 'friendship' and even of the aid of our socialist friends." [19] By March, he was traveling to Moscow and Peking, there to warn Hanoi's patrons that Cambodian neutrality must be respected lest "pro-American rightists" like Prime Minister Lon Nol seize power and force his own abdication as Head of State.[20]

For the ailing Sihanouk, however, worn by his efforts to walk the neutral tightrope, time had already run out. The country's economy had virtually stagnated after the Prince had summarily rejected American aid in 1963; discontent among unemployed university graduates had at length grown increasingly vocal; and, casting these problems into sharp relief, was the glittering court affected by Sihanouk and his Eurasian wife. The Prince's eccentric, personalized style of rule—at first charming and refreshing to his people—had begun to grate on the nerves of those responsible for the day-to-day administration of Cambodian affairs. And although Sihanouk himself seemed above reproach, there were rumors of avarice and corruption within the royal family.

Against this background, and against the background of Cambodia's historic fear of Vietnamese encroachment, the anti-Communist demonstrations that had been wracking Phnom Penh turned, with the apparent encouragement of the Cambodian Army, into outright rioting. On March 16, North Vietnamese and P.R.G. representatives met with Cambodian officials to discuss the issues of Communist troop withdrawals and recompense for damage incurred by the North Vietnamese and Vietcong legations in the course of the demonstrations. That same day in Moscow, Sihanouk elicited a Soviet pledge of support for Cambodian neutrality without, however, receiving any assurances that Hanoi had been persuaded to pull back its troops.[21] In fact, it was evident that the issues had moved beyond the point of negotiated agreement. For almost two months the Cambodian Army, apparently on its own initiative, had already been fighting Communist guerrillas in the eastern regions of the country, and on March 17 a Cambodian Army unit had reportedly called in South Vietnamese artillery in support of its effort to drive a battalion of Vietcong troops back across the border. Meanwhile, at the negotiations in Phnom Penh, the Communist representatives seemed less interested in finding a way to preserve the country's neutrality than in forcing Cambodian officials to call off the anti-Communist rioting and pay for damages already incurred.

Thus on March 18, just as he was emplaning from Moscow en route to Peking, a somewhat stunned Sihanouk received word of his ouster in a coup led by General Lon Nol, his own hand-picked Premier, and by his First Deputy Premier, Prince Sisowath Sirik Matak, a royal cousin. Next day, before a joint session of the Cambodian National Assembly, Sihanouk was formally accused of nepotism, ineptitude, corruption, and the crime of shipping weapons to the Vietcong, and unanimously relieved of office. National Assembly President Cheng Heng was continued as Acting Head of State until constitutionally provided elections could take place and General Lon Nol was voted "full powers" to govern the nation in the meantime. In Peking, Sihanouk denounced his ouster as illegal, called for a popular referendum to be conducted under the auspices of the three-nation International Control Commission (I.C.C.) for Cambodia (whose presence he had suspended in December 1969 on grounds of costliness), and appealed to his subjects to resist the new regime by force.[22]

The way now appeared open for a decisive resolution of the issue of Cambodian neutrality, but initially at least Sihanouk's ouster seemed to raise more questions than it answered. In Phnom Penh, the new leadership swiftly pledged not to change the country's basic policies, including its strict adherence to neutrality.[23] But the question naturally arose that if the new government wanted no changes, why had it bothered to get rid of Sihanouk? The question must have been of particular concern to Hanoi. Lon Nol was known as an anti-Communist. For several months, as Commander of the Army, he had been fighting Hanoi's forces and it was he who had tolerated—if not encouraged—the anti-Communist rioting in Phnom Penh. Could Hanoi now expect him to prove another Sihanouk, neutral in theory but friendly in practice? Similar questions were puzzling officials in Washington. On the one hand, they knew Lon Nol to be friendly. On the other hand, they were hesitant to write off Sihanouk, and some even wondered whether this particular Prince had stolen a page from Machiavelli, engineering his own coup as a mock exercise in order to strengthen his hand against his internal enemies. Above all, there was the question of a widened war. Would the new regime seek to restore Cambodia's neutrality by waging all-out war against encroaching Communist forces in the eastern provinces? Could its ragtag, volunteer army hope to win such a fight?

Such puzzlement was reflected by President Nixon at his news conference of March 21.[24] "As you know . . . , the Cambodian political situation, to put it conservatively, is quite unpredictable and quite fluid," the President said, while revealing that the United States had "established relations on a temporary basis" with the new government and expressing the hope that "whatever government eventually prevails there, . . . would recognize that the United States' interest is the protection of its neutrality."

Even as Nixon spoke, however, it was already becoming clear that Lon Nol's version of neutrality did not include the presence of 40,000 Communist troops on Cambodian soil, even if (or perhaps in large part because) they outnumbered the poorly trained and equipped Cambodian force of 35,000. On March 22, the government asked for a prompt return of I.C.C. observers in an effort to persuade the Communists to leave, and the next day Lon Nol himself stressed the need to expand the Cambodian Army, although he professed to favor a peaceful solution through the talks with Communist representatives that were still under way. That possibility was dashed, however, when Hanoi and the Vietcong on March 25 announced the recall of all their diplomats from Phnom Penh. In the days that followed, as clashes between government and Communist forces grew, it became increasingly apparent that the war in Vietnam had spilled over and that a broader war for all of Indochina was getting under way.

19 : Nixon Takes the Plunge

In his April 20 speech, Nixon had warned against any stepped-up enemy activity in Laos and Cambodia, as well as Vietnam,[25] and now he was confronted by the fact that the enemy had apparently picked up the gauntlet. In Laos, Communist Pathet Lao and North Vietnamese forces had earlier launched a spring offensive, pushing across the strategic Plain of Jars, capturing the key supply base of Sam Thong and threatening the last Royal Laotian stronghold held by General Vang Pao at Long Tieng. The drive, involving an estimated 67,000 North Vietnamese troops in Laos, carried the enemy farther south than at any time since 1962, and posed a threat to Vientiane, the administrative capital. So alarmed were the neighboring Thais that they reportedly airlifted two battalions of their own troops to help defend Long Tieng (using U.S. planes in the process) in an effort to stay the Communist tide. The general gravity of the situation was underscored on March 19 when Secretary Laird advocated continued U.S. bombing of the Ho Chi Minh Trail in Laos even if a Communist government came to power there and demanded a halt.[26]

With the downfall of Sihanouk, moreover, another Communist advance soon threatened the Cambodian capital. While Hanoi had with-drawn its diplomats, it had withdrawn none of its troops, and on March 29, Cambodia charged that Communist forces were intensifying their invasion, moving west from the frontier and adding more troops to the 40,000 already on hand. Though militarily weak, Cambodia had by now moved to cut off supplies flowing to the Communists from the port of Sihanoukville (renamed Kompong Som), had stepped up coordination of its military efforts with South Vietnamese forces (which had struck across the border on March 27 and 28 in raids encouraged by Cambodia), and had reportedly sounded out Washington about providing military aid (but not U.S. intervention). By mid-April, Cambodia was charging that Communist forces had more than doubled the area under their control, occupying three eastern provinces and more than half of five others, and were pushing to within twenty miles of Phnom Penh itself. With the capital threatened, Cambodian soldiers now began taking revenge on the Vietnamese civilians living among them, massacring about 100, in-cluding 30 children, in what appeared to be a general roundup, while hundreds of bodies of other Vietnamese floated down the Mekong River. At the same time, Lon Nol continued his urgent appeals for defensive arms from any nation that would supply them, even though the indiscriminate attacks on Vietnamese civilians were blackening the eye of his regime around the world and were putting new political pressures on Saigon to limit its already existing cooperation.

By the time of President Nixon's April 20 address, the military situation in Laos and Cambodia shaped up as follows: After a brief occupation of Sam Thong, Communist forces in Laos appeared to be withdrawing from the south, with as many as 15,000 crossing into the northernmost provinces of Cambodia. The pressure on Long Tieng had eased, and Royal Laotian troops seemed once again in control of the southern panhandle region, although Communist troops con-tinued to occupy the Plain of Jars. In Cambodia, the Communist ad-vance toward Phnom Penh continued despite almost daily cross-border raids by South Vietnamese troops and planes and despite a hurried call-up of 18,000 new recruits and reserves by the Cambodian govern-ment. There were also some indications that Cambodians in the north were heeding Sihanouk's continuing call for resistance to the new regime, though the bulk of the population seemed more confused than committed by the events taking place around them. In Phnom Penh, civil servants and workers could be seen drilling and otherwise engaged in military exercises during their lunch hours, in preparation for the defense of the capital from imminent attack.

On April 21, in the face of unsuccessful efforts to repulse the enemy advance, Lon Nol issued a personal and urgent appeal to President Nixon, for the first time specifically requesting arms, equipment, and the intervention of American-trained Cambodian mercenaries led by Green Berets in South Vietnam.[27] In the view of some U.S. military experts, Cambodia now teetered on the verge of collapse, and a debate broke out within the administration as to just what, if anything, the United States should do.[28] Already by the middle of April, the Commander of American forces in South Vietnam, General Creighton W. Abrams, and U.S. Ambassador Ellsworth Bunker had sent parallel recommendations to the Departments of Defense and State. These urged an American attack into the Fishhook region, where enemy troop concentrations were known to be great. They also urged joint attacks with the South Vietnamese against other enemy sanctuaries.[29] By April 17, the President himself had approved a secret shipment of 6,000 captured Soviet AK-47 rifles to the Cambodian Army and had encouraged the South Vietnamese to increase the scope and frequency of their cross-border raids in an effort to divert the enemy advance on Phnom Penh.

The President was aware that the collapse of Cambodia (and perhaps Laos, as well) would gravely imperil the Vietnamization program, but he also knew that an American thrust into Cambodia would have the effect of widening a war he had promised to wind down, with all the domestic repercussions that might entail. He could not be sure whether the enemy's new efforts in Cambodia were merely hit-and-run tactics, designed to give the impression of civil war, as the State Department maintained, or a concerted drive to isolate and capture Phnom Penh and its new government, as the Defense Department was inclined to believe.[30] The President did know that congressional sentiment ran strongly against supplying Lon Nol with even the $500 million in military aid that the latter had requested, but he also knew that his own efforts to contain the Cambodian situation through diplomacy were meeting with little success. Like Sihanouk before him, General Lon Nol had tried to work out a live-and-let-live arrangement with Hanoi by which the North Vietnamese would both reduce their military presence in Cambodia and the flow of supplies reaching them through Kompong Som (Sihanoukville). Nixon had sought to signal Hanoi through Asian intermediaries that the United States would respect any deal Lon Nol could strike. He had also signaled Moscow that now might be the time to reconvene the Geneva Conference of 1954, as France had proposed on April 1 [31] and as Soviet Ambassador to the U.N. Yakov A. Malik had himself intimated on April 16.[32]

Either these signals got scrambeld, however, or they were deliberately ignored by Hanoi, and Lon Nol's search for an accommodation was rejected. In the days immediately following the Nixon speech of April 20, Sihanouk met with Chinese Premier Chou En-lai and the leaders of North Vietnam, the Vietcong, and the Pathet Lao somewhere in south China to plan a united front for the "liberation" of all Indochina, to denounce the United States as the villain behind the Cambodian coup, and to urge a stepped-up fight against American "imperialism" and its "lackeys" in Laos, Cambodia, and Vietnam.[33] At about the same time, the Russians made clear their lack of interest in a new Geneva conference, despite Malik's earlier intimation, and it appeared that force rather than compromise would continue to dictate any solution to the area's problems.

With these developments in mind, President Nixon summoned a meeting of the National Security Council (N.S.C.) on April 22, apparently already determined to "do something," for the possibility of an American attack into the Fishhook was discussed.[34] On April 23–24, the Washington Special Action Group, headed by Kissinger, took up the problem and began preparing a series of options upon which the President could act. With the monsoon rains due to begin in a month and with Hanoi looking either to topple Lon Nol or clear a supply corridor along Cambodia's eastern borders or both, the time for action was short. On the 24th, the President called for operational plans from the Military Assistance Command, Vietnam (M.A.C.V.) for an American thrust into the Fishhook to be delivered within 24 hours and at the same time scheduled a secret meeting of the N.S.C. for the 26th, a Sunday. According to various inside chronicles of these events that subsequently appeared in the press, most of the President's key advisers, including Secretaries Laird and Rogers and even General Wheeler, were dubious of any direct U.S. involvement in a Cambodian operation.[35] They feared, among other things, a setback at home for the President's Vietnam policies, which had gained a measure of public support; the possible collapse of the Paris talks; a Communist seizure of Phnom Penh; or even a major North Vietnamese attack across the demilitarized zone (D.M.Z.) into South Vietnam. But the President was said to believe that time was running out for the Lon Nol government, that Hanoi was in danger of seriously miscalculating his own resolve in the conduct of the war, and that the deep divisions stirred at home by American intervention could initially be borne and would gradually dissipate as Vietnamization gained a surer footing.

On April 27, Secretary Rogers testified on the Cambodian situation before a closed session of the Senate Foreign Relations Committee, where he encountered strong bipartisan opposition to any military aid at all for the Lon Nol regime. The sentiment of the Committee, Senator Fulbright said, was that any such aid would result in a widening of the war and make it "more difficult to carry out disengagement." [36] For his part, Rogers told the Committee that the administration was as yet undecided on the question of arms aid. What Rogers failed to mention was that the President was rapidly moving toward a far bolder course of action. Indeed, the very next morning Nixon's decision came down: In a series of consecutive assaults on enemy base areas, combined U.S. and South Vietnamese forces would attack in the Fishhook while U.S. ground advisers would accompany South Vietnamese troops into the region known as Parrot's Beak, 33 miles west of Saigon. To counter the possibility of an enemy counterstrike across the D.M.Z., the President subsequently ordered four air raids over North Vietnam, the first such sorties since the U.S. bombing halt in 1968.

Backed by U.S. air and artillery support, South Vietnamese forces began a drive into the Cambodian sanctuaries on April 29, and on the following day President Nixon explained his decision in a nationwide television address. [37] "This is not an invasion of Cambodia," the President said. "The areas in which these attacks will be launched are completely occupied and controlled by North Vietnamese forces. Our purpose is not to occupy the areas. Once enemy forces are driven out of these sanctuaries and once their military supplies are destroyed, we will withdraw." A majority of Americans, the President said, want to end the war rather than have it drag on interminably. By depriving the enemy of his privileged sanctuaries, the Cambodian action would serve that purpose. Describing Hanoi's "massive military aggression in Laos and Cambodia," he warned that "We will not react to this threat to American lives merely by plaintive diplomatic protests. If we did, the credibility of the United States would be destroyed in every area of the world where only the power of the United States deters aggression." From the wording of his speech, it was evident that the President viewed the events in Cambodia as a major test, not only of the Vietnamization program, but of his own will and character as well. It was clear he was determined to meet that test whatever the advice of his closest aides, whatever the sentiment in Congress, and whatever, even, the reaction of American public opinion. In the President's words, "Whether I may be a one-term President is insignificant compared to whether by our failure to act in this crisis the United States proves itself to be unworthy to lead the forces of freedom in this critical period of world history."

20 : Aftermath: Laments and Limits

Surprisingly enough, the initial reaction in Congress to the President's speech was not so devastating as earlier intimations from the Senate Foreign Relations Committee might have indicated. Most key congressmen accepted the President's argument that a limited action in Cambodia would serve to protect the future of Vietnamization and insure the prospect of American withdrawal from the war, and the White House reported that telephone calls were running 6 to 1 in favor of what the President had done.[38] To be sure, some antiwar Senators were hotly critical of the President's action, but there were no immediate cries of "impeachment" (despite congressional sensitivity on the issue of troop commitments abroad), and initially it appeared that the President had made his case convincingly and well.

The impression did not last, however, and public and congressional unrest soon began mounting. In part, this could be attributed to the slayings at Kent State University,[39] but in part too, the President's own rhetoric seemed to be at the root of his troubles. In his eagerness to justify the Cambodian decision, the President had also tended to oversell both the nature of the crisis and the effects to be expected from his action. In his April 30 speech, for example, he had warned that the enemy "is concentrating his main forces in these sanctuaries . . . where they are building up to launch massive attacks

on our forces and those of South Vietnam." Yet, in the first week of
Operation Rock Crusher (as the Cambodian incursion was called),
when a combined force of 10,000 American and South Vietnamese
troops plunged into the sanctuaries, no such concentrations could be
found and it appeared that, if anything, Communist forces had been
withdrawing. The President had also dramatically announced that
"Tonight, American and South Vietnamese units will attack the headquarters for the entire Communist military operation in South Vietnam [C.O.S.V.N.]." But again neither the headquarters nor any of its
occupants were ever uncovered, and after a week or so of apparently
vain searching all mention of C.O.S.V.N. was dropped from military
briefings by M.A.C.V.[40] On the other hand, the President had said
nothing whatever in his speech about a resumption of heavy air strikes
against North Vietnam. When those strikes took place on May 2–5,
the Pentagon quickly dubbed them "protective reaction" measures
designed to silence enemy antiaircraft fire at U.S. reconnaissance
planes, even though enemy supplies and troop concentrations were
among the targets.[41] A bewildered public was thus left wondering
whether or not the war was indeed widening in more ways than
Nixon had specified.

The President had long stressed his efforts to be "completely candid
with the American public and Congress" about the war,[42] but now a
"credibility gap" appeared to be opening within his own administration. In late December of 1969, Secretary Rogers had given assurances
that "we're not about to get involved in any other war or any other
situation like Viet-Nam unless we have the full support of the Congress
and the American people." [43] In March, he had told the Senate Foreign
Relations Committee that the United States had no plans to commit
ground combat troops to the fighting in Laos (forbidden anyway by
act of Congress), even if that country were overrun by the Communists.[44] Now the President's decision on Cambodia appeared to
belie such remarks, and on May 3 Rogers was again stressing that
fundamental administration policy had not changed and that the Cambodian operation was strictly limited in "extent, purpose, and duration. . . . It's only going to last 6 or 8 weeks." [45]

This was the theme struck by the President during a televised news
conference on May 8 when he said that the first American units would
be withdrawn from Cambodia by the middle of the following week,
with the great majority out by the second week in June and all of

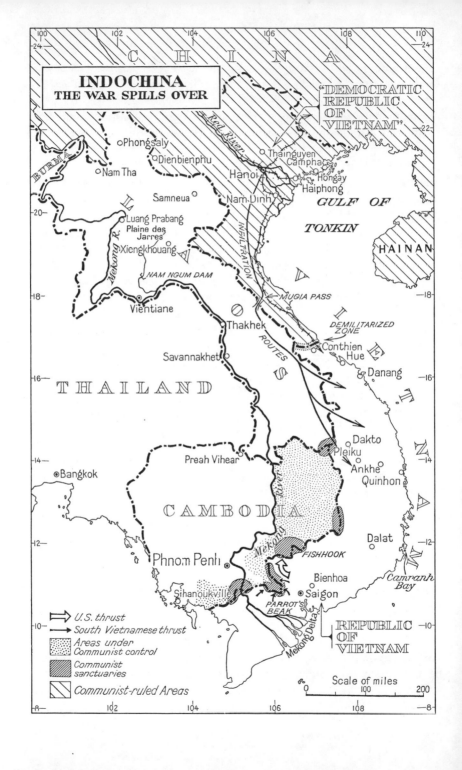

INDOCHINA
THE WAR SPILLS OVER

CHINA

"DEMOCRATIC REPUBLIC OF VIETNAM"

Red River

Phongsaly

Dienbienphu

Nam Tha

BURMA

Samneua

Thainguyen
Campha
Hanoi
Hongay
Haiphong
Nam Dinh

GULF OF TONKIN

HAINAN

Luang Prabang
Plaine des Jarres
Xiengkhouang

Mekong R.

NAM NGUM DAM

Vientiane

INFILTRATION

MUGIA PASS

DEMILITARIZED ZONE

Conthien
Hue

Thakhek

ROUTES

Savannakhet

Danang

THAILAND

Dakto
Pleiku

Preah Vihear

Mekong River

Ankhe
Quinhon

Bangkok

CAMBODIA

FISHHOOK

Dalat

Mekong

Phnom Penh

Bienhoa

Camranh Bay

Sihanoukville

Saigon

PARROT'S BEAK

Mekong Delta

REPUBLIC OF VIETNAM

U.S. thrust
South Vietnamese thrust
Areas under Communist control
Communist sanctuaries
Communist-ruled Areas

Scale of miles
0   100   200

them withdrawn by June 30, at which time he would report to the nation on the entire operation. As to the essential wisdom of his decision, the President observed that it was his belief, "based on what we have accomplished to date, that we have bought at least 6 months and probably 8 months of time for the training of the ARVN, the Army of [the Republic of] South Vietnam. We have also saved, I think, hundreds, if not thousands, of Americans. . . . Rockets by the thousands and small arms ammunition by the millions have already been captured and those rockets and small arms will not be killing Americans in these next few months." [46]

In Cambodia itself, meanwhile, U.S. field commanders, who had just begun exploiting their offensive and counting up arms caches, expressed shock over Nixon's new deadlines for withdrawal and dismay over his order to penetrate no further than 21.7 miles into Cambodian territory. [47] With the enemy fading back into the jungle in traditional style, they feared that political pressures at home would once again rob them of an opportunity (eliminating the enemy's sanctuaries) for which they had waited five years. To be sure, Nixon had imposed no such limitations on South Vietnamese forces, but the question arose as to how the A.R.V.N. could be expected to fight on alone in Cambodia when they were as yet unable to hold their own in South Vietnam. Nor could the government in Phnom Penh look with particular favor upon the prospect of thousands of South Vietnamese soldiers roaming its eastern provinces any more than it had earlier welcomed the presence of North Vietnamese in the same area. Although the Cambodian government had not been informed in advance of the Nixon decision to intervene, it promptly approved the President's move. But it was clearly less enthusiastic about the South Vietnamese role in the rescue effort than the American.

Meanwhile, on May 6, Cambodia had thrown aside its neutralist stance, breaking diplomatic ties with China, North Vietnam, and North Korea, while its relations with Russia and France (viewed as a key supporter of Sihanouk) drifted to a low ebb. On May 16, the Lon Nol government had urged an 11-nation conference of Asian Foreign Ministers meeting in Jakarta, Indonesia (and boycotted by the Communists) to send troops to its aid. [48] But only Thailand (already allied with South Vietnam in the fighting and, at any rate, suspect in Phnom Penh of harboring territorial designs on Cambodian territory) pledged a volunteer force of ethnic Cambodians, armed and equipped by the United States. On May 27, following three days of negotiations in Saigon, the Foreign Ministers of Cambodia and South Vietnam issued a joint communiqué declaring that A.R.V.N. forces had entered Cambodia with the permission of the Cambodian government and that the troops would leave only when their task was completed.[49] At the same time, President Thieu made it clear that South Vietnamese forces would continue to operate in Cambodia for an indefinite period and would require continued U.S. logistical support.[50]

Yet it could hardly be said that Phnom Penh gained a new sense of security from the efforts of its new-found friends, for the military situation around the Cambodian capital continued to deteriorate despite the allied thrust in the east. Allied naval forces, including 30 U.S. gunboats, had begun a drive on May 9 up the Mekong River with the aim of reaching the besieged capital, and on May 12 other U.S. naval forces began a blockade of the Cambodian coastline designed to intercept incoming North Vietnamese supply boats. Yet enemy guerrilla units appeared to be tightening the ring around the capital, ranging within ten miles of its outskirts, and cutting most of the key roads leading into the city. By the time the June 30 deadline for the U.S. withdrawal rolled around, virtually half of Cambodia's territory was under enemy control, as the last remaining army garrisons were abandoned to Communist forces in the northeast and all available troops were concentrated for the defense of Phnom Penh.

The continuing plight of the Lon Nol regime was a subject President Nixon passed over in his otherwise optimistic report to the nation on June 30.[51] "Ten major operations were launched against a dozen of the most significant base areas," the President noted, "with 32,000 American troops and 48,000 South Vietnamese participating at various times. As of today, all Americans, including logistics personnel and advisers, have withdrawn, as have a majority of the South Vietnamese forces." He described the captured supplies and equipment as being "enough to equip about 25 full-strength North Vietnamese infantry battalions; . . . enough to feed all the enemy combat battalions estimated to be in South Vietnam for about four months," and went on to cite these major accomplishments of the operation: elimination of any immediate threat to U.S. forces and to South Vietnam's security; a heavy toll of enemy casualties (11,349 killed, 2,328 captured); an end to "the concept of Cambodian sanctuaries, immune from attack, upon which the enemy military had relied for five years"; disruption of Hanoi's supply lines and general strategy in the Saigon and Mekong Delta areas; separation, for the time being, of enemy main-force units from guerrillas operating in the southern part of South Vietnam; the guaranteeing of continued U.S. troop withdrawal; and more time for South Vietnam to strengthen its defenses against further enemy attack. In a special tribute to the South Vietnamese troops, the President added: "We have witnessed visible proof of the success of Vietnamization as the South Vietnamese performed with skill and valor and competence far beyond the expectation of our commanders or American advisers. The morale and self-confidence of the Army of South Vietnam is higher than ever before."

With that particular point, at least, most observers could agree. Operation Rock Crusher had clearly lifted the spirits of the Saigon government, even if it had done relatively little to ease the military squeeze on Phnom Penh.[52] Apparently affected by the scope and intensity of the public protests against his decision, the President offered relatively little by way of future help to the Lon Nol regime. He pledged only to "conduct—with the approval of the Cambodian Government—air interdiction missions against the enemy efforts to move supplies and personnel through Cambodia toward South Vietnam and to reestablish base areas relevant to the war in Vietnam. We do this," he stressed, "to protect our forces in South Vietnam." At the same time, he promised that the United States would turn over captured materiel to Cambodia for its defense; that it would supply military assistance to Cambodia "in the form of small arms and relatively unsophisticated equipment"; and that he would encourage other countries in Asia, in line with the Nixon Doctrine, to provide moral and material support. But for Lon Nol, the implication was clear: he would have to sink or swim as best he could, without the kind of American commitment that had helped South Vietnam preserve its independence but made it a nightmare for the American people.

Thus from the President's viewpoint, the Cambodian operation, to the extent that it had bought time for the crucial Vietnamization process, had proved an unqualified success. Yet the price had been high as well. Aside from the widespread protests engendered both at home and abroad, which betokened a setback in public confidence for Nixon's Vietnamization strategy, more than 300 additional Americans had been killed and another 1,300 wounded. In addition, the 39,000 A.R.V.N. troops that initially remained behind after June 30 (more, according to press reports, than the President had indicated), represented something of a drain on Saigon's home defense efforts, which the administration was above all trying to bolster. Though relatively quiescent for a time, moreover, the antiwar forces in Congress were now stirred to new heights of activity, pressing forward with renewed energy their efforts to limit the President's power to conduct war and undertake overseas commitments.[53] At the same time, America's adversaries abroad seemed on the whole less impressed by the boldness and courage of the Nixon decision to intervene than by the ensuing hue and cry aimed at forcing him to withdraw. In an unusual press conference on May 4, Premier Kosygin had roundly denounced the U.S. incursion as a further sign of Washington's "imperialist, aggressive aims." Is it possible, he asked, "to speak seriously about the desire of the United States President for fruitful negotiations to solve pressing international problems while the United States is grossly flouting the Geneva Agreements of 1954 and 1962, to which it is a party, and undertaking one new act after another undermining the foundations of international security?" Finally, the Soviet leader had warned that his government would "draw the appropriate conclusions for its policy from this course of action." [54] The remarks presaged a general stiffening in the Soviet attitude and were followed on June 11 by a pledge of stepped-up economic and military aid to Hanoi stemming directly from the U.S. move in Cambodia.[55] In the meantime, moreover, Peking had moved to cancel a meeting scheduled for May 20 between its own envoy and that of the United States in Warsaw.[55a]

Still another effect of the incursion had been to draw the pro-Communist forces in all Indochina into the kind of informal strategic alliance which had hitherto been neglected, and to draw them closer to Peking's hard line on the conduct of the war as well. As General Giap put it in June, the peoples of Vietnam were now duty-bound to fight alongside "the fraternal peoples" of Laos and Cambodia in an integrated military effort to free all Indochina from the American grip.[56] And, indeed, Hanoi was moving swiftly to secure a hold on supply routes through southern Laos and northern Cambodia, in an apparent effort to insure logistical bases in those areas and replace the routes they had lost. Sihanouk, in the meantime, had announced on May 5 the launching of a new left-wing political movement called the

"National United Front of Kampuchea [Cambodia]" (FUNK), which enjoyed the backing of Communist China, North Vietnam, and the Communist movements in South Vietnam, Laos, and Cambodia. At the same time, he formed a Royal Government of National Union, headed by former Prime Minister Penn Nouth, which openly rested on Communist support and purportedly included representatives of the Communist "Red Khmer" guerrilla movement. Though provisionally based in China, this government-in-exile soon claimed to have advance echelons operating in "liberated" areas of Cambodia itself, and was promptly recognized by a number of Communist states, though not by the U.S.S.R., which continued to maintain its Embassy in Phnom Penh.

In Cambodia itself, officials disappointed with the extent and effectiveness of the allied incursion now moved desperately to increase the beleaguered nation's self-defense efforts by issuing a general mobilization decree on June 25 and raising the number of its still poorly trained and equipped troops to 150,000.[57] With Vietnamese from North and South now warring throughout the countryside, the economy, which had been ailing under Sihanouk, moved even nearer the brink of disaster and by July all development projects (many of them Communist-backed) were shut down. By early August, Cambodian officials were warning that the new government could last only six more months without more substantial U.S. economic and military aid.[58] Yet, for all its troubles, the Cambodian government continued to show a remarkable degree of unity and by contrast with South Vietnam appeared to enjoy a solid base of support among the nation's youth and intellectuals. On July 5, the discredited Sihanouk was found guilty of treason and corruption by a specially convened tribunal and sentenced to death in absentia. On October 9, by unanimous vote of parliament, Cambodia officially proclaimed itself the Khmer Republic.[59] By year's end, with only 8,000 to 10,000 South Vietnamese troops left in the land, the country had raised its own self-defense effort to 165,000 troops, and there was scattered talk in this nation of less than 7 million people, of mustering an ultimate force of 610,000 troops, although Phnom Penh continued under siege and much of the countryside remained in Communist hands.

For Washington, Cambodia's seeming determination in the face of such peril presented yet another cruel irony in a part of the world where agonizing dilemmas had become an almost commonplace fact of life. Long committed to a less than popular and militarily ineffective regime in Saigon, the United States now seemed to be turning its back on a country which showed both the will and the popular support for a determined—if unequal—fight against the common enemy. A key corollary of the Nixon Doctrine was that those countries making strenuous efforts to help themselves would find a willing partner in the United States. But could the "small arms and relatively unsophisticated equipment," with which the President had pledged to aid Cambodia, truly reflect the kind of meager assistance that Washington had in mind? Apparently not, as events soon made clear.

On August 20, the two nations signed an agreement concerning the regulation of military assistance furnished to Cambodia; [60] and Vice-President Agnew, following his Asian trip (which included a stopover in Phnom Penh), confirmed on September 1 that the U.S. would provide $40 million in military assistance funds.[61] On December 22, Congress approved the administration's request for an additional $255 million in military and economic aid for fiscal year 1971.[62] And there were even numerous press reports that, despite Nixon's announced limitations on U.S. involvement, American planes were in fact repeatedly involved in close combat support operations with Cambodian troops on the ground and even that numbers of civilian-clad U.S. military advisers were openly working with Cambodian forces in and around the capital.[63] On the diplomatic side, Emory C. Swank was sworn in September 3 as the first U.S. Ambassador to Cambodia since 1965, replacing Lloyd Rives who had been appointed *chargé d'affaires* in 1969 when U.S.-Cambodian relations were reestablished.

On the whole (and despite the administration's own reluctance), the United States seemed to have gained another heavily dependent client in Southeast Asia—not to mention a widening of the war in the bargain. If the President, by his decision to intervene in Cambodia, had bought time for Vietnamization, he had also riled anew his critics at home, complicated his efforts to reach an understanding with the U.S.S.R. (if the Soviet reaction could be taken as literal), jeopardized the search for better relations with Peking, and in the end gained little guarantee that the North Vietnamese would not eventually reinfiltrate the so-called sanctuaries that the allied effort had been designed to clear. To be sure, the feared North Vietnamese attack on Phnom Penh or across the D.M.Z. into South Vietnam never came. But North

Vietnamese and P.R.G. representatives did cancel the 66th plenary session of the Paris peace talks scheduled for May 6, in protest against renewed U.S. bombing of the North, and shortly thereafter both Xuan Thuy, the chief North Vietnamese negotiator, and Mrs. Nguyen Thi Binh, chief delegate of the P.R.G., withdrew from the talks altogether, although the ostensible reason was attributed more to Washington's failure to name a high-ranking successor to Henry Cabot Lodge, who had resigned as head of the U.S. delegation on December 8, 1969, than to the Cambodian incursion *per se.*

Yet it was possible that events in Cambodia, like so many other events in the history of the Vietnam conflict, had undermined that delicate, almost indefinable moment when the wings of peace are poised for possible flight. As one observer told staff members of the Senate Foreign Relations Committee, "in all international negotiations the moment at which success can be achieved arrives when two conditions exist. The first is that all the principal parties must believe that they can yield and not have their concessions interpreted by others as having been made under pressure from a position of weakness. The second is that the principal parties must be willing to forego [*sic*] certain and important gains in order to reach a settlement . . . as a result of recent events in Cambodia, the moment when these two conditions will exist lies even further in the future." [64] The Cambodian incursion, in short, seemed not only to have complicated the war but may have detoured the road to a peaceful settlement as well.

21 : The Search for Peace

They were called "peace talks," but there was certainly no peace and at times very little talking. In Paris, the dreary repetition of previously rejected proposals by each side ground on, even as 1970 began, around that oval conference table whose very configuration had proved the subject of intense bargaining and a forewarning of the difficulties that lay ahead. At the 50th plenary session of the talks on January 15, [65] Hanoi and the P.R.G. firmly and categorically rejected Nixon's three criteria for the withdrawal of U.S. forces—i.e., progress in the negotiations, enemy restraint in the fighting, and progress in Vietnamization—saying they could never be met and once again demanding the unconditional withdrawal of American troops so that the

Vietnamese people could "settle their own affairs." [66] Yet at the same time the Communist representatives, having earlier agreed to negotiate with Saigon's delegation, now refused even to recognize that delegation's existence, and addressed their litany on the need for U.S. withdrawal only to the acting head of the American delegation, Philip C. Habib.

Habib, for his part, was concentrating his efforts on an attempt to halt the open polemics and return the talks to restricted, secret session —a strategy based on the assumption that American opinion had now rallied to the President's side and that Vietnamization itself was succeeding.[67] "You seem to prefer using these meetings to advance demands for unilateral actions on our part without any indication of what you are prepared to do," he said at the 50th meeting. "You have abused these meetings for propaganda purposes. As I said last week, the continuation of sterile plenary sessions does not serve the cause of a negotiated settlement." [68] On February 11, however, Xuan Thuy made it clear that secret talks could not resume until Habib had been replaced by a representative of "elevated rank" to head the American delegation,[69] and so the sessions dragged fruitlessly on well into the summer, with both sides accusing each other of deliberately expanding the war, and with prospects for any settlement in a seemingly hopeless state of deadlock.

Not unexpectedly, in such circumstances, the focus for peacemaking tended to shift away from the polemics in Paris and back toward outside intermediaries—or would-be intermediaries—where it had rested before the Paris sessions got under way in 1968. As already noted, in the wake of Sihanouk's ouster and the stepped-up fighting in Laos, France had issued its call for a general peace conference on all Indochina, presumably designed to supersede the near-comatose state of the talks it was already hosting in Paris. After mulling the idea over for several weeks, however, Hanoi and the P.R.G. responded negatively—though politely. Then on April 16, Ambassador Malik had set forth his suggestion for a new Geneva conference—something the Soviets had long opposed. But within a week, Malik was backtracking on his own idea, terming it unrealistic in the current circumstances.[70]

Next, Indonesian Foreign Minister Adam Malik proposed a 20-nation conference of Asian and Pacific countries, including North and South Vietnam, North and South Korea, and Communist China, with the more modest aim of working out an agreement to preserve

Cambodia's neutrality. When that conference convened on May 16–17 in Jakarta, however, the Communist states were absent, and little by way of a concrete solution was set forth by the 11 states which did attend. Their major recommendations called for a reactivation of international peace-keeping machinery, an early reconvening of the Geneva conference, and further diplomatic efforts through the U.N.[71] On May 5, in fact, Secretary-General Thant had already issued one of his own periodic world-wide appeals for peace in the area, in which he called for a Geneva-type international conference and mildly reproved the Soviet delegate for his opposition to the idea in the Security Council.[72] The next day, Secretary Rogers blandly welcomed the appeal,[73] followed shortly by affirmative responses from Britain and France, though the U.S.S.R. remained silent. Finally, on June 13, Hanoi's representatives in Paris thoroughly shattered Thant's bid by blasting the Secretary-General personally, terming him pro-Lon Nol, and denouncing his proposal as "sheer hypocrisy." The talks, said Hanoi, were in a deeper impasse than ever as a result of the American invasion of Cambodia.[74]

Only in Laos did it appear that concrete steps toward some sort of partial truce were possible. Like Indochina as a whole, that country had long been divided into two warring factions—the supposedly neutralist Royal Laotian Government, headed by Prince Souvanna Phouma, whose Army was aided by some 1,040 U.S. advisory forces operating in the country;[75] and the so-called Lao Patriotic Front headed by Souvanna Phouma's half-brother, Prince Souphanouvong, and backed by an estimated 60,000 North Vietnamese troops. In February, as Communist troops stormed across the Plain of Jars, Prince Souvanna announced he would ask Britain and the Soviet Union, as co-chairmen of the 1962 Geneva Conference on Laos,[76] to hold new meetings in order to dampen the flames of conflict that were again spreading through the country. This was followed on March 6 by President Nixon's statement[77] announcing that he also had written to Prime Minister Wilson and Premier Kosygin, echoing Souvanna's plea and spelling out in considerable detail U.S. policy aims toward Laos. The United States, Nixon said, had no intention of introducing ground combat forces into Laos. It sought only the protection of its own troops in South Vietnam through the bombing of the Ho Chi Minh Trail and the protection of the legal government's neutrality.

The next day, in apparent response to these appeals, the Pathet

Lao broadcast its own five-point peace plan, calling among other things for the complete withdrawal of all U.S. forces from the country, the formation of a new coalition government, the eventual election of a new neutralist government of national union, and the establishment of a demilitarized zone where talks toward these ends could be held by the interested parties.[78] Souvanna now had to decide whether the Pathet Lao plan represented a sincere effort at negotiated settlement or a diversionary move designed to discourage any reconvening of the Geneva meeting while the Communist military offensive ground on. On March 9, with the apparent encouragement of Washington, the government agreed to exchange messages with Pathet Lao representatives regarding the latter's plan, while the U.S. indicated the next day it had no objections to direct negotiations along the lines proposed by the Communists.[79] Having regained the diplomatic initiative, however, the Pathet Lao now decided to let Souvanna cool his heels in Vientiane, while awaiting the suddenly elusive Communist messenger. At the same time, they moved to raise the stakes by announcing that no talks could be held until the United States ceased all bombing raids. This condition was seconded by Premier Kosygin in his March 15 reply [80] to the Nixon letter concerning U.S. aims in Laos, and was officially conveyed to Souvanna in the message that finally arrived from Souphanouvong on March 20.[81] Considerably put out by this turn of events, the government in Vientiane promptly rejected any such precondition to negotiations, and prospects for any kind of settlement appeared to dim swiftly. They grew dimmer still as the war proceeded to spill over into Cambodia, where the focus of diplomatic concern in the area shifted during April and May. Though nominally neutral, Souvanna himself seemed more convinced than ever that Hanoi's ultimate aim was the domination of all Indochina,[82] and for a time at least he appeared to lose hope that Laos could bargain its way out of the fighting through a separately negotiated agreement. By October, however, he had come around to the view that if there were any chance at all for a partial cease-fire anywhere in Southeast Asia, that cease-fire would come first in Laos. The prospect for truce talks was still alive, though bogged down in a dispute over the makeup of each side's delegation, and government officials in Vientiane were pinning their hopes on a limited cease-fire covering only the northern part of the country, where Hanoi would be asked to reduce the number of its troops in return for a halt in

U.S. bombing of the area.[83] By year's end, however, even this constrained vision of a narrowly limited agreement seemed to be getting nowhere, while the Laotian government's military position had grown considerably worse.

There remained, it seemed, only the peace talks in Paris, and when the dust from the Cambodian incursion had settled on June 30, President Nixon turned once more to dispelling the anemia with which these negotiations were afflicted. "For our part," he had told the nation in announcing the withdrawal of the last American troops, "we shall renew our efforts to bring about genuine negotiations both in Paris and for all of Indochina." [84] The next day, he moved to restore high-level status to the talks by announcing the appointment of "one of America's most distinguished diplomats," David K. E. Bruce, as the new head of the U.S. delegation.[85] A Democrat with a long record of service under five Presidents, Bruce was the only diplomat in U.S. history to have been Ambassador to Britain, France, and Germany in the course of his career. He would, the President said, assume his post in Paris on or about August 1 and "will have great flexibility in the conduct of his talks. We hope that this move on our part will be reciprocated by a similar move on the part of the North Vietnamese in attempts to find a peaceful solution to the war in Vietnam."

It was not until September 17, however, that all four delegations in Paris were represented by their regular chiefs—Bruce for the United States, Pham Dang Lam for South Vietnam, Mrs. Binh for the P.R.G., and Xuan Thuy for North Vietnam—and on that date the Communists did respond by setting forth the first substantive initiative in more than sixteen months of plenary sessions. In an eight-point statement,[86] Mrs. Binh proposed that in exchange for an agreement on the withdrawal of all American and other foreign forces from South Vietnam by June 30, 1971, the Communist side would refrain from attacking the withdrawing forces and would engage at once in discussions on measures to insure the safety of the withdrawing troops and the release of captured prisoners. Asked what would happen with regard to South Vietnamese troops, a Vietcong delegate later said that if they chose to continue hostilities the Communists would fight back; but if they ceased all combat, the Communists would also refrain.

In two key respects, however, the Communists had not budged from the demands they had repeated week after week since the presentation of their first ten-point peace plan on May 8, 1969.[87] They still insisted on total withdrawal of American and non-Vietnamese troops, including weapons and war materiel and the dismantling of their bases, and on the replacement of the Thieu-Ky government in Saigon with a coalition composed of P.R.G. representatives and other Vietnamese "really standing for peace, independence, neutrality, and democracy," [88] though this latter demand was less sweepingly stated than in the past. On July 30, President Nixon had already made clear his own opposition to either an "imposed" or a "negotiated" coalition of the type the Communists sought,[89] and the initial reaction of Ambassador Bruce to the Vietcong proposals was that they amounted to "old wine in new bottles." [90] At the 85th plenary session on September 24, Bruce told the Communist delegates that "While you have rearranged some of the elements of your earlier proposals and added certain detail to them, it would appear that your fundamental demands remain unchanged." [91] He called for clarification of the Communist position and urged abandonment of "language of preconditions and unilateral demands."

The Communists having nonetheless tried in their own way to break the deadlock—and having failed—it was now the turn of the Americans. After conferring with Bruce in Ireland on October 4, President Nixon once again went before a nationwide television audience on October 7 to announce a new five-point plan for ending the war.[92] For months public and private groups and individuals had been urging the President to call for a cease-fire and standstill throughout all Indochina, despite the administration's skepticism about the enforceability of such an arrangement under conditions of guerrilla warfare and despite its reluctance to give the enemy any "breathing space" in which to regroup and resupply. Ever since its eight-point initiative for peace had been presented May 14, 1969,[93] the administration had preferred to stress the importance of mutual troop withdrawals (i.e., U.S. and North Vietnamese) as a way to end the war. With its Vietnamization program under way, however, the United States was now withdrawing its forces unilaterally, and it appeared that the time might be ripe to reexamine the possibilities of a standstill cease-fire. Such a proposal was, in fact, the key element in the President's plan of October 7.

"This would be a 'cease-fire-in-place,'" the President said. "It would not in itself be an end to the conflict, but it would accomplish one goal all of us have been working toward: an end to the killing."

He was not asking for any preconditions to the proposal. But to be effective, he noted, the cease-fire should be supervised by international observers, as well as by the parties themselves; it should not be used by either side as an opportunity to build military strength; it should apply to all kinds of warfare, including bombing and acts of terror; it should encompass not only Vietnam but all of Indochina; and it should "be part of a general move to end the war in Indochina." This last-mentioned factor brought the President to his second point: an international conference "to deal with the conflict in all three states of Indochina." Until such a conference could get under way, Nixon said, the Paris talks would continue as the primary forum of the negotiations.

The President's third point was designed to deal with the Communist demand for a complete withdrawal of all American troops. "We are ready now," Nixon declared, "to negotiate an agreed time-table for complete withdrawals as part of an overall settlement." It was evident from the context in which he spoke that he was referring to U.S. withdrawals and not to the "mutual" withdrawal of U.S. and North Vietnamese forces which he had stressed in the past. As a fourth point, the President asked for a political solution in South Vietnam that "reflects the will of the South Vietnamese people" and also reflects "the existing relationship of political forces in South Vietnam." He promised that the United States would abide by the outcome of whatever political process was agreed upon. Finally, the President proposed "the immediate and unconditional release of all prisoners of war held by both sides."

In presenting the Nixon plan in Paris the next day, Ambassador Bruce referred to it as "bold and comprehensive," [94] and to the extent that it won back for the administration some of the domestic support that had slipped away at the time of the Cambodian incursion, that seemed to be true. Senator Mansfield was frank in his praise of the President's initiative, and the Senate itself adopted a resolution supporting Nixon's stand.[95] A survey of the U.S. press showed almost unanimous editorial backing for the plan,[96] and Secretary Rogers termed the domestic response "uniformly favorable" and the international reaction as a whole "most encouraging." [97]

Unfortunately, however, the response from Hanoi was somewhat more withering. On the very day Bruce was setting forth the initiative, the North Vietnamese and P.R.G. delegates were denouncing it as a "maneuver" and insisting again on unconditional withdrawal of American troops and the ouster of the Thieu regime as the only way to peace. The United States had already publicly urged the Soviet Union to attempt to persuade Hanoi of the value of the Nixon plan, but on October 10 Moscow termed the President's offer a "great fraud," while Communist representatives in Paris excoriated it as a "swindle" designed to help the Republicans in the November elections.[98] The plan, in short, was officially and "resolutely" rejected and "buried," as far as the Communists were concerned, and Hanoi flatly declared that a cease-fire before a settlement was like an open admission that U.S. "aggressors" had a right to be where they had placed themselves by force.[99]

For a time, Ambassador Bruce patiently refused to take these varying and colorful degrees of "no" for an answer, stressing a continued U.S. willingness to compromise and nurturing a faint hope that the Communists were ready to come to terms. But by the end of October he was clearly experiencing the same sort of deadlock that had frustrated his predecessor and was reportedly feeling some of the discouragement that had led Lodge to resign. At the 91st session of the talks on November 5, both sides bitterly accused each other of discourtesy and walked away as far apart on issues of substance as they had been at any time in the 30-month history of the discussions.[100] If there was any comfort at all to be drawn from the talks, it was that the Nixon administration seemed unilaterally on the way to reducing one formidable point—that of U.S. withdrawal—to a non-issue. Even in that connection, however, President Nixon was moved to warn on December 10 that he would order renewed bombing of North Vietnam if Hanoi took advantage of U.S. withdrawals either to threaten the forces that remained or to step up the fighting in the South, or if it fired on U.S. reconnaissance aircraft over the North.[101]

It was increasingly evident, however, that the Thieu government and its perpetuation was more and more becoming the crucial point around which war would continue or peace be made—at least as far as Hanoi was concerned. As for Thieu himself, in a speech of October 31 marking the third anniversary of his term in office, the South Vietnamese leader stressed that he would never accept a coalition government and declared that peace could only come to his country by way of the battlefield and not in Paris. Taking an unusually hard line, and passing over Nixon's five-point plan, Thieu labeled advocates of compromise as cowards and warned that even after the fighting stopped all Communists would be expelled from the country and the war against their views would go on.[102]

22 : And the War Goes on

So the war continued throughout the year, with no appreciable end to the killing in sight. To its credit, the Nixon administration could claim some significant achievements through its own policies, despite the lack of a breakthrough in negotiations. Authorized troop levels in South Vietnam, which stood at 484,000 as the year began, were down to 344,000 as the year ended and were scheduled to drop further in the months ahead.[103] In addition, U.S. combat deaths had fallen to their lowest point in four years, totaling 4,183 for the year as a whole, or an average of 80 a week. At the same time, the dollars-and-cents cost of the war, which had been running at approximately $22 billion a year when Nixon assumed office, had dropped to almost half that amount,[104] though it was clear that South Vietnam, as well as Cambodia, would require billions more in aid in the years ahead.

There were obvious gains within South Vietnam also. Inflation, which had climbed at the rate of 50 per cent in the twelve months up to mid-1970, fell to only 4 per cent in the last half of the year, after Saigon instituted strong fiscal and monetary measures under emergency powers reluctantly granted by the National Assembly. Saigon was now fielding an army of 1.1 million men, who accounted for a growing bulk of the combat engagements (16 major engagements to every one for U.S. forces). They were taking over more and more bases as the Americans withdrew, had assumed complete responsibility for naval operations inside the country, and were flying almost half the combat air strikes within South Vietnam as well.[105] The level of fighting had also continued to drop significantly, particularly in the southern portions of South Vietnam, due in part, no doubt, to strategic decisions made in Hanoi but partly attributable, also, to the growing strength and effectiveness of Saigon's own security forces. By year's end, in fact, the focal point of the war seemed to have shifted out of South Vietnam entirely and centered in the panhandle region of Laos, where Communist forces were engaged in a major effort to build alternate supply and infiltration routes and where so many U.S. B-52 bomber raids were taking place that M.A.C.V. reportedly had to establish traffic control patterns similar to those in effect at major U.S. airports.[106]

Yet there were also signs that the Communist forces were edging their way back into the Cambodian "sanctuaries," and there was no denying, even in official Washington, that the war itself continued to take a grim toll in human suffering and slaughter. In March 1971, Senator Edward M. Kennedy estimated that at least 25,000 South Vietnamese civilians had been killed in the course of the fighting in 1970 and that another 100,000 had been wounded—figures that were not disputed by Pentagon officials. "By this yardstick alone," the Senator said, "we can see that the war in Indochina is not 'winding down' for the peoples of the area." [107] Nor did it appear that the people of South Vietnam were taking kindly to their American protectors. In July, the U.S. Embassy in Saigon was forced to warn its staff against traveling alone in the capital because of anti-American violence on the part of students and anti-regime protestors. In August, *The New York Times* reported that Americans working in South Vietnam were finding themselves hated by the population, with opposition deputies in the National Assembly openly espousing anti-American slogans in their campaign against Thieu.[108]

From the viewpoint of many Americans, of course, the sacrifices being made by the United States on behalf of South Vietnam had long seemed a poor bargain, and now there were reports that growing numbers of American troops were returning from the war addicted to drugs like heroin, which were easily available in the region's major cities. There were repeated tales of venality and corruption among South Vietnamese officials and continuing persecution by President Thieu of his political opponents. To top it off, at a time when American concern for U.S. prisoners of war held by Hanoi was on the rise, there were revelations that the South Vietnamese themselves had subjected Communist prisoners to torture and other forms of inhuman treatment in the so-called "tiger cages" that served as cells at Con Son prison.

This last was a problem of especially grave concern to the United States. For several years the wives and families of American prisoners had been petitioning Hanoi through its delegation in Paris, through the Soviet Union, and in other ways to release a list of captives and provide information about their treatment, state of health, etc. At the beginning of 1970, there were an estimated 1,400 U.S. soldiers missing in action in Vietnam, of whom 430 were believed to be held in the North. Some of these had written their families, but many had not been heard from either by mail or through information released by North Vietnamese authorities, or through the auspices of the International Red Cross, which had failed to gain a representative in Hanoi. In June, North Vietnam had informed representatives of an American peace group that it held 334 Americans captive,[109] but Pentagon officials disputed the accuracy of the list and official Washington seemed increasingly convinced that American POW's were being used by Hanoi as political hostages to a negotiated settlement.

As concern over the fate of these prisoners mounted, President Nixon named astronaut Frank Borman as his Special Representative on Prisoners of War,[110] and in August Borman undertook a 25-day journey to 14 nations in an effort to establish contact with Hanoi and bring pressure on it to accept Red Cross inspection of its POW camps. In his report to a joint session of Congress on September 22,[111] Borman stated there were now about 1,500 U.S. citizens missing in Southeast Asia. "We have received letters from 323 prisoners in North Viet-Nam, and one held by the Viet Cong in South Viet-Nam. From propaganda broadcasts, pictures, and returnees, we have reason to believe that there are about 376 Americans incarcerated in North Viet-Nam, 78 in South Viet-Nam, and three in Laos, making a total of 457 that we know were at one time alive out of the 1,500 that are missing." So far, he added, nine U.S. prisoners had been released by the North and 23 in the South. "I wish I could tell you we were able to go to Hanoi—we were prepared to—to discuss the situation," but "I can only report American anguish and human tragedy."

The failure of the Borman mission and the continuing fear in Washington that U.S. prisoners were being used as a trump card in the negotiations by Hanoi led the Nixon administration to bolder steps later in the year. On November 21, a small U.S. Army and Air Force task force landed at Sontay prison camp compound, 23 miles west of Hanoi in North Vietnam, in a daring effort to free the prisoners thought to be held there. At the time, U.S. bombing raids against the North resumed for a 24-hour period, apparently in concert with the POW camp raid, but attributed by Secretary Laird to retaliation for the downing of a U.S. reconnaissance plane nine days earlier.[112] Whatever the case, the effort proved in vain, for no prisoners were found by the rescue team in the vacated camp.

Like almost everything else in this war, the raid and its accompanying bomber attacks stirred a storm of controversy both at home and abroad. President Nixon hailed the effort as "a mission of mercy, an attempt to rescue . . . fellow Americans who were being held captive in North Vietnam under the most barbaric conditions." [113] But there were those in Congress who believed that the lives of American POW's may have been endangered by a reckless action that ended in failure and imperiled the course of the peace talks as well. Senator Fulbright, for one, compared it to the administration's Vietnamization effort as a whole: ". . . it was ineffective and it did not get results." [114]

And so it went. At the 94th session of the Paris peace talks on December 10, the U.S. and South Vietnamese delegates offered to exchange immediately all prisoners of war with North Vietnam and the P.R.G., an exchange that would have traded 8,000 North Vietnamese for 800 American and allied troops. The Communist delegates countered with a proposal for an immediate cease-fire if the United States would agree to withdraw its forces from South Vietnam by June 30, 1971.[115] That deadlock remained. The United States did, however, succeed in getting the U.N. General Assembly to adopt a resolution on December 9 calling for the humane treatment of war prisoners by all parties to a conflict.[116] In an open letter of December 26 to families of American POW's, President Nixon wrote that "As we approach 1971 we face above all the question of the release of our men. . . . I can do no less than pledge to you that we will not rest until every prisoner has returned to his family and the missing have been accounted for." [117]

That, of course, was far from the only problem the President faced in Southeast Asia as 1971 approached. In the year that was ending, he had seen the war spread and the peace talks flounder. The intransigence of the enemy continued, even as he had struggled unilaterally to disengage. As it had from the start, the Vietnam conflict was proving the most ruthless test of endurance—or folly—that the nation had encountered as it wound its way along the difficult path to a peaceful world.

6 : China and the Rim of Asia

During his tour of Asia in the summer of 1969, Richard Nixon had spoken at length about America's role in the Pacific, about the limits being placed on it, and about the need for more self-help and mutual cooperation among the countries of the area in their own defense. Significantly enough, however, he had said next to nothing about the one country which had for 20 years been the focal point of U.S. policy in the Far East and whose shadow still loomed large over every stop on the Asian leg of the President's journey. The People's Republic of China (P.R.C.) was not only the world's most populous nation; it was a nuclear power with a demonstrated capacity to engage its supposed enemies on the field of battle. In the short two decades of its existence, the P.R.C. had engaged U.S.-U.N. troops in Korea and fought border actions against both India and the Soviet Union, its two largest neighbors. It was supporting Hanoi in its struggle against "American imperialism" and had even lent aid to the Palestinian commandos in their war on Israel. If its official statements were to be taken literally, it was the avowed enemy of almost every government on the face of the earth, the revolutionary storm center of a new and turbulent epoch in the history of man, and the one power in Asia which no bourgeois leader could safely ignore.

Yet there was Nixon, traveling on the rim of this Communist giant and acting for all the world as though it hardly existed. In fact, of course, Communist China was very much on the President's mind, and his failure to engage it in the usual polemics was a matter of some considerable significance in itself—rather like the story of the dog that failed to bark in the Sherlock Holmes mystery. Nixon had come to Asia bent on establishing new lines for American policy—what would soon come to be known as the Nixon Doctrine. It was obvious that a new policy for Asia meant a new policy for China as well. Ever since its founding in 1949, the People's Republic had been at the center of American Far Eastern concerns. It was largely to contain China that Washington had imposed a strict trade embargo, formed the Southeast Asia Treaty Organization (SEATO), entered bilateral defense pacts with the Republic of Korea and the Republic of China on Taiwan, and worked assiduously to block Peking's membership in such organs of the world community as the U.N. But even before the Nixon administration assumed office, it was evident that U.S. policy toward the regime of Mao Tse-tung was undergoing a change. By 1965, some 51 nations, including many U.S. allies, had extended diplomatic recognition to Peking, and it seemed clear that the Communist regime could no longer be regarded as a "passing" phenomenon. In 1966, the Johnson administration quietly initiated a new approach designed to improve relations and dispel the implacable hostility of previous years, though the Chinese themselves, in this instance, hardly seemed to notice the change.

On assuming office President Nixon nonetheless picked up these threads and sought to weave them into a broader tapestry. In July 1969, travel restrictions to the mainland were eased and the trade embargo was modified to allow American tourists to bring home up to $100-worth of Communist Chinese goods. In December, the $100-ceiling was removed on noncommercial goods brought into the U.S. by individuals or nonprofit institutions. At the same time, foreign subsidiaries of American firms were allowed to conduct nonstrategic trade with the mainland for the first time.[1] By the time President Nixon delivered his first State of the World message to Congress in February 1970, he was referring to the Chinese as "a great and vital people who should not remain isolated from the international community. In the long run," he said, "no stable and enduring international order is conceivable without the contribution of this nation of more than 700 million people." The President went on to warn that "We will not ignore hostile acts. We intend to maintain our treaty commitment to the defense of the Republic of China. But we will seek to promote understandings which can establish a new pattern of mutually beneficial actions." [2]

23 : China Picks up the Pieces

As 1970 opened, Peking seemed cautiously prepared to explore these developments with an eye to seeing what Washington had to offer. To be sure, Chinese editorials greeted the new year with a withering propaganda blast at the West, stressing the possibility of nuclear war and urging a Maoist-style revolutionary war to counter it.[3] But these were the kind of hostile accusations (as opposed to "hostile acts") which the Nixon administration appeared ready to overlook in its general quest for accommodation. Not only Washington but Moscow and other capitals had long since grown accustomed to such verbal fusillades, which seemed on the whole less indicative of Chinese intransigence toward the outside world than of continuing insecurities and problems stemming from within. More revealing of the Chinese attitude, in Washington's view, was the agreement to resume talks between Peking's envoy in Warsaw and the U.S. ambassador on January 20, the substance of which was not revealed but the mere scheduling of which was indicative of a shift in Peking's outlook.

From a broader perspective, moreover, there were ample grounds to explain such a shift. By the end of 1969, tensions along the Sino-Soviet border had reached crisis proportions, and Peking seemed genuinely concerned over the possibility of a military confrontation with Moscow. Inside China itself, it was also apparent by now that the tumultuous Cultural Revolution, together with the disruptive effects it had had on Peking's relations with the outside world, had essentially run their course. The leftist elements which had led the upheaval seemed increasingly on the defensive. In January 1970 reports claimed that leftist leaders were encountering resistance from military men and former party hierarchs to their demands for automatic inclusion in the new party structure that was in the process of being built. Then in March, the P.R.C. State Council or Cabinet held its first publicized meeting since 1966, ostensibly to launch a new production drive for grain and cotton but more probably to underscore the reemergence of stability and continuity in state affairs.[4] There were also indications that the economy had recovered from the blows it had suffered, with experts estimating that the gross national product for 1970 would probably exceed that of 1966, when the disruptions began. In September, and also for the first time since 1966, the universities resumed regular classes, with emphasis on technical subjects as opposed to the liberal arts, and on the whole China appeared to be settling back on that road to nation-building from which it had so abruptly departed.

This seemed especially apparent after the Central Committee of the Communist Party met from August 23 to September 6 to approve (somewhat belatedly) the economic plan for 1970 and to announce that a new National People's Congress, which had not been convened since 1965, would meet "at an appropriate time." [5] According to Nationalist Chinese sources, the party leaders unveiled a new draft constitution at the same meeting, named Mao the Great Leader of the People of All Nationalities, Head of State Under the Dictatorship of the Proletariat, and Supreme Commander of the Whole Nation and the Whole Army for life, and confirmed Defense Minister Lin Piao as his successor. The new charter also reportedly confirmed one result of the Cultural Revolution by perpetuating the role of the military at almost every level of Chinese national life.[6]

Not that the Cultural Revolution had been designed to bring the Army to power. On the contrary, as the causes and effects of that once bewildering phenomenon became clearer, it seemed more and more evident that the Army had gained ground principally because, with the party and state apparatus in disarray, it alone possessed the authority to restore stability. As Professor Michel Oksenberg of Columbia University described the process: "The PLA garrison commanders assumed the burden of arbitrating among competing groups, deciding which, if any, to support and reconciling conflicting claims. In early 1967, Peking often intervened in this process, accusing the commanders of settling disputes unfairly. But as the chaos spread, the garrison commanders were able to secure greater latitude in handling local affairs. This decisive shift in power away from Peking, in favor of garrison commanders, occurred in September 1967 and represented perhaps the decisive turning point in the Cultural Revolution." [7] Throughout 1970, it remained evident that the centralized machinery of both party and state had been gravely weakened and that power continued to shift toward these provincial Army commanders. In the summer and fall, continuing shakeups in the administrative leadership of certain provinces—particularly those bordering on the U.S.S.R.—showed steady gains for People's Liberation Army (P.L.A.) officers at the expense of Maoist activists, while exhortations to the people to emulate the Army (as well as the thoughts of Chairman Mao) continued as a key propaganda theme.

In the meantime, nonetheless, a certain placidity had returned to domestic life, and there were signs that the regime was once again turning its attention to the outside world from which it had virtually sealed itself off since 1966. Two events, in particular, seemed to hasten the reemergence of Chinese diplomacy in 1970, in both of which the hand of Premier Chou En-lai was evident. Following the Cambodian coup on March 18, the Peking government not only gave haven and support to the Sihanouk government-in-exile but also to a conference in May at which representatives of the Communist movements in Vietnam, Laos, and Cambodia sought, with Chou, to forge a more united front for all of Indochina.[8] These moves gave a considerable boost to Peking's influence in Hanoi at a time when the Russians appeared somewhat left out in the cold by Southeast Asia's most dramatic development of the year.

The second event was related to Chou's apparent success in detaching North Korea from its close alignment with Moscow and drawing it closer to Peking's orbit. The Kremlin itself provided the opening by a series of steps designed to improve its relations with Japan, North Korea's ancient enemy, and by further suggesting that Pyongyang join in the maneuvers. Despite past tensions between Peking's leadership and North Korea's Premier and party leader, Kim Il Sung, Chou made it a point to visit Pyongyang in April, there to reaffirm Chinese-Korean friendship and, in an oblique criticism of Soviet policy, to warn sharply against the revival of Japanese "militarism" and "reaction." In a joint communiqué the two powers charged that "Japanese militarism is vainly trying to realize its old dream of a 'Greater East Asia Co-prosperity Sphere' and has openly embarked on the road of aggressions against the people of Asia." [9]

By June, therefore, Peking had managed to strengthen its ties with the Communist regimes in Asia at the expense of Moscow, had enhanced its international prestige by launching a 380-pound space satellite on April 25, and, most importantly, was moving to restaff its 45 ambassadorial posts, which had been thinned as a result of the

Cultural Revolution. In June the process of reemergence continued, as Peking provided a warm welcome for Rumanian Vice-President Emil Bodnaras, and pledged $23 million in material aid for Rumanian flood relief.[10] In July came an official two-week visit, at Peking's invitation, by French Minister for Cultural Affairs André Bettencourt and the significant announcement that Peking and Moscow had agreed, despite their unresolved border problems, to exchange ambassadors.[11] There were other stirrings as well—the continued reception and fêting of such foreign leaders as Sudanese President al-Nimeri and former French Premier Maurice Couve de Murville; the release from prolonged detention of several British citizens and even of Bishop James E. Walsh, the 79-year-old American Roman Catholic who had been imprisoned for twelve years on alleged spying charges, the prompt relief aid proffer to Peru when a disastrous earthquake struck there at the end of May, and so on.

On the whole, the world reacted to these varied moves with unconcealed pleasure and a sense of relief, for if the Cultural Revolution had accomplished little else, it had at least aroused international concern lest a fifth of mankind head off in some unfathomable direction all its own. If any additional proof were needed that China was indeed mooring once more amidst the other ships of state, it came in October, when Canada announced its intention of establishing diplomatic ties with the mainland. Negotiations toward that end had been under way for 20 months, during most of which time Peking had consistently demanded Canada's endorsement of its sovereignty over Taiwan as a "price" of recognition and Canada had just as consistently refused it. It was the Chinese, therefore, who broke the impasse by agreeing to a formula on Taiwan which Canada had been urging. In a joint communiqué issued at the conclusion of the talks, Canada recognized the People's Republic as the sole legal government of China, taking "official note" of Peking's claim to Taiwan as an "integral part" of the mainland without, however, either endorsing or challenging that position.[12] While in the end this formulation proved acceptable to Peking, it was not to the Republic of China on Taiwan itself, and the latter proceeded to break its relations with Ottawa.

Peking's concession to Canada nonetheless opened the gates to similar agreements with a number of other countries. On November 6, Italy announced that it would exchange ambassadors with Peking within three months.[13] At the same time, both Austria and Belgium, as well as Luxembourg and Ethiopia, were moving to establish ties on a similar basis. Even Pope Paul VI, who undertook a ten-day, 30,000-mile journey on November 27 to nine cities in Asia and the Western Pacific, sought to direct a conciliatory message of his own to Chinese people "everywhere" during a stopover in Hong Kong.[14]

Still another result of Peking's carefully timed concession to Canada became apparent during the perennial debate over China's seat in the U.N. in November. The annual U.S.-sponsored resolution, stipulating that any proposal to change Chinese representation constituted an "important question" requiring a two-thirds majority, was adopted by the General Assembly on November 20 by a vote of 66 in favor, 52 against, with 7 abstentions.[14a] Concurrently, the Assembly resolution to admit Peking failed of adoption by a vote of 51 in favor, 49 against, with 25 abstentions.[15] But for the first time, the pro-Peking vote received a simple majority, and not a few delegates seemed of the opinion that the tide had decisively turned at last in Peking's favor. To some extent, a shift in the U.S. position on the issue was a factor in all this. During the course of the U.N. debate, U.S. Deputy Representative Christopher H. Phillips had argued narrowly that Nationalist China, as a good and faithful member of the organization and the effective government of Taiwan's 14 million people, should not by rights be expelled from its Security Council seat. But he pointedly refrained from commenting on Peking's right to be seated, raising none of the old arguments that had served so well in the past.[16] It was thus apparent that the United States was itself in the process of reassessing its traditional stand on this most traditional of cold war issues.

Whether a comparable reassessment of the United States was under way in Peking, however, seemed doubtful for the moment. While American and Chinese representatives in Warsaw had resumed private discussions on January 20, after a two-year hiatus, and though a second meeting—the 136th between the two governments—had taken place one month later to the day, a third scheduled meeting was nonetheless cancelled by the Chinese in the aftermath of the Cambodian incursion. Instead, on May 20, Chairman Mao issued a solemn statement entitled "People of the World, Unite and Defeat the U.S. Aggressors and All Their Running Dogs!"—filled with all the old polemics and leaving scant grounds for any hope that the Chinese attitude might be softening.[17] Despite Mao's polemics, however, the Department of State expressed regret over the last-minute torpedoing of the Warsaw talks and voiced the hope that discussions would resume again in the near future.[18] In a televised interview in Tokyo on July 8, Secretary Rogers stated his belief that Peking held "the key to the future of Indochina" and urged the Communist regime to "talk sensibly about a settlement" there. Declaring that the United States had done "everything we can to improve our relations with China," the Secretary noted that the Chinese, for their part, had "given some indication they might like to improve relations, but so far the progress has been very slow." [19]

In addition to the steps the Nixon administration had taken in 1969 to ease trade and travel restrictions on the mainland, there were further conciliatory gestures during 1970. The U.S. announcement in March that Americans could henceforth travel to the mainland for any legitimate purpose was followed in April by moves to permit shipment of American-made components of foreign-made nonstrategic goods previously banned.[20] In another unilateral step in August, the administration authorized the bunkering of free-world ships carrying nonstrategic cargoes to China, provided that non-American petroleum products were used.[21] These were small steps in themselves, but they were designed to have a cumulative effect. In addition, the United States was pressing forward with troop withdrawals from Vietnam and was generally proceeding, to the considerable distress of its allies, to implement the Nixon Doctrine throughout the Western Pacific. Although the Warsaw talks remained suspended at Chinese insistence, U.S. trade and travel remained at a minimum, and such matters as cultural relations had yet to be discussed, President Nixon nonetheless failed to show signs of discouragement. At his news conference on December 10, he said he was "going to continue the initiative that I have begun, . . . having in mind the fact that looking long toward the future we must have some communication and eventually relations with Communist China." [22]

24 : The Nixon Doctrine: Repercussions

Even the most slowly paced change in a nation's foreign policy can bring prompt repercussions among other nations affected by it, and such certainly seemed to be the case with many of America's Far Eastern allies. For twenty years, they had toed Washington's basic line against Peking, and now with the Nixon Doctrine in effect and a low-key U.S. flirtation with Peking going forward, they tended to feel cast adrift in a sea of uncertainty. This was especially true of Taiwan, where the impact of any reconciliation between Peking and Washington would undoubtedly be felt the most, but it applied as well to other nations in the area which had tied their defenses to the United States.

For the Nixon administration, the task of reconciling both the doctrine enunciated at Guam [23] and the new approach to Peking with its professed intention to stand by its Far Eastern allies was a delicate one. As the year began Vice-President Agnew was in the midst of a three-week, eleven-nation tour of the area, designed to reassure Asian leaders of America's continuing role as a Pacific power. In Taipei, he told President Chiang that the United States was "pledged to stand firm in the commitments we have made to our allies," adding that "As President Nixon has emphasized, however, the future of East Asia is appropriately in the hands of Asian leaders and their peoples. The United States wishes to assist them in their endeavors, but the essential ingredients of will, of imagination, of common purpose, can only be found here." [24] It was a message the Vice-President repeated at stops in Thailand, Australia, and elsewhere. At a state dinner in Auckland, New Zealand, he defined the Nixon Doctrine as an attempt "to deemphasize paternalism and to emphasize partnership. . . . We intend to provide the shield of our nuclear ability. . . ," the Vice-President said, "On the other hand, we do not feel it wise for us to interject ourselves into every dispute that might arise within a nation concerning political development or concerning changes in its system." [25]

Following his return to Washington on January 19, Agnew told a press conference that the Asian leaders he had visited accepted the Nixon Doctrine, viewing it as "flexible enough and yet clear enough to allow an understanding of our commitment." [26] There were scattered indications that the regional self-help efforts the doctrine sought to encourage were gaining some ground. During the summer, Singapore and Malaysia were said to be considering the establishment of a five-power defensive arrangement with Australia, New Zealand, and Britain, following the latter's decision to maintain a token military presence in the area as part of a Commonwealth defense force. In addition, the five members of the Association of Southeast Asian

States (ASEAN), having successfully helped to ease the dispute between Malaysia and the Philippines over the status of the Malaysian state of Sabah in December 1969, appeared to be moving toward greater regional economic cooperation.

There were even some signs that Taiwan was reluctantly adjusting itself to the new American outlook. On July 28, the Nationalist regime was reported to be acceding to U.S. pressure to cut its own armed forces from 600,000 to 550,000, with a promise of more cuts to come, while President Chiang's son and apparent successor, Vice-Premier Chiang Ching-kuo, was stressing economic progress (over the proverbial recapture of the mainland) as the country's main task.[27] On the surface, Taiwan's defense cuts may have appeared to run counter to the administration's emphasis on greater self-help efforts, but in a broader sense, they reflected the U.S. desire not only to lower its profile in the area but to ease tensions generally as a means of beating a smoother path to Peking's doorstep.

Yet throughout the year, it also remained evident that the Nixon Doctrine and all its corollaries had struck America's Far Eastern allies less like a gift of partnership than like a ton of bricks. In February, Foreign Minister Thanat Khoman of Thailand, smarting from the doctrine's implications and from congressional criticisms of U.S. aid to his government, warned fellow Asians that they must make haste to develop a regional security system without reliance on U.S. troops. "We cannot sit with arms folded waiting for doomsday," he declared.[28] During a visit to Washington April 21–23, Chiang Ching-kuo himself cautioned U.S. officials against overtures to Peking and urged a minimal withdrawal of American forces from the Far East.[29] And in early June, South Korea brusquely informed a Cambodian military mission that it was unable to aid the beleaguered Lon Nol regime because of its own problems with Communist forces in the north and its commitment of some 50,000 troops to South Vietnam—the implication being that, if Washington could not help, Seoul could do even less.

There were times, in fact, when the Nixon Doctrine seemed to be encouraging Asian states to look less toward mutual self-help efforts than to saving their own individual skins. When Secretary Rogers flew to Manila to attend the fifteenth session of the SEATO Ministerial Council held July 2–3, he was greeted somewhat like an erring father who had announced his intention of abandoning his children. Filipinos,

Australians, New Zealanders—delegates from around the periphery of China urged him to go slow on U.S. military, economic, and political cutbacks in the Western Pacific. Even Japan (though not a SEATO member) had reportedly communicated its doubts about the essential course of U.S. policy.[30] Obviously on the defensive, Rogers took pains to reassure fellow delegates that the United States was not about to walk away from its responsibilities. The Nixon Doctrine, he said, "means that we will remain a Pacific power and a member of the Pacific community. It means that we will support the efforts of our Asian friends to maintain their own sovereignty and security. It does not mean that we will turn our back on our international policies or withdraw into a shell of isolationism." [31]

In a joint communiqué July 3, the SEATO Ministers duly "noted President Nixon's important formulation of United States policy in Asia, in the terms of the 'Nixon Doctrine.' The Council considered this to be fully in accord with the spirit and terms of the Manila [SEATO] Treaty." [32] Such words hardly constituted a ringing endorsement, but by 1970 SEATO seemed somewhat less than capable of taking a firm stand on any significant issue. Founded largely to thwart Chinese expansionism, its inner logic had gradually unravelled as the Chinese turned their energies first against Moscow and then against the alleged shortcomings of their own society. France had been boycotting the organization's activities for years, while Pakistan, which refused to sign the communiqué, for all intents and purposes had also become a SEATO dropout. The Council meeting itself was marked by an intemperate exchange between the United States and Thailand, stemming from Thanat's bitter counterattack on U.S. Senate doves and continued Thai reluctance to supply troops to Cambodia, despite a pledge of U.S. financing.[33]

Back in Washington, Secretary Rogers nonetheless described the meeting as "successful," citing in particular the reassuring announcement by Britain's new Conservative government that it would continue to maintain a military presence east of Suez in the Malaysia-Singapore area. Like Vice-President Agnew before him, Rogers also stressed the understanding with which the Nixon Doctrine was being received.[34] Yet despite these two missions—one by the Vice-President and one by the Secretary of State—doubts lingered and nerves remained frayed. On July 8, the State Department officially informed South Korea of Washington's intention to withdraw 20,000 of its authorized 63,000 troops in that country over the course of the next year,[35] and within a week, Seoul's Prime Minister Paek Tu Chin was threatening the resignation of the entire South Korean Cabinet if the United States went ahead with the plan. The announcement July 24 of a planned reduction of U.S. military personnel—mostly Air Force—in the Philippines, that would scale down the number of troops from 24,400 to 18,400 by June 1971, brought similar cries of alarm in Manila,[36] despite long-standing discontent arising out of the presence of U.S. forces.

If Washington was sincere about lowering its profile in the area, however, there was little it could do by way of reassurance except to dispatch still another good-will mission, and that the White House proceeded to do. On August 22, Vice-President Agnew flew off for another round of talks, this time touching down in South Korea, Taiwan, South Vietnam, and Thailand, throwing in, on the spur of the moment, a five-hour stop in Phnom Penh. While the Vice-President carried with him renewed assurances of continued U.S. support, he was now also instructed to make it clear that the Nixon Doctrine meant business and that the burden of Asian defense had shifted to Asian hands. As he winged toward his first stop in Seoul, the Vice-President gave accompanying reporters what amounted to the most sweeping definition of the Nixon Doctrine to date. "It is not compatible with our philosophy," he said, "to have large contingents of our forces permanently stationed in any country." [37]

It was a message Agnew hammered away at throughout his talks in Seoul. Convinced he could no longer forestall a U.S. troop reduction, President Park Chung Hee sought to tie U.S. withdrawals to explicit promises of substantial U.S. aid to modernize the 620,000 South Korean armed forces. In a planned two-hour meeting between Park and Agnew that stretched to six, the Vice-President demonstrated that he could be just as stubborn as his Korean hosts, who were renowned for their tenacity in negotiations. Agnew did promise substantial aid for South Korean forces, but flatly refused to link their moderniza-tion to U.S. withdrawals. American forces in Korea would be reduced as scheduled, he reportedly said, and all U.S. ground troops might well be gone from the peninsula in as little as five years.[38] In a press briefing of August 26, the Vice-President described these talks as "a very frank exchange of views concerning the pace of modernization and the relationship between the reduction of American forces and modernization. The United States takes the position that reduction is not contingent upon modernization nor is modernization contingent upon reduction. Nonetheless, we would not reduce forces . . . [below] a level that would keep the security of Korea intact." [39]

Whether the South Koreans were satisfied with these terms seemed doubtful, to say the least, but it was clear that Agnew was bringing home to Asians as never before the practical implications of the Nixon Doctrine. After the hard bargaining in Seoul, the other stops on the Vice-President's intinerary were relatively ceremonial. Although Foreign Minister Thanat was still smoldering over those Senate doves who, he said, "would like nothing better than to push Southeast Asia into Communist hands," [40] Bangkok at the same time began adopting its own version of the Nixon Doctrine by announcing that it would pull its 12,000-man Black Leopard division out of South Vietnam as soon as possible.[41] Even so, however, the government of Prime Minister Thanom Kittikachorn seemed satisfied with Agnew's assurance that the Nixon administration would do all it could to prevent any reduction in the $30 million in economic and $60 million in military aid that Thailand received annually. The Thais, said Agnew, "were very careful to make clear to me that they were not asking for an increase in their funds, they simply would hope that because of their added responsibilities in connection with Cambodia and the insurgencies in their own country, near Laos and Cambodia, they would not have to take any severe cuts at this time. I found them extremely understanding of the American position." [42]

Significantly, much of the ferment unloosed by the Nixon Doctrine was taking place at a time when many of the countries of Asia were continuing to make substantial economic gains and were thus better able to provide for their own defense. In fact, one of the cheerier notes struck at the annual three-nation ANZUS Council meeting in Washington on September 26 was the final communiqué's reference to "the remarkable economic growth and social development of Asian nations with free economies. The nations of the Western Pacific were increasingly able to assume the primary responsibility and initiative in the affairs of their region." [43] This seemed particularly true of such countries as Taiwan and South Korea, where economic growth had been climbing at the exceptional rate of 10 per cent or more a year. From another perspective, however, it was precisely South Korea's model record of economic development which may have prompted

North Korea to begin raids and infiltration tactics against the South. These tactics had been intensified since 1967 and continued in 1970, and they argued strongly, in Seoul's view, against any rushed withdrawal by the United States.

Economic prospects for Thailand, Singapore, and Malaysia also looked reasonably hopeful, even though Thailand and Malaysia continued to suffer small-scale Communist insurgencies. Only the Philippines, with its rising levels of political corruption, economic mismanagement, and street rioting (much of it anti-American in tone), stood apart in the area as a source of concern to both its neighbors and Washington. In Indonesia, on the other hand, continuing progress under the anti-Communist regime of General Suharto served to strengthen Washington's hope for the eventual stabilization of Southeast Asia outside a Communist framework. Following earlier visits to Thailand and Malaysia, President Suharto arrived for a state visit in Washington on May 26–27, where President Nixon hailed "the role you and your Government have played and are continuing to play for peace in the Pacific." [44] The remark could be seen as a tribute to Suharto's own efforts to end his nation's self-imposed isolation and return it to the swim of world politics by sponsoring, for example, the 11-nation conference of Asian Foreign Ministers on Cambodia. Suharto, in turn, paid tribute of sorts to evolving U.S. policy goals by assuring Nixon that "The nations of Asia have started to take it upon themselves to meet the challenges that Asia faces today." [45]

It appeared evident, therefore, that the Nixon Doctrine was gaining virtually unanimous rhetorical acceptance throughout non-Communist Asia by the end of 1970. Whether it was also gaining acceptance as a matter of practical application, however, very much remained to be seen. Nations like South Korea, the Philippines, and Taiwan had long been tied so closely to the United States, had long been in such a state of dependency, that it seemed only natural they should take fright at the prospect of walking alone. Others, like Thailand, were reassessing their relations with China as a hedge against the day when U.S. troops would be gone. Even Malaysia was easing away from its long-standing orientation toward British policy. When the country's popular Prime Minister Tunku Abdul Rahman voluntarily retired in September, his successor, Tun Abdul Razak, promptly began steering a more neutralist course. Such reactions were hardly surprising, given the essential aims of the Nixon administration's policies—the wooing of Peking, the withdrawal from Vietnam, the lowered profile elsewhere. Such policies clearly foreshadowed, if not an end to American commitments in the area, at least a substantial reduction of the American presence. Washington was obviously gambling that, given its own preoccupations, Peking would not move to fill the vacuum. But Washington also knew that another nation—a friendly one at that—was also on the rise in Asia, outweighing even the 750 million people of mainland China in its astonishing display of vigor and power.

25 : Focus on Japan

Ever since his days as Vice-President in the 1950's, Richard Nixon had advocated a strong role for Japan in the Western Pacific and a strengthening of Japanese defenses. As President, he seemed all the more eager to give full rein to these views. ". . . Japan," he had observed in the State of the World message,[46] "will be crucial to our efforts to help other Asian nations develop in peace. Japan's partnership with us will be a key to the success of the Nixon Doctrine in Asia." Indeed, as the President described it, he had faced a crucial decision with respect to Japan upon entering office, namely: "What did we consider more important—the maintenance of American administration of Okinawa with no adjustments in the conditions under which we operate our bases, or the strengthening of our relationship with Japan over the long term?" In choosing the latter option, the President maintained, "We have thereby laid the foundation for US-Japanese cooperation in the 1970's."

That foundation had been established in November 1969, when Prime Minister Eisaku Sato paid an official visit to Washington for the express purpose of settling the Okinawa issue.[47] For 25 years since the end of World War II, the United States had occupied that island in the Ryukyus, gradually transforming it into a powerful strategic outpost on the rim of Asia, equipped to handle nuclear devices. The symbolic significance of such devices, given the vivid Japanese memories of Hiroshima and Nagasaki, was not lost on a nation anxious for a full return of sovereignty and acceptance into the fold of nations. In agreeing to return administrative control of Okinawa to Japan by 1972, the Nixon administration also agreed to subject its bases on the island to the same far-reaching restrictions that governed American bases on Japan proper, *i.e.,* the stationing of nuclear weapons would be barred without express Japanese consent. In return, Prime Minister Sato agreed to expand and improve aid programs in Asia, and for the first time publicly linked Okinawa's security to that of South Korea and Taiwan. He also promised to accelerate the reduction and removal of restrictions on trade and the movement of foreign capital into Japan, and, implicitly, to assume greater responsibility for Japan's own defense. More immediately, the Nixon-Sato agreement served to alleviate the threat that Japan's leftist opposition would be able to block the continuance in force of the 1960 U.S.-Japanese Security Treaty, which was to become subject to denunciation by either side as of June 23, 1970.

That Japan was fully capable of shouldering a world role by 1970 seemed more than evident to the thousands of foreign visitors who flocked to "Expo '70," described by Secretary Rogers as "the greatest world's fair of all time." [48] Already the world's third greatest industrial power (after the U.S. and U.S.S.R.), Japan's unmatched record of economic growth showed few, if any, signs of faltering. Indeed, at least two books published in 1970 were almost solely devoted to reminding the world that from the ashes of World War II a new superstate had arisen that could not help but count weightily in international politics in the years ahead. One, by French journalist Robert Guillain, contended that the Japanese were proving through hard work and exceptional organizational skills that a nation could win international influence and respect without a classic resort to military prowess—could achieve, in Guillain's words, "greatness without the bomb." [49] The other, by the American strategic analyst Herman Kahn, foresaw Japan's possible emergence as the world's most powerful nation, economically, by the end of the 20th or early 21st century, but worried whether Japan could successfully defend its economic gains without reversion to the Samurai spirit of the past—without, in short, a rebirth of militarism. [50]

The problem was already preoccupying Japan's neighbors and even the Japanese themselves. In a public warning in April against the dangers of "great-powerism," Prime Minister Sato cited fears that the country's growing strength might lead to behavior disturbing of the international equilibrium. "It is entirely a new case," he said, "that a country such as Japan, possessing great economic strength, has no significant military power and yet makes its presence felt throughout the world." [51] To some extent, the Prime Minister's concern seemed justified. Japan, after all, was a unique case—a great power which spent less than 1 per cent of its gross national product on its defense, which lacked for nothing except the political will to build an arsenal of weapons of mass destruction, if it so desired. There were, moreover, right-wing elements within the nation which seemed determined to change this posture. In January, shortly after the December 1969 elections, which registered substantial gains for Sato's Liberal Democratic party, police authorities issued a warning against the militant tactics of right-wing groups and extreme nationalists whose influence in the elections had been small but whose threat to public security was deemed large.[52] In November came the disturbing news that the noted Japanese novelist, Yukio Mishima, founder of the right-wing, paramilitary *Tate No Kai* (Shield Society), had committed ritual suicide after he and five colleagues had staged a dramatic assault on Japan's Self-Defense Force's East Army Headquarters in Tokyo and harangued its soldiers on corruption in Japanese politics.

Such stirrings were for the moment minuscule compared to the strong pacifist leanings of the Japanese as a whole and to the power and influence of the country's sizable leftist opposition, but they nonetheless struck an ominous note in the nation's generalized debate on its future role in Asia and the world. At least one element in that debate moved toward resolution when Japan became the 94th nation to sign the nuclear nonproliferation treaty on February 3.[53] At the same time, however, the Japanese registered their objections to what they called the treaty's "discrimination" against non-nuclear states and withheld ratification pending developments in the disarmament negotiations under way between the United States and Russia and at the U.N. Meanwhile, it was increasingly evident that the Japanese were moving to bolster their conventional defense forces within the limits imposed by the constitution. In a Cabinet reshuffle January 14, Sato appointed Yasashiro Nakasone as State Minister and Director-General of the Defense Agency—a gesture designed to please advocates of a larger defense establishment, of whom Nakasone himself was a leading spokesman. In addition, the 1970 budget called for a sharp rise in defense outlays to $1.6 billion (still, it should be noted, less than 1 per cent of Japan's $200 billion G.N.P.). In a white paper issued October 20, the government renewed its promise to avoid becoming a military threat and conditionally reaffirmed its non-nuclear principles, but as commentators in Peking were quick to point out the paper also urged special efforts to expand Japan's Navy and Air Force, to strengthen the Army's fire power and mobility, and to expand its guided missile units and the development of offensive weaponry.[54]

If there seemed to be an element of schizophrenia in all this, it is probably because such an element was present. Having proved to its own satisfaction that the yen was indeed mightier than the sword, Japan seemed in no rush to assume those security burdens in Asia which Washington was in the process of relinquishing. No less than President Nixon, Prime Minister Sato placed great value on close U.S.-Japanese cooperation. Japan's decision on June 22 to maintain the Security Treaty [55] in face of relatively muted protests from leftists in the streets was evidence of its desire for continuity in such matters. But Japan also appeared to value its trade relations with mainland China, its growing commercial ties to the Soviet Union,[56] and, above all, the lesson it had learned from its course of military adventurism in World War II. In 1970, Japan was the only major power whose foreign aid expenditures—pledged at $1.4 billion by Finance Minister Takeo Fukuda—came near to matching what it was spending on defense.[57]

From Peking's viewpoint, however, the issue of Japan's world role had been decisively settled in the Nixon-Sato talks of November 1969, with Japan having more or less agreed to serve as American "imperialism's gendarme in Asia." [58] Sato's references to the security needs of Taiwan and South Korea had irked, in particular, apparently reinforcing China's growing sense of isolation and encirclement. At any rate, throughout 1970 it was evident from the harsh pronouncements of Peking's propagandists that Japan had taken its place alongside the United States and the Soviet Union as an especially worrisome "enemy" of the Chinese people.

From the United States' viewpoint, Japan's modest steps toward rearmament posed no such problem. In a speech before the American Academy of Political and Social Science on April 10,[59] Under Secretary of State for Political Affairs U. Alexis Johnson pointed out that "Japan has already assumed responsibility for its own conventional defense, and it is doubtful whether there is much more that it could do that would directly relieve United States military responsibilities in Japan, almost all of which are related to regional commitments."

As an island nation, Johnson said, Japan was naturally concerned with protecting its air and sea approaches. Accordingly, it was modernizing its air defense system by adding new Nike-Hawk and Nike-Hercules batteries built by the Japanese themselves. The F-4 Phantom jet, coproduced under a licensing agreement with American manufacturers, would also soon be added to its arsenal, with the Japanese Navy undertaking a program of expansion and modernization as well. But, said Johnson, "What Japan is accomplishing for its own defense is, of course, entirely proper and reasonable for a great nation." In reducing its own military profile in Asia, he added, including the scheduled withdrawal of 12,000 of the 45,000 U.S. troops on Japan proper and the 5,000 of the 45,000 on Okinawa, the United States had "no intention of trying to push Japan into the assumption of security responsibilities for which Japan and its neighbors are not prepared."

Of greater immediate concern to the United States than the issue of Japanese rearmament was the issue of Japan's economic and trade policies toward other developed countries and especially toward its largest trading partner, the United States. Here was a problem which Under Secretary Johnson was forced to discuss in less reassuring terms. "I am sure that most of my friends in the Japanese business community will agree with me," he said, "that the era has passed during which Japan could claim special privileges and that if Japan is going to continue its spectacular economic development, Japan must be willing to grant to others that same freedom of economic enterprise within Japan that Japan is seeking and in large degree receiving in other economically developed countries, especially in the United States." To be sure, by 1970 Japan had gradually begun to ease the stringent restrictions on foreign capital which had prevented American business from investing substantially in Japanese firms. And in February, the Sato government had also moved to lift quotas previously imposed on nine different import items. But about 100 other quotas restricting imports remained in effect, all of them in violation of the rules laid down by the General Agreement on Tariffs and Trade (GATT), to which Japan was a party. And meanwhile the Japanese were strongly resisting American pressure to impose voluntary export quotas on their own sales of noncotton textiles (synthetic or wool fibered) to the United States.

It was this last issue which came to epitomize the economic tensions that had grown up between the two countries, casting doubt on Prime Minister Sato's conviction that the 1970's would mark a decade of close and fruitful U.S.-Japanese relations. As is sometimes the case in such matters, internal political pressures in both countries seemed to set the problem in motion. During his 1968 campaign for the presidency, Nixon had promised relief to U.S. textile manufacturers and workers from the inroads being made by foreign competition. What the President wanted was a system of voluntary restrictions on noncotton textile exports to the United States, similar to the one already in effect for cotton textiles. What the President apparently failed to reckon with was the strength of the countervailing internal political pressures against such restrictions within leading export countries like Japan and including, in the Far East, Taiwan and South Korea as well.

Behind these mutually antagonistic political pressures lay deeper economic problems. At a time when the United States was struggling to right its own balance-of-payments problems, Japan was racking up major surpluses—in part at American expense. In 1969, for example, Japan enjoyed a payments surplus of $2.28 billion and an even larger trade surplus of $3.75 billion. About a third of the trade surplus came through merchandise trade with the United States. It was Washington's aim to redress this imbalance, and textiles seemed, for political reasons if nothing else, a good place to start. With the Japanese resisting voluntary quotas of the kind and duration that Washington desired, however, the issue mushroomed into something of a confrontation. In April, Chairman Wilbur D. Mills of the House Ways and Means Committee introduced legislation designed to set textile quotas by law,[60] and the protectionist mood in the U.S. Congress indicated he had broad support. In June, talks on a voluntary quota system between U.S. and Japanese representatives broke off without agreement, and the stage seemed set for what newspaper accounts described as a looming trade war.

While struggling to allay those internal pressures which had fueled the confrontation, however, it was evident that neither the United States nor Japan wanted to spark a trade war from which it seemed probable that neither country would benefit. If the United States constituted Japan's largest foreign market, Japan was second only to Canada as a market for U.S. exports. As a nation heavily dependent on trade for its economic livelihood, moreover, Japan looked to the

United States not only as its major market abroad but as its prime source of most raw materials and advanced manufactured products and as its key source of patent rights and technological licensing as well. With this mutually profitable relationship serving as a backdrop, negotiations on the textile issue were later resumed and continued through the end of the year. Even so, however, successive U.S. proposals and Japanese counterproposals, based on voluntary limitations in one form or another, continued to be unacceptable in turn, and the issue of a possible trade war remained the foremost problem confronting the two nations in their mutual relations as 1971 began.

26 : The Teeming Subcontinent

While American interests in the Far East were focusing increasingly on its alliance with Japan and its efforts at *rapprochement* with China, the populous Indo-Pakistani subcontinent continued its seeming drift toward despair and disintegration. The area's two largest states— India with more than 500 million people and Pakistan with more than 130 million—had been chastised in Nixon's State of the World message for what the President called "the waste of their limited resources in an arms race." [61] However, events in 1970 seemed to indicate that the two nations had more to fear from internal strife than from mutual hostility toward each other, although the two tended to go hand-in-hand. In India, the continued split in the ruling Congress party left Prime Minister Indira Gandhi dependent on the pro-Moscow wing of the Indian Communist party and other opposition groups in her efforts to cope with rising prices, increased social unrest, and sharpening political violence.

A series of bombings and political assassinations fomented by Mao-quoting Naxalites (so-called from a peasant uprising in Naxalbari, West Bengal in 1967) helped force the breakup of the leftist "United Front" government in West Bengal in March, bringing on the subsequent imposition of direct rule by the central government. In random terrorist attacks on policemen and political opponents (mostly other Marxists), the Naxalites had virtually brought Calcutta, already India's most problem-ridden city, to its knees and were gaining popularity in the countryside through a campaign of land seizures and landlord executions on behalf of impoverished peasants. Ironically, peasant sympathy for the Naxalite cause appeared to stem less from the movement's terrorist tactics than from certain secondary effects of the so-called green revolution, designed to make India self-sufficient in food by 1974. The undeniable improvements in agricultural techniques and output were unfortunately speeding tenant foreclosures, as landlords found their land increasingly valuable and the price of foodstuffs continued to rise.

Meanwhile, in face of such political fragmentation and social strife, Mrs. Gandhi was increasingly hard-pressed to cope with the nation's mounting problems. She did manage to wring legislative enactment of the $29.9 billion Fourth Five-Year Plan and of a scheme, initially knocked down by the Supreme Court, to nationalize the country's 14 largest banks. But efforts to enact meaningful land reforms continued to founder and attempts to divest India's 279 princes or rajas of their privileged status and privy purses was blocked both by the Upper House and later by the Supreme Court. Wearied but unbowed, the Prime Minister took the unprecedented and risky step on December 22 of dissolving the Lower House and calling for new elections, despite the split in her own party and the political ferment evident throughout the country. In struggling to steer a course toward moderate socialism, Mrs. Gandhi hoped to avert an ultimate swing toward Communism or some other extreme.

Internationally, with Soviet influence clearly on the rise and American influence—and aid—dwindling, India's long-term drift to the left continued. Responding to left-wing pressure, the government began closing United States information libraries and centers in cities where no U.S. consulates operated, in line with its effort to keep parity between the U.S. and the U.S.S.R. in such services.[62] On August 8, it announced agreement with East Germany to establish relations at the consular level, and there were even reports in October that relations with Communist China were moving into a more propitious phase, due largely to Mrs. Gandhi's reported conviction that the worst of the Cultural Revolution had passed.[63] When, also in October, the United States announced its intention of resuming the sale of an unspecified amount of arms to Pakistan for the first time since military aid to both India and Pakistan had been suspended in 1965, Indian authorities reacted with unusual indignation.[64] Although Mrs. Gandhi denied it, one possible result of the U.S. decision was her refusal to attend President Nixon's dinner October 24 in honor of delegates attending the 25th anniversary session of the United Nations in New York.[65]

Nor, despite this "one-time, limited exception" to the arms embargo, as American officials described it,[66] could United States relations with Pakistan be described as any smoother. Ever since its clash with India over Kashmir in 1965, Pakistan had been leaning increasingly on Peking for its prime military support. On November 11, President Mohammad Yahya Khan was grandly welcomed in the Chinese capital, where his hosts reportedly promised him an interest-free loan of $200 million toward the support of Pakistan's $17.4 billion Fourth Five-Year Plan, which began July 1. In the meantime, as already noted, Pakistan had dropped out of meaningful participation in CENTO and SEATO, and had virtually eliminated itself as a client of the United States in the sometimes confusing and often shifting line-up of Asian states. Yet, like India, Pakistan's most critical problems appeared to stem from within rather than without. Ever since the downfall of President Ayub Khan's regime in March 1969, Pakistan had been governed by a Martial Law Administration headed by General Yahya Khan, whose twofold aim was to overcome wide-spread dissatisfaction at the uneven rate of social and economic progress achieved under Ayub and to return the country to civilian, parliamentary rule under a new and equitable constitution designed to hold in check the rising antipathy between the Eastern and Western portions of the country. In January 1970, political parties were al-lowed to resume legal activity under a martial law regulation passed he previous December, which was designed to pave the way toward general elections scheduled for October 5.

Almost immediately, political fighting flared in Dacca, the East Pakistani capital, followed by manifestations of student violence in both the Eastern and Western portions of this country separated by 1,000 miles of Indian territory. After several postponements, the elections were finally held December 7 and the results confirmed the worst fears of those Pakistanis who had warned against the nation's division along regional lines. The vote reflected East Pakistan's long-standing contention that it had been denied a legitimate share in the national government, that the bulk of foreign aid had been unfairly invested in the West, and that it had been exploited by Western-based business concerns. Thus the 71 million people of East Pakistan voted overwhelmingly for the pro-autonomy Awami League led by Sheikh Mujibur Rahman, giving that party an absolute majority in the National Assembly whose key duty would be to lay the foundations of a new constitution within 120 days of its meeting. The 61 million people of West Pakistan gave the lion's share of their votes to the leftist Pakistan People's party led by former Foreign Minister Zulfikar Ali Bhutto, a nationalist critical of autonomous sentiments in East Pakistan and much in favor of a strong central government. The stage therefore was set for a decisive clash between East and West over the shape and nature of the future government, with a hint of possible civil war already in the air. Nor had grievances in the East been assuaged by the advent of natural disaster—a cyclone and tidal wave which struck in mid-November, leaving 200,000 East Pakistanis dead and some 600,000 missing—or by what Easterners considered the negligent response of the central government in coming to their aid.

It can only be said that developments in Ceylon added verisimilitude to this generally dreary picture of South Asia. In May, that country handed an overwhelming victory to a three-party coalition headed by Mrs. Sirimavo R. D. Bandaranaike, ending a five-year period of moderate rule under Dudley Senanayake and ushering in a new era of "socialist" domestic and international policy for the nation. From then on, Ceylon's already sluggish economy appeared to slide steadily downhill, while Mrs. Bandaranaike pressed ahead with plans to recognize North Vietnam, North Korea, the Vietcong's P.R.G., and East Germany; to break relations with Israel; to expel the U.S. Peace Corps; and to nationalize all foreign banks and other key sectors of the economy. At another time, under other circumstances, the United States might well have sounded the alarm over such obviously antipathetic steps by a nation normally considered outside the sphere of Communist power and influence. But in 1970, events in Ceylon, like those in India and Pakistan, hardly seemed to cause a ripple of concern in the American capital. The Nixon Doctrine and all that went into it appeared, indeed, to be taking effect in more ways than one.

7 : The Americas:
Left and Right Take Center Stage

No one has really satisfactorily explained why it is that so many people in the United States find events in Latin America of so little interest, although the fact that Rio de Janeiro, Montevideo, and Buenos Aires are all farther from New York than London, Paris, or Madrid may have something to do with it. Occasionally, of course, some development south of the border catches the American eye—as when, for example, Mexico moved in 1970 to abolish the "quickie divorce" for which Juarez and Tijuana had become famous.[1] By and large, however, most Americans seemed more concerned with what was going on in Europe, Asia, and the Middle East than with what was happening in their own hemisphere. This was especially puzzling since two of the most dramatic American foreign policy developments of the 1960's focused on Latin America—the Cuban missile crisis of 1962 and Washington's intervention in the Dominican Republic in 1965. There were those who believed, moreover, that if trends toward political violence and polarization continued, Latin America could well become an object of momentous *yanqui* concern in the 1970's.

Certainly, the events of 1970 itself seemed to point in that direction. It was as though the rising level of political kidnappings, assassinations, and general gun play constituted some sort of bid for world attention. Even nature lent a hand in Peru, provoking at the end of May one of the worst earthquakes on record, a violent tremor that took the lives of an estimated 50,000 people and left hundreds of thousands home-less.[2] From a more Olympian perspective, Latin America could be said to be going through another of those apparently cyclical phases marked by a general disillusionment with democracy and a turn toward extremist solutions on the left and right. Once again military rule became the vogue, with its accompanying police excesses, torture of political prisoners, repression of criticism in the press, and its con-comitant resort to counterviolence by opponents at the opposite ex-treme. If it had by 1970 become a cliché that Latin America enjoyed a new breed of military rulers—the left-leaning generals of Peru, the middle-class technocrats of Brazil, the leftist-nationalists of Bolivia—in contrast to the traditional caudillos of old, it was also true that Latin America was experiencing a new style of revolutionary opposition, one aptly characterized by former Brazilian congressman Carlos Marighella. His *Minimanual of the Urban Guerrilla*[3] had become something of a classic by 1970, although Marighella himself had been killed in a police ambush in November 1969.

"The urban guerrilla," Marighella had written, "is an implacable enemy of the government and systematically inflicts damage on the authorities and on the men who dominate the country and exercise power. The principal task of the urban guerrilla is to distract, to wear out, to demoralize the militarists, the military dictatorship and its repressive forces, and also to attack and destroy the wealth and prop-erty of the North Americans, the foreign managers, and the Brazilian upper class." One of the key tactics he recommended was the kid-napping of foreigners, police agents, or any "notorious and dangerous enemy of the revolutionary movement" with the aim of embarrassing the oppressor and undercutting his morale. "Kidnapping is used to exchange or liberate imprisoned revolutionary comrades, or to force suspension of torture in the jail cells of the military dictatorship," Marighella wrote. "The kidnapping of North American residents or visitors in Brazil constitutes a form of protest against the penetration and domination of United States imperialism in our country. . . ."

For their part, many North Americans had long since found them-selves as out of sympathy with the sometimes rapacious ways of Latin America's upper class as any follower of Marighella, but they were also less than enthusiastic about the remedies the urban guerrillas were seeking to effect—particularly when it involved, as it did in Brazil, Uruguay, Guatemala, and the Dominican Republic, the kidnapping and even the execution of American citizens. In such an atmosphere, prudence seemed to dictate that the wisest policy would be one of lying low until the bullets stopped whizzing. In fact, it could be said that by 1970 United States policy toward Latin America had entered, in the euphemistic phrase, "a period of transition" during which policy seemed to hang suspended while Washington on the one hand and various Latin American capitals on the other sorted out their thoughts. In his State of the World message, President Nixon implied a reduced role for the United States when he spoke of "a new partnership in the Americas . . . in which all voices are heard and none is predominant." "As elsewhere in the world," the President said, hinting at a broadening application of the Nixon Doctrine, "our basic role is to persuade and supplement, not to prescribe." [4] The President emphasized what he called "action for progress," but called it "only a beginning. There is a long way to go." [5]

27 : *Shaping U.S. Policy*

In a sense, Washington's policy had already come a long way. Fired by the portent of Fidel Castro's takeover in Cuba, the United States had moved energetically and deeply into Latin American affairs during the 1960's, attempting through the Alliance for Progress to help lift a whole continent out of decades of lethargy and neglect. However, as with so many of Washington's policies in the 'sixties, a credibility gap soon surfaced—a gap between what the Alliance promised by way of social, political and economic progress and what was actually taking place. The decade had opened with a surge of democratically inclined, popularly elected presidents, but it closed with more generals and colonels manning the posts of power than at any time in recent memory. To be sure, the Cuban blueprint had faded considerably as an attractive means of solving the area's problems. Yet 1970 did see the hemisphere's first freely elected Marxist president, Salvador Allende Gossens, take office in Chile—that supposed model of Latin American stability and middle-class virtue. If one were searching for ironies with which to cap the Alliance's record, one would surely have to look no further than that.

From the point of view of the United States, something had obviously gone wrong, and in President Nixon's word "a new spirit and a new approach were needed" if inter-American relations were once again to be set aright.[6] Yet even among Latin Americans there was a predominant feeling of ambivalence as to precisely what, if anything, Washington could or should do. Against an apparently growing belief that Washington was being too "pushy," that it was throwing its weight around in an "imperial" manner by designing programs *for* its neighbors rather than *with* them, there was also a feeling that the United States "no longer cared." At a time when Latin American problems were becoming more complex and intensive, Washington's concern did indeed seem to be cooling—and cooling at a time when Latin America's own problems were on the rise. Along with the United States, Western Europe, and Japan, Latin America was becoming one of the world's most highly urbanized areas, and its explosive population growth rate of 2.9 per cent a year meant in all likelihood that the slums which already ringed its principal cities would go right on spreading, that the squeeze on education, health, and housing would grow even more acute in the years ahead. In such a context, political and social unrest went hand-in-glove with authoritarian solutions and anti-*yanqui* nationalism, as Latin Americans cast about for both the source of their trouble and an end to it. In President Nixon's words, "The state of the hemisphere and of our relationship was satisfying neither to North or to South Americans." [7]

The President nonetheless recognized that, however clouded by problems, a "special relationship" did in fact exist between the United States and its sister republics. Early in his administration he had asked Governor Nelson A. Rockefeller of New York to undertake a fact-finding mission throughout the region, with the aim of establishing new guidelines for Washington's inter-American policies. After extensive talks with some 3,000 leaders in 20 countries, the Rockefeller team delivered its report to the President in September 1969.[8] "We went to visit neighbors and found brothers," it began. "We went to listen to the spokesmen of our sister republics and heard the voices of a hemisphere. We went to annotate, to document, and to record. We did so; and we also learned, grew, and changed."

One thing the Rockefeller team apparently learned that had not changed, however, was the supposed threat of Communism to the hemisphere and the need for continuing U.S. military aid (increasingly opposed by members of Congress) to keep it at bay. In line with such considerations, the report also emphasized the special nature of the relationship that existed between Washington and the rest of the hemisphere and warned dramatically that "The moral and spiritual strength of the United States in the world, the political credibility of our leadership, the security of our nation, the future of our social and economic progress are now at stake" in Latin America. Such a crisis situation obviously required a commensurate program of action to deal with it, and the report was generous in recommending steps that could be taken. These included creation of the post of "Secretary of Western Hemisphere Affairs" to serve as a focal point within the government on all matters involving the hemisphere; establishment of yet another "Economic and Social Development Agency" to supplant the Agency for International Development (AID); establishment of a "Western Hemisphere Security Council" to deal with subversion, an "Institute for Education, Science and Culture," and even (hopping aboard the ecological bandwagon) an "Inter-American Institute of Natural Resource Conservation."

Such a proliferation of bureaucratic institutions seemed hardly designed to warm the heart of a Republican administration. Even so, the administration did ask Congress on March 18, 1970 for implementing legislation to establish the position of Under Secretary of State for Western Hemisphere Affairs,[9] although no action was taken by Congress during 1970. However, the President skipped over the suggestions for a Western Hemisphere Security Council and assorted other agencies, drawing instead for the broad outlines of his policy on the work of the Special Commission on Latin American Coordination (CECLA).

That group of 21 Latin American states had met in Viña del Mar, Chile in May 1969 to hammer out a common Latin American position on trade, aid, and investment *vis-à-vis* the United States. Their recommendations, embodied in 35 specific proposals, known as the "Consensus of Viña del Mar," [10] covered the gamut of obstacles that they considered impediments to inter-American relations. They wanted a liberalized U.S. trade policy—lower tariffs and quotas on their exports and price stabilization agreements; easier terms—lower interest rates, longer periods of repayment—for development loans; and elimination of the requirement "tying" aid to the purchase of goods and services from the United States. Finally, they wanted a greater voice in the distribution of aid—less through bilateral channels like AID and the Export-Import Bank and more through such mulitlateral institutions as the Inter-American Development Bank (I.D.B.) and the International Bank for Reconstruction and Development (I.B.R.D.).

On the whole, what the Latin Americans were seeking was a greater sense of participation—a more active role for themselves—in the determination of their own destiny. In line with his generally emerging foreign policy position around the world, President Nixon was only too willing to pass the initiative along to those who were clamoring for it. He would insure, he said, "that the shaping of the Western Hemisphere's future reflects the will of the other nations of this hemisphere" and that the "nations of the hemisphere evolve an effective multilateral mechanism for bilateral assistance." [11] Thus at its meetings of November 1969 and February 1970, the Inter-American Economic and Social Council (IA-ECOSOC) had, with United States backing, urged the Inter-American Committee for the Alliance for Progress (CIAP) and the I.D.B. to explore ways of stepping up their roles in development decisions. The goal, according to Nixon, was "to enable the other Western Hemisphere nations to assume a primary role in setting priorities within the hemisphere, developing realistic programs and keeping their own performance under critical review." [12] As will be seen in Chapter Ten, multilateral aid-giving appeared to be one of those ideas whose time had come in 1970. But the Nixon approach to Latin America involved more than this long-proposed effort to minimize the aid donor's self-interested interference in the development process. It stressed as well the need for recipient nations themselves to become actively involved in the way in which aid was distributed. In line with this approach, the President agreed to submit U.S. economic and financial programs for the hemisphere to CIAP for review on a regular basis, as was already the case with other participating countries, and stated his intention of developing additional mechanisms for direct Latin American participation in the aid-allocation process.

Nor was that all. In a further effort to lower the U.S. profile in the hemisphere, the President had already ordered on November 1, 1969 the partial "untying" of U.S. aid to Latin America from the need to make purchases in the United States. Thenceforth, Latin Americans were free to spend up to 50 per cent of their loan dollars (as opposed to the former 10 per cent) outside the hemisphere, provided the remaining 50 per cent was spent in North or South America. In addition, the administration was pressing ahead with its plan for a generalized system of tariff preferences for all developing countries, first announced—in a Latin American context—in Nixon's speech of October 31, 1969 before the Inter American Press Association in Washington.[13] At its February meeting, IA-ECOSOC agreed to move the process a step farther by establishing the Special Committee for Consultation and Negotiation (CECON), which, together with CIAP, would consult regularly on trade and development policies for the hemisphere as a whole.[14] To that end, CIAP did conduct its first full-scale review of U.S. social and economic programs in October, one result of which was a U.S. pledge to seek ways of increasing Latin American imports by more than $350 million a year.[15] (The Latin American share of the U.S. market had dropped by about one-third since 1960.)

These were steps that Latin Americans themselves had long been urging, and by acceding to them the administration was, in part at least, assuaging a generalized sense of disillusionment resulting from a decade of goal-setting by Washington. This seemed equally evident in the revised Charter of the Organization of American States (O.A.S.) that went into effect on February 27, although its origins reached back to the Johnson administration. Formed out of the old Pan American Union in 1948 and comprising 24 members by 1970, the O.A.S. was the oldest regional organization to which the United States was a party, just as the Rio treaty of 1947 was the oldest security pact still in effect. For a number of years the effectiveness of the O.A.S. had been limited by the cross-purposes at which its members were acting. Preoccupied by the Cuban and Communist threats, the United States wanted the organization to lay greater stress on the hemisphere's security problems. Preoccupied by their internal troubles, the Latin American states wanted it—and by extension Washington—to pay more attention to their economic and social needs.

The extensive reorganization of the O.A.S., embodied in the Protocol of Amendment to the Charter of the Organization of American States (or "Protocol of Buenos Aires"), had been signed on February 27, 1967 at the Third Special Inter-American Conference held in Buenos Aires.[16] With the subsequent ratification by 20 member states, the Protocol entered into force February 27, 1970, and represented a major shift in the organization's focus toward accommodating Latin American demands. Changes included enlarged responsibility for IA-ECOSOC, creation of the Inter-American Council for Education, Science and Culture to replace the old Inter-American Cultural Council, replacement of the former Inter-American Conference by a General Assembly, and improvements in the peace-making and peace-keeping functions of the organization.

Despite these changes, it would nonetheless be wrong to conclude that Washington's new stance toward inter-American affairs had become wholly passive or compliant. For one thing, the urgings of Latin Americans were too often disparate or contradictory for that to be possible, the "Consensus of Viña del Mar" notwithstanding. In a message to the Eighth Special Meeting of IA-ECOSOC,[17] held on February 3–6 in Caracas, Venezuela, moreover, President Nixon went out of his way to dispel any sense of U.S. indifference or apathy toward the course of inter-American relations. "I take this occasion," he told the assembled delegates through Assistant Secretary of State for Inter-American Affairs Charles A. Meyer, "to pledge to the peoples of America that my Administration will strive to demonstrate in action our commitment to progress and to the enhancement of the dignity of life in this Hemisphere." He went on to outline some of his budget recommendations to Congress, among which were "a contingency account of $540 million to provide for expanded multilateral assistance through international financial institutions," a large part of which would be channeled to meet hemisphere needs; "$556 million in AID funds for the hemisphere . . . an increase of about 20% over the 1970 appropriation levels"; and finally, a decision "to advance the request for funds to fill the United States subscription of $206 million to the callable capital of the Inter-American Development Bank," originally scheduled for 1971.

Since the administration's over-all foreign aid request in 1970 was $509 million below that of the previous year, such sums could be taken as a fair indication of the administration's priority concern for Latin American needs. Yet, as Latin Americans knew, what the President requested by way of aid and what the Congress provided could be two very different things. At the eleventh annual meeting of the Board of Governors of the I.D.B. held in Punta del Este, Uruguay April 20–24, Secretary of the Treasury David M. Kennedy announced that "with full Latin American support, we would be prepared to approach the U.S. Congress promptly for increases in both our ordinary Capital subscription and our contribution to the Fund for Special Operations." [18] While the President was able to praise Congress on December 31 for having provided "an expansion of over $800 million in the United States subscription to the Bank's ordinary capital," he was forced to regret that the lawmakers had thus far authorized only $100 million of a planned $1 billion three-year pledge for the Bank's Fund for Special Operations.[19]

With foreign aid caught up in a general tug-of-war between Congress and the President over foreign policy issues, there were those who believed that Latin America might fare even less well in the years ahead. In a speech on April 10, Senator Frank Church, Chairman of the Western Hemisphere Affairs subcommittee, gave vent to growing congressional sentiment when he described the aid program for Latin America as a "net loss" and proposed that the Agency for International Development "be shut down and the keys thrown away." [20] Attributing the "alarming deterioration in inter-American relations" to "our meddling" and to budgetary support "for notoriously authoritarian" regimes, the Senator urged a policy of nonintervention and disengagement in the area's affairs. At the same time, he cautioned that the United States must not turn its back on Latin American needs. "What is necessary," Senator Church said, "is that we first get off the backs of our neighbors. We must learn to hold ourselves at arm's length; we must come to terms with the inevitable, letting changes take place without insisting upon managing or manipulating them. We must begin to show some self-restraint."

Such a ringing call for policy revision may well have struck administration officials as gratuitous, since U.S. policy was moving in precisely the direction Senator Church demanded. To be sure, the military regime of General Emilio Garrastazú Médici in Brazil was still receiving one of the largest portions of U.S. aid in the hemisphere (Colombia got the most), but on a per capita basis the left-leaning Christian Democratic government of President Eduardo Frei Montalva in Chile was receiving even more. Concurrently, the administration was moving to cut back drastically military aid and arms shipments to the area. Total military aid for 17 republics for fiscal year 1971, for example, stood at $16.1 million as compared to more than $80 million in such aid five years before.[21] Indeed, the most heavily armed and modernly equipped military establishment in the entire region belonged to Cuba, which had received nothing by way of U.S. assistance since 1960, but regarding which Senator Church nonetheless saw fit to urge an easing of U.S. curbs beginning with travel restrictions.[22]

The implications of such congressional stirrings were not lost on

Latin America. During an official visit to Washington June 2–4, President Rafael Caldera Rodríguez of Venezuela told a joint session of Congress that "It is not enough that Presidents exchange ideas; it is necessary that their agreements receive full backing from the Congress, and that it in turn may rely on the support of the citizens." [23] President Caldera did some blunt talking about other issues vexing inter-American relations. "Producers of raw materials see their prices stagnating or declining," he said, "while the prices of manufactured goods rise. How many schools and hospitals will close, how many workers be dismissed, how much pain be inflicted, how many rebellions engendered in peace-loving nations, by the reduction of a single cent per pound of coffee, bananas, lead, or copper? . . . The formula for achieving cordial relations . . . cannot be the merciless attempts at forever lowering the prices of our goods while increasing the price of the commodities we have to import. The thesis that more trade diminishes the need for aid is correct as long as the trade is a just one and is converted into a greater possibility for attaining the urgently needed changes in developing nations."

Yet, with the U.S. economy suffering a downward swing, Congress was no more inclined to go along with administration proposals on preferential trade treatment than it was to loosen the purse strings for more aid. Even the administration itself appeared reluctant to expand commodity agreements in order to insure Latin Americans a measure of price stability for major raw materials. Despite President Nixon's pledge to help ease Latin America's chronic foreign debt problems,[24] the terms of many U.S. development loans remained relatively "hard" (though somewhat more generous than comparable loans from other developed countries), and Latin Americans continued to bear a debt-servicing burden averaging one-sixth of their total export earnings. The result was that, despite its aid and other investments, the United States enjoyed a net annual flow of funds from Latin America of about $500 million—a condition which prompted some Latin Americans to wonder precisely who was aiding whom. Little wonder, perhaps, that more and more Latin American governments were coming to view U.S. private investments in the area and the profits repatriated therefrom less as a boon to their economic development than as a drain on their resources.

28 : The Perils of Militant Nationalism

The history of inter-American diplomacy is regrettably replete with instances of bad timing, and that unfortunate tradition seemed to be running true to form in 1970. Just when the Nixon administration was moving both to expand aid and to give Latin Americans greater voice in its distribution, for example, certain influential members of Congress were talking in terms of cutting it out altogether. And just when the United States appeared ready to adopt a more cooperative, less domineering stance toward its neighbors, Latin Americans in a number of countries were rushing to embrace a brand of militant nationalism that threatened to unravel the threads of hemispheric accord. Nor was it the somewhat worn banner of "Fidelismo" that led the way. In 1970, a growing number of Latin Americans referred admiringly to "Peruanismo" as the latest trend-setter in a region longing for radical change. The Peruvian generals who had seized power in 1968 took as the chief symbol of their revolutionary regime the Inca leader Tupac Amaru, who had been torn to pieces in the square at Cuzco after staging the last Indian uprising against the Spanish *conquistadores* in the late 18th century. *"Campesino, the padrón* will no longer feed off your poverty,"* Tupac Amaru had told his impoverished followers, and that had become the rallying cry of President Juan Velasco Alvarado's "Revolutionary Government of the Armed Forces." [25] In Uruguay, too, the memory of Tupac Amaru, contracted into Tupamaro, had provided a rallying symbol for the band of young terrorists who made international headlines in their violent efforts to bring down what had long been Latin America's most placid and democratic government. But it was in Peru that the self-proclaimed revolutionaries had first attained power and in Peru that their radical reforms were being put to the test.

Only a few years earlier, in 1965 and 1966, the Peruvian Army had been busily crushing guerrillas of the Leftist Revolutionary Movement in the central and southern Andes. But the campaign had been an eye-opener for an army already aware that 83 per cent of Peru's arable land was held by a mere 0.8 per cent of the country's 13 million people —the so-called 40 families whose domineering hand in state affairs made Peru a prototype of the oligarchic system. Velasco himself had loyally served conservative and reformist regimes alike in the past. But when he took power on October 3, 1968, he quickly acted to dispel the notion that yet another self-serving junta had been spawned on the Latin American scene. Within six days Velasco had confiscated (without intent to compensate) the oil fields of the International Petroleum Company (I.P.C.), a subsidiary of Standard Oil of New Jersey and the biggest U.S. investment in the nation. Within four months he had established diplomatic relations with the Soviet Union, and within a year he had launched sweeping agrarian reforms designed to expropriate some 3.25 million hectares from landowner control.

Coupling such moves with vaguely Marxist utterings, anti-imperialist preachments, and harassment of conservative elements in the press, Velasco moved ahead with even bolder measures in 1970. In June, the regime seized control of *Banco Popular del Peru,* thereby becoming the country's second largest commercial banker and acquiring in the bargain control over many industries owing money to the bank.[26] In July, a new industrial law forced Peruvian firms to give 10 per cent of their annual pre-tax net profits to workers while setting aside another 15 per cent of company earnings for the eventual purchase of 50 per cent of the firms' shares in the name of the workers.[27] At the same time, the government made clear its intention of socializing all first-priority basic industries, such as iron, steel, chemicals, and cement, and of "Peruvianizing" firms established exclusively with foreign capital until 66.66 per cent of their stock came under national ownership. In August, the regime set such stiff new requirements for companies operating mineral concessions that a number of them were forced to forfeit some of their holdings, including American Smelting and Refining, Lampa Mining, and Cerro de Pasco.[28] By this time, Peruvians were referring admiringly to the "Velasco Doctrine," which to them meant the progressive reversion of foreign-controlled firms to national ownership.

Not since Castro assumed power in Cuba had a Latin American government moved so harshly against U.S. private enterprise within its borders, and precisely how the Nixon administration viewed these developments remained for a time unclear. In his State of the World message, the President had cautioned that "Foreign investments are the most exposed targets of frustration, irrational politics, misguided nationalism. Their potential for mutual benefits will only be realized through mutual perception and tact." [29] That was hardly a ringing defense of U.S. interests, but then some of those interests—for example, those of I.P.C.—were proving hard to defend. To the State Department's considerable dismay, the Peruvian seizure of I.P.C. had tripped into effect the so-called Hickenlooper amendment, which called for automatic suspension of aid to nations which expropriated U.S. property without just compensation.[30] In this particular case, the amendment had the effect of placing the United States in the embarrassing position of having to cut off aid to what appeared to be a genuinely reformist regime. Only because Peru discreetly refrained from requesting additional development loans was a U.S.-Peruvian confrontation on that issue avoided. Other tensions had arisen in connection with Peru's claim to sovereignty over 200 miles of ocean off its shores—a claim it shared with Chile and Ecuador and one which both Peru and Ecuador had sought to enforce by seizing U.S. fishing vessels caught within the 200-mile limit. The United States, which recognized a three-mile limit, was still struggling to negotiate a satisfactory compromise on this off-shore fishing issue as 1970 came to an end.

On the whole, then, it could be said that U.S.-Peruvian relations had fallen under considerable strain. Yet, as Washington recognized, the Velasco regime appeared to offer hope for the kind of genuine reform that many in the United States believed essential if Latin America were not to explode in violence. It could even be argued —and was—that Peru's soldier-nationalists of the left had every reason to embrace an enlightened social and economic policy because they were motivated by the same instinct for self-preservation that characterized their rightist brethren elsewhere in the hemisphere. Here, after all, was a country of 13 million people, only three million of whom were estimated to live within the money economy. The rest, mostly Quechua or Aymara Indians, lived in the appalling poverty of the slums around Lima and other large cities or scraped out a bare existence from the rocky soil of the Andes. It was characteristic of their general plight that when some 50,000 of these Peruvians perished in the May earthquake, their deaths were said to have had virtually no impact at all on the nation's economy. In such combustible circumstances, the Army could logically argue that by rescuing *"los pobres"* it was also rescuing the country itself from violent upheaval —and by coincidence saving its own skin.

Following a visit from Assistant Secretary Meyer in mid-March, the Peruvian government again went out of its way to deny any Communist links and reported that the cloud over U.S.-Peruvian relations had "cleared." [31] In June, these relations took another step forward when Mrs. Nixon flew into Lima with two planeloads of emergency relief supplies for the earthquake victims and received an exceptionally warm reception from Peruvian officials.[32] (A Soviet airlift of supplies halted abruptly after one of its planes crashed en route.) On the whole, the United States seemed disposed to help Peru, not only through the disaster prompted by the earthquake, but through its Nasser-like experiment in social revolution run by men in uniform.

Washington seemed no less tolerant of a similar experiment under way in Bolivia, which had begun in late 1969 and was only briefly interrupted when that country's left-leaning, nationalist leader, General Alfredo Ovando Candía, was ousted under near-civil war conditions on October 6 by a rightist junta under the leadership of General Rogelio Miranda. But on October 7, the militant leftist General Juan José Torres in turn seized power and promptly pledged a government based on peasants, workers, students, and the armed forces. It was the radical "anti-imperialist" students who had played a major role in bringing Torres to power, virtually paralyzing police operations in an unrestrained campaign of terror and inflicting some $36,000-worth of property damage against U.S.-owned facilities. Torres rewarded them by ordering the release on December 23 of the French Marxist writer and revolutionary, Régis Debray. In other respects, however, the new President surprised outside observers and angered some of his followers by ousting two ultraleftists from the Cabinet, installing moderates in their place, and playing down talk of stepped-up nationalization. The United States, for its part, quietly continued diplomatic ties with the new government and overlooked the outburst of youthful terrorism, apparently trusting in the hope that General Torres would be more inclined to follow the Peruvian example than a Communist one.

In the long run the generals of Peru and Bolivia may have been shaping Latin America's most significant developments in 1970, but the Chilean election certainly comprised the year's most electrifying event. In a three-way race for the presidency on September 4, Allende won a narrow (36.3 per cent) plurality over his Christian Democratic and National party rivals, and for a moment the shadow of a leftist, anti-U.S. west Andean axis (comprising Peru, Bolivia, and Chile and possibly tied to Cuba) must have passed darkly over Washington.

A staid, middle-class country with a long and respected tradition of democratic rule, Chile had made considerable progress toward the Christian Democratic party's proclaimed goal of a "Revolution in Liberty" under the six-year term of President Frei. A moderate leftist, Frei had done much to improve the income, education, and housing of the urban and rural poor, pushing through substantial land reform measures. By buying up to 51 per cent of their shares, he gradually "Chileanized" U.S.-owned copper mines, which accounted for some 80 per cent of the nation's foreign exchange earnings. No less than the Alliance for Progress itself, however, Frei's Revolution in Liberty had apparently raised expectations faster than they could be fulfilled. Constitutionally barred from succeeding himself, the popular Frei backed fellow Christian Democrat Radomiro Tomic for the office he was leading. Rallying to the Nationalist party banner, Chile's conservatives backed former President Jorge Alessandri Rodríguez. In the end, it was the wealthy Socialist Senator and four-time presidential contender, Allende, who emerged victorious.

As a Marxist, Allende seemed to fit the 19th century romantic mold better than that of the 20th century commissar-bureaucrat. The Socialist party from which he sprang ranged in composition from moderate Social Democrats to fiery Castro-style revolutionaries, but on the whole stood to the left of the staid, Moscow-oriented Communist party with which it was allied.[33] Allende himself was a friend and admirer of Fidel Castro, but he had also served for years within Chile's established democratic framework and did not strike those who followed his career as a potential dictator. The staying power of the coalition he led (called *"Unidad Popular"*), moreover, was almost wholly dependent both on Allende's popularity and reputation and on the Christian Democrats, who still comprised the largest bloc in the legislature. Thus only after Allende promised the Christian Democrats that he would adhere to constitutional processes did the Chilean Congress vote to confirm his election on October 24. The new President appointed a Cabinet in which the Ministries of Defense and Education went to Radical party allies, while the Communists received the potentially less troublesome posts in Labor, Public Works, and Finance. The powerful Interior Ministry went to a trusted confidant from the Socialist party and Foreign Affairs was handed to Clodomiro Almeyda, a former university professor and also a Socialist.

In a speech to the nation on November 5, two days afer his

inauguration, Allende blamed the country's ills on the capitalist system and promised to establish a working-class republic. "I won't be just another President," he said. "I will be the first President of the first really democratic, popular, national and revolutionary government in the history of Chile." [34] Strong words, but Allende's program indicated that he meant it. Economically, the state would become the commanding force through outright nationalization of the copper mines, state ownership of financial institutions (including insurance), foreign trade, strategic industrial monopolies, and the infrastructure (electricity, transport, communications, gas, heavy industry). That would leave only medium and small concerns to be run privately though in cooperation with the state. [35] Politically, the regime sought a new constitution which would establish a unicameral legislature, universal suffrage (abolition of the literacy requirement), and provision for the popular recall of legislators. It pledged concurrently to respect civil liberties and the electoral process. Socially, the program would carry his predecessor's reforms to their ultimate fruition—expropriation of the landed estates, a massive drive to improve education, concentration on low-cost housing, etc. Finally, if its campaign promises were to be fulfilled, the new government would have to take some of its boldest steps in the field of foreign policy. The *Unidad Popular* had urged that the O.A.S. be disbanded and replaced by a "non-imperialist" institution; it had called for the rejection of politically conditioned aid, the establishment of diplomatic ties with Cuba, Communist China, East Germany, North Vietnam, and North Korea, and "support" for such national "liberation" movements as those formed by the Palestinian terrorists. [36]

In his first months in office, Allende showed that he was approaching his declared tasks with caution, seeking friendly relations with all states, and struggling to contend with a domestic business slump and a flight of capital. His main problem seemed to be less one of holding the country together (most Chileans respected the legality of his leadership) than of keeping the sometimes unruly factions composing his coalition in line. Many of his primary objectives—the nationalization of copper, the recognition of Cuba, etc.—were deemed to reflect the popular will and, in some cases, were simple extensions of Christian Democratic policy. Frei himself had moved toward renewed diplomatic and trade ties with Cuba, for example, so that Allende's prompt action in establishing such ties on November 12 hardly shocked the

Chileans.[37] In other respects, the new Marxist government was acting in a spirit of accord with its immediate neighbors. On December 14–31, its representatives met in Lima with other members of the so-called Andean Group (including Peru, Bolivia, Ecuador, and Colombia), which on Chilean urging successfully reached agreement on a unified approach to foreign capital investment. Among other things, the agreement provided that after January 1, 1971 all industrial or commercial firms established within the regional market must within 15 years draw at least 51 per cent of their capitalization from the region itself.[38]

Initially, the U.S. reaction to the Chilean changeover was low-keyed, if far from enthusiastic. Discussing events in Chile during a television interview in late December, President Nixon commented that "what happened in Chile is not something that we welcomed, although . . . we were very careful to point out that that was the decision of the people of Chile, and that therefore we accepted that decision and that our programs with Chile—we still recognize the government, we still have our People-to-People program, we still have our Peace Corps program—those programs would continue as long as Chile's foreign policy was not antagonistic to our interests. . . . I haven't given up on Chile or on the Chilean people, and we are going to keep our contact with them." [39]

In breaking the O.A.S. embargo on Cuba without advance warning or consultation, however, the Allende government had aroused the first mild criticism of its policies in Washington, where the White House promptly took the opportunity to warn that such measures "caused uncertainties in the relations between the United States and Chile." [40] That Washington still considered Cuba something of a menace in the hemisphere was evident as early as March, when the State Department reportedly circulated notes to O.A.S. members urging Latin Americans not to relax their curbs against Castro's regime in the face of stepped-up Soviet military activity on the island and of what Washington deemed the continuing threat of Castro's subversive policies.[41] If anything, that concern mounted later in the year, when conflicting reports about an alleged Soviet submarine base at Cienfuegos began to circulate. In a sense, however, the free election of Allende in Chile (as well as the revolutionary course being followed by the generals in Peru and Bolivia) appeared to mock both Castro's publicized effort to export guerrilla warfare and Washington's great fear of its spread.

Castro himself, in a speech marking the centennial of Lenin's birth on April 22, had clearly shifted his own position on the value of such tactics, bringing himself more in line with the orthodox Moscow view. He sarcastically berated his former Latin American disciples as "superrevolutionary theoreticians, superleftists, veritable supermen," and denounced their refusal to acknowledge the importance of Soviet help. Above all, he stressed Cuba's critical need to devote all its energies to its own economic development.[42]

Even the urban terrorists who sometimes invoked his name had to admit that the latter point was well taken. With all its difficulties, including continued dependence on Soviet aid, Cuba had hardly proved an attractive model of Latin American revolutionary development. In an anniversary speech to the nation on July 26, Castro painted the bleakest picture yet of the Cuban economy, taking full blame for the nation's problems and offering to resign if the people so desired. Sector-by-sector, the report was a grim accounting of goals unachieved and targets missed. There were shortfalls in consumer goods and drops in food production. Most disastrous of all, failure of the massive effort to achieve a record 10-million-ton sugar crop absorbed and drained the country's manpower resources without yielding the anticipated benefits. The 1970 harvest was still a record 8.5 million tons, but the economic chaos unloosed in bringing it in had set the economy as a whole back instead of pushing it forward. As a result, the Cubans were forced to agree to the creation of a joint Cuban-Soviet economic commission, whose existence would give Moscow a firmer hand in the economic life of the country. At the same time, the Cuban military assumed increasing powers over economic and educational affairs, falling in line with the general trend already noted throughout the area.

If in the midst of these trials Cuba had the energy left to try to export its tarnished system by violent means, few Latin Americans seemed aware of it. Castro himself summed up the country's problems this way: "The road is difficult, yes. It is more difficult than . . . we expected. Yes, imperialists, it is hard to build socialism." [43] Indeed, about the only source of interstate violence in the area was the still smoldering dispute between Honduras and El Salvador, which had erupted in 1969 (and flared up again in January 1970) in the aftermath of a soccer game, but which actually focused on the presence in Honduras of some 300,000 Salvadoran laborers. The "soccer war," as it was called, struck a near-mortal blow at the once prospering Central American Common Market (C.A.C.M.) when Honduras, still smarting from the conflict's effects, revoked late in 1970 the common tariff provisions to which it had adhered. But the war did afford an opportunity for the O.A.S. to exercise, indirectly though effectively, its little-used peace-keeping powers by establishing in mid-July a demilitarized zone along the borders, to be patrolled by military observers. As Secretary Rogers noted in an address to the First Special Session of the O.A.S. General Assembly held in Washington June 25–July 8: "The special OAS committee dispatched to the scene [in 1969] secured a cease-fire within 5 days. Since then the continuing involvement of the O.A.S. has helped preserve the peace and advance the prospect of settlement. We can also take satisfaction from the new frontier pacification plan formulated and agreed to with the participation of the Central American Foreign Ministers." [44]

The Secretary also praised the Latin American initiative which resulted in the establishment of the world's first international instrument for a nuclear-free zone. By mid-1970, the Treaty for the Prohibition of Nuclear Weapons in Latin America (the Treaty of Tlatelolco) of February 14, 1967 [45] had been ratified by and entered into force for 17 of the 22 signatory states. (Cuba refused to sign the document and Guyana's right to sign was in dispute.) On August 13, 1970, President Nixon asked Senate approval for the ratification of Additional Protocol II to the treaty,[46] which in the President's words called on nuclear-weapons states "to respect the denuclearized status of Latin America, not to contribute to violation of the Treaty, and not to use or threaten to use nuclear weapons against the Treaty parties." [47] While the Senate took no action toward ratification in 1970, ultimate U.S. adherence to the Protocol was not in doubt, and the O.A.S. could take pride in the unique initiative it had successfully set before the world.

29 : Coping with Urban Terrorism

The O.A.S. confronted a more perplexing task, however, in its efforts to stem the tide of urban kidnapping and terrorism. On April 14, U.S. Ambassador to the O.A.S. Joseph J. Jova joined with the Argentine delegation in asking the organization's Permanent Council to consider this problem.[48] The immediate reason for the appeal had been the kidnapping March 31 and subsequent murder on April 5 of Count Karl von Spreti, the West German Ambassador to Guatemala, after the Guatemalan government refused to accede to terrorist demands for the release of 25 "political prisoners" and $700,000 in cash. But the practice had already become widespread enough to engender governmental concern throughout the hemisphere. A rundown of incidents in early 1970 showed that leftist guerrillas in Venezuela kidnapped (and released on payment of $160,000 ransom) the twelve-year-old son of a wealthy businessman in January; that Guatemala agreed to release a captured guerrilla in exchange for the liberty of its own Foreign Minister in February, and in March released two more terrorists in exchange for U.S. Embassy aide Sean M. Holly; that five political prisoners were flown from Brazil to Mexico that same month in return for the release of the Japanese Consul General; and that the Dominican Republic freed 20 more such prisoners, also in March, in return for the life of the U.S. Air Force attaché.

Thus, by the time the hapless von Spreti was slain, government attitudes were growing tougher. Argentina had already bluntly refused to release any political prisoners following the kidnapping in March of the Paraguayan Consul, who was subsequently released unharmed. The hard line worked less well in the case of former Argentine President Pedro Eugenio Aramburu, who was kidnapped in May and murdered sometime in June, apparently by revolutionaries sympathetic to ex-dictator Juan Perón. In the meantime, the guerrillas were raising the stakes as well. When the West German Ambassador to Brazil, Ehrenfried von Holleben, was seized in June, the Brazilian government was so fearful of a repeat of the Guatemalan episode that it flew a planeload of 40 prisoners to political asylum in Mexico—the highest ransom yet paid. In Uruguay, the Tupamaros launched the boldest move of all. On July 31, they kidnapped both U.S. police adviser Dan A. Mitrione and the Brazilian Consul, injured two other U.S. aides in the process, and proceeded to demand the release of *all* political prisoners in that country in exchange for the two foreigners. When the government of President Jorge Pacheco Areco refused to negotiate, the guerrillas added U.S. agronomist Claude L. Fly to their catch on August 7 and three days later, in an apparent show of seriousness, fatally shot Mitrione.

In a statement on the death of Mitrione, Secretary Rogers lashed out at the "inhumanity" of the killers and said that "The spread of terrorism, which cloaks common crimes in politicial fanaticism, must meet with the repudiation of all men of decency and good will everywhere. The authors and supporters of such vicious acts merit the scorn and contempt of the entire world." [49] Eleven days prior to the shooting of Mitrione, the First Special Session of the new O.A.S. General Assembly, meeting in Washington, had unanimously condemned such acts of terrorism and extortion as crimes against humanity and requested the Inter-American Juridical Committee to find ways of combating them. [50] But it was difficult to see precisely what governments confronted by such tactics could do. In July, the International Commission of Jurists accused Brazil of using "systematic and scientifically developed" torture of political prisoners in an effort to break the back of the terrorist underground, obviously to no avail. [51] In Guatemala's presidential and congressional elections of March 1, the voters, presumably fed up with the tactics of urban terrorists, supported the hard-line rightist candidacy of Colonel Carlos Arana Osorio, who campaigned in a bullet-proof limousine but spoke to the people like a man on horseback. "We are going to act with energy and without restraint," the tough-talking Colonel told a victory rally. "The whole weight of the law will fall on those who stand outside the law." [52] By year's end, however, neither Arana's get-tough policies nor his promises of social reform had slackened what seemed to be a steadily mounting wave of political violence and terrorism.

In fact, the problem of urban guerrilla warfare offered no easy solution. Except for Uruguay, with its strong tradition of weak, middle-class rule, the urban guerrillas appeared to thrive most under rightist regimes such as those of Brazil, Argentina, the Dominican Republic, and Guatemala. Ironically, some of these countries were scoring the highest economic growth rates in their history—Brazil, for example, with a high of 9.5 per cent in G.N.P. growth for 1970, compared to a low of 2.5 per cent in Chile, with its severe inflation and increasing unemployment. [53] Politically, however, there appeared to be no correlation between economic progress and internal unrest. In Colombia, where the economy grew by a healthy 7 per cent, the government was forced to declare a state of siege and martial law after former dictator General Gustavo Rojas Pinilla, running as a populist candidate for the presidency, was narrowly defeated at the polls by the National Front's Misael Pastrana Borrero. When Pastrana was sworn in on August 7, he pledged "reforms in continuity" and an open door to foreign investment; [54] but he, too, had to contend not only with the threat of violent action by the rightist supporters of Rojas Pinilla, but also with leftist guerrilla groups operating in the mountains, including a new breed of young Catholic priests calling themselves the "Golconda group."

In Ecuador, where the economic growth rate equalled Brazil's, President José María Velasco Ibarra nonetheless had to quell student unrest and deal with runaway inflation and a loss of reserves. In an effort to enforce economic reforms, he rescinded the constitution on July 22, dismissed Vice-President Jorge Zavala Baquerizo, dissolved the Congress, and declared himself "supreme leader" until the end of his term on August 31, 1972. In Argentina, where the economy increased 4.8 per cent after years of industrial stagnation, a resurgent Peronist movement, abetted by leftist revolutionaries and their allies in the Catholic clergy, contributed to the state of national crisis which led to the ouster on June 8 of General Juan Carlos Onganía. His successor, General Roberto Marcelo Levingston, assumed office on June 18 and proceeded to ease some of the harsher curbs that Onganía had employed to deal with popular unrest. By late December, he moved in Peruvian style to "Argentinize" the economy, having earlier warned that elections and a return to civilian rule were at least four or five years in the offing.

The problem facing rightist regimes in general seemed typified by events in the Dominican Republic, where the strains of the 1965 civil war were still very much in evidence. On May 16, President Joaquín Balaguer, who represented conservative, pro-American interests, was reelected to a second four-year term, although some 40 per cent of the voters stayed away from the polls in apparent sympathy with the boycott waged by former President Juan Bosch's Dominican Revolutionary party. When Balaguer began his second term on August 16, he pledged renewed efforts to achieve agrarian reform, improve conditions in education and housing, and enact other measures of social justice.[55] However, his inauguration coincided with the onset of an epidemic of political assassinations and police countermeasures, all of which either distracted the regime from its promised reforms or gave it an excuse to evade them.

What the Peronists of Argentina, the populists of Colombia, and even the Dominican revolutionaries had in common was that same sense of economic nationalism and hostility to U.S. "economic imperialism" that was so evident among the generals of Peru, Bolivia, and even to some extent of Argentina and Brazil. The number of Latin American countries openly welcoming United States capital investment had already shrunk considerably, and in 1970 it shrank still more. Among the newly independent states of the Caribbean, meanwhile, another form of nationalism, also containing anti-American overtones, was making itself felt. In April, the United States dispatched a planeload of small arms and ammunition to the government of Prime Minister Eric Eustace Williams in Trinidad and Tobago after street rioting and demonstrations by "black power" advocates had triggered an attack on an arms depot and an attempted coup by rebel armed forces. Similar stirrings were also under way in Jamaica, as well as in the Bahamas and various smaller West Indian islands. Both Williams and Jamaican Prime Minister Hugh Shearer were black men, and indications were that the "black power" cries being raised against them stemmed more from social and economic than from racial problems. Nonetheless, they were additional evidence of the radicalization process going forward in the hemisphere.

Although good neighbors seemed increasingly hard to come by from the point of view of the United States, Secretary Rogers was able to single out Mexican-American relations as "a model of the type of mature relationship which is our objective throughout the Americas." [56] A "guided democracy" under the tutelage of the Institutional Revolutionary party, Mexico had developed a consistent record of economic growth while carefully regulating foreign investment and keeping it subservient to majority Mexican control. It had certainly experienced periods of tension and discord with Washington. However, its own revolution had long since become institutionalized and, as Rogers pointed out, relations by 1970 could hardly have been better. The two countries were pressing forward with "Operation Cooperation," instituted in 1969 in an effort to control marijuana and drug traffic. On July 16, 1970, they signed a treaty to control the illegal trafficking in archaeological artifacts; [57] they successfully negotiated an amended and extended civil air transport agreement on July 31; [58] and, on November 23, they signed a treaty settling all boundary differences and establishing procedures for averting such differences in the future.[59] On November 13, Luis Echeverría Álvarez, who had been chosen to succeed Gustavo Díaz Ordaz in the July 5 elections, met informally with President Nixon at the White House.[60] The meeting, prior to Echeverría's December 1 inauguration, continued the long-standing tradition of close personal relations between the leaders of the two countries.

30 : Québec Libre?

Oddly enough, the two trends that were sweeping Latin America in 1970—nationalism and the onslaught of urban violence—were precisely those besetting the United States' neighbor to the north as well. One says "oddly" because Canada had for years borne the image of a tranquil, "proper" country, somewhat out of the world's mainstream in terms either of critical problems or spectacular achievements. Stable, and secure, it had gone its way peacefully, prosperously, but in the shadow of its massive, over-awing neighbor to the south. Beneath this surface tranquility, however, problems had long been festering. Canadians had often complained about United States cultural hegemony in their country, and they seemed even more annoyed by the steadily rising level of U.S. economic control. With some $27 billion invested, Americans owned an estimated two-thirds of Canada's manufacturing industries, forests, oil production, and mining concerns.[61] The country's energetic Prime Minister, Pierre Elliot Trudeau, had attained office on a pledge of greater Canadian independence, and by 1970 his efforts, no less than those of some Latin American governments, were sparking certain frictions in U.S.-Canadian relations.

In addition to the cutback in its forces assigned to NATO (announced in 1969), Canada was in the process of reducing its armed forces by some 18 per cent—down to 82,000—over a three-year period. It had already announced its general intention of reducing the American cultural and economic presence in the nation's life, and in March, in a move obviously designed to prevent U.S. control, it officially limited new foreign investment in uranium mining to a one-third interest.[62] In an even bolder step on May 31, Canada symbolically declared its economic independence by unpegging its currency from the U.S. dollar and allowing it to float free of the 92.5-cent parity that had been in effect since 1962.[63] By year's end, the Canadian dollar had floated upward to U.S. $.98.

That Washington would suffer such moves, including Canada's recognition of Communist China,[64] without some irritation seemed too much to expect. Canadians themselves were quick to note that they had gained not even so much as a mention in President Nixon's lengthy and definitive State of the World message. They were further irked in March following Nixon's announcement of a stiff quota on oil imports from Canada, a move seen as a U.S. counterbargaining step for long-range concessions on access to Canadian fuels, including uranium.[65] The two countries did reach agreement on mutual efforts to control pollution in the Great Lakes,[66] but they were sharply at odds over Canada's extension of its territorial sea to 12 miles, including the waters surrounding its Arctic islands.[67] At the meeting of the Joint United States-Canadian Committee on Trade and Economic Affairs held in Ottawa November 23–24,[68] Secretary Rogers wryly observed that he had seen a lapel button with the slogan, "I'm for an independent Canada," though he quickly sought to endorse that sentiment. "We recognize the sensitivities that Canadians have about a large measure of Canadian trade and Canada's domestic investment represented by exchanges with the United States and by the actions of American investors," he said. "However, I would like an independent Canada and would wish to continue to have an independent, united prospering Canadian neighbor." [69]

That wish was nonetheless being undermined, in the American view, by more than Canada's emerging sense of economic nationalism. By the end of 1970, for example, the rate of Canadian unemployment stood at 6.6 per cent, partly as a result of Trudeau's drive against inflation. Far more serious, however, was the explosion of separatist sentiment in the French-speaking province of Quebec that took place in October.

For years, Quebec's French-speaking majority had grumbled against the cultural and economic predominance of English-speaking Canada, but not until the 1960's had their discontent assumed violent proportions. The notorious Front for the Liberation of Quebec (F.L.Q.), whose aim was to achieve separation through violent means, had taken a leaf from Marighella's minimanual, robbing banks, bombing establishment institutions, and, on October 5, kidnapping James R. Cross, a British consular aide in Montreal. When the Trudeau government rejected the F.L.Q.'s characteristic demands for the release of "political prisoners" together with $500,000 in gold as ransom for Cross, the F.L.Q. seized Quebec Labor Minister Pierre Laporte for good measure. Canada now faced in double measure the same ago-

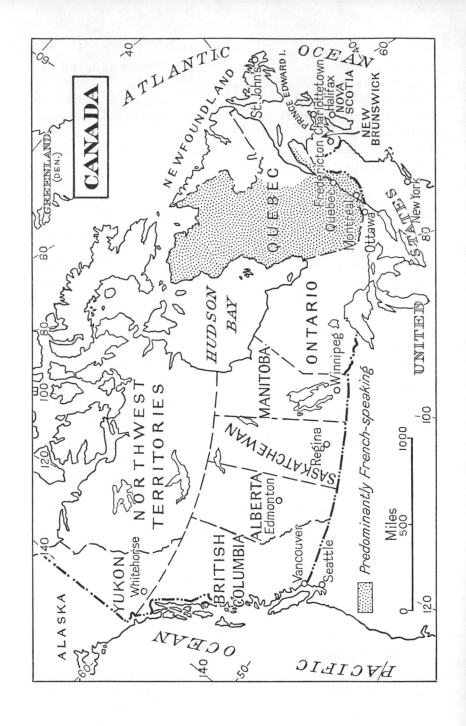

CANADA

nizing problems that had confronted various Latin American governments through the year.

Despite his reputation as a stanch civil libertarian, Trudeau adopted a hard line against the F.L.Q. On October 16, he invoked the emergency War Measures Act, placing Quebec under what amounted to martial law under which 250 suspects were arrested and held without bail. On the following day, the terrorists replied by murdering Laporte and directing police to his body in the trunk of an automobile south of Montreal. Amidst mounting criticism of his handling of the affair, Trudeau now renewed his offer of safe conduct for the kidnappers to Cuba in return for the life of Cross, but it was not until December 3 that the terrorists complied. After releasing Cross unharmed on December 4 into the technical custody of the acting Cuban Consul, they boarded a plane, together with some of their relatives, and flew to asylum in Cuba.

Clearly shaken by these events, Canadians now wondered about the future of their bilingual country. Earlier, on April 29, Quebec voters had gone to the polls and handed a decisive, if not necessarily conclusive, setback to the outright separatist *Parti Québécois*. Later, during the height of the kidnapping crisis, Montreal overwhelmingly reelected its hard-line Mayor, Jean Drapeau, who had backed Trudeau's controversial invocation of emergency powers to the hilt. If such indications were reliable, most French Canadians apparently wanted to preserve the federal union of which they were a part. But the question remained for Canada as it remained for the hemisphere as a whole: How could governments deal effectively with a handful of criminal terrorists, who used the kidnapping of innocent persons as their primary tactic, without eroding those very freedoms the terrorists themselves professed to demand?

8 : Africa: The Second Decade

In 1970, the bulk of newly independent Africa entered upon its second decade of self-rule. Within a nine-month period in 1960, some 17 former colonial territories had been granted their independence in a rush of nationhood. Ten years and some 30 coups later, only seven of the original 17 heads of state were still around to guide the destinies of their fledgling countries. Most had fallen victim to the armies they had proudly nurtured as a symbol of sovereignty. Two—Sir Abubakar Tafawa Balewa of Nigeria and Sylvanus Olympio of Togo—had been murdered. Others were exiled or imprisoned. There were some observers who saw in all this shades of another Latin America—the colonial heritage, the endemic poverty, the predilection for charismatic leaders, and even resort to rule by men in uniform.[1]

Yet it could be said of Africa in 1970—as it could not be said of Latin America—that many of its countries seemed on the way to mastering some of their most formidable problems. The Democratic Republic of the Congo (Kinshasa), for example, had barely achieved independence on June 30, 1960 before being plunged into chaos by a civil war that threatened to involve the great powers and a U.N. fighting force. By 1970, it had settled down to a fruitful exploitation of its rich economic potential, reestablishing close economic ties with Belgium and attracting substantial new investments from the United States, Japan, and Western Europe. Politically, Kinshasa took its first tentative steps toward institutionalized rule by naming the man responsible for it all, Lieutenant General Joseph D. Mobutu, as President in an uncontested popular election on October 31–November 1. The election of a one-party Parliament on November 30 continued the trend toward legitimacy, although it remained apparent that behind the newly established republican façade Mobutu's autocratic hold on the nation remained unimpaired.

Ghana, too, had made a propitious about-face. After years of dictatorial rule under Kwame Nkrumah, whose extravagant policies had brought the country to the brink of economic ruin, a four-year transitional military government had paved the way toward a National Assembly in 1969 and the election on August 31, 1970 for a four-year term of former Chief Justice Edward Akufo-Addo as President. Having rescheduled part of its enormous external debt, and with the prospect of additional relief from its creditors, Ghana saw the revival of both its ambitions for development and its hope for democratic norms.

To be sure, Africa as a whole was hardly free of critical problems. Far more than Latin America it felt the weight of severe underdevelopment. Racist policies in white-controlled southern Africa also spread tension and animosity across the continent, and in black-ruled Kenya, Uganda, and Malawi there were official campaigns under way to divest Asians of their businesses and drive them back across the sea. At least three countries found themselves at war internally. In Chad, nomadic Muslim tribesmen backed by Libya were battling the government of President François Tombalbaye and the 3,500 French troops who supported him. In the Sudan, tribal warriors in the south continued their 15-year-old rebellion against the Muslim-dominated central government in Khartoum, led since May 1969 by the pan-Arabist revolutionary, General Jafar Muhammad al-Nimeri. And in Ethiopia, where Emperor Haile Selassie I celebrated the 40th anniversary of his accession to the throne, a Muslim-oriented and Arab-supported insurrection by the so-called Eritrean Liberation Front forced the government to declare a state of emergency throughout most of the Eritrean province on December 16.[2]

Political strife in varying degrees of severity dotted the continent elsewhere. In Lesotho, Prime Minister Leabua Jonathan annulled the parliamentary elections of January 27 and began arresting his opponents three days later after preliminary returns from the balloting indicated that the ruling Basutoland National party had lost its majority in the National Assembly. In chronically unstable Dahomey, elections were also annulled on April 3 under threat of civil war, resulting in a patchwork arrangement whereby Hubert Maga assumed the Presidency May 7 on a rotating basis with his two leading rivals, Justin Ahomadegbe and Sourou-Migan Apithy. In Somalia, the leftist Supreme Revolutionary Council, led by Major General Mohamed Siad Barre, thwarted an attempted coup on April 27 led by the former security chief.[3] Fully three quarters of the continent was under one-party or military rule, and in many countries tribalism continued to tear at the delicate fabric of national unity.

Yet for all of this, there was hope in 1970 that the worst of Africa's post-independence troubles were over. Nigeria, the continent's largest nation with more than 60 million people, was a case in point. On October 1, 1960, it had gained independence from Britain amidst pomp, pageantry, and what may have been the highest hopes for success ever accorded a newly sovereign state. Within five years, however, the disintegrating influences of tribal and regional animosities led to a military seizure of power in January 1966 and a second military coup by a different tribal faction barely six months later. Even then, the Supreme Military Council, headed by Major General Yakubu Gowon proved unable to hold the country together. Dissatisfied with their share of federal revenues and perquisites, and fearful of renewed massacres and further exploitation at the hands of their now dominant tribal enemies, Ibo leaders in Eastern Nigeria proclaimed the independent "Republic of Biafra" in July 1967, and, as 1970 opened, Africa's worst civil war in post-colonial history was dragging into its 30th month.

Despite superior technical and organizational skills, the Ibo forces led by General Odumegwu Ojukwu, had found themselves not only outnumbered but progressively starved both for food and the materials of war. The United States had pronounced itself neutral in the contest, and the only aid it supplied was in the form of humanitarian relief for the sick and starving. Of the major powers only France had come to the Ibos' aid, while in Africa itself, Biafra had gained recognition of but four states—Gabon, the Ivory Coast, Tanzania, and Zambia. Backed by Soviet and British aid, on the other hand, federal troops were slowly closing the ring on the breakaway Eastern Region. On January 11, authorities in Lagos confirmed that they had taken the Biafran capital of Owerri and were moving on the Uli air strip through which Biafra's last trickle of supplies was being funneled. On January

12, the short-lived republic threw in the towel, thus ending a conflict that cost an estimated 2 million lives (mostly through starvation) and over $1 billion. With Ojukwu in hiding in the Ivory Coast, the interim Biafran leader Brigadier Philip Effiong formally surrendered, pledged loyalty to the central government, and awaited the fate of the rebel forces.

Upon accepting the rebel surrender "in good faith," Gowon called for the safety of civilians and for humane treatment of the surrendering forces.[4] His government had already announced, however, that it would accept no assistance from France, Portugal, South Africa, Rhodesia, or any other country which had supported Biafra and that all relief and aid supplies would have to be channeled through authorities in Lagos,[5] giving rise to fears of political manipulation designed to gain revenge. The world now anxiously awaited signs of the "genocide" that some spokesmen claimed would befall the peoples of the Eastern Region in the wake of the central government's victory. A good deal of lawlessness and disorder there was, but after a two-day unscheduled stop in Lagos January 18–19 during the course of an official visit to 11 West African countries, Secretary-General Thant reported no evidence of any systematic mistreatment or reprisals, while Henrik Beer, the Secretary-General of the Red Cross, praised the conduct of the Lagos authorities.[6] In the months that followed, it did appear that Lagos had remained true to its promises. Though still beset by cases of starvation and malnutrition, the Ibos were gradually returning to the national fold and picking up the threads of normal existence.

By the time Nigeria celebrated its tenth anniversary of independence on October 1, the wounds of the civil war appeared to have healed with surprising swiftness. Ibos were returning to their former places of employment in the predominantly Moslem north (from whence they had fled when the civil war began; they were, however, less well received among hostile tribesmen in the Eastern Region itself), and the nation's economy seemed hardly the worse for wear. General Gowon, who was emerging as one of Africa's most underrated leaders, announced a four-year, $4.4 billion economic development plan, relying heavily on rapid expansion of oil production (primarily in the Eastern Region) with a projected over-all growth rate of 7 per cent annually.[7] Although he warned that a return to civilian rule would in all probability not be possible before 1976, few Nigerians, including the reconciled Ibos, voiced immediate objections. In their eyes, General Gowon had proved himself the one leader capable of drawing a badly rent nation back together. As Gowon knew, moreover, if Nigeria were not to tear itself asunder once again, broadly based political parties would have to be nurtured that would not rely for their key support on regional or tribal interests.

By year's end, Gowon had also moved to mend relations with the four African states that had recognized the rebels (the Ivory Coast, in the meantime, having expelled the fugitive Ojukwu). Furthermore, despite initial fears that Soviet influence might grow in proportion to its heavy support of the central government, General Gowon opened the door once again to Western private investment, sought military aid from the United States, and declared a foreign policy of strict nonalignment.[8] Thus, as with the Congo earlier in the decade, Nigeria had met the gravest possible threat to its nationhood and emerged not only intact but apparently stronger than before. The tribal fragmentation that posed a threat to much of Africa had accordingly been dealt an important setback, and the continent could enter upon its second decade of independence wiser in the knowledge it had gained and with increased confidence in the future.

31 : Whitest Africa Carries On

Another salutary result of the Nigerian settlement was the enhancement of prospects for unity within such pan-African organizations as the Afro-Malagasy Joint Organization (OCAM) and the Organization of African Unity (O.A.U.). Both of these bodies had split internally over the Biafra issue, which, once resolved, left them free to devote full energies once again to the continuing affront posed by white racist rule in southern Africa and in the remaining Portuguese colonies of Angola, Mozambique, and Portuguese Guinea. At the Seventh Session of the O.A.U. Assembly of Heads of State and Government in Addis Ababa, Ethiopia, September 1–3, the 41-nation organization sharply attacked Britain's plan to resume arms sales to the government of Prime Minister Balthazar Johannes Vorster in South Africa,[9] in apparent defiance of long-standing U.N. resolutions. The U.N. Security Council had already approved a tightening of that embargo on July 23 by a vote of 12 in favor to none opposed, with the U.S., the U.K., and France abstaining,[10] and on October 16, an O.A.U. delegation led by President Kenneth Kaunda of Zambia met with Prime Minister

Heath in London in further protest of the proposed sales. By this time Britain, whose level of trade with black African states exceeded that with the white-ruled regimes in the south, showed signs of having second thoughts,[11] and Kaunda's party moved on to France, which was already in the process of selling an estimated half billion dollars in arms to the Vorster government.[12]

In the meantime, however, the predominantly French-speaking 15-nation OCAM, having accepted the small Indian Ocean state of Mauritius as a member in January, was entertaining proposals from a few of its members for increased contact with the white-ruled African states. With the backing of Madagascar, President Félix Houphouët-Boigny of the Ivory Coast proposed the opening of a "dialogue" with South Africa, apparently in the wake of certain encouraging signals from the white rulers themselves.[13] Having resolved their quarrel over Nigeria, therefore, OCAM and the O.A.U. now faced the uncertain prospect of a quarrel over the right way of dealing with the regime they had so long and unanimously condemned.

The Republic of South Africa was the symbolic leader of some nine states or territories lying south of the Zambezi River and encompassing a total population of about 40 million people. Five of these nine—South Africa itself, Angola, Mozambique, Rhodesia (Zimbabwe), and South West Africa (Namibia)—were under direct European (white) control and the four others—Swaziland, Lesotho, Botswana, and Malawi—were under considerable white influence and pressure. By far the most prosperous and economically advanced of all the countries in Africa, South Africa continued to enjoy a substantial economic growth rate of some 8 per cent a year, despite the boycotts and embargos leveled against it. Yet, while its rigid policy of *apartheid* had gained virtually world-wide condemnation, its strategic and economic significance had grown with the closing of the Suez Canal (in the first 18 months after the Canal was closed in June 1967, some 10,000 ships were diverted to the Cape route around Africa and made use of South African ports),[14] and the growing Soviet naval presence in the Indian Ocean. It was such considerations (in addition to the hard currency being earned by France) that had helped to impel the new Heath government to rethink Britain's arms sales policies, particularly with regard to the gun boats which South Africa found to be increasingly necessary to its maritime defense.

If strategic factors were pointing toward a breach of the arms

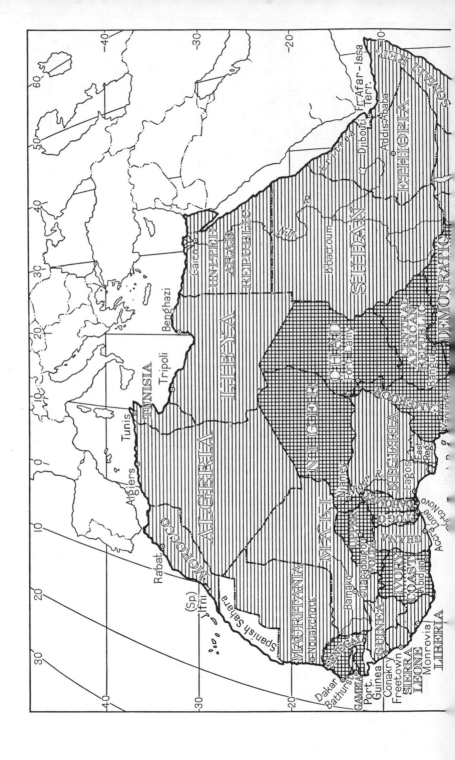

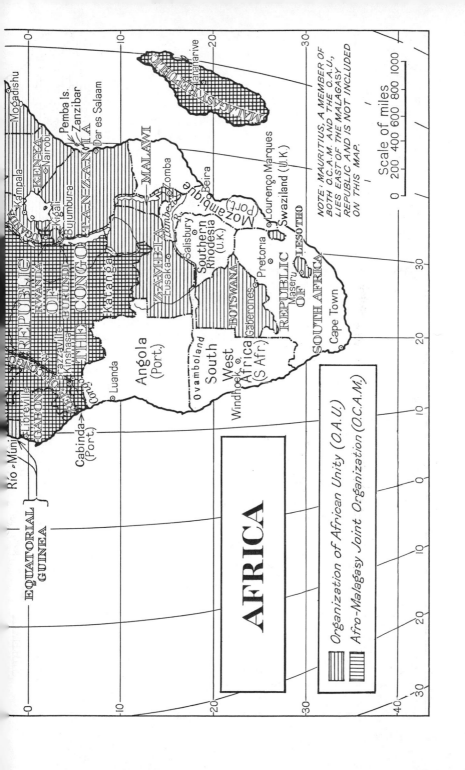

AFRICA

Organization of African Unity (O.A.U.)

Afro-Malagasy Joint Organization (O.C.A.M.)

NOTE: MAURITIUS, A MEMBER OF BOTH O.C.A.M. AND THE O.A.U., LIES EAST OF THE MALAGASY REPUBLIC AND IS NOT INCLUDED ON THIS MAP.

Scale of miles
0   200 400 600 800 1000

Mogadishu

Pemba Is.
Zanzibar
Dar es Salaam

KENYA
Nairobi
Kampala
Kigali
Bujumbura

RWANDA
BURUNDI

TANZANIA

MALAWI
Zomba

DEMOCRATIC REPUBLIC OR CONGO
Kinshasa
Brazzaville
Libreville

GABON
CONGO

Katanga

Cabinda
(Port.)

Río Muni

EQUATORIAL GUINEA

Luanda

Angola
(Port.)

Ovamboland

South West Africa
(S Afr.)

Windhoek

BOTSWANA
Gaberones

ZAMBIA
Lusaka
Zambezi R.

Southern Rhodesia
(U.K.)
Salisbury

Mozambique
(Port.)

Beira

Lourenço Marques

Swaziland (U.K.)

Pretoria

REPUBLIC OF SOUTH AFRICA

Maseru
LESOTHO

Cape Town

MADAGASCAR
(Port.)
Tananarive

embargo, however, developments within South Africa itself were pointing, albeit imperceptibly, toward a crack in the government's racial policies. White South African sportsmen were increasingly irritated by the world-wide boycott which kept their teams on the sidelines in international sports events, so much so that by 1970 many of them were seriously questioning the wisdom of the government's stringent efforts to keep sports racially compartmentalized. At the same time, the very prosperity of the white-dominated economy led to a severe labor shortage, emphasizing the extent to which black African labor was being underutilized, while making the nation's 15 million blacks themselves more and more aware of their own economic power within the system. Though the Vorster government continued to adhere inflexibly to the *apartheid* line, the gradual erosion of its electoral support among the 3.8 million white voters in 1970 may have constituted a harbinger of more flexible policies to come. In the parliamentary elections of April 22, the ruling National party's majority was reduced by five seats in the House of Assembly and the ultraconservative Reconstituted National party of Albert Herzog was eliminated altogether. This turn of events gave a considerable boost to the more moderate but still heavily outnumbered United party led by Sir De Villiers Graaff, while Mrs. Helen Suzman of the more vigorously anti-*apartheid* Progressive party was reelected to her party's single seat. Though the National party still held a commanding lead of 117 out of 166 seats in the Assembly, the gains of the United party were seen as evidence of a slight electoral trend toward moderation. The trend was bolstered during provincial elections in October, when the United party scored another vigorous gain.

For its part, the Vorster government was meanwhile quietly trying to persuade black African regimes that policies of cooperation offered more than those of confrontation. To this end, it began stepping up contacts with such governments as part of a general "outward looking" foreign policy. How South Africa proposed to do this without eventually having to make similar conciliatory gestures toward its own black population was not made clear, but it was clear that among less militant black states the economic lure of some kind of South African tie proved hard to resist. There were indications that both Madagascar and Mauritius, each of which had accepted South African economic investments, would follow Malawi's example and establish diplomatic ties for the immediate economic advantage involved.[15] Thus while South Africa was hardly gaining converts to its own abhorred system, it was forcing cracks in what had been a united black front. It only remained to be seen whether its own solidly racist system might be similarly cracked in the process.

If South Africa was testing a course of reconciliation, however, Portugal was pursuing a tougher line. Unlike South Africa, Portugal did not espouse a racially segregated policy in its African colonies. But it did pose an affront to such organizations as the O.A.U. by its lingering colonial presence on the continent. Having at least temporarily checked the various liberation movements in Mozambique and Angola,[16] the Portuguese were still experiencing considerable difficulty in Portuguese Guinea, where the local independence movement was strongly supported by the adjacent Republic of Guinea under President Sékou Touré. Touré's maverick policies had irritated many African leaders, but when he reported to the U.N. Security Council that a force of mercenaries, including elements of the Portuguese armed forces, had attacked the capital city of Conakry early on November 22, even some of his more skeptical opponents displayed a sense of shock and sympathy. On November 23, the Security Council promptly and unanimously called for "the immediate withdrawal of all external armed forces and mercenaries," and decided to send a special mission to Guinea to look into the situation.[17]

In its report of December 4,[18] the U.N. mission verified that the amphibious force of some 350 men who invaded Guinea included not only Guinean exiles hostile to the Touré regime but also regulars of the Portuguese armed forces. Although Portugal strongly denied any hand in the affair, it seemed evident from the attacks of the raiding party—the freeing of political prisoners, the assault on the headquarters of the so-called African Party for the Independence of [Portuguese] Guinea and Cape Verde—that Portuguese elements were involved. Despite Lisbon's denials, the Security Council on December 8 endorsed the findings of the special mission, specifically condemned Portugal for the invasion (ultimately repulsed by Guinea's own, Chinese-trained "people's militia"), and demanded that Portugal pay full compensation to Guinea for the damages caused by the attack.[19] Three days later, the O.A.U. Ministerial Council held an emergency meeting in Lagos, and issued a series of resolutions charging NATO (of which Portugal is a member) with complicity in the invasion and calling for the elimination of the use of mercenaries in Africa generally.[20]

Although the United States abstained from voting on the condemnation of Portugal in the December 8 Security Council resolution, it did act decisively when Britain's break-away colony of Southern Rhodesia formally declared itself a republic on March 2, thereby severing its last tenuous tie to the British crown.[21] Since its Unilateral Declaration of Independence from Britain in 1965, the Rhodesian government of Prime Minister Ian D. Smith had made clear its intention of following the South African model by virtually excluding the country's 5 million black and mixed population from the governing process, which would be dominated by Rhodesia's 250,000 white settlers. Once the final step was taken, the United States was confronted by the prospect of either closing its consulate in Salisbury, the Rhodesian capital, in sympathy with both British and black African sentiments or keeping it open to serve the 1,200 Americans and their dependents living there as missionaries or officials of U.S. chrome interests. After some initial hesitation, Washington announced that the consulate would be closed by March 17,[22] and by year's end only South Africa continued to recognize the "rebels" in Salisbury as the legitimate government of Rhodesia. Although it continued to maintain its consulate in the Rhodesian capital, even Portugal withheld diplomatic recognition from the Smith regime out of deference to Britain, its NATO ally.

32 : Washington Seeks a Policy

Despite its action on Rhodesia, U.S. policy toward Africa, and especially southern Africa, remained far from clear. On March 17, the very day that Washington closed its consulate in Salisbury, the U.S. found it necessary to cast its first veto in the Security Council against a five-power draft resolution that would have condemned the U.K. for not using force against the Smith regime and would have required U.N. members to sever all communications with Southern Rhodesia.[23] "We have repeatedly stated the view that force is not the answer to this problem," Ambassador Yost remarked in explanation. "For this reason we oppose a resolution condemning the United Kingdom for failure to use it." [24] However, the U.S. did back a compromise resolution of March 18 that, among other things, condemned the policies of the Smith regime, called for enforcement of existing U.N. sanctions, and urged increased "moral and material assistance" to the black majority in the struggle against white domination.[25] Despite such condemnations, Smith's popularity among white Rhodesian voters reached an all-time high when his Rhodesian Front party won all 50 of the white seats at stake in the April 10 elections.

In his State of the World message on February 18, President Nixon had spelled out U.S. policy toward southern Africa in these terms: "Clearly there is no question of the United States condoning, or acquiescing in, the racial policies of the white-ruled regimes. For moral as well as historical reasons, the United States stands firmly for the principles of racial equality and self-determination." The President also added, however, that "we cannot agree that progressive change in Southern Africa is furthered by force. The history of the area shows all too starkly that violence and the counter-violence it inevitably provokes will only make more difficult the task of those on both sides working for progress on the racial question." [26] When Secretary Rogers became the first American Secretary of State to visit sub-Saharan Africa February 7–22 on a ten-nation tour, he repeatedly sounded these themes before black African audiences. The Secretary undertook the trip in order, as he put it, to listen to the views of African leaders concerning "the relationship in the future between Africa and the United States." Out of that process, he said, the United States would then be ready "to enunciate a new policy toward Africa." [27]

Listen the Secretary did, but he did some talking as well. In Addis Ababa, Rogers set forth the "four basic convictions" that underlay U.S. policy formulation.[28] First was U.S. opposition to "the continuation in Africa of systems based on racial discrimination." Second was respect for the independence of African nations. "We have no desire for any domination of any country or any area," declared Rogers. "We have no desire for any special influence in Africa, except the influence that naturally and mutually develops among friends." The third factor seemed more a warning—or cautionary advice—than a conviction: The U.S., "as a developed nation," recognizes "the special obligations to assist in the economic development of Africa." However, the Secretary added, "our resources and our capacity are not unlimited. We have many demands at home." All of which pointed to the probability that Washington would continue to let Western Europe bear the lion's share of responsibility for the economic development of the continent. Finally, Rogers said, "We do not believe that Africa should be the scene of a major-power conflict. We on our part do not propose to make it so. In our bilateral relations we will be motivated by what we can do, not what others may do." After stops that included Kenya, Zambia, and the Congo (Kinshasa), Rogers concluded that "Most of the leaders in Africa believe in these things too." [29]

However, the policy statement submitted by Secretary Rogers to President Nixon on March 26 contained very little by way of significant change in U.S. policy toward Africa.[30] The Secretary again stressed that "We want no military allies, no spheres of influence, no big power competition in Africa." He again cited the "limitations on our [assistance] capacities and our resources" and the special European role in African development. "We have also determined not to recognize the white-minority regime in Salisbury and will continue to support UN economic sanctions." "We are maintaining our arms embargo" on South Africa and, he went on, "We oppose their continued administration of Namibia (South West Africa) and their implementation of apartheid and other repressive legislation there." And, he said, the U.S. would continue to maintain an embargo against the shipment of arms to Portugal for use in the Portuguese territories. Past U.S. policies, in short, would pretty much continue in force.

There were a few new straws in the wind, however. Secretary Rogers noted that the United States would seek to provide "economic alternatives" for the small independent states in southern Africa such as Botswana, Lesotho, and Swaziland. He indicated that U.S. economic aid would increase its emphasis on regional programs and projects, such as those undertaken by the East African Community (Kenya, Tanzania, and Uganda), and that more of it would be funneled through multilateral institutions like the U.N. Development Program, the International Development Association, and the recently founded African Development Bank. He cited President Nixon's already announced goal of seeking preferential trade treatment for all developing countries, and noted its special application to the African states. In a subsequent statement on May 20, U.S. Assistant Secretary of State for African Affairs David D. Newsom announced that the United States had decided officially to discourage investment in South West Africa by U.S. nationals. Such investments, Newsom said, "shall not receive U.S. Government assistance in protection . . . against claims of a future lawful government of South-West Africa. Moreover, we shall no longer make available Export-Import Bank credit guarantees for trade with South-West Africa." [31] Washington went a step farther on July 29 when it voted in favor of two U.N. Security Council resolutions concerning South West Africa. The first called for a worldwide diplomatic, commercial and industrial boycott against the continued presence of South Africa in the country.[32] In the second resolution,[33] the Security Council decided to seek an advisory opinion from the International Court of Justice on "the legal consequences for States of the continued presence of South Africa in Namibia" in face of its resolution of January 30 condemning that presence as illegal.[34]

On the whole, however, the Secretary of State had forged little by way of genuinely new policies as a result of his African trip. To be sure, he had established a personal rapport with various African leaders and had no doubt gained significant insight into their attitudes and feelings, particularly as applied to South Africa. Even before he left, however, influential voices both within and without the United States were beginning to question some of the assumptions upon which U.S. policy toward the area was based.[35] In his book, *The Great Powers and Africa,*[36] published early in 1970, Waldemar A. Nielsen had urged a review of Portugal's NATO membership precisely because of its intense and occasionally violent involvement in African affairs. He had also advocated a critical study of the whole range of U.S. trade, diplomatic, and investment links with the white-ruled regimes in southern Africa. On the other hand, other influential voices were questioning whether the blacks of southern Africa were really being helped by the boycotts and sanctions aimed at the governments that ruled them. Was the isolation being imposed upon South Africa in danger of causing *apartheid* to feed upon itself for want of a proper airing in the international community? And what of Soviet intentions in the area—its growing Indian Ocean presence, its considerable influence in such African states as Somalia, the Congo (Brazzaville), and Tanzania? In Zambia and Tanzania, moreover, the Chinese People's Republic was building a $412-milion, 1,116-mile railroad for the express purpose of relieving Zambia's dependence on southern Africa for an outlet to the sea.[37] Might not Chinese penetration also pose a problem?

It was clear from Rogers' statements that the United States now viewed such issues as relatively insignificant. Washington's attitude toward the TanZam railroad was one of benign indifference. U.S. officials questioned the economic value of such a project, but understood the political reasons for it. Certainly Washington had by now concluded that any great power competition for African influence was at best an expensive game, and often a losing one. And based on the evidence, the Soviets had reason to agree. Their considerable help to the Nigerian central government really gained them very little once the civil war was over. Farther north, the Algerian government of President Houari Boumediene was also stepping up trade with the United States (despite the absence of diplomatic relations since the 1967 Arab-Israeli war) and simultaneously cooling its dependence on the U.S.S.R. At the same time, the socialist Boumediene began smoothing relations with other Arab states, particularly Arab monarchies, by inviting King Faysal of Saudi Arabia on an official visit June 20 and by settling a long-festering border dispute with King Hassan II of Morocco over iron deposits of the Tindouf area.[38] However, Algerian-French relations took a turn for the worse in July when Boumediene unilaterally increased the posted price of oil extracted by French companies by 50 per cent.[39]

Such developments served as reminders that most of Africa's newly independent states were above all interested in their own economic development in a politically independent climate. In such circumstances, any great power seeking deliberately to meddle or manipulate would likely get its fingers burned. As the events of 1970 appeared to reveal, Africa had become less of an international battleground and more of a testing ground for the development problems which almost all its countries continued to face.

9 : *Western Europe:*
A Rebirth of Diplomacy

That Europe had more than recovered from the war was hardly news by 1970. That it appeared to be regaining some of its old preeminence in the art and exercise of diplomacy was another matter, however. In proclaiming the end of the postwar era, President Nixon had recognized as much. "Our *common* success in rebuilding Western Europe had restored our allies to their proper strength and status," he said. "It was time that our own leadership, in its substance and its manner, took account of this fact." [1] And, indeed, history may record that the United States, with its preoccupations in Vietnam and the Middle East, was straggling on the diplomatic sidelines in 1970 while Western Europe moved to initiate the "new era" of which President Nixon spoke. Britain was making its third—and by all indications its most auspicious—bid to join the European Economic Community (E.E.C.), an effort, which, if crowned with success, could alter the whole of international relations as perhaps nothing else since World War II. In lieu of a final peace treaty, West German Chancellor Willy Brandt was moving on his own initiative toward a policy of reconciliation with his eastern neighbors—the so-called *Ostpolitik,* designed to normalize the Federal Republic's postwar status and usher in a new era in German foreign policy. Even France seemed to be setting its sights on a new role as a key Mediterranean power, bolstering its ties to Spain and Greece, warming its relations with Italy, the Maghreb, Egypt, and Lebanon, and concluding a controversial arms deal under which Libya's revolutionary government would receive 100 advanced military aircraft over the next four years.[2]

To be sure, such European initiatives were invariably accompanied by nods of consultation or other gestures of benign intent toward the United States, whose role as Europe's postwar nanny still apparently merited some respect. There was the usual parade of leaders through White House doors—Harold Wilson of the United Kingdom in January, Georges Pompidou of France in February, Brandt in April, and Edward Heath, Wilson's successor as Prime Minister, in December. There were the periodic celebrations of togetherness at meetings of the NATO Ministerial Council in May and December and at a meeting of the 22-nation Organization for Economic Cooperation and Development (O.E.C.D.) in May. There were the usual murmurs of encouragement regarding Nixon's efforts at disengagement from Vietnam, particularly his five-point peace proposal of October 7, and even the usual shouts of dismay when the President appeared to be widening that war into Cambodia.[3] Any development which appeared to deflect the United States from its course of trans-Atlantic partnership seemed universally deplored, while the Nixon administration itself—not to mention a host of politicians and pundits on both sides of the Atlantic —never tired of declaiming that Western Europe was and would continue to be America's first foreign policy concern.

For all of that, however, a feeling of mutual detachment seemed subtly to be gaining ground throughout the year. Although Washington repeatedly denied any intention of cutting back on the 310,000 troops committed to NATO's European command, the impression remained widespread that some reductions were only a matter of time. Coincidentally, the fear of any East-West confrontation in the heart of Europe—a fear which had always provided the mainspring for NATO's existence—continued to fade, not only because of President Pompidou's cordial visit to the Soviet Union in October,[4] or the successfully concluded Bonn-Moscow treaty renouncing the use of force,[5] or even the SALT talks in which U.S. and Soviet representatives were engaged alternately in Vienna and Helsinki,[6] but also because of the advanced state of Russia's military preoccupation with a supposed Chinese threat in the Far East. Indeed, one could speculate that, given

France's growing nuclear arsenal and the prospective entry of a nuclear-armed Britain into the European Community itself, the day might eventually come when Washington would be inclined to fold its own nuclear umbrella and silently steal away.

33 : Looking Inward

Such currents swam against the prevailing tide of rhetoric and gave strength to the notion that the Nixon Doctrine would eventually find a European corollary to make it whole. No less than the United States, moreover, the countries of Western Europe had their own internal problems and external interests to attend to. If the United States was turning inward by dint of necessity, Europe too reflected the mood of self-absorption.

Even Sweden, whose prosperous welfare state had become something of a model for advanced, industrial societies, seemed afflicted by those "diseases of affluence" besetting various nations of the North Atlantic region. The Social Democratic government of Prime Minister Olof Palme was struggling unsuccessfully to cope with runaway inflation and a series of wildcat strikes that stemmed, primarily, from its own highly egalitarian efforts to minimize income differentials between workers and white collar professionals. Apparently more irritated than inspired by Palme's program, Swedish voters dealt the ruling Social Democrats a substantial setback in parliamentary elections on September 20, reducing the party's share of the popular vote to a minority 45.3 per cent and forcing Palme to rely on Communist support for aspects of his program opposed by the "bourgeois" parties of the right and center.

Such manifestations of internal stress did not prevent the Palme government from pressing ahead with plans to affiliate Sweden with the E.E.C. on terms compatible with the country's traditional neutrality, but they did serve to lessen Sweden's international celebrity as a well-planned and ordered society. Nor was that image enhanced by the reception accorded the new U.S. Ambassador, Jerome Holland, a black, on his arrival in Stockholm in April. For several years, much to Washington's irritation, Sweden had been tendering humanitarian aid to North Vietnam while providing political asylum to American deserters and draft dodgers, and when Ambassador Holland was greeted by jeers and racial epithets and later subjected to an egg-throwing attack, Sweden's posture of moral rectitude appeared to sag reciprocally. Holland himself sharply rebuked his detractors five days prior to Palme's departure June 1 for an unofficial ten-day tour of the United States,[7] and the continuing strain in U.S.-Swedish relations was evident in Nixon's subsequent decision not to receive Palme at the White House.[8] Although relations improved somewhat in the months following Palme's visit, internal problems continued to absorb the energies of his government. It was evident that Sweden, no less than the United States, had found faults enough at home to preoccupy its leadership as 1970 drew to a close.

That Italy had long had more than its share of internal problems was denied by no one, least of all the Italians. But Italy, too, was under extraordinary stress during 1970. A late-blooming beneficiary of postwar reconstruction, it had in the 1960's registered remarkable economic gains, stabilizing its currency and advancing its industry to a position of competitive leadership among the E.E.C. six. By 1970 the bloom appeared to be fading, however, and the nation's underlying problems—a calcified bureaucracy, social unrest, and a system of rule by coalition that seemed increasingly unable to invoke needed reforms—were glaringly revealed in the political paralysis that beset the country throughout much of the year. The interim all-Christian Democratic Cabinet that had ruled the country under Prime Minister Mariano Rumor since July 1969, broke apart in February, delivering Italy into its 30th governmental crisis of the postwar period.

It was an old story in the history of parliamentary democracies facing on the Mediterranean: of government operating in a pressure cooker of discontent, of factions united as to the need for reforms but divided over their shape and implementation, of discontent growing as the government floundered. On March 27, Rumor formed a new Center-Left coalition, bringing back into play the four-party alliance that had ruled the nation on-and-off since 1963, but the arrangement was not to last. Among the coalition's factions a dispute had been brewing over the advisability of cooperation with the Italian Communist party, the largest in the West and the second largest political party in Italy next to the Christian Democrats. The dispute came to a head in the June 7–8 elections to choose candidates for some 690 seats in 15 newly created regional parliaments. These were Italy's first major regional elections in the postwar period, designed to grant a measure of the decentralization and regional autonomy promised in the 1948 constitution, and there were those who feared that vengeful voters would seize the opportunity to deal the Center-Left parties a crushing blow. As it turned out, none of the fiercely contending political parties was able to chalk up any significant gains. Indeed, despite their squabbles (or perhaps because of them), the parties of the Center-Left scored a modest gain, while the Communists, for the first time since World War II, suffered a slight setback. But the Communists did show traditional strength in the so-called "Red belt," winning an outright majority of seats in Emilia-Romagna and falling only two seats short of a majority in both Tuscany and Umbria.[9]

When returns from the regional elections were in, the Socialist party promptly joined with the Communists to form governments in Tuscany and Umbria. Since the Socialists were partners in Rumor's coalition in Rome, they now faced charges of bigamy—consorting with Communists at the regional level while wedded to Christian Democrats, Unitary Socialists, and Republicans at the national level. The issue posed no moral dilemma for the majority of Socialists, who had been advocating an "opening to the Communists" even before the regional elections took place. But it proved too much for an adamant minority in that party and for the other parties of the alliance to bear. On July 6, the Cabinet fell, the issue of cooperation with the Communists having become, for the moment at least, something of a storm center in Italian coalition politics. It was not until August 6 that a former Finance Minister, the Christian Democrat Emilio Colombo, was able to patch over differences and form a new Cabinet based on the old Center-Left formula.

Together with his reluctant partners, Colombo now struggled to push through a package of emergency economic measures designed to spur investment, raise tax revenues, and temper the pace of inflation. That accomplished, he turned to negotiations with organized labor on housing and public health reforms, nailing down preliminary agreement on these issues by the end of the year. However, a wave of wildcat strikes, which shut down banks, ministries, and newspapers, left garbage uncollected, mail undelivered, and transportation disrupted, continued to afflict the country. And scattered incidents of mob violence continued to occur, particularly in the southern city of Reggio Calabria, where a dispute over the designation of a regional capital touched off an explosion of accumulated social and economic tensions, reflecting not only Rome's long-standing neglect of the *mezzogiorno* but also the apparent vitality of right-wing, antidemocratic forces. The coalition was also severely tested in October by the passage of Italy's first divorce law, a nongovernmental measure backed by Communists, Socialists, and some smaller parties while bitterly opposed by the Christian Democrats and the Vatican.[10] But the major source of strain on the governing alliance continued to revolve around the issue of an opening to the Communists, with the feeling apparently growing that only by coopting the Communist party could the government push through the major reforms so clearly required. The dilemma led one American observer to declare pessimistically that "Italy shows mounting symptoms of becoming the Czechoslovakia of NATO, a country of uncertain political and even foreign orientation." [11]

Colombo's troubles at home forced him to cancel a planned trip to the United States in October, although President Nixon took the opportunity to touch base with the new Premier on his tour of the Mediterranean in September.[12] The President observed that Italy, with "the longest coastline of any nation in the Mediterranean," had a "tremendous stake in peace in the Mediterranean." [13] In Naples, he accordingly put in a plug for NATO at a time when "instability seems to be the order of the day. . . . What we must realize," the President said, "is that in a period of instability, of uncertainty, and of possible lack of confidence, that what is needed is an institution that is stable, that men and women can hang onto, and NATO is such an institution." [14]

That Italy might some day have to choose between internal order (through cooperation with the Communists) and its ties to NATO (the probable price of such cooperation) was obviously of considerable concern to Washington. Italy, after all, was the key southern anchor of NATO at a time when France had withdrawn from the military side of the alliance, when anti-American sentiment was on the rise in Turkey, and when the Soviet presence throughout the Eastern Mediterranean had increased dramatically. In such circumstances, a pep talk on NATO's virtues by the President of the United States seemed to be a start, at least, toward repairing the alliance's southern flank. Nor, in such circumstances, was it altogether surprising that Nixon should choose to extend his Mediterranean tour, gracing the controversial regime of General Francisco Franco in Spain with an official visit on October 2–3.[15]

Spain, too, was deeply caught up in internal tribulations during 1970. Aging and infirm, the 78-year-old Franco was confronted by what appeared to be the gravest threats to his regime in 30 years. Politically divided and ridden by financial scandal, the ruling National Movement (Falange) was itself beset on all sides by pressure for change from student and labor groups, elements of the business community, and even Catholic religious leaders. In July, the bloodiest police-worker confrontation in a decade left three demonstrators dead in Granada. In November, widespread strikes on behalf of political prisoners afflicted Madrid and other key cities. In December came the notorious trial of 15 Basque nationalists, accused of complicity in the murder of a police official, amidst more strikes and demonstrations and a world-wide outcry against the rigged and repressive atmosphere in which the trial was going forward. When a military court on December 28 sentenced six of the accused to death and the remainder to long prison terms, the world reacted with shocked indignation, while Spain itself was churned by fears of a revolutionary outbreak or a military coup, forcing the regime to impose a nationwide state of emergency. Although General Franco commuted the death sentences to 30-year prison terms on December 30, it seemed clear that Spain had come to that inevitable crossroads awaiting all authoritarian regimes where a choice between a turn toward liberalization or increased repression had become the question of the hour.

Yet, in strategic terms, Spain commanded the western aprpoach to that same sea whose eastern stretches were falling more and more under Soviet influence. Despite the authoritarian reputation of Franco and his followers, therefore, Secretary Rogers cordially received Spanish Foreign Minister Gregorio López Bravo in March,[16] and by mid-April had reportedly agreed with him on the broad outlines of a new five-year mutual defense agreement to replace the one due to expire September 26.[17] In May, Rogers conferred with Franco himself in Madrid,[18] and on August 6, the new "Agreement on Friendship and Cooperation" was signed and made public, initiating, in the words of a joint statement, "a new era in partnership between the United States and Spain." [19]

The agreement provided for stepped-up cooperation in such fields as education, science and technology, agriculture and trade, but its most significant and controversial sections related to cooperation in defense. Under the terms of Chapter VIII, the United States agreed "to support Spanish defense efforts, as necessary and appropriate, by contributing to the modernization of Spanish defense industries, as well as granting military assistance to Spain." In return, the United States would continue to operate jointly with Spain two Air Force bases and a submarine installation, petroleum and other storage facilities, and a network of communications and navigation support facilities. The cost to Washington: a pledge of $3 million in economic aid and some $300 million in grants and credits for military assistance, including the delivery of 36 used Phantom jet fighter-bombers. In addition, the United States would support Spain's effort to achieve "full integration" into the E.E.C. and, although Secretary Rogers denied it was part of the agreement,[20] would also press informally for Spain's eventual membership in NATO.

The agreement went into effect on September 26, but not without protests and recriminations from opposition groups in both countries. While in Spain, Rogers refused to discuss the issue with opponents of the Franco regime, who had petitioned him for a hearing. In Washington, Senator Fulbright complained that the administration was seeking to achieve by executive agreement what by all logic was a treaty requiring the Senate's advice and consent before it could enter into force.[21] Senator Church wanted to know why the old agreement could not simply have been extended for another two years as in the past. Other members of Congress expressed concern that the new agreement would "commit" the United States to the defense of Spain in the event of an outbreak of hostilities. Still others complained that if war broke out in, say, the Middle East, the United States would have to "consult" with Spain before being allowed to use the bases.[22] The Senators did not object to such consultation *per se,* but they wondered what the value of the bases could be if their use depended on Franco's consent.

Senator Fulbright summed up the doubts afflicting many members of Congress when he said: "What is the threat facing Spain today that requires an additional 36 of the most potent fighter bombers in the world? I make that remark noting that Spain has recently purchased 30 Mirages from France; that it already has F-5s and F-104s; and that the United States has 54 of its own F-4s stationed on Spanish soil. I submit that that presents an extraordinary force of jet combat aircraft for a country at war with no one, whose territory borders on two allies and who, as far as I can see, faces no threat requiring such a formidable air combat force." [23]

In response to these congressional challenges, Under Secretary Johnson firmly denied that the new agreement committed the United States in any way to Spain's defense. Such a commitment, Johnson said, could only be undertaken by treaty.[24] He also stressed that the agreement "enables us to maintain a presence in the Mediterranean that we otherwise would not be able to do." And, the Under Secretary noted, the United States "would very much hope that Spain could eventually join NATO." [25] Since Defense Secretary Laird had already expressed the same hope in June,[26] it seemed evident that the administration's concern for the security of NATO's southern flank had reached the point of overriding whatever doubts it might have had as to the advisability of a formal alliance with Spain's antidemocratic regime.

Given their memories of Franco's association with Hitler and Mussolini, however, most of America's NATO allies did not share such sentiments. Many of them, in fact, had already turned a cold shoulder to Greece, a NATO member, precisely because that ancient seat of Western democracy had fallen under the sway of a military-backed rightist clique which showed no more concern than Franco Spain for the rights and liberties of the people. Under the threat of expulsion Greece had withdrawn from the Council of Europe in December 1969, and the latter on April 15, through its European Commission on Human Rights, denounced the regime's continuing torture of political prisoners and, with France and Cyprus abstaining, demanded a prompt end to such practices.[27] Meanwhile, as further evidence of European disapproval, the country's associated ties to E.E.C. showed progressive signs of deterioration, despite occasional French support.

In fact, shortly before its third anniversary in power on April 21, the regime of Premier Georgios Papadopoulos announced an easing of martial law and the restoration of some constitutional rights, including due process in cases of arrest and imprisonment.[28] In June, it freed 73 prisoners (although an estimated 1,200 remained behind bars or on island prison camps), but in November it proceeded to denounce a year-old pact giving the Red Cross access to those being detained, apparently out of pique over continuing reports criticizing the manner in which the prisoners were being treated. Although the government spoke vaguely of an eventual return to democratic rule, there were no concrete signs that it was moving in such a direction. On November 29, a carefully chosen 56-member Advisory Council was named to offer advice on legislative proposals. On the whole, however, progress toward democratic, constitutional rule seemed as often reversed as speeded, and the regime made no secret of its firm intention to stay on until Greece had been thoroughly purged of those elements deemed subversive in its eyes.

As with Spain, therefore, it was difficult to tell whether Greece suffered more from its inherent political and economic ills or from the government which seemed to perpetuate them. From Washington's viewpoint, however, the strategic requirements of a secure Mediterranean again apparently overrode the issue of ideological niceties. In April, *The New York Times* reported that the Pentagon had been secretly shipping to Greece double the military aid authorized by Congress,[29] thereby circumventing to a large extent the ban imposed in 1967 and partially relaxed following the Czechoslovak crisis in 1968. On September 22, the State Department announced that, after an 18-month review of U.S. policy toward Greece, the administration had decided to resume normal military shipments to that country. "The resumption of such shipments will enhance the ability of the Greek forces to carry out their responsibilities in defense of the NATO area, and thus contribute importantly to the cohesion and strength of the southern flank of NATO," the announcement said. "The decision to resume the shipment of suspended items rests entirely on these considerations." [30]

In early October, while President Nixon was toasting General Franco in Spain, Defense Secretary Laird was on hand in Greece to reassure Papadopoulos of continued U.S. military backing in the face of Russia's naval challenge in nearby waters.[31] With U.S. support thus assured, and with his opposition both at home and abroad badly splintered, Papadopoulos and the Colonels around him seemed, for the time, firmly in control. But the United States had once again found itself confronted by a choice whose familiar dimensions had helped turn an entire generation (or so it appeared) away from the painful moral dilemmas inherent in great power rivalry. For all its talk about a lower profile abroad, the Nixon administration had extended the hand of support to two regimes widely regarded as unsavory, all with the aim of attaining an added margin of security for its Mediterranean interests. In doing so, it had edged away from the predominant sentiment in Western Europe itself, adding perhaps new strains to the alliance it was seeking to bolster. Yet, in the administration's view there was little else that could be done. The old cold war tensions had no doubt eased considerably in the heart of Europe, but they were alive and kicking on its southern shores.

Not surprisingly, Secretary Rogers flew on from his end-of-May talks with Franco to Portugal, where the status of another agreement governing U.S. bases in the Azores remained to be discussed.[32] Portugal was still another country beset by internal troubles in 1970, but even more than Spain or Greece it had gained the obloquy of world opinion—in this case for its colonial policies in Africa. This did not deter Rogers from his visit, but it did apparently defer any immediate effort to regularize the status of the bases which the United States was leasing. In any case, the Portuguese had enough problems to occupy them without adding the issue of any long-term defense arrangement with the United States. For 36 years, the country had lived in the shadow of its all-powerful leader, Antonio de Oliveira Salazar, and his death on July 27, after two years of retirement and physical incapacity, brought to the surface long-developing tensions between those who would perpetuate Salazar's "corporate" system and those who would turn a new page in the nation's political evolution. Caught as he was between the past and the future, however, Salazar's successor, Prime Minister Marcello Caetano, appeared to opt for the relative safety of the past. There was no sharp break with Salazar's legacy, no move to encourage an organized political opposition, no effort to free the "overseas provinces" which had cost the nation so heavily in blood and treasure (though in December, Caetano did propose to grant them a greater measure of internal autonomy).[33] On the whole, Portugal remained an essentially closed society in which pressure for fundamental change, both at home and in its colonies, seemed increasingly confined to radical underground groups advocating revolution. As such, it also remained among the weaker links in NATO's European chain of command.

Portugal, Greece, Spain, and Italy may have been preoccupied, by dint of necessity, with their internal problems, yet it could be said that none of them seemed so inwardly oriented or self-absorbed as France. Not that France itself was undergoing any grave political or economic crisis in 1970. On the contrary, it appeared that the nation's mood of introspection was almost wholly a psychological phenomenon, the result, perhaps, of many years of Gaullist image-building and self-congratulation, so that Frenchmen were at length inclined to wonder what they and their country were really like. As with the passing of Salazar in Portugal, the death of former President Charles de Gaulle on November 10 afforded the opportunity for new directions in national policy, had the General's followers deemed it wise. Aside from a more cordial attitude toward Britain's bid for membership in the E.E.C. (already signaled) and a cooler attitude toward those French-speaking African states with whose leaders de Gaulle had maintained personal ties of friendship, President Pompidou was expected to remain basically faithful to the grand lines of Gaullist policy as already laid down. The search for East-West *détente* would go on, as would the courting of the Arab states, to the continued consternation of Israel. And despite its heavy cost ($5 billion out of the $16.7 billion, five-year defense budget approved in October),[34] France's nuclear *force de frappe* would continue its course toward expansion and improvement.

Even during de Gaulle's own last months in power, however, relations with the United States had resumed on a more even keel. On an eight-day tour of the United States, February 23–March 3, President Pompidou told a gathering on the White House lawn that France wanted to strengthen its ties with Washington and hoped the United States would continue to maintain its military and economic presence in Europe, observing that the door to U.S. investments in his country, once partially closed, was now fully open.[35] In Chicago, an irritated Pompidou was subjected to some close-quarter heckling by crowds protesting France's sale of jet fighters to Libya, but President Nixon was quick to issue an official apology and subsequently made the unusual gesture of flying to New York, where the French leader had been denied an official reception, to attend a farewell dinner in Pompidou's honor.[36]

The Mideast policies which had stirred such angry demonstrations in the United States also left France's Jews feeling somewhat insecure, but French Premier Jacques Chaban-Delmas had argued that the 100 jets consigned to Libya were being supplied solely for Mediterranean defense, that they were not to be deployed in the conflict with Israel, and that should any of them turn up on the Arab-Israeli front, further deliveries would be halted.[37] The United States and France had long disagreed on Middle East policy, but to the extent that French officials were now evidencing a broad concern over the Mediterranean's security, their policies appeared to be running parallel to Washington's.

In February, several months before Washington officially resumed its own arms shipments, Pompidou was reported willing to provide the Greek regime with the heavy arms it found unobtainable elsewhere.[38] That same month Spain and France signed a new contract under which Madrid would purchase 30 Mirage jet fighters—a move also said to reflect the two countries' joint interest in the Mediterranean.[39] Short of military reintegration, moreover, France was also evidencing a more cooperative spirit toward NATO, a development traceable, in the view of some observers, to Pompidou's talks with Nixon earlier in the year. As a nation bordering on the Mediterranean and with interests of its own to pursue there, France seemed no less alarmed by the teetering power balance in that ancient sea than the United States.

34 : Britain Looks to Europe

With de Gaulle's abrupt retirement to his country home at Colombey-les-Deux-Eglises in April 1969, the more abrasive aspects of French foreign policy—those that had so irritated Washington—had apparently passed from the scene. If Pompidou was hurt and puzzled by the demonstrations against him in the United States, he was nonetheless pleased by his talks with Nixon and by the courtesy afforded him in addressing a joint session of the U.S. Congress.[40] In May, Premier Chaban-Delmas reported that the American incursion into Cambodia had not worsened U.S.-French relations, that France fully endorsed the efforts of Brandt in Germany to reach accord with his eastern neighbors, and even that France would no longer oppose the attempt of the United Kingdom to join the E.E.C. The French, it appeared, were no longer ruffling and disconcerting their allies by the simple expedient of saying "no."

For the United Kingdom, in particular, the shift in the French attitude opened new and happier vistas to the future. For years, Britain had afforded the world the spectacle of a once great empire in decline, its self-confidence shaken, its economy in perpetual crisis, its Commonwealth torn by internal dissension, and its entreaties to join the Common Market effectively rebuffed by an ancient enemy across the English Channel. The fall from the pinnacle of world power had been bad enough, but to have a French President instruct the British on the need to put their house in order before becoming "eligible" to join Europe, and to gain first their "independence" from their former colony, the United States, had been especially wounding to Anglo-Saxon pride. Britain, it was said, had lost an empire but had not yet found a role.

By 1970, however, Britain showed distinct signs of emerging from its post-imperial wanderings in the wilderness. By contrast with many of its internally troubled and preoccupied neighbors on the Continent, the nation's social and economic fabric seemed well-knit and hardier than the British themselves once imagined. To be sure, there were mounting indications of trouble in the autonomous province of Northern Ireland, where a Catholic minority, not unlike the French in Quebec, saw themselves the victims of discrimination and abuse at the hands of their Protestant neighbors. In June and July, rioting in Belfast and Londonderry resulted in at least 13 dead and another 350 seriously wounded, forcing the Ulster government of Prime Minister James Chichester-Clark to impose a ban on parades and demonstrations for the next six months. On the whole, however, the British were experiencing good news through most of the year.

In January, Prime Minister Wilson's Labor government announced a foreign trade surplus for the third straight month and reported that the nation's gold reserves had risen in ten out of the 12 months in 1969.[41] By March, Defense Minister Denis Healey could inform Parliament that the 4,500 troops withdrawn from West Germany as an economy measure in 1968 could be returned to NATO duty,[42] while the new strength of sterling and continued improvements in the trade balance afforded a cut in the bank rate from 8 per cent to 7½ per cent.[43] Buoyed by still more signs of a full economic recovery and sensing a propitious moment, Wilson on May 18, called for general elections to be held one month from that date, confident that a grateful British electorate would sweep him back into office on the strength of a resurgent economy.

It may have been Wilson's worst political mistake. When the returns were in on June 18, it was the Conservative party led by Edward Heath that rolled up a 30-seat majority in the House of Commons—a stunning upset which most observers attributed unconvincingly to a low voter turnout. Next day, Heath set about organizing the first Conservative government since 1964, eventually designating Sir Alec Douglas-Home as Foreign Secretary, Anthony Barber as Chancellor of the Exchequer, Lord Carrington as Secretary of State for Defense, and Geoffrey Rippon as the Minister in charge of negotiations with the Common Market. Waged under the slogan, "A Better Tomorrow," Heath's campaign had emphasized private enterprise, lower taxes, trade union reform, and greater attention to British interests abroad, including a pledge to press forward with Common Market entry which was echoed by the Labor opposition. The proposed program must have had its appeal, for Heath drew proportionately about as many votes among the newly enfranchised 18- to 21-year-old voters as among older elements of the electorate.

Promptly upon assuming office, Heath moved to "attend to British interests abroad" by announcing the government's intention to resume arms sales to South Africa and by declaring a continued presence for British troops east of Suez in Malaysia.[44] In a special budget speech in October, Barber announced plans for tax reductions and cuts in government spending. At the same time he revealed the extent of the new government's determination to clear away obstacles in the path of E.E.C. membership by reporting that Britain intended to abandon its system of support for agriculture—mainly through deficiency payments to farmers—in favor of the Common Market's system of support—mainly through levies on imports.[45] This would be a wrenching process for British consumers, more accustomed to lower food prices than their counterparts on the Continent, but it was a clear signal to the continental Six that Britain would make whatever sacrifices necessary to join them.

The path to British entry had been opened in December 1969, when leaders of the Community's members (France, West Germany, Italy, Belgium, Luxembourg, and the Netherlands) met at The Hague for a decisive round of talks on the Community's future.[46] In addition to agreeing on steps toward a full economic and monetary union, with the object of establishing a common Community currency by 1980, the leaders also declared the E.E.C.'s readiness to open negotiations for membership with the United Kingdom, Ireland, Norway, and Denmark. After several years of drift as the result of Gaullist foot-dragging and opposition, the E.E.C. now seemed prepared to begin an energetic course of expansion, both in terms of its quest for unification and in terms of broadening its membership.

In 1970, these objectives gained steady momentum. At a meeting of the Council of Ministers at Brussels on February 7–8, the E.E.C.

Foreign Ministers hammered out a package of agreements regarded as among the most significant since the forging of the Treaty of Rome establishing the Common Market in 1957. For the first time, the Community was provided with certain independent financial resources, derived from industrial tariffs, farm levies, and a percentage of indirect taxes collected by the national governments—all of which were eventually expected to total more than $4 billion a year. In addition, and despite French reluctance, the European Parliament in Strasbourg, a consultative body with the potential function of acting as the Community's supranational legislature, was slated to achieve its first real powers by 1975, when control over 3½ per cent of the Community's budget would be shifted to it.[47] In March, these historic steps were followed up by agreement in principle to establish common foreign policies, with initial emphasis on European security and the Middle East. A study group was formed to report on these issues, while Britain and other applicants were invited to join in the preliminary discussions.[48]

Efforts toward an economic and monetary union encountered somewhat rougher sledding however. A draft plan for monetary union was taken up by the Council of Ministers on December 14–15, but agreement to institute the plan's initial stages was not immediately forthcoming.[49] In the meantime, however, the Community's Finance Ministers had agreed in principle to limit the range within which their currencies could fluctuate on foreign exchange markets and had instituted procedures for mutual balance-of-payments aid as part of their over-all scheme for monetary integration.[50]

While these steps were going forward, the Community continued its policy of negotiating associate memberships and preferential trade agreements with other nations in Europe, the Mediterranean region, and Africa. Preferential trade agreements were signed with Israel and Spain on June 29, and Malta's accession to associated status was negotiated in December. A multilateral convention with the E.E.C.'s 18 associated states in Africa, the so-called second Convention of Yaoundé, was fully ratified in December and was scheduled to enter into force on January 1, 1971, as was a similar agreement (the Arusha Convention) with the East African Community states of Kenya, Tanzania, and Uganda. Overshadowing these peripheral arrangements, however, were the applications of Britain, Denmark, Norway, and Ireland for full membership and the negotiations related thereto which got under way in Luxembourg on June 30.

In a White Paper published on February 10,[51] the Wilson government had estimated that food prices in Britain might rise by as much as 25 per cent, and that the nation's balance of payments could come under heavy strain, should Britain's application end in success. Wilson himself still favored entry as a long-term good, foreseeing eventual gains for British industry and a new and important political role for Britain in the councils of Europe. But there were also indications that the British public was growing even cooler to the idea, the nation's economic outlook having taken a turn for the better on a go-it-alone basis, and some members of Wilson's own party were reported uneasy at the prospects. With negotiations already under way in September, in fact, a Labor party conference barely commanded sufficient votes to reject a measure against Britain's application which had strong support from the Transport Workers Union.[52]

At the opening round of talks on June 30, Britain's Anthony Barber promptly cut to the crux of his country's difficulties by elaborating the expected cost to Britain of its accession to the Community's common agricultural policy.[53] When in mid-October the British negotiators announced that a six-year transition period would be required for Britain to adapt to E.E.C. farm rules, France responded by rejecting the time span out-of-hand as too lengthy, and there were fears that a possible deadlock might doom the talks. But by year's end, the British had yielded to a speedier timetable (five years instead of six), all key issues, including the thorny problems posed by New Zealand butter and Commonwealth sugar, were out on the table, and a favorable solution was being predicted for sometime in mid-1971.

From Washington's viewpoint, the long-heralded hour of West European integration now seemed imminent. For years the United States had encouraged successive British governments to move toward accommodation with the Common Market, while lending strong backing to the E.E.C. in its quest for greater unification. As the time of Britain's nuptials approached, however, Washington had begun to evince a certain nervousness that reflected its own uncertainty as to what such a union might hold in store. In February, for example, the senior U.S. representative to E.E.C., J. Robert Schaetzel, voiced his concern over the slow rate of growth in American agricultural exports to E.E.C., complained that E.E.C. was dumping its own agricultural products in some traditional U.S. markets, and assailed the growing circle of E.E.C. preferential trade agreements as threatening fatally to undermine the provisions of the General Agreement on Tariffs and

Trade (GATT).[54] Such practices, Schaetzel warned, were bound to affect America's ability to maintain its share of NATO force levels in Europe. In October, Deputy Under Secretary of State for Economic Affairs Nathaniel Samuels underscored the toughening U.S. attitude when he warned that Britain's entry into E.E.C. should not provide the basis for more preferential arrangements and discriminatory treatment of U.S. goods. The United States, he indicated, was also worried about the international monetary implications of the U.K. bid, given the fact that sterling still financed about a third of world trade and the dollar's role as an international medium of exchange was still under pressure.[55] The big question appeared to be how Britain's indebtedness would be affected by imports from other E.E.C. countries and how that debt burden, in turn, would affect the role of the pound.

No less than when the E.E.C. was founded in 1957, the United States recognized that there were risks as well as opportunities involved in the expansion of the Common Market and the consolidation of Western Europe into an economic unit. One reason Washington had so strongly backed the British bid initially was the prevailing U.S. view that the United Kingdom, with its outward orientation and its special ties to the United States, would act as a counterweight within the E.E.C. to the inward, protectionist impulses evident in French policy. But now France itself, concerned by the growing economic and political weight within the Community of a resurgent West Germany, was bidding Britain enter as a prospective counterweight to Bonn. With the Gaullist imprint on various E.E.C. policies already established, Washington was growing worried lest an expanded Community emerge less as a twin pillar of a strengthened North Atlantic relationship than as a formidable economic rival of the United States.

35 : The Federal Republic Looks East

Exactly which would be the case now seemed to depend less perhaps on Great Britain or even France than on the Community's most economically powerful partner, the Federal Republic of Germany. At the Common Market summit meeting in December 1969 at The Hague,[56] all eyes had been focused on the newest member present, Chancellor Brandt, who had taken office at the head of a coalition of Social Democrats and Free Democrats just six weeks earlier. Brandt himself had seized the opportunity to exhort his fellow West European leaders to get the E.E.C. moving again toward closer political and economic cooperation and toward negotiations with Britain and other Western European applicants. With France now willing to go along, the other E.E.C. leaders had quickly fallen into line, a development which signaled not only a revitalization of the Common Market itself but the emergence of a new and politically more powerful role for West Germany in North Atlantic affairs.

That Germany had, in the 25 years since World War II, successfully reconciled itself—and, indeed, moved into a position of mutual confidence—with its Western allies was generally conceded by 1970. But there had been virtually no progress in a similar direction with Germany's Eastern neighbors, although Moscow had exchanged diplomatic missions with Bonn as early as 1955. For a long time, the cold war had precluded any reconciliation between a Western-allied German Federal Republic and a Communist-oriented bloc in East Europe. But it was Brandt's notion that an alleviation of the "German problem" should come not in the wake of a generalized East-West *détente* but as an integral part of it. On assuming office in October 1969, Brandt had affirmed his determination to seek a reconciliation with the East, not only as a means of easing tensions between the two Germanys but as a contribution to the broad "European peace order" of which he repeatedly spoke.[57] On March 19, 1970, he made a precedent-shattering journey across the East-West boundary to Erfurt in the German Democratic Republic, there to set his new *Ostpolitik* in motion.

A *New York Times* correspondent described what happened as Brandt drove with his East German counterpart, Premier Willi Stoph, from the Erfurt railroad station to the nearby conference site. "A hoarse cry suddenly went up from a crowd of several thousand which had been held back out of sight . . . ," he wrote. "It was far more than a welcoming cheer. It was an elemental sound from deep down in the guts—a shout to and for Germans in every part of the land that seemed to say: 'We are one people.' "[58] It was also an ironic commentary on the times that Brandt's reception in Erfurt could be interpreted either as a singularly welcome omen for his *Ostpolitik* or as an ominous signal to his Eastern neighbors of the dangers lurking behind any reciprocal opening, on their part, to the West.

In a total of two meetings with Stoph (another followed on May 21 at Kassel, West Germany), Brandt encountered only a series of rebuffs to his political overtures, although East Germany's Walter Ulbricht did hint that the two Germanys might exchange low-level diplomatic missions and that they might apply separately for membership in the U.N.[59] On the whole, however, Brandt found the Ulbricht conditions for any "normalization" of relations far too difficult to meet—the call for recognition of West Berlin as an "independent political entity," for example, and, above all, the demand for Bonn's signature on a treaty recognizing East Germany as a sovereign and separate state. Even so, Brandt himself was not reluctant to press unilaterally toward that normalization of affairs which recognized the political realities of the hour in postwar German life. He quietly buried the so-called Hallstein doctrine, under which Bonn had denied or withdrawn recognition to most governments with diplomatic ties to the Ulbricht regime. He changed the name of the Ministry for All-German Questions to that for Internal German Relations, and ceased referring to Germany's other half as the Soviet or Eastern "zone," preferring the term "German Democratic Republic" instead.

In a sense, Brandt's magnanimity was rooted in shrewd political calculation, for there were other fish in his *Ostpolitik* frying pan besides the Ulbricht species. Simultaneously with his approach to East Germany, Brandt's ministers were fanning out toward Moscow and Warsaw, there to undertake similar missions of reconciliation and there to be received more cordially than by Ulbricht and his aides. It was said that the East Germans had been pushed kicking and screaming to the conference table with Brandt, but from all outward appearances both Russia and Poland were eager recipients of the Bonn emissaries. There were several reasons why this should be so. To the extent that Communist fears of German "revanchism" were rooted in genuine anxiety stemming from experience, the anti-Nazi record of Brandt and his Social Democratic party was reassuring. Brandt had also moved swiftly upon taking office to sign the nuclear nonproliferation treaty and had clearly signaled his intention of accepting the territorial and political *status quo* in Central and Eastern Europe, both of which actions allowed the Russians and Poles to breathe additional sighs of relief.

In February, the Poles, with apparent Russian backing, agreed to open exploratory talks with Bonn aimed at a normalization of the two countries' relations. From Poland's viewpoint, this meant primarily that West Germany recognize the Oder-Neisse frontier, behind which some 40,000 square miles of prewar German territory had been placed under Polish administration, as the final and permanent border. From West Germany's viewpoint, it meant that Poland would accord full diplomatic recognition to Bonn, together with all those other perquisites that a "normalization" of relations implied. For all practical purposes the West Germans had already recognized the Oder-Neisse as a *de facto* boundary in Central Europe. *De jure* recognition was one trump card Brandt would now play to win his *quid pro quo.* By July it was evident that the two sides had reached virtual agreement, but the focus of diplomacy now shifted to the talks under way between Bonn and Moscow.[60]

These clearly held the key to the success or failure of Brandt's *Ostpolitik.* Initially, at least, the talks centered on the issue of a mutual renunciation of force by both sides, based on a recognition of the political and territorial *status quo* in Eastern Europe. From the Soviet viewpoint, such a treaty would effectively seal the territorial and political gains accruing to Russia from World War II, would open the door to stepped-up trade with the booming German economy, would speed the flow of German technology eastward, and would, as some observers saw it, free Moscow's hand in the event of trouble on its eastern frontiers with China. For West Germany, the treaty would help clear the atmosphere of suspicion and distrust that had grown up in the heart of Europe since the war; it would open the door to improved relations not only with Moscow but with Moscow's East European allies; hopefully, it would help the West Germans establish contact with their brothers in the East, perhaps even fostering improvements in their situation; and, finally, in the broadest terms, it would be a step toward the eventual peaceful reconciliation of the two Germanys themselves.

By June, a draft of such a treaty had been hammered out by Egon Bahr, an aide to Brandt, and Foreign Minister Gromyko. At this point, however, German domestic politics intervened and for a time threatened to wreck the entire course of Brandt's diplomatic offensive. Together with his Free Democratic allies, Brandt held a slim 12-seat majority in the 496-member *Bundestag,* and it was clear that a slight defection either by his coalition partners or by members of his own party could imperil ratification of any treaty that might be negotiated, and perhaps doom the government itself. In June, West German newspapers had leaked the draft of the proposed treaty with Moscow, and Brandt's Christian Democratic opponents promptly accused the government of concocting a "sell-out" which would give the Soviets all they were seeking, consign the two Germanys to permanent division, and get nothing by way of an improved status for West Berlin in return. As a result of these charges, Brandt's *Ostpolitik* became a key issue in regional elections held in North Rhine-Westphalia, Lower Saxony, and the Saar on June 14. When the results were in it was apparent that Brandt's coalition partners, the Free Democrats, led by Foreign Minister Walter Scheel, had suffered a grave setback when their representation in two states was eliminated entirely. This result, in turn, led to the defection of three Free Democrats with seats in the *Bundestag* at the party's convention in October, reducing Brandt's already small majority from 12 to six.

By this time, however, Scheel himself had already traveled to Moscow to forge revisions in the treaty's final draft that would meet some of the Christian Democratic criticisms, although members of the opposition broke precedent and refused to accompany Scheel on his mission. On August 12, Brandt was in Moscow putting his signature to the historic pact along with Premier Kosygin. But even as he prepared to sign, the German Chancellor warned his Soviet hosts that there would be no ratification of the document by the *Bundestag* unless concrete progress could be shown in the four-power talks on Berlin's status.[61]

The treaty itself was a short document, consisting of a preamble, five articles, and two appended letters, but its various clauses went considerably beyond a mere renunciation of force by both sides.[62] In return for Bonn's pledge to expand economic, scientific, and technological relations and "to respect without restriction the territorial integrity of all States in Europe within their present frontiers," including the Oder-Neisse line in Poland, Moscow acceded, in conformity with the two appended letters, to the principle of ultimate German unity "in free self-determination," relinquished the right it had claimed to intervene in West German affairs (based on two articles in the U.N. Charter which Bonn's Western allies had long considered obsolete), and formally acknowledged that, in the absence of a World War II peace treaty, ultimate responsibility for *both* Germanys and for *all* of Berlin rested with the Big Four.

Within less than a year the foundation of Brandt's *Ostpolitik* had thus been set into place, and the way was open for the conclusion of the Bonn-Warsaw pact, which was duly signed in Warsaw on December 7,[63] and for the negotiation of similar agreements normalizing

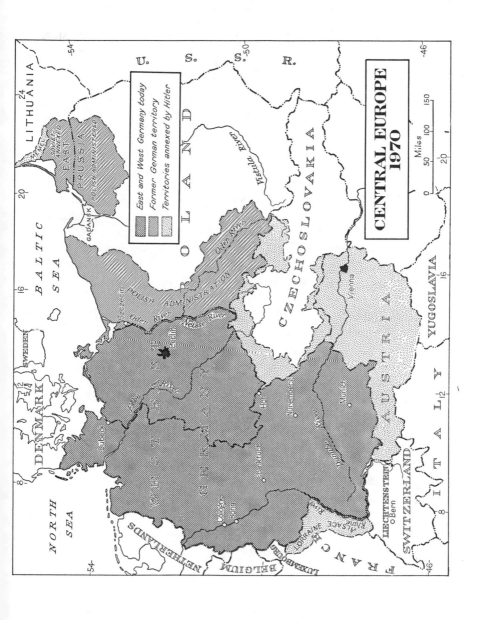

CENTRAL EUROPE
1970

East and West Germany today
Former German territory
Territories annexed by Hitler

Miles
0   50   100   150
20

NORTH
SEA

BALTIC
SEA

SWEDEN

DENMARK

NETHERLANDS

BELGIUM

LUXEMBOURG

FRANCE

ALSACE

LORRAINE

Rhine River

Cologne
Bonn

Frankfurt

WEST

GERMANY

Elbe River

Lübeck

Berlin

Nuremberg

Munich

Danube River

SWITZERLAND

LIECHTENSTEIN
o Bern

ITALY

AUSTRIA

Vienna

CZECHOSLOVAKIA

YUGOSLAVIA

POLAND

POLISH ADMINISTRATION

Oder River

Oder River

Neisse River

Szczecin

GDANSK

EAST
PRUSSIA

SOVIET
ANNEXED

POLISH ADMINISTERED

MEMEL

LITHUANIA

Vistula River

U. S. S. R.

-54

-50

-46

20

16

12

8

54

-54

16

12

8

-46

24

West Germany's relations with other East European states. In broader political terms, the way was now also open for a new four-power agreement on Berlin, perhaps also for the convening of that European security conference for which the Russians had been pressing but which West Germany's allies had made contingent upon progress in the Bonn-Moscow talks, and for the realization of NATO's periodic offers to negotiate mutual balanced force reductions in Europe.

Everything, however, appeared to hinge on Berlin, whose status appeared increasingly vulnerable with each step by East Germany toward its own legitimacy. The Ambassadors of the United States, the Soviet Union, France and Britain had been meeting in the divided city since March 26, but until Brandt put his signature to the Bonn-Moscow pact they had accomplished little more than to agree on a broad range of disagreements.[64] The Western allies wanted a written Soviet commitment that civilian traffic on West Berlin's access routes across East Germany would move unimpaired. In addition, they sought easier communication between East and West Berliners and a degree of normalization in the city's economic and political links with the Federal Republic. The Soviets had long insisted, however, that East Germany had sole responsibility for the Western traffic across 110 miles of its territory, and with Ulbricht bent on keeping matters that way it looked as though agreement would not be easy to come by. In the fall, the old harassment of Western traffic in and out of the city was sporadically renewed, and by December the allies detected a general stiffening in the Soviet position. Nonetheless, the Soviets were keenly aware that without a Berlin accord the treaty they had signed with Brandt stood little chance of entering into effect. The momentum of their own efforts toward improved relations with West Germany, therefore, seemed to point toward an ultimate settlement of the city's future, even if it had to come over the proverbial "dead body" of Walter Ulbricht.

36 : The United States and Europe

With the signing of the Bonn-Moscow pact, the diplomatic icejam that had accumulated through 25 years of cold war in Europe appeared to be breaking up. The efforts of the United States to negotiate an arms limitation agreement with the Soviet Union [65] was running in tandem with Brandt's own efforts at *rapprochement* with the East. It was hardly surprising, then, that Washington lent its generalized support to the *Ostpolitik* campaign, although the vagueness of that support occasionally irritated Brandt's followers. In his State of the World message, President Nixon had observed that "Our German ally has also undertaken steps to seek normalization of its relations with its Eastern neighbors. Since the problem of Germany remains the key to East-West problems in Europe, we would welcome such a normalization." [66] Brandt himself was in Washington for consultations on April 4–10, and repeatedly stressed that his negotiations with the East were going forward in the context of close consultation with West Germany's allies and his country's firm commitment to NATO.[67]

Nonetheless, there were persistent murmurings to the effect that Washington was less than pleased with both the pace and substance of Bonn's efforts, that a number of respected "elder statesmen" like Dean Acheson and George W. Ball were uneasy at the prospects, and that there were those in America who saw the specter of another Rapallo in the offing. Questioned about this on German television in April, Secretary Rogers flatly denied the existence of such sentiments in official quarters. "I don't see any friction at all developing," he said.[68] When the treaty itself was signed on August 12, Rogers issued a statement expressing the United States' official "satisfaction" and reiterating U.S. "confidence and support" for the policies of the Federal Republic.[69] At the same time, the State Department made public the second appended note of the treaty, a letter from the Federal Republic to the United States reporting on the "imminent signing" of the treaty and putting to rest the notion that either Russia or West Germany were about to infringe in any way on Allied rights. "Since the settlement of a peace treaty is still outstanding," the note said, "both sides take the position that the agreement under consideration does not affect the rights and responsibilities of the French Republic, the United Kingdom of Great Britain and Northern Ireland, the Union of Soviet Socialist Republics and the United States of America." [70]

If there were any reservations in Washington, they appeared to stem from the Nixon administration's frequently expressed concern for the continued viability of NATO in a rapidly changing diplomatic environment. As Richard F. Pedersen, Counselor of the State Department, put it in a speech of April 21: "We must seek every opportunity for improving relations with the countries of Eastern Europe. But we must not succumb to 'detente fever' or a sense of ennui from the welcome fact that NATO's military power has never had to be used." [71]

To be sure, as the fear of war in Central Europe continued to fade from day to day, NATO had come to resemble some sort of modern-day ark of the covenant—sacred and untouchable, but something of a relic nonetheless. Afflicted with the same mild case of schizophrenia that beset Western policy generally, the alliance had, since the Harmel report on its "future tasks" in 1967,[72] followed a two-track course of maintaining, on the one hand, its military strength and political solidarity while moving, on the other, toward *détente* with the East. The strains generated in pursuit of these divergent if complementary goals were still very much in evidence through much of 1970. Few people, for example, could have been more aware than the NATO Ministers of the increasingly global reach of Soviet power, of the Kremlin's maritime build-up, or of its thrust into the Mediterranean. Yet at the meeting of the organization's Defense Planning Committee in Brussels on December 2, the organization was forced to take note that its members had been devoting a decreasing share of their respective G.N.P.'s to defense and that the defense expenditures of the NATO countries had actually declined in real terms by 4 per cent from 1964 to 1969.[73]

That the *détente* track seemed somewhat faster than the defense track was not surprising, given the emphasis that NATO Foreign Ministers had placed on a reduction of East-West tensions at its Council meeting December 4–5, 1969 in Brussels.[74] At the May 26–27 meeting of the Council in Rome in 1970, the emphasis was even more apparent, with Italian Premier Rumor calling for prompt and forthright conversations between NATO and Warsaw Pact members while British Foreign Minister Michael Stewart was pushing for the establishment of a standing committee to deal with East-West affairs in Europe.[75] Secretary Rogers himself had taken the occasion to endorse once again the proposal of his European allies for negotiations toward mutual and balanced force reductions with the East.[76] In a joint declaration at the conclusion of the meeting, the Council Ministers issued an invitation to "interested states to hold exploratory talks" on the matter, suggesting four "considerations" on which the discussions could be based: (1) that the reductions "not operate to the military disadvantage of either side having regard for the differences arising from geographical and other considerations"; (2) that they be carried forward on "a basis of reciprocity"; (3) that they include both "stationed and indigenous forces" in the central European area; and (4) that an adequate system of "verification and controls" be established to enforce the agreement.[77] On the whole, it was the most far-reaching invitation yet issued to the Soviet bloc; and when no response was forthcoming in subsequent months, the NATO Ministers, undiscouraged, proceeded to renew their call at the Council meeting in Brussels on December 3–4, adding that they would also be ready to explore the matter of a European security conference as soon as the four-power talks on Berlin achieved a satisfactory conclusion.[78]

With so many doves of peace taking wing, there were indeed legitimate grounds for the fear that NATO's security function might get derailed. As the year began, total NATO troop strength in Europe stood at 2,225,000 against the Warsaw Pact's 2,390,000, with the latter heavily superior in tanks and planes.[79] In Germany, the U.S. 7th Army, cut from 285,000 to 165,000 during the 1960's, felt particularly vulnerable and neglected, while Washington was abuzz with talk of further cutbacks to come. When the eight-power NATO Nuclear Planning Group met in Venice, June 8–9, Secretary Laird faced pressure from his European counterparts to approve a strategic "second strike" against Soviet targets if an initial tactical nuclear response failed to halt any Soviet advance.[80] The suggestion, though not adopted, reflected European anxieties that a weakened NATO conventional defense would collapse should a real test come.

For its part, the Nixon administration was fully aware of the problems besetting NATO conventional defense forces. On September 30, President Nixon told NATO Secretary-General Manlio Brosio that he wanted the Europeans to increase their own troop commitments to NATO rather than supply the increased cash support for U.S. forces which some European governments were offering.[81] On October 1, Western Europe's Defense Ministers (the so-called "Eurogroup") met to discuss the burden-sharing issue but failed to agree on increased force levels. Backed by Italy and the Netherlands, the Federal Republic's Helmut Schmidt proposed an annual donation of $250 million to $300 million to help ease the cost of maintaining American forces. Closer to Nixon's view, the United Kingdom said it would consider increasing its own defense effort.[82]

These differences were at least partially resolved in the course of the year. Shortly before the December NATO Council meeting, the

Defense Planning Committee adopted a document entitled "Alliance Defense for the Seventies," a broad set of force-level recommendations that had been in preparation since early in the year.[83] At the same time, the ten-nation Eurogroup approved a "defense improvement program" that would channel nearly a billion dollars into the alliance's military capability over the next five years, designed to improve bases, forces, and weapons.[84] Under these programs, allied armor, tactical air, and antisubmarine forces were singled out for improvement, as were NATO's conventional forces in the Mediterranean. At the same time, the 24 existing divisions in Central and Northern Europe would be raised to something approaching war strength.

Commenting on these developments, Secretary Laird was quick to hail the "new spirit" of the alliance and "the move toward a more proper sharing of the military defense burden," while Secretary Rogers praised the meeting as "one of the most important in the history of the alliance." [85] In his December 3 message to the NATO Council, President Nixon echoed his own satisfaction with the defense improvement program. "We have agreed that NATO's conventional forces must not only be maintained, but in certain key areas strengthened," he said. "Given a similar approach by our Allies, the United States will maintain and improve its own forces in Europe and will not reduce them unless there is reciprocal action from our adversaries." [86]

This was a bold pledge for the President to make, given the fact that more than half of the U.S. Senate was on record in support of the so-called Mansfield resolution introduced in 1966, but never formally acted upon. It stated that "a substantial reduction of United States forces permanently stationed in Europe can be made without adversely affecting either our resolve or ability to meet our commitment under the North Atlantic Treaty." [87] Nor had Senator Mansfield been put off by the talk of mutual and balanced force reductions that occupied NATO circles in 1970. In April, shortly after Brandt had been in Washington urging no troop reductions by the U.S., Mansfield was arguing that "there has been no indication whatsoever that the Soviet Union has been interested in negotiation of a mutual reduction. The prospects for its realization are extremely remote and for all practical purposes irrelevant." [88] Mansfield advised that the United States alone—and not West Germany or the Soviet Union—should determine U.S. policy on the number of American troops maintained on the Continent, and he favored a reduction in line with his greater emphasis on U.S. domestic needs.

If the administration was equally aware of the balance-of-payments burdens and domestic needs that so concerned Senator Mansfield and others, however, it was clearly not prepared to reduce unilaterally its commitments to Europe in order to ease the strain. "We can no more disengage from Europe than from Alaska," Nixon had said in the State of the World message,[89] and the President's steadfast support of the alliance's military preparedness throughout the year was more than a token of his sincerity. Like many Americans, the President was nonetheless aware that Europe itself was changing and that the North Atlantic relationship was clearly entering a new and uncertain phase. For the moment, Europe and America remained bound by their common fears, as well as their common hopes. But Europe and America alike had their own internal interests to pursue and their own domestic troubles to attend to, and the lure of East-West *détente* appeared to offer tempting answers to a number of their mutual problems.

10 : Dollars, Trade, and Aid

Frenchmen hailed it as a vintage year for wines, the best some said since 1945. But for the American economy, 1970 was a year of trial, tension, and turmoil—a highly unfitting climax to what had, until 1969 at least, been a vintage decade of surging growth and prosperity in America's economic history. When the year began, unemployment stood at 3.9 per cent of the labor force, consumer prices were rising at the rate of 6 per cent or more a year, and the administration's budget for fiscal year 1971 was projecting a $53-billion growth in the gross national product (G.N.P.) together with a theoretical surplus in federal income over expenditures of some $1.3 billion.[1] When it ended, unemployment stood at 6 per cent, inflation had abated somewhat (although it still exceeded 5 per cent), the projected budget surplus had turned into a newly projected deficit of more than $20 billion, and for all intents and purposes the economy had failed to register any real growth at all.

From the administration's viewpoint, the troubles were clearly traceable to the guns-*and*-butter decisions of the Johnson presidency,[2] when the nation sought simultaneously to carry on a business-as-usual policy at home while spending $20 billion or more a year on the Vietnam war abroad. And, indeed, by 1970 there were few economists around who were denying that this "untaxed" war had come to place an intolerable strain on the American economy, belying in the

252

process the traditional Marxist view that in capitalist societies war is always "good business." As Nixon contended in his budget message of February 2: "Government spending rose by more than 50% from 1964 to 1968, fanning the flames of inflation with a 4-year deficit of $39 billion." [3]

For the President's Democratic opponents, however, the real fault could be traced less to past occupants of the White House than to the current one. It was the Nixon administration, after all, which had advertised its FY 1971 budget as "anti-inflationary," which had promised balanced growth with price stability, and which, in the end, had delivered none of these. On the contrary, as far as the President's critics could see, he had only succeeded in adding a new and increasingly serious problem to the inflationary spiral already at hand—a full-fledged business recession and a rising tide of unemployment.

Wherever the blame might lie, it was clear that the economy had entered an extraordinary and perplexing phase in which rising prices and rising joblessness seemed to go hand in hand. For various and widely debated reasons, moreover, prices appeared reluctant to respond to the traditional applications of fiscal and monetary restraints. As the Organization for Economic Cooperation and Development (O.E.C.D.) pointed out in its December 1970 survey, ". . . there are also disquieting signs that the problem of inflation may have got worse in the sense that, where traditional restrictive policies have been applied, the effect on prices has been less rapid and less long-lasting than in the past." The report went on to warn that "It may not be easy for the United States to achieve in the 1970s the degree of price stability which in the past was associated with an undesirable high level of unemployment." [4]

Through most of the year, the approach of the administration seemed to emphasize a gradual application of brakes combined with a great deal of talk about rosier economic prospects ahead, the latter apparently designed to spur business and consumer confidence. In January, for example, the Chairman of the President's Council of Economic Advisers, Paul W. McCracken, was forecasting a drop in the rate of inflation to 3.5 per cent by year's end while maintaining that the increase in unemployment would not be large.[5] By late June, however, with the stock market falling sharply and unemployment rising to 5 per cent, McCracken was telling the nation that things would probably get worse before they got better.[6] As late as mid-July, the President was predicting that the last half of 1970 would "definitely see the economy turning up," [7] but by then administration policy itself had begun to shift away from deflationary tactics as economic activity continued to sag. The altered policy was to accept a growing budget deficit as a means of limiting the slowdown and to accept as well some moderate increases in federal expenditures beyond those allotted in the original budget. With an eye on the wage-price spiral, however, the administration continued to resist strongly any program expansion which would substantially raise federal outlays beyond 1970.[8]

Since the President himself had repeatedly ruled out any resort to wage and price controls, the immediate success of his anti-inflation drive now seemed cast into doubt. Even before 1970 began, economists outside the government, such as former Under Secretary of the Treasury Robert V. Roosa, had been calling for some sort of wage-price controls to bank the inflationary fires.[9] The new Federal Reserve Board Chairman, Arthur F. Burns, who had been appointed in January to replace the retiring William McChesney Martin, Jr., announced in May that he was in favor of a modest incomes policy, while Secretary of Housing and Urban Development George Romney called for a new federal commission to ride herd on wage and price increases, saying the clamp on spending and credit had not been enough.[10] These views were discreetly echoed by an O.E.C.D. report urging the use of formal wage-price guidelines.[11] In June, Treasury Secretary David M. Kennedy again rejected these suggestions,[12] but in a major televised address on the economy later that month, President Nixon, while barring use of emergency wage-price controls which Congress was preparing to grant him, appealed to the "social responsibility of business and labor" and announced a series of periodic "inflation alerts" to be prepared by the Council of Economic Advisers. These alerts, the President said, would "spotlight the significant areas of wage and price increases and objectively analyze their impact on the price level." [13] As such, they would act as a sort of public check on private business and labor practice and in that sense signaled a step toward the kind of governmental regulation which the President, to that point, had rigorously eschewed.

In the months that followed the Council of Economic Advisers issued two inflation alerts, one in August and one in December, criticizing "inflationary" wage and price increases in such industries as construction, automobiles, and oil.[14] But the alerts appeared to have little impact in terms of slowing the rise in prices. On December 14, the President announced that he would appoint Secretary Kennedy Ambassador-at-Large, effective February 1, and would designate Governor John B. Connally of Texas, a Democrat, as the new Secretary of the Treasury.[15] The move was seen, in part at least, as an effort by the President to cast a fresh approach to the economic problems facing the nation and to recruit to his cabinet a strong and politically significant figure to aid in the process. With a prominent Democrat heading the Treasury, moreover, the President may have hoped to undercut at least some of the criticism of his policies building among his Democratic opponents in Congress.

37 : The Dollar and the World

Congress was not the only place where concern over the President's policies was being felt, however. Because of its preeminent role in world trade and finance, and because of the dollar's key role as a reserve currency, a medium of exchange, and a standard of value in the international monetary system, the United States had for many years been required to manage its own economy with international as well as domestic factors in mind. Inflation or contraction at home could have disruptive effects abroad, particularly at a time when many other advanced, industrialized nations were struggling to cope with inflationary pressures of their own. As the President pointed out in his State of the World message: "In the economic sphere, more than in almost any other area, what we do has a tremendous impact on the rest of the world. Steady non-inflationary growth in our domestic economy will promote steady non-inflationary growth in the world as a whole. The stability of our dollar is essential to the stability of the world monetary system." [16]

That system, with its heavy reliance on the dollar, had already been subject to a number of disruptions and crises throughout the 1960's, stemming in part from the difficulties of individual countries and in part from inadequate international adjustment mechanisms by which excessive and prolonged payments imbalances could be avoided. The size and persistence of the U.S. payments deficit in many of those years had also called forth frequent expressions of foreign concern. Yet despite the internal difficulties besetting the American economy and the continued weakening of the dollar through inflation, 1970 proved a year of relative calm on the international monetary front. To a large extent, this was attributable to reforms emerging out of crisis situations in the past. In 1969, particularly, the world took what President Nixon described as "a step of profound importance" [17] when it moved, under the auspices of the International Monetary Fund (I.M.F.), to create a new form of reserve asset—the so-called Special Drawing Rights (S.D.R.'s) or "paper gold" as they came to be called.[18]

As a basic supplement to gold and the dollar, S.D.R.'s were designed to assure a more adequate supply of internationally acceptable money to meet the reserve needs of a steadily growing world economy, and there was hope that someday they would become the world's primary source of reserve growth. Gold had long ceased to be an adequate source of new reserves; the separation of the private and official markets for gold in 1968 had further diminished its importance in the international monetary system. Nor was it feasible that the world be forced to rely more heavily on dollars flowing from a U.S. balance-of-payments deficit to meet its expanding needs. While the mere existence of S.D.R.'s could not guarantee an adequate supply of international money, their continuous and periodic creation by conscious decision of the international community (through the I.M.F.) would lend a measure of rationality and flexibility to an international monetary system that had, in the view of various experts, too long been lacking in both. The first $3.4 billion in S.D.R.'s were distributed among 105 of the 115 member states of the I.M.F. on January 1, 1970, with the United States, as the Fund's largest contributor, drawing the largest share—about $850 million. Another $2.9 billion were set for distribution on January 1, 1971, and a like amount on January 1, 1972.

It was the creation of S.D.R.'s which, in the administration's view,[19] underlay the atmosphere of tranquility which prevailed in foreign exchange markets as 1970 opened. And it was their widespread acceptance which contributed to the relative calm in international monetary affairs that prevailed throughout the year. The United States both accepted and paid out S.D.R.'s to finance its payments position in 1970, and the intent was to continue doing so in the years ahead. But there were other factors contributing to greater stability as well. The U.S. balance of payments, on the official settlements basis, had shown a surplus for the years 1968 and 1969, after a prolonged period of worrisome deficits. While much of the surplus was attributable to an inflow of short-term foreign capital seeking the higher interest rates that prevailed in the United States in those years, the turnaround was nonetheless welcome news. In 1969, moreover, U.S. official gold holdings, which had been dwindling in years past, rose by $967 million, while the U.S. gold tranche position in the I.M.F. improved by $1,034 million.

Given the spirit of international cooperation which had manifested itself in the creation of S.D.R.'s, then, there was reason to hope that other problems afflicting the international monetary system could also be resolved. And, indeed, the international financial community took advantage of the relatively crisis-free atmosphere of 1970 to undertake additional improvements. On February 9, the I.M.F. Board of Governors, in a step designed to augment the Fund's ability to deal with financial emergencies, voted a substantial increase in members' quotas that would have the effect of raising total I.M.F. reserves from $21,372 million to a possible maximum of $28,900 million.[20] Some 107 of the Fund's members consented to the specified increases in their quotas, the United States share rising by $1.54 billion, of which $385 million in gold was paid into the Fund at year's end.[21]

The need for more flexible techniques and practices that could help improve the adjustment mechanisms governing payments imbalances was also occupying the interest of the I.M.F.'s Executive Directors. Experience had shown that revaluations of national currencies were too frequently resisted as a means of rectifying payments imbalances either for reasons of politics or national prestige or because of the sometimes wrenching and painful consequences for national economies of altering exchange rates. Yet adjustments were clearly necessary if chronic payments imbalances were to be avoided. In a report entitled, *The Role of Exchange Rates in the Adjustments of International Payments,*[22] the Executive Directors singled out three possible means of improvement: a widening of the margins within which exchange rates could fluctuate around their par values (thus reducing the need for revaluations); more frequent (and therefore smaller) changes in the par values themselves, thereby avoiding the discomforts associated with long-delayed and substantial revaluations; and the temporary use of floating exchange rates, with appropriate safeguards, to facilitate transitions from one par value to another.

At the annual meeting of the I.M.F. Board of Governors in Copenhagen on September 21–25, the United States supported continued exploration of ways of making the adjustment mechanism more flexible and also called for an examination of the possible use of S.D.R.'s to help in financing development efforts in the less developed countries.[23] No immediate decisions were reached on these various proposals by the assembled delegates, although they endorsed the broad conclusions drawn in the Executive Directors' report. Inasmuch as inflationary pressures had been the most frequent source of exchange rate difficulties, many delegates also focused their concern on the need for member states to pursue internal policies that would keep aggregate demand within the bounds of available resources. This was a problem of particular concern in 1970, since inflationary pressures were rampant in much of the world; it was also a problem of special concern and relevance to the United States.

As noted above, the United States had experienced a massive inflow of short-term foreign capital during 1968 and 1969, when tight money policies were in effect as a curb on inflation, pushing the payments balance for both years into the black. With an easing of money and credit restrictions beginning early in 1970, however, the process reversed itself. As the growth of the Eurodollar market had shown, the world had an immense stock of mobile funds that were highly sensitive to changes in interest rates in the advanced countries. In 1970, some $6 billion of short-term funds flowed out of the United States to Western Europe, where tight money and credit policies still continued in effect. The flow helped restore needed reserves to some countries—notably Britain and France—and added still further to the strong reserve position of West Germany. But it also contributed to a record 1970 balance-of-payments deficit for the United States of $9.8 billion on the official settlements basis. Such flows of liquid funds were not inspired by financial crises or necessarily by speculation in anticipation of revaluation of certain currencies, but they constituted a major problem nonetheless, complicating the management of both domestic and international monetary policy among the countries affected.

While the I.M.F. moved to develop ways of counteracting these volatile flows of liquid funds, the international financial community began to express anew its concern over the U.S. payments deficit to which the flows were now contributing. At a time when S.D.R.'s had been introduced with a view toward ending the world's dependence on continued dollar deficits to finance the expansion of trade and investment, such massive deficits as the one recorded in 1970 could only serve to distort orderly monetary arrangements, feeding inflationary pressures that were already world-wide in scope. The continuing build-up of liquid claims on the United States, moreover— claims which had for many years exceeded America's international reserves, was seen by some Europeans as a gathering menace to the stability of the international monetary system as a whole. Sooner or later, they reasoned, creditor countries might refuse to accept still more dollars, with a resultant breakdown in the system so laboriously and painstakingly constructed since World War II.[24] As the Managing Director of the I.M.F., Pierre-Paul Schweitzer, put it in remarks at the Board of Governors meeting in September, "From the standpoint of the functioning of the international system, by far the most important problem is posed by the deficit in the balance of payments of the United States." [25]

From the American viewpoint, the balance-of-payments position of the United States depended not only on the state of its domestic economy and on the economic policies of the administration but on the economic performance and policies of other countries, as well, including foreign decisions about such fundamental matters as exchange rates.[26] In that sense, no matter what constraints the U.S. government imposed on the domestic economy, and no matter how many measures it adopted to alter or control individual categories of international transactions, the United States would not be able to abolish its payments deficits if many of its major trading partners maintained exchange rates or followed balance-of-payments policies that enabled them to accumulate surpluses over and above their S.D.R. allocations.

Despite the prevailing calm and the efforts toward reform in 1970, therefore, it remained evident that the international monetary system was still fraught with unsolved and potentially explosive problems. There was an obvious and pressing need for the United States to emerge from its recession and bring a halt, simultaneously, to its inflation, thereby restoring balance to its own economy and reducing the pressures on its international payments position, as well. If 1970 were any measure, however, that prospect looked more distant than many central bankers would have hoped. Much appeared to depend on a continuing and healthy growth in world trade, but in 1970 grow-

ing protectionist sentiment within the United States itself was placing
even that possibility in danger.

38 : The Shadow of Protectionism

In 1970, the United States enjoyed a surplus in its balance of trade
with other nations of some $2.1 billion, more than triple the $638
million surplus in merchandise trade of 1969. Economists had been
fond of pointing out, however, that certain unusual factors lay behind
1970's whopping $9.8 billion payments deficit, and it was entirely
possible that other nonrecurring factors were lurking behind the improved trade surplus as well. In fact, when U.S. exports jumped ahead
by a surprising 15 per cent in 1970 (to a total of $42 billion), the rise
was promptly attributed in part to such special factors as a sudden
leap in aircraft sales and a bulge in agricultural exports. The 11 per
cent increase in imports (to $40 billion) was attributable largely to
another sharp rise in the purchase of foreign consumer goods.[27]

There was a comparable surge in the dollar value of world trade
as a whole in 1970, due in part to the effects of widespread inflation
but attributable also to continuing tariff cuts under the Kennedy
Round of trade concessions negotiated in 1967 under the auspices of
the General Agreement on Tariffs and Trade (GATT). On January 1,
1970, the third of five staged duty reductions agreed to in those
negotiations went into effect, with the fourth and fifth cuts due on
January 1, 1971 and January 1, 1972, respectively.[28] This brought 26
of the world's most advanced industrial nations to the 60 per cent
stage of the over-all reductions, under which tariffs on thousands of
nonagricultural products would ultimately be slashed by an average
of 35 per cent, with duties on many items reduced by 50 per cent
and more.

These were rosy figures that augured well for the continued expansion of world trade, but from the Nixon administration's viewpoint the time for complacency had hardly arrived. With protectionist
sentiment on the rise again in the United States, the President moved
in May to order the U.S. Tariff Commission to conduct an inquiry
into the competitive posture of U.S. industry,[29] less with an eye to
establishing the strength of U.S. exports than to assessing the impact
on the economy of the country's rising imports.[30] In October, Secretary of Commerce Maurice Stans predicted a trade surplus in excess of

$3 billion for the United States in 1970 but warned simultaneously that increased competition coupled with foreign trade barriers could soon have a deleterious impact on America's trade balance, its economy, and its world role.[31]

These scattered indications of trouble brewing on the horizon had not been reflected in the administration's own trade bill submitted to Congress in November 1969.[32] It was a relatively modest measure in the "free trade" tradition, granting the President limited authority to reduce tariffs, eliminate the protective American Selling Price (A.S.P.) system of customs valuation for certain products, and improve the granting of "adjustment assistance" to workers and companies harmed by import competition. Even while this bill was being written, however, it was evident that Secretary Stans was encountering difficulties in his effort to negotiate voluntary quotas on non-cotton textiles with the countries of Western Europe, Japan, and other Asian suppliers (cotton textiles themselves had been subject to quota restrictions for a number of years). President Nixon had come to office pledging special relief in that regard to American textile workers and manufacturers, and one of the more significant developments of 1970 was the way in which this campaign pledge had unloosed the gates to a generalized outpouring of protectionist sentiment.

The administration itself ultimately and ruefully recognized that the issue had snowballed entirely out of hand. In January, on precisely the day GATT officials were launching an attack on non-tariff barriers and calling for their elimination, the Chairman of the powerful House Ways and Means Committee, Wilbur D. Mills, was warning that textile quotas would have to be imposed by legislation unless voluntary agreement with exporting countries could be reached promptly.[33] In February, Secretary Stans himself fed protectionist hopes when he announced that some sort of quota—if not voluntary, then legislative—would have to be imposed by the end of the year.[34] During the annual session of the Contracting Parties of GATT, held in Geneva February 17 to 27, the United States fully endorsed Director-General Olivier Long's call for major reductions in non-tariff barriers,[35] but the administration's own refusal to end import quotas on oil could be taken as evidence that its own councils were divided on the issue and that the divisions were weakening its general posture in support of freer trade.

It would be an exaggeration to say that this was all that those hungering for a degree of protection against the rising tide of imports needed. Nonetheless, on April 13, Representative Mills introduced revised trade legislation (the so-called Mills bill),[36] which set quotas not only for non-cotton textiles but for shoes as well, limiting their import by country of origin and by category but allowing for a margin beyond the fixed limitations to be agreed upon through bilateral consultation. In addition, the bill liberalized the provisions for relief by import restrictions when a domestic industry could show injury from imports, under the so-called "escape clause" provision of existing trade legislation. In the hearings that followed, other industries seeking protection urged still broader applications of the quota device, and the door to further restrictive trade practices seemed to swing wide open. By July 1, the Ways and Means Committee was judging relief for textiles and shoes alone as unfair to other, equally hard-pressed industries, and Mills himself was calling for a "trigger" device that would impose import quotas on any product having a disruptive impact on domestic business.[37]

On July 14, the Committee approved and sent to the floor of the House what was generally thought to be the most restrictive piece of trade legislation seriously considered by Congress in 35 years. In its final version, the House bill not only imposed mandatory quotas on textiles and shoes, broadened the escape clause provisions of old legislation, and adopted Mills' trigger device; it also sought to toughen anti-dumping rules and to stiffen the so-called countervailing duties which the United States could impose upon findings that foreign nations were unfairly subsidizing their exports.[38] There was more to come, however. In October, the Senate Finance Committee voted out similar legislation that was even more restrictive, denying to the President the power to remove the A.S.P. method of customs valuation which the House had granted.[39] To veto-proof its bill, moreover, the Senate Committee attached it as an amendment to the Social Security bill, which the President could refuse to sign only at his political peril.

For its part, the Nixon administration had long since expressed its own concern that such restrictive legislation would open the door to a trade war that would benefit no one, and its warnings had been echoed ominously by America's trading partners, particularly the E.E.C. In his own letter to Chairman Mills on May 11, prior to hearings on the proposed legislation, the President wrote that "Progress toward freer trade should continue. We must encourage it. Without the strong support of the United States, the world's largest trader, this progress could falter." [40] When the Mills bill was reported out of committee in July, administration officials denounced it and warned that its restrictions on imports could fan the flames of inflation in the United States.[41] When Kenneth N. Davis, Jr., Assistant Secretary of Commerce for Domestic and International Business, urged the President in June to back legislation limiting imports of textiles, apparel, and footwear, declaring that voluntary quotas would not work,[42] he was promptly repudiated by Secretary Stans, who then announced Davis' resignation.

Despite these efforts to halt the protectionist trend, however, the administration had also "reluctantly" agreed to a legislated quota on textiles, and there were some who thought it secretly welcomed the Mills bill—which, after all, had not yet become law—as a means of gaining concessions from trading partners.[43] When the U.S.-Japanese textile talks broke off in June, moreover, the President simultaneously announced that the domestic shoe industry would be eligible for "adjustment assistance" and in an unusual step asked the Tariff Commission to look into whatever damage that industry might be suffering under the escape clause proviso.[44] There was also a certain ambivalence present in the testimony of administration officials before the Senate Finance Committee in the fall. Secretary Stans, for example, questioned whether the Mills bill would invite a loss of U.S. exports through foreign retaliation, while Secretary Rogers was sure that it would.[45] To Senator Fulbright, such ambivalence seemed to stem as much from the administration's "southern strategy" as from any natural antagonism between the State Department's primary concerns and those of the Department of Commerce.[46] With a fair concentration of textile plants in the South, the President was perhaps doubly mindful of his unfulfilled campaign pledge.

Whatever the case, Congress in the end passed no trade legislation at all in 1970, leaving the volatile issue for consideration at its next session. On the surface, at least, the President had been spared the embarrassment of a final test on the protectionist issue. Nonetheless, it was clear that the vague isolationist sentiments which afflicted and at times infested American foreign policy in 1970 had become equally evident in the nation's trade policies as well. Discussing the rise of protectionist attitudes before a gathering of dignitaries at Malmö, Sweden on October 30, Ambassador Joseph A. Greenwald, the

Permanent U.S. Representative to the O.E.C.D., told his listeners: [47] "I would like to be able to tell you today that this is mainly smoke and that no real fire lies behind it. If I did, it would be misleading and perhaps dangerous."

As Greenwald explained, protectionist sentiment had struck firmer roots in the United States than the mere presence of a recession or of chronic balance-of-payments problems could explain. A great many Americans were not only questioning their own role in the world, they were also questioning the world's attitude toward America. They saw their allies in Europe invoking restrictive agricultural policies at a time when the United States itself was struggling to put its agriculture on a market basis. With agricultural products accounting for 17.4 per cent of total American exports, they resented the fact that Europe's highly subsidized farmers were capturing foreign markets that had traditionally been the preserve of the United States. They saw the value-added tax being introduced by the E.E.C. as another devious effort by Europeans to raise border charges against U.S. goods. They wondered why the United States should play by the international rules laid down by GATT when the E.E.C. had woven a network of preferential trade agreements embracing two dozen countries and when a nation like Japan maintained not only a larger number of import quotas than any other industrialized country but also restricted the entry of capital investment from abroad.

To be sure, the United States was not free of restrictive practices itself. There was the A.S.P. system which Nixon had asked Congress to eliminate. There were "buy American" rules and a growing list of technical standards and quality certification procedures which acted as non-tariff barriers to trade. And now there was the prospect of additional quotas on imports, although under the circumstances that device ran counter to GATT rules. Even so, however, some Americans seemed to feel that the equality and partnership concepts which the President was stressing in his foreign policy pronouncements were not being reciprocated by the nation's allies. With the A.F.L./ C.I.O. backing import quotas as a means of saving American jobs,[48] even organized labor had shifted to an unequivocal stand against trade liberalization.

If the logic of comparative advantage argued for freer trade, therefore, the passions of the times did not. And, indeed, it could be argued that the nation had relatively little to gain from any further reduction in trade barriers—at least in terms of manufactured goods—because, in any case, a decreased proportion of U.S. earnings from abroad in the years to come would derive from exports of manufactured products. In a paper prepared for the Atlantic Conference in Puerto Rico, economist Lawrence Krause pointed out that the United States was moving rapidly toward a service-oriented economy, as opposed to one dominated by the production of goods.[49] In such an economy, goods for export could be expected to constitute a diminishing role in the trade balance. In support of his contention, Krause cited a Labor Department study which indicated that more than two-thirds of the American work force would be employed in service industries such as education, government, finance, health, etc. by 1980. By that same year, Krause suggested, the returns from massive private American investments abroad would have become so great as to obviate the need for a favorable trade balance in the over-all balance-of-payments posture of the nation. Already in 1970 such investments were returning almost $9 billion to the plus side of America's balance-of-payments ledger. (At the same time, a total of $5.8 billion in private funds was being added to the nation's direct and portfolio investments abroad.) While Krause pointed out that U.S. agricultural exports—and U.S. consumers, generally—would still definitely stand to gain from freer trade, his remarks nonetheless raised questions about the urgent necessity for freer trade policies for the United States, given the existence of certain long-run trends.

In the long run, of course, as a noted economist once observed, we are all dead. The immediate problem for the United States in 1970 was clearly to curb the inflationary trend which, if left unchecked, could only erode the nation's trade and payments posture further. It was chiefly a domestic problem, and it showed the profound impact which domestic economic decisions could have on America's international economic and political role. In 1970 the President was obviously determined to slay the inflationary dragon, but in the peculiar economic circumstances of the time it seemed increasingly likely that he had unleashed the dragon of unemployment in the process. The key question facing his administration at year's end was how great a political risk any renewed dampening of the economy would entail. If unemployment continued to rise—and prices as well—the President appeared to have little choice but to turn to some form of those wage and price controls he had so stoutly resisted since taking office.

39 : Aid in the Out-Basket

Given such gloomy economic prospects at home, it might have seemed altogether natural in 1970 that foreign aid should turn up on the presidential—and congressional—chopping block as well. In fact, however, a trend of dwindling assistance to the less developed countries had been under way for some time, related less to the financial and economic problems that had come to press upon the nation than to a generalized sense of frustration as to what aid could accomplish and a growing skepticism as to the kind of commitment it entailed.

When the U.N.-proclaimed Decade of Development [50] got under way early in the 1960's there were widespread hopes that a worldwide effort to bridge the poverty gap between rich and poor nations could succeed. The less developed countries themselves—many of them in the first blush of independence after years of colonial rule—seemed determined to forge ahead. Many had drawn up ambitious development plans stressing self-help and acknowledging the need for sweeping social changes. Spurred both by cold war competition and their own rising levels of prosperity, the developed nations seemed ready and willing to help. The United States had paved the way with its Mutual Security programs of the 1950's. The Soviet Union was following suit with its own aid program, while the recovered nations of Western Europe and Japan were also pitching in. At the multilateral level, such organizations as the World Bank and the U.N. Development Program were expanding their activities.

Against this background of hope and determination, the U.N. goals set for the First Development Decade seemed modest and entirely within reach. They called initially for a 5 per cent annual growth rate in national income for the developing countries by 1970 (later changed to 5 per cent in G.N.P.) and for a yearly contribution by the rich nations of 1 per cent of their national income (later G.N.P.) to help make it possible. Though modest, these goals were only partially achieved. While developing countries exceeded the 5 per cent growth rate, developed countries consistently failed to achieve their 1 per cent target. As a percentage of G.N.P., in fact, contributions to the development effort by the rich nations had actually been declining, and there were many poor nations which had not even begun to lay the foundations of development. As the U.N. General Assembly pointed out in a resolution adopted October 24, 1970: ". . . the level of living of countless millions of people in the developing part of the world is still pitifully low. Those people are often still under-nourished, uneducated, unemployed and wanting in many other basic amenities of life. While a part of the world lives in great comfort and even affluence, much of the larger part suffers from abject poverty, and in fact the disparity is continuing to widen. This lamentable situation has contributed to the aggravation of world tension.[51]

To an extent, the Decade of Development had become a decade of disillusionment. The vision of a world-wide effort, in which rich and poor alike would join hands to conquer poverty, had proved both eminently practical and discouragingly naive. It was practical because it worked so well for nations like South Korea and the Republic of China, the latter eventually even joining the ranks of aid-givers as opposed to aid-recipients. It was naive because so many deep-rooted social and political obstacles—rapid population growth, corruption, tribal rivalries, unyielding traditions, and resistance to change among them—stood so often and so unexpectedly in the way of economic progress.

In its *World Economic Survey, 1969–1970,* the U.N.'s Department of Social and Economic Affairs reported that of 56 less developed countries with development plans in operation, almost two-thirds had failed to achieve their goals.[52] The report noted that there were also a large number of shortfalls in terms of per capita consumption, with some countries actually experiencing a reduction in the figures. "In almost a third of the developing countries for which measurements can be made," the Department said, "the increase in private consumption between 1960 and 1967 did not keep pace with the expansion in popu-lation. . . ." On the other hand, the Department also pointed out that "at the other end of the scale, in rather more than one fourth of the countries, the rise in private consumption was at least twice as fast as the growth in population." [53] The report did note that the 1960's saw widespread improvement in infant mortality rates, per capita food consumption, primary and secondary school enrollment, and agricultural output. But it observed that the gross inequities in the distribution of income that were present when the 1960's began were still present and virtually unchanged when the decade drew to a close. On the whole, the average annual rate of growth in the G.N.P.'s of all developing countries for the years 1960 to 1967 was estimated to be 4.7 per cent, a figure halved on a per capita basis because of continuing sharp increases in population growth.

Nor had the developed countries lived up to their end of the bargain with any greater degree of success. According to the Development Assistance Committee of the O.E.C.D., only six countries (Australia, Belgium, France, the Netherlands, Portugal, and the United Kingdom) provided total net flows to developing countries in 1970 which exceeded the officially accepted target of 1 per cent of G.N.P.[54] The total net flow of resources to the less developed countries in 1970, the Committee reported, was $15.6 billion, or about $1 billion higher than in 1969. However, the Committee noted that "price increases in most countries have been such that the real resources transferred per person in 1970 were little, if at all, higher than ten years earlier." The Committee also observed that the United States was among ten countries to increase their net flows in 1970 as compared to 1969. But it also noted that the United States ranked 16th—ahead only of Norway—among donor nations in terms of the percentage of its G.N.P. going into the development effort. In terms of official development assistance (as opposed to total net flows, including private investment) the U.S. contribution actually shrank in 1970 to $3.1 billion— the lowest amount since 1961. As a percentage of G.N.P., it dropped from 0.33 per cent in 1969 to 0.31 per cent in 1970.

In his budget message to Congress on February 2,[55] President Nixon recalled the efforts of his administration "to identify more effective ways to encourage international development and stability with a limited availability of Government funds. I have concluded," he said, "that the answers lie in greater initiatives by the countries we assist, more trade, a larger role for private enterprise, and increased reliance on cooperative, multilateral efforts." In terms of the Agency for International Development (AID), this meant that the agency's own budget authority would be reduced to the lowest level on record— $1.8 billion—a move prompted in part, the President explained, by an effort to forestall cutting of the agency's budget by Congress. In any event, the House in June proceeded to cut even this record low figure by 25 per cent,[56] while some Senators even toyed with the idea of doing away with AID altogether.[57]

In his budget message, the President also asked for reduced allocations for the Export-Import Bank, the Peace Corps, and the Food for Peace program, although Congress acceded to his request that U.S.

contributions to multilateral financial institutions be raised substantially.[58] In November, the administration went back to the Congress with a supplemental request for $1 billion in additional economic and military aid for Cambodia, Israel, South Korea, Jordan, Lebanon, and Indonesia, of which $340 million was for military assistance (bringing the total military assistance program funds requested for FY 1971 to $775 million) and another $500 million was to finance military credit sales to Israel.[59] A bill authorizing the bulk of these funds was approved by the Congress and sent to the White House for the President's signature early in 1971.[60]

As might be expected, these over-all cutbacks in U.S. aid were not received warmly abroad, either by donor nations or aid recipients. In a speech to the World Bank's Board of Governors in September, Bank President Robert S. McNamara declared it "inconceivable that the American people will accept for long a situation in which they—forming 6 per cent of the world's population but consuming 40 per cent of the world's resources—contribute less than their fair share to the development of the emerging nations." [61] The former Secretary of Defense found it ironic that the United States spent 20 times as much on military power as on aid to the less developed countries when, he claimed, a fractional shift of military funds to economic development purposes could serve to reduce those sources of international tension and conflict which made military budgets so lopsided in the first place.

To an extent, the administration itself appeared to sympathize with these sentiments. "We in the United States cannot ignore this worldwide problem and concentrate only on domestic concerns," AID Administrator John A. Hannah told a gathering at Ohio State University on October 30.[62] "It is unrealistic to think that 30 years from now 300 million Americans can live comfortably here while across the continents of Asia, Africa, and Latin America, more than twice the present population—some 7 billions of people—struggle to eke out an existence."

Accordingly, when preparations for the Second United Nations Development Decade were getting under way at the U.N. General Assembly in November, Senator Jacob K. Javits, a U.S. delegate to the Second Committee, reaffirmed the United States' commitment to devote 1 per cent of its G.N.P. to development assistance, although his statement doing so was couched in so many qualifications that the pledge itself seemed questionable. "The United States faces staggering domestic needs," Javits said,[63] "which have given rise to a national debate, still unresolved, on how to apply limited public and private resources to seemingly limitless requirements. The combination of these internal requirements and of the enormous burdens carried by us externally, plus the frustrations, as well as the successes, of nation-building in the developing world have brought a profound reexamination of aid policy in the United States and the best means for conducting it in the future. We are thus unable now to say when the United States may meet the 1-percent aid objective, or even whether our efforts toward this objective will be successful. . . . [But we] are prepared to make our best efforts to increase both official and private flows and we hope we can be successful in moving closer to the aid objective. It is in this spirit that we are willing to join in the international reaffirmation of the aid target."

Offering something akin to a *quid pro quo,* the U.N. resolution setting forth an "International Development Strategy for the Second United Nations Development Decade," [64] adopted October 24, gave obeisance to the prevailing U.S. attitude when it said: "Developing countries must, and do, bear the main responsibility for financing their development. They will, therefore, continue to adopt vigorous measures for a fuller mobilization of the whole range of their domestic financial resources and for ensuring the most effective use of available resources, both internal and external."

All that was clearly in line with administration philosophy, but given the steady and seemingly irreversible decline in official U.S. aid, it may have appeared highly wishful, if not downright equivocal, for the United States to enter upon another decade of promises it might not be able to keep. Yet it should be said that the Nixon administration clearly had hopes of stepping up the private flow of funds to less developed areas, even if official flows continued to shrink. The President himself had been pressing for a generalized system of trade preferences for all less developed countries, and in March the United States had concluded talks with E.E.C. members on such a preferential system encompassing manufactured and semi-manufactured goods, agreeing on basic objectives but divided to some degree over methods. At a meeting of the Special Preferences Committee of the United Nations Conference on Trade and Development (UNCTAD) later that month in Geneva, Edwin M. Cronk, Deputy Assistant Secretary of

State for International Trade Policy, set forth in considerable detail the U.S. position.[65] Noting that the developing countries' share of world trade had declined from 25 per cent in 1955 to 18 per cent in 1968, Cronk calculated that, had the exports of developing countries kept pace with those of developed countries between 1960 and 1968 alone, the exports of the less developed states would have been worth $11 billion more in 1968 than they actually were. In effect, a "normal" growth in their trade would almost have doubled net flows from rich to poor nations in one year alone.

The United States, Cronk said, had proposed "a preference scheme which would eliminate tariffs over the broadest possible commodity range and without limits on preferential imports. We have also pressed other developed countries to do the same." But there were several caveats. For one thing, the United States wanted the elimination of existing reverse preferences, such as those received by E.E.C. in its preferential arrangements with other countries. For another, said Cronk, the United States had of necessity "to avoid serious disruption of our domestic industries. We feel we have done so by limiting our exceptions to petroleum and petroleum products, textiles, and shoes and by providing for use of our standard escape-clause and adjustment assistance procedures."

Between 1964, when the less developed countries first proposed a preference system, and 1969, when President Nixon announced a definite shift in U.S. policy, the United States had been among the few industrialized countries to stand in opposition to the preferential treatment idea. With the conversion of Washington, the way was open to agreement at last, and at another UNCTAD meeting in October a report of the Special Preferences Committee indicated that a "breakthrough" was at hand. Though no binding document was signed and no formal vote was taken, the less developed countries saw in the Committee's report a commitment by the rich nations to establish as soon as possible a system of special tariff cuts for the poor, to be put in effect over a ten-year trial period. The Soviet bloc also indicated that it would undertake a special drive to increase its imports from the less developed states. The United States was still at odds with E.E.C. and the United Kingdom over reverse preference systems but there was apparent confidence that concrete measures toward a preferential system could be reached sometime in 1971.[66]

While all this had been going on, the Nixon administration had also been moving toward one of those periodic overhauls of the entire foreign aid structure. On March 8, Rudolph A. Peterson, President of the Bank of America and Chairman of the Presidential Task Force on International Development, submitted a 48-page report recommending that the Agency for International Development be scrapped, its functions split up and transferred to new agencies, and that increasing amounts of U.S. aid be channeled through such multilateral institutions as the World Bank.[67] It was the sixth such officially sponsored critique in the tortured, 22-year history of the U.S. foreign aid program, and it came on the heels of another highly critical private report drawn up for Secretary Rogers by U.S. Ambassador to Chile Edward M. Korry, who charged that past aid policies had been misguided and self-defeating.[68] Both the Korry and Peterson reports called, not for less U.S. aid, but for less U.S. visibility in its administration—a point of view that clearly squared with President Nixon's over-all effort to lower the U.S. profile abroad.

"For the first time in history," the Peterson report said, "it appears feasible to approach this world problem on a worldwide basis. International development can become a truly cooperative venture—with the countries that receive help eventually achieving the ability themselves to help others." [69] To this end, the task force recommended that the developing countries be placed "at the center of the international development effort, establishing their own priorities and receiving assistance in relation to the efforts they are making on their own behalf." It suggested that international lending institutions become the major channel for aid-giving, that U.S. bilateral assistance be provided largely within this multilateral framework, and that the United States separate its economic program from its military assistance efforts, eventually phasing out the latter altogether. To carry out these recommendations, the report called for the establishment of a U.S. International Development Bank to oversee capital lending and related technical assistance loans, a U.S. International Development Institute to seek new breakthroughs in the application of science and technology to development needs, an Overseas Private Investment Corporation (OPIC—already authorized by Congress) to mobilize private American capital and business skills, and a U.S. International Development Council to coordinate U.S. trade, investment, financial, agricultural, and export-promotion policies in the development effort.

"It should be a cardinal aim of U.S. foreign policy to help build an equitable political and economic order in which the world's people, their governments, and other institutions can effectively share resources and knowledge," the report said. "The downward trend in U.S. development assistance appropriations should be reversed."

In his September 15 message to Congress,[70] entitled "Foreign Assistance for the 'Seventies" and embodying many of the Peterson recommendations, President Nixon also spoke of the continuing need for aid. "The answer is not to stop foreign aid or to slash it further," he said. "The answer is to reform our foreign assistance programs and do our share to meet the needs of the 'Seventies." Accordingly, the President called for "a set of fundamental and sweeping reforms to overhaul completely our entire foreign assistance operation to make it fit a new foreign policy." In line with the Peterson report, the President urged a scrapping of AID, although he proposed only two new agencies (aside from OPIC) to take its place: a U.S. International Development Corporation "to handle our bilateral lending on a more businesslike basis," and a U.S. International Development Institute with the same aims as those suggested by Peterson. He also called for a greater emphasis on multilateral aid-giving, declaring it his hope that "we shall eventually be able to channel most of our development assistance through these international institutions." But, with the requirements of the Nixon Doctrine in mind, the President also proposed a "freshly conceived" International Security Assistance Program whose objective would be to help other countries assume greater responsibility for their own defense and thus help reduce the U.S. presence abroad. At the same time, the President revealed his faith in private as opposed to official contributions to the development process by urging steps to expand private investment in and trade with less developed countries, having already made clear his administration's commitment to a system of tariff preferences.

Despite the talk of a "major transformation," however, there was little that was really new in the President's message, aside from his call for the dismantlement of AID. The United States had already been shifting its assistance efforts to multilateral institutions, in some cases, about as fast as the increased contributions of other donor nations would allow. Similarly, as early as 1966 the Johnson administration had recognized that economic aid programs were being tainted by close association with the military effort in Vietnam, and so moved to separate out the military aid program for Southeast Asia as a whole. The hope for increased private-sector contributions to the development effort had been kicking around in Washington for years, but with many less developed countries growing wary of private foreign investment (or foreign domination, as they more often put it) and with many U.S. investors equally wary of the risks involved, there were not many who foresaw major gains in that area.

As for Congress, the reactions were predictable. Senator Fulbright, who had plumped for multilateral aid-giving for years, was generally in sympathy, while Congressman Passman, who wanted control over what the taxpayers were "giving away" kept in U.S. hands, was scandalized.[71] As the fifth in a string of administering agencies for the foreign aid program since 1948, AID itself could take wistful pride in the fact that it had survived the game of musical chairs for at least nine years. Though ensnarled by congressional restrictions and the inevitable bureaucratic malaise, it had gathered to itself considerable expertise on such critical development problems as family planning and improved agricultural techniques, and there were those who wondered where that expertise would go once the agency was shut down. President Nixon gave at least a partial answer in his message on the subject to Congress. The new agencies and guidelines he was seeking, he said, would enable him "to reduce significantly the number of overseas U.S. Government personnel working on development." [72] Like America's official presence elsewhere in the world in 1970, it seemed, its presence among the less developed nations would soon be winding down as well.

11 : The World Takes Stock

For the United Nations 1970 should have been a year of festive celebration marking the organization's silver anniversary—25 years of achievement, frustration, and sheer survival. In fact, a special commemorative ten-day session of the General Assembly was held in New York, October 14–24, with speeches and special resolutions. But it seemed indicative of the general state of neglect and demoralization into which the organization had fallen that few of the more prominent world leaders showed up for the occasion and that President Nixon himself upstaged the proceedings by giving a state dinner for assembled dignitaries in far-away Washington. As Secretary-General U Thant somewhat ruefully observed on October 24: "The United Nations born of the Charter has done well, but it has not done well enough. . . . It is unforgivable that so many problems from the past are still with us, absorbing vast energies and resources desperately needed for nobler purposes." [1]

Earlier, in May 1969, Thant had warned the world that the U.N. had at most ten years in which to reform itself or face collapse,[2] a view poignantly echoed by Emperor Haile Selassie of Ethiopia in his anniversary address before the world body in 1970. Recalling the fate of the old League of Nations and the paralysis of inaction that eventually destroyed it, Selassie declared that the U.N. must strengthen itself or face similar prospects.[3] Taking a somewhat longer-range view in May, Canada's Lester B. Pearson, a former President of the General Assembly, warned at a privately-sponsored conference in New York that as then constituted the U.N. would not survive to see its 50th anniversary. Pearson revived the call for a permanent U.N. military force to help keep the peace, and he urged the creation of a three-man task force to appraise the organization and recommend changes for its greater effectiveness.[4]

In their heart of hearts, few servants of the organization were unaware that the U.N. remained odd-man-out in a world which, for all the talk of multinational corporations, "spaceship earth," and the "global village," remained dominated by the nation-state system. Flailing in a sea of troubles, it lacked even the capacity to deal with limited conflicts on a systematic basis. To be sure, there were those who recognized the importance of the work of the U.N.'s specialized agencies and who valued the political side of the organization as a great forum for talking out problems. Yet it had to be asked whether the interminable debates that went on there—between the Arab states and Israel, between South Africa and the black African states—were really conducive to a peaceful solution of these problems, however much they followed in the enlightened tradition of John Stuart Mill.

Charging that the U.N. had "developed neither the power nor the moral authority to cope with its members' proclivity toward violence and their quest for security in ever bigger, more dangerous and more expensive armaments," two U.S. congressmen who had served on the U.S. delegation to the 24th Regular Session of the General Assembly in 1969 concluded that the world body was limping along only as "a passive witness to events." In their report to the House Committee on Foreign Affairs in February, Representatives Dante B. Fascell of Florida and J. Irving Whalley of Pennsylvania raised the question as to whether the United States should continue trying to work through the U.N. or begin looking to other means for solving international problems.[5]

40 : The U.S. and the U.N.

A Gallup poll taken on the occasion of the special anniversary session in October found that most Americans favored the creation of a U.N. peace-keeping army of 100,000 men and that, despite reservations, most believed it very important that the United States continue its own efforts to make the U.N. a success.[6] In its public pronouncements the Nixon administration heartily agreed. Yet it was also apparent that throughout 1970 the administration was essentially of two minds about the U.N.'s future. On the one hand, it was vexed, as were numerous other governments, about the organization's failures and shortcomings—its patent inability to cope with limited (not to mention "great power") conflicts, its tangled finances, its cumbersome, inefficient system of administration, the tendency of its political organs to talk on and on without effect and to no apparent conclusion. On the other hand, it was also apparent that Washington clearly valued the U.N.'s existence, that it hoped for a genuine strengthening of the organization's effectiveness, and that it was contributing no insignificant measure of its own energies toward that end. In March, the United States had broken tradition by casting its first veto in the Security Council, against a resolution that condemned Britain for not forcefully ousting the breakaway, racist government of Ian Smith in Southern Rhodesia.[7] One could conclude either that the United States was at last taking a realistic view of its role in the organization, without impugning its support for U.N. principles, or that the veto was but another way of indicating that the world body no longer merited Washington's scrupulous regard. Both attitudes were discussed at the time, and, indeed, both may have been reflected in the veto.

The duality of this attitude was fully expressed in President Nixon's State of the World message to Congress, transmitted in February. "The United Nations is both a symbol of the worldwide hopes for peace," the President said, "and a reflection of the tensions and conflicts that have frustrated these hopes." The U.N.'s achievements had been "impressive," Nixon said, and the United States would continue to lend its "strong support" to the organization. But the time had also come "to acknowledge its realistic possibilities and to devise ways to expand them." [8]

In his statement before the Subcommittee on International Organizations and Movements of the House Committee on Foreign Affairs on August 6, Secretary Rogers proceeded to spell out precisely what the administration had in mind by way of U.N. reforms.[9] In his 1969 address to the General Assembly,[10] Rogers said, Nixon had already urged the world body to apply its resources not only to peace-keeping but to such activities as protecting the world environment, sharing the benefits of space technology, fostering the interrelated objectives of economic development and population control, and securing the safety of international air travel from airplane hijackings. Now, Rogers said, the administration was urging the examination of "four key areas in which we believe that steps could be taken to make the U.N. a more effective instrument. . . ."

The first order of business in Rogers' view was the strengthening of the U.N.'s capacity to deal with political crises, to take emergency peace-keeping action, and to promote the peaceful settlement of disputes. While there were limits to what could be expected of the U.N. in this field, Rogers said, the time was nonetheless ripe for a new effort to establish reliable ground rules and procedures, and to that end the United States was already engaged in direct conversations with the Soviet Union whereby "the Security Council would authorize and define the mandate of peacekeeping operations and the Secretary General would implement the mandate in consultation with member governments most concerned." Agreement along these lines would clear the way, Rogers indicated, for adequate advance arrangements on military contingents and logistical support. At the same time a special effort was being made to revitalize provisions of the Charter which would draw the Secretary-General into the early stages of international disputes and enable both the Security Council and the General Assembly to take timely action in recommending methods for their solution.

The second area of the U.N.'s work that required bolstering, Rogers said, was the role of the International Court of Justice. "The Court did not have a single case on its docket until a week ago [when it was asked for an advisory opinion on the legal status of South West Africa (Namibia) [11]]," Rogers declared, "and a revival of the Court's functions is long overdue." Blaming the Court's forced inactivity on the failure of states to place their disputes before it, Rogers noted that the United States was "examining various disputes to which we are a party to determine whether the Court might be brought into play." Concurrently, the United States was urging that the Court establish regional chambers outside The Hague, particularly in the developing world, and that it give regional organizations access to its hearings, in an effort to broaden its role and impart a greater sense of proximity to its work.

The third area of reform related to U.N. procedures and institutions—better budget planning, a more efficient use of resources, a streamlining of parliamentary procedures, better management practices, etc. Along with other nations, Rogers said, the United States was "increasingly concerned about rising costs and about the need to insure adequate accountability on the part of the U.N. and specialized agencies for the uses made of our contributions." In this connection the Secretary cited the 1969 report of Sir Robert Jackson of Australia,[12] proposing an overhaul of the U.N. Development Program designed to centralize the Program's authority, provide it with better management procedures, and give coordinated direction to the various specialized agencies which operated in the development field. "We have strongly supported these reforms," Rogers said, "and I am pleased to report that good progress had been made in achieving a wide consensus among member governments in support of those reforms we consider essential."

Finally, the United States wanted to see an expanding role for the U.N. in the fields of technological cooperation, population control, protection of the environment, drug and narcotics regulation, and resource sharing. "For the near future," Rogers said, "a principal value of the U.N. may well be its ability to draft rules and provide a mechanism for facilitating international cooperation in dealing with new technology. We want to strengthen its capacities in this field, with urgent priority to the international task of protecting man's environment, to the dangers of excessive population growth, and to the need to halt the epidemic of abuse of dangerous drugs." Noting that some thought the U.N. to be facing a crisis of confidence, Secretary Rogers concluded that "The only realistic choice we have . . . is to make it more effective; to renew its confidence; to help it gain greater public support."

On July 9, President Nixon had signed an Executive Order establishing a Commission for the Observance of the Twenty-fifth Anniversary of the United Nations, with the aim of eliciting recommendations for ways of strengthening the world organization and U.S. participation therein.[13] Chaired by a former Permanent Representative to the U.N., Ambassador Henry Cabot Lodge, the Commission submitted its first Interim Report on September 14,[14] and its tentative recommendations more or less paralleled those already set forth by Secretary Rogers. The cumulative impact of these and other pronouncements clearly gave the impression that the United States was making a determined—perhaps last ditch—effort to infuse the U.N. with new life. Yet it remained questionable exactly how seriously the administration took this organization celebrating its 25th birthday, or even the proposals for reform being set forth to improve it. Secretary Rogers had vowed to examine international disputes to which the United States was a party with the aim of providing the International Court of Justice with more business, yet he knew as well as anyone that the United States reserved by law (the so-called Connally Amendment) the right to refuse the Court's jurisdiction in matters of domestic jurisdiction as defined by the United States itself.[15] Nor had the Secretary proposed that reforms go so far as to touch upon this aspect of U.S. law.

Moreover, the United States had established something of a tradition in appointing eminent men to the post of U.N. Ambassador— ex-Senators, a former Supreme Court Justice, and even a former presidential candidate. A distinguished career diplomat, Charles W. Yost, was named Ambassador when Nixon came to office, but he was summarily dropped toward the end of 1970, to be replaced by a conservative Republican Representative from Texas, George H. W. Bush, who had lost a bid for a Senate seat earlier in the year. There were those who promptly and caustically equated the appointment of this virtually unknown and diplomatically unpracticed congressman with the President's regard for the U.N. as a whole. It was also clear that the administration was not about to join those voices calling for a complete revision of the U.N. Charter, although the assumed goal of such an undertaking in the U.N.'s 25th anniversary year would have been a general strengthening of the organization's muscle and its ability to act decisively in the interests of peace. This too could be seen as evidence of the administration's basic reluctance to go beyond a patch-work reform job for an organization in need, as some saw it, of a sweeping overhaul.

Yet there was also logic in the administration's contention that Charter review and revision were not the answer. As Ambassador Yost stated on February 18, "Personally I see no need to go through the arduous—unpromising—process of amending the charter in the near future. It already contains the powers that are required, if the member governments will agree to their being used." [16] In that light, the administration's reform efforts could be interpreted as a realistic approach to problems within a viable, existing framework, and it must be said that Washington sought conscientiously to follow through on its proposals. Secretary Rogers had noted in his testimony before the House subcommittee that U.S.-Soviet discussions on means of improving U.N. peace-keeping operations were "business-like" and "continuing," and that the United States was pressing its views within the U.N.'s Special Committee on Peace-keeping Operations as well.[17] These reform proposals did not meet with success in the U.N.'s 25th anniversary year, as the United States had hoped, but it was not for want of trying on the part of U.S. delegates.

Under the leadership of Ambassador Francisco Cuevas-Cancino of Mexico, the Special Committee on Peace-keeping Operations had been laboring for two years at the task of developing systematic guidelines for the peace-keeping function. On September 8–10 the Third Conference of Non-Aligned Countries had met at Lusaka, Zambia, and issued what Ambassador Yost described as a "strong declaration" [18] in favor of action on the peace-keeping issue at the 25th Regular Session of the General Assembly scheduled to begin September 15. At this time, the United States' own proposals were already before the Special Committee, and a consensus for reform appeared to be building. The U.S. proposals stressed a plan by which the Secretary-General could obtain from member states advance information on the personnel and equipment the members would be prepared to provide for peace-keeping operations authorized by the Security Council. Such information would include the number and type of contingents, military observers, and auxiliary personnel available, as well as their state of readiness. The Secretary-General could then compile a register of availabilities, locate any potential gaps, and issue an appeal to all members aimed at filling them. The plan would by no means resolve the problem of when, where, or how the forces could be used, but it would constitute a dramatic step toward, and further impetus for, a standing U.N. peace-keeping force. As Ambassador Yost described it, "This type of proposal would be completed without prejudice to the known position of any party. . . . Consequently, we believe such action could have been taken at this session without prejudice to the work on reaching agreement on general guidelines for peacekeeping." [19]

The Committee remained at loggerheads, however, over the procedural issue of responsibility for the establishment and control of peace-keeping operations, as well as the means of financing them, and the best the General Assembly could do was to pass unanimously on December 8 a resolution calling on the Committee to intensify its efforts toward agreement with a view to reporting on its progress by May 1, 1971.[20] "I shall not hide our disappointment," Ambassador Yost said, "that we could not commemorate the 25th anniversary of the United Nations by taking concrete actions to strengthen U.N. peacekeeping." [21]

The United States nonetheless continued its efforts in this area. It had urged the reactivation of those U.N. Charter provisions calling for conciliation and for early warning of impending conflicts, and it sought the establishment, under Article 33, of a panel of U.N. fact-finders who would be available to the Secretary-General and member states for travel to the scene of tension or conflict in order to make inquiries and report on the facts of the situation.[22] It also lent strong support to a Finnish-sponsored request that the Security Council hold periodic, private meetings at the foreign ministers' level for the purpose of a broad exchange of views on both the international situation and the responsibilities of the U.N.[23] Pursuant to this suggestion, the first such meeting was held on October 21 in New York, where those attending urged a further strengthening of the Security Council's peace-keeping role and agreed that the holding of periodic meetings of foreign ministers constituted a step in that direction.[24]

If on the whole the United States could take little satisfaction from its efforts to bolster the U.N.'s peace-keeping functions, however, it experienced still more frustration in its efforts to promote reform in the organization's financial, administrative, and procedural structure. In his opening address before the General Assembly on September 30, Ambassador Yost had warned that the organization was in danger of suffocating "under an avalanche of paper," that the continuing application for membership by very small states—or "ministates"— was hampering the organization's effectiveness, and that "The persistence of the United Nations financial deficit undermines confidence in the organization, threatens its capabilities in many fields, and casts a cloud over its future." [25]

The United States wanted the problem of ministates solved by a form of "associated membership" in which very small countries could enjoy the benefits of the U.N. without having to assume the membership burdens which the Charter stipulated. It wanted Sir Robert Jackson's proposals for strengthening the U.N.D.P. placed in effect. It wanted senior posts in the Secretariat filled as the Charter prescribed—according to "the highest standards of efficiency, competence, and integrity" and "on as wide a geographical basis as possible." In the same vein, it wanted seats in the Security Council filled in line with the prospective member's contribution to international peace and security. And finally, it wanted the organization and procedures of the General Assembly streamlined and administrative and budgetary control improved throughout the organization.

In most instances, such administrative and procedural reforms failed of accomplishment, though it remained possible that subsequent years might eventually bring success. On October 13 Fiji, a small island nation in the South Pacific with a population the size of Seattle's, was admitted as the 127th member of the U.N., despite U.S. misgivings.[26] The Jackson report, though praised by most delegations as a step toward greater control and efficiency in the administration of specialized programs, ran into stubborn opposition from those specialized agencies jealous of their own powers and independence. Few of its recommendations were actually put into effect in 1970. The broad survey of U.N. manpower utilization and deployment which had begun in 1969 was roughly 60 per cent completed by the end of 1970,[27] but the problem of translating its findings into appropriate reforms remained to be tackled. And above all the organization's budget problems continued on their dreary, downhill course.

As U Thant put it in the introduction to his annual report on the U.N.'s work: "The Organization's financial situation is worse than ever before and steadily deteriorating." [28] Unpaid assessed contributions totalled a record $135.5 million as of June 30, the Secretary-General said, and particularly heavy deficits remained in the financing of the U.N. Emergency Force in the Middle East (ended in 1967) and the U.N. Peace-keeping Force in Cyprus (still functioning in 1970). In addition, Thant reported, the U.N. still owed $32.2 million toward its peace-keeping operation in the Congo, ended almost a decade earlier. In the meantime, the organization's regular budget was rising steeply, from $168.4 million in the financial year 1970 to $192.1 million in 1971.

The United States, which contributed almost a third of the regular budget's funds and which was fully paid up in its assessments, found these problems as thoroughly deplorable as did the Secretary-General. In a statement before the U.N. Committee on Administrative and

Budgetary Questions (Committee V) on October 21,[29] the U.S. Assistant Secretary of State for International Organization Affairs, Samuel De Palma, decried the "critical" state of the U.N.'s finances and called upon member states to "face up to the pressing needs of the situation." He also urged the U.N. itself to "produce substantial savings while improving the overall performance of our organization" by cutting down, for one thing, on "the plethora of conferences and documentation." The General Assembly's own review of budget requests from specialized agencies had been "all too cursory," De Palma added, while the Fifth Committee itself "seldom considers the substantive aspect of activities, how necessary they are, how urgent," etc. in its own assessment of the organization's financial needs. There was, in short, no rational sense of priority in the way the U.N. spent its money, and more than anything else, perhaps, De Palma's stern statement provided an accurate measure of both Washington's concern for the U.N.'s future and its dissatisfaction with the organization's existing state.

There was, however, one area of progress in which the United States and other U.N. members could take satisfaction. If the organization's political tasks were largely frustrated, its economic and social efforts continued to develop and expand, more or less in line with Secretary Rogers' emphasis on technological cooperation, population control, protection of the environment, drug and narcotics regulation, and resource sharing. As already noted, the United States had for several years been shifting the emphasis of its own foreign aid efforts toward a multilateral framework, had renewed, even if somewhat ambiguously, its pledge to strive to commit 1 per cent of its G.N.P. to the development effort, and had agreed in principle at a United Nations Conference on Trade and Development to a system of preferential tariffs for the manufactured and semi-manufactured goods of the less developed world.[30] In a special message to Congress in 1969, President Nixon had also urged that "the United Nations, its specialized agencies, and other international bodies should take the leadership in responding to world population growth. The United States," he said, "will cooperate fully with their programs."[31] In addition to supporting bilateral population control programs with 31 less developed countries, therefore, the United States in 1970 pledged $7.5 million to the newly established U.N. Fund for Population Activities, in line with Secretary-General Thant's own view that population pressures represented "the greatest challenge facing the United Nations and the world today." [32]

It was in 1969, also, that President Nixon had pledged U.S. backing of an Iranian proposal for the establishment of an International Volunteer Service Corps under U.N. auspices, which would enlist young people from many countries in the cause of development.[33] On December 7, 1970 the General Assembly voted to establish such a Corps (to be called, "United Nations Volunteers") within the U.N.D.P. and called upon member nations for voluntary contributions in its support.[34] The United States also gained U.N. endorsement of its pleas for stronger international measures to control international traffic in narcotics and dangerous drugs. On July 25 and November 11, the Economic and Social Council passed resolutions providing, among other things, for an action program aimed at countering drug abuse and establishing a U.N. Fund for Drug Abuse Control, to be financed out of voluntary contributions.[35] In December the General Assembly "strongly endorsed" these decisions [36] and called upon member states to enact "legislation providing severe penalties for those engaged in illicit trade and trafficking of narcotic drugs." [37]

41 : The Sky Above, the Sea Below

For many long-time observers of the U.N., the real future of the organization seemed to lie in these expanding economic and social functions—in agencies like the Development Program headed by Paul G. Hoffman, in the work of the Industrial Development Board, UNCTAD, the Food and Agricultural Organization, the regional economic commissions, and even in the ground-breaking exercise represented by the planned Conference on the Human Environment to be held in Sweden in 1972.[38] With the Security Council hobbled by the veto, with the General Assembly swamped by a sea of delegates from 127 countries (holding at times, it seemed, 127 different points of view), and with the world at large at the mercy of great powers for whatever measure of peace lay in store, the U.N.'s political capacities, if not wholly atrophied, seemed at least to be withering on the vine. It was symptomatic of the organization's drawing power that its 25th birthday party opened with many countries represented by only a single delegate, with the Russians, the French, and the Arab states unrepresented at the highest level, and with only 42 top leaders on hand for the special commemorative session. There was the usual speech-making, laid on, as *The New York Times* ironically observed, against a background of nuclear-testing by the United States, the Soviet Union, and China.[39] And even the special resolutions adopted for the occasion seemed somewhat flat and predictable, given their heavy emphasis on the concerns of the less developed countries, which composed the vast majority of General Assembly delegates, and their repetition of past homilies.

In its Declaration on the Occasion of the Twenty-fifth Anniversary of the United Nations, adopted at the close of the commemorative session on October 24, the General Assembly reaffirmed its "deter-mination to respect the principles of international law concerning friendly relations and co-operation among States," acclaimed "the role of the United Nations in the past twenty-five years in the process of the liberation of peoples of colonial, Trust and other Non-Self-Governing Territories," strongly condemned "the evil policy of apartheid," pledged "a continued and determined struggle against all violations of the rights and fundamental freedoms of human beings," proclaimed its conviction that "economic and social development is essential to peace, international security and justice," and hailed the 1970's as "the Second United Nations Development Decade, which coincides with and is linked to the Disarmament Decade." [40]

Under the leadership of President Edvard Hambro of Norway, the 25th Regular Session of the General Assembly passed two additional resolutions specifically condemning the remnants of colonialism, par-ticularly as practiced by Portugal, South Africa, and the illegal govern-ment in Southern Rhodesia.[41] It passed seven others urging detailed and strong actions against South Africa's policy of *apartheid* and its government.[42] As a climax to its special ten-day commemorative session, it adopted a long-pending declaration on the principles of international law, exhorting member states to practice friendly rela-tions and cooperation in the spirit of the U.N. Charter.[43] But this was largely overshadowed by the Assembly's action in proclaiming the 1970's as the Second United Nations Development Decade and in its adoption of an international development strategy aimed at reducing the poverty gap among nations.[44]

Although not all the targets of the First Development Decade had been met,[45] the strategy for the Second Decade nonetheless called for the achievement of still higher goals and objectives. The average annual rate of growth in the G.N.P.'s of developing countries as a whole were set at at least 6 per cent, with the possibility of a higher rate during the second half of the decade based on a mid-term review. In terms of per capita G.N.P., this meant an average growth rate of about 3.5 per cent annually, and even that would have to rise, the strategy indicated, if the gap between rich and poor nations was to begin to close. In pursuit of these goals, developing countries were urged to reduce income disparities within their own borders, to trim illiteracy, expand educational facilities, establish minimum health and public sanitation programs, improve their planning mechanisms, including statistical services, and strive to absorb increasing numbers of the unemployed into an expanding labor force. Developed countries, for their part, were urged by 1972 or at latest by 1975 to supply net annual transfers of at least 1 per cent of the G.N.P.'s to the less developed states, with a major part of those transfers to be provided in the form of official development assistance—or 0.7 per cent of G.N.P. by mid-decade. In addition, developed countries were expected to channel increased amounts of their aid through multilateral institutions and were asked to adopt trade policies beneficial to the poorer states in line with recent UNCTAD agreements.[46]

These were optimistic goals, but it must be noted that they were put forward with dead seriousness, for the discussions upon which the development strategy was based were prolonged, deliberate, and carefully weighed. Indeed, it may be said that however much the outside world faulted it, the U.N. could, even in such delicate political matters as the use of the seabed or the regulation of outer space, take pride in its day-to-day efforts and achievements. Unquestionably, the most significant disarmament agreement of 1970 was negotiated through the U.N.-sponsored Conference of the Committee on Disarmament in Geneva and commended, 104 to 2 with 2 abstentions, by the General Assembly on December 7.[47] A draft Treaty on the Prohibition of the Emplacement of Nuclear Weapons and Other Weapons of Mass Destruction on the Sea-Bed and the Ocean Floor and in the Subsoil Thereof, sponsored jointly by the United States and the Soviet Union, had been submitted to the 24th session of the General Assembly in October 1969, at which time certain amendments were recommended by Canada, Argentina, Brazil, and Yugoslavia, among others.[48] The second revised draft, submitted on September 1,[49] incorporated the suggested changes and, with the expected signature and ratification of the leading nuclear powers, effectively prohibited the stationing of such weapons on or under the ocean floor, with the proviso that verification activities could be conducted by any and all signatories.

Nor did the nuclear prohibition treaty end what had become a wide-ranging U.N. concern with the uses of the seabed. For several years the delegate from Malta, in particular, had been urging a broadly based treaty reserving the wealth and riches of the seabed for the benefit of all mankind and not just for those with the technological resources to develop them. This was perhaps the most complex and ambitious task of law-making ever undertaken by the organization, since it involved at once conflicting claims among nations to offshore territorial limits, the depths at which the old law-of-the-sea governing the limits of the continental shelf ended and the new law of the seabed began, and the kind of institutions or administrative mechanisms that would most effectively promote the seabed's use for all mankind. These extraordinary complexities had been in the process of being thrashed out in the U.N. Committee on the Peaceful Uses of the Sea-Bed and the Ocean Floor beyond the Limits of National Jurisdiction for two years, and the United States, no less than other nations, had occasionally raised its voice in opposition, not so much to the principles toward which the Committee was striving, as to the law-making by which it proposed to get there.

On May 23, in a major policy statement, President Nixon outlined U.S. policy in the area and announced that his representative would introduce specific proposals at the next meeting of the Seabeds Committee.[50] These proposals, Nixon indicated, would require the renunciation of all national claims over the natural resources of the seabed "beyond the point where the high seas reach a depth of 200 meters," earmarking such resources as "the common heritage of mankind." The exploitation of these resources "for international community purposes, particularly economic assistance to developing countries," would be carried forward by two types of international regime—one in which coastal nations would act as trustees over the exploitation of continental margins beyond the 200-meter depth off their coasts; another to authorize and regulate exploration and use of the seabed beyond the continental margins. Until such machinery could be established, Nixon said, all permits for exploration and exploitation of the seabed should be issued "subject to the international regime to be agreed upon," with a substantial portion of the revenues therefrom turned over to an international development agency for assistance to developing countries. Finally, Nixon said, negotiations toward a new law-of-the-sea treaty, establishing a 12-mile limit for territorial seas and providing for free transit through international straits, should be undertaken to "assure unfettered and harmonious use of the oceans as an avenue of commerce and transportation, and as a source of food."

In Geneva on August 3, the United States duly submitted its "Draft U.N. Convention on the International Seabed Area" to the Seabeds Committee,[51] spelling out in detail the President's policy goals and including the proposed establishment of both a Trusteeship system and a high-powered International Seabed Resource Authority, composed of an Assembly of all the contracting parties, a balanced Council of 24, and an independent Tribunal. On December 17 the U.N. General Assembly, taking note of the Seabeds Committee's work, passed a series of resolutions delineating the seabed as "the common heritage of mankind," and reflecting in large measure U.S. views.[52] These called upon the Secretary-General, in cooperation with UNCTAD, to determine the economic impact a regulated exploitation of the seabed would have upon developing countries in particular; instructed the Secretary-General—again in collaboration with UNCTAD—to prepare a report on the special problems of land-locked countries relating to their exploration and exploitation of the seabed's riches; ordered the convening, in 1973, of an international conference on the law of the sea to deal with the establishment of an international regime for the seabed and related issues; and instructed the Seabeds Committee to hold two meetings in 1971 in order to prepare draft treaties for consideration by the law-of-the-sea conference in 1973.[53]

Even as the U.N. was moving to cope with the technological advances that made wealth beneath the sea an object of increasing international concern, it was also striving to rationalize and regulate man's use of the space around earth so that benefits of the new aeronautical technology could be turned to the advantage of all nations as well. The space exploits of the United States and the Soviet Union had opened new vistas in international communication, meteorology, and methods for surveying the earth's resources, and the developing countries again seemed eager to explore their applicability to the development effort as a whole. In line with the Nixon administration's stress on a balanced budget, the U.S. space program in 1970 was undergoing something of a belt-tightening process, with the National Aeronautics and Space Administration eliminating 50,000 jobs and stretching out its existing projects to accommodate a cut in funds. Nonetheless, at the U.N., the United States continued to lend lively support to the proposal, first put forward by President Nixon in 1969,[54] for a survey of the earth's resources by the so-called Earth Resource Technology Satellites, while being preoccupied, as well, with the future of direct television broadcasting from satellites and the drafting of a liability convention covering man-made objects reentering the atmosphere from space.

In his statement before the U.N. Committee on the Peaceful Uses of Outer Space on September 1, the U.S. representative, Ward P. Allen, commended a proposal by Secretary-General Thant to establish a working panel on the applications of space technology and invited member states to submit their own proposals for experiments by the first of two planned Earth Resource Technology Satellites by April 15, 1971.[55] While noting that adequate technology for direct satellite broadcasting to homes was still some 15 years in the offing, Allen urged continued efforts by the so-called Direct Broadcast Working Group of the Outer Space Committee toward preliminary developments of international cooperation in the area, but also noted with regret the inability of the Outer Space Legal Subcommittee, after six years of trying, to complete the drafting of a liability convention. In that connection, he said, only two substantive issues remained to be resolved. One concerned the binding nature of damage claims that had been awarded; the other related to fair standards of compensation. The United States, Allen said, looked forward to a successful compromise on both issues, the urgency of which, it might be added, was underscored by the fact that with the launching of the Apollo 13 moon shot on April 10 the 4,371st man-made object had been hurtled into space.

In a series of resolutions on international cooperation in the peaceful uses of outer space, passed December 16, the General Assembly urged its various specialized agencies and committees to continue their efforts at promoting satellite broadcasting, particularly as an educational and informational tool in less developed areas. It also called upon the Outer Space Committee's Technical and Scientific Subcommittee to consider at its next meeting the establishment of a working group on earth resources surveying, with special reference to satellite application. But it expressed deep regret that, notwithstanding certain progress, the draft of a convention on liability was not yet completed in acceptable form, and it urged a "decisive effort" to reach agreement by the time of the 26th session.[56]

Having thus reaffirmed its growing interest in aeronautical technology, the U.N. also in 1970 was forced to come to grips with the more mundane problems of aerial hijackings and political extortion as practiced against the world's commercial airlines. In 1970, there had been more than 30 instances of air piracy in the Western Hemisphere alone, most of the commandeered flights ending up in Cuba. But the incidents that moved the international community toward concerted action took place on a remote airfield in the Jordanian desert in September, when Palestinian terrorists first hijacked and then held for ransom three commercial airliners and their frightened passengers against demands for the release of fellow terrorists from prisons in Israel, Switzerland, Germany, and England.[57] In prompt response to these incidents, President Nixon announced a six-point program designed to meet what he called "the menace of air piracy . . . immediately and effectively." [58] First, he said, specially trained and armed United States marshals would thenceforth "ride shotgun" on flights of U.S.-flag airlines. Second, U.S. commercial carriers would be provided with federal enforcement officers to extend the use of electronic surveillance equipment at airports, to conduct searches when appropriate, and to make arrests. Third, concerned federal agencies were ordered to accelerate their efforts to develop improved security measures. Fourth, the President said, the United States would consult fully with foreign governments on the full range of techniques used to foil hijackers. Fifth, he urged all countries to adhere to a draft convention providing for the extradition or punishment of hijackers and called upon the international community to suspend air service to those countries which refused to do so. And finally, he praised and lent full U.S. support to a U.N. Security Council resolution of September 9 [59] calling for all possible legal steps to prevent further hijacking or any other interference with international civil air travel.

At the request of the United States, a special meeting of the Council of the International Civil Aviation Organization (I.C.A.O.) was then held in Montreal on September 18. Following a statement by U.S.

Secretary of Transportation John A. Volpe, the United States submitted the draft of a resolution urging contracting states to suspend
civil air services to any country failing to extradite or prosecute a
hijacker or detaining any passengers, crew, or aircraft which had been
unlawfully seized.[60] A watered-down version of this resolution, calling
upon contracting parties to "consult" promptly "with a view to deciding what joint action should be undertaken," was adopted by the
I.C.A.O. Council on October 1.[61] In addition, the resolution called for
I.C.A.O.'s Legal Committee to consider the advisability of drawing up
an international convention governing such instances of air piracy
and blackmail and imposing the kind of sanctions which Washington
favored.

On November 25, the U.N General Assembly passed a resolution
calling upon states to "take joint and separate action . . . to ensure
that passengers, crew and aircraft engaged in civil aviation are not
used as a means of extorting advantage of any kind," and urging "full
support for the current efforts of the International Civil Aviation
Organization towards the development and co-ordination, in accordance with its competence, of effective measures in respect of interference with civil air travel." [62] Accordingly, from December 1 to 16, a
77-nation conference on air laws met at The Hague, under I.C.A.O.
auspices, for the express purpose of drafting a Convention for the
Suppression of Unlawful Seizure of Aircraft. Again the United States
pressed for strong action both against hijackers and against any state
which might afford them, wittingly or not, some form of refuge. In
the compromise text finally approved, the convention provided that
if a state does not extradite a hijacker, it must then submit the case,
without exception, to its own authorities for prosecution. It further
provided that the crime of hijacking must be subject to severe penalties
in all states. Taking a leaf from similar, older conventions to combat
piracy on the high seas, in short, the text provided for universal
criminal jurisdiction over hijackers, wherever found, by obligating contracting states either to extradite them or to prosecute them under
severe penalties. Finally, the convention took steps to facilitate extradition of hijackers between contracting states.[63]

In his statement to the conference on December 16, John B. Rhine-
lander, Deputy Legal Adviser and acting chief U.S. delegate, declared
that "My delegation believes this convention marks an important international reaction to lawless acts which, regardless of motivation, must

be punished," and urged the 77 nations present "to bring this convention into effect at the earliest possible moment." [64] Yet it remained to be seen whether even the severest penalties could bring what was an epidemic of hijacking to a halt. For while the world at large in 1970 may have been looking to modern technology, as applied both in the sky above and the sea below, to redound to the benefit of all mankind, the world had also seen how such advanced and luxurious products of man's technological ingenuity as jet passenger aircraft could be converted into gleaming metal death traps by a small band of political fanatics who appeared to care little if at all about the penalties that might await their crime.

42 : A Year of Contradictions

In his address before the 25th anniversary session of the General Assembly, President Nixon had observed that "Since the birth of the United Nations—for the first time in this century—the world's people will have lived through 25 years without a war. Let us resolve together," the President said, "that the second quarter century of the United Nations shall offer the world what its people yearn for, and what they deserve: a world without any war, a full generation of peace." [65] Such lofty sentiments were hardly out of keeping with either the occasion or the audience of dignitaries before whom the President stood. Yet there was more than a touch of irony in the fact that men spoke repeatedly of peace before a body whose efforts to organize the peace were clearly in a state of shambles. From the President's own viewpoint, it was the doctrine of nuclear sufficiency, far more than the U.N. Charter, which held the key to a world without war. And the fact that in 1970 the world as a whole spent more than $200 billion on military arms—an amount equivalent to the combined Gross National Products of almost a hundred less developed countries—indicated he was far from alone in his reliance on military strength.

Nor could it really be said that a generation of older, cynical men were at fault for this dreary state of affairs, despite the world-wide cries of youth for a greater role in determining the destiny of mankind. As part of its silver jubilee in July, the U.N. had brought some 650 young people from 113 states to its New York chambers for a World

Youth Assembly, there to draft a message embodying the hopes of youth for the world at large. The result was a replay in miniature of the same lamentable conditions which afflicted the world body as a whole. While the smaller commissions dealing with such topics as education and the environment drafted their recommendations wisely and well, in an atmosphere of relative calm and reason, the larger political meetings were beset by shouts, table-pounding, and general tumult, so much so that many delegates did not even get a chance to speak. When representatives from South Vietnam and Nationalist China were rudely denied the platform, 30 delegates from 19 countries walked out of the conference in protest, proving that youth had found no better way to bridge the world's differences than the elders they so frequently condemned.

In the uneven struggle for a better world, such contradictions were hardly new. For ages men had talked of peace while arming to the teeth for war, and 1970 was certainly no exception. As with every year, its trends were contradictory, its results by-and-large inconclusive. Though the United States had moved to expand the Indochina war into Cambodia, it was also moving to wind down the scale of that conflict and reduce its own participation. Though the Soviets were thrusting toward a global reach for their military power, they were also talking seriously with the United States about limiting the strategic arms race and bringing a measure of stability and accommodation to Central Europe and Berlin. Though a peaceful settlement had yet to come to the Middle East, the shooting at least had stopped. And if in the name of peace men continued to gird for war, there were also signs that economic necessity and the need to tend to long neglected internal disparities might soon impose a ceiling of their own. In such contradictory ways, the world appeared to be moving into a more tranquil— perhaps even better—phase, and men could hope that, for all their troubles, a generation of peace might indeed lay in store.

Chronology of Major Events

JANUARY 1—DECEMBER 31, 1970

N.B. Italicized references are to sections of the text which provide additional information or background data.

The following symbols are used as cross references to other entries within the Chronology:

P—High-level contact with the U.S. President, listed under "The United States."

G—U.N. General Assembly action, listed under "The United Nations."

S—U.N. Security Council action, listed under "The United Nations."

1. THE UNITED STATES

MAJOR TREATIES AND AGREEMENTS [1]

Entered into force:

Feb. 27. Protocol of Amendment to the Charter of the Organization of American States (Protocol of Buenos Aires), signed at Buenos Aires Feb. 27, 1967 (TIAS 6847). (*Sec. 27*)

Mar. 5. Treaty on the Non-Proliferation of Nuclear Weapons, signed at Washington, London, and Moscow, July 1, 1968 (TIAS 6839). (*Ch. 3*)

Apr. 29. Convention on the Privileges and Immunities of the United Nations,

---

[1] The initials TIAS refer to Treaties and Other International Acts Series published by the U.S. Department of State.

approved by the General Assembly Feb. 13, 1946; entered into force Sept. 17, 1946; for the U.S. Apr. 29, 1970. (TIAS 6900)
Sept. 26. Agreement of Friendship and Cooperation Between the U.S. and Spain, signed at Washington Aug. 6, 1970 (TIAS 6924); supersedes defense agreement of Sept. 26, 1953. (*Sec. 33*)

Signed:

Feb. 10. Agreement with the U.S.S.R. on cultural exchanges (done at Washington (TIAS 6878). (*Sec. 2*)
June 19. International Patent Cooperation Treaty, done at Washington.
Dec. 16. Convention for the Suppression of Unlawful Seizure of Aircraft, done at The Hague. (*Sec. 41*)

Transmitted to Senate:

Feb. 19. Convention on the Prevention and Punishment of the Crime of Genocide (entered into force Jan. 12, 1951; previously submitted to the Senate in 1949).
Aug. 19. Protocol for the Prohibition of the Use in War of Asphyxiating, Poisonous or Other Gases, and of Bacteriological Methods of Warfare, signed at Geneva June 17, 1925; first transmitted in 1926. (*Ch. 3*)
Sept. 24. Nice Agreement Concerning the International Classification of Goods and Services to Which Trademarks Are Applied, signed at Nice June 15, 1957.

PRESIDENTIAL VISITORS

Following is a list of the principal heads of states, governments, and international organizations received by President Richard M. Nixon during 1970 (in Washington unless otherwise noted):
Jan. 27–28—Prime Minister Harold Wilson, United Kingdom. (*Ch. 9*)
Feb. 24–26—President Georges Pompidou, France. (*Sec. 33*)
Apr. 10–11—Chancellor Willy Brandt, Federal Republic of Germany. (*Sec. 35*)
Apr. 14–15—Prime Minister Hilmar Baunsgaard, Denmark.
May 26–27—President Suharto, Indonesia (*Sec. 24*)
June 2–4—President Rafael Caldera Rodríguez, Venezuela. (*Sec. 27*)
June 4—Prime Minister Ahmed Laraki, Morocco.
July 23–24—President Urho K. Kekkonen, Finland.
Aug. 4—President Joseph D. Mobutu, Congo (Kinshasa).
Aug. 11—Prime Minister Hugh L. Shearer, Jamaica.
Sept. 3—President Gustavo Díaz Ordaz, Mexico (at Coronado, Calif.).
Sept. 18–19—Premier Golda Meir, Israel.
Oct. 21—Prince Souvanna Phouma, Laos.
Oct. 24—Premier Eisaku Sato, Japan.
Oct. 25—Head of State Cheng Yeng, Cambodia; Prime Minister C. K. Yen, Republic of China; Archbishop Makarios II, President of Cyprus; Emperor Haile Selassie I, Ethiopia; President Yahya Khan, Pakistan; President Demetrio B. Lakas, Panama.
Oct. 26—President Nicolae Ceauşescu, Rumania.
Nov. 5—Prime Minister Lee Kuan Yew, Singapore.
Nov. 13—President-elect Lúis Echeverría Álvarez, Mexico. (*Sec. 29*)

Dec. 8—King Hussein, Jordan.
Dec. 17-18—Prime Minister Edward Heath, United Kingdom. (*Ch. 9*)

PRESIDENTIAL TRAVELS

Aug. 20-21. The President visits Puerto Vallarta, Mexico, with President Gustavo Díaz Ordaz.
Sept. 27–Oct. 5. The President visits Italy (Sept. 27-28), the Vatican (Sept. 28), NATO Southern Command, Naples (Sept. 29-30), Yugoslavia (Sept. 30–Oct. 1), Spain (Oct. 2-3), United Kingdom (Oct. 3), Ireland (Oct. 3-5). (*Secs. 7, 8, 33*)
Nov. 12. The President attends the funeral of President Charles de Gaulle and confers with President Pompidou.

THE CONGRESS

Jan. 19, 1970–Jan. 2, 1971. The 91st Congress holds its Second Session and adopts the following major enactments affecting foreign affairs (with Public Law numbers and dates of presidential approval):
P.L. 91-194, Feb. 9 (H.R. 15149). Foreign Assistance and Related Programs Appropriation Act, 1970. (*Sec. 39*)
P.L. 91-217, Mar. 19 (H.R. 14944). Authorizing increased police protection for the White House and foreign embassies.
P.L. 91-246, May 12 (S.3544). Extending the Arms Control and Disarmament Agency authorization for FY 1971 and FY 1972.
P.L. 91-273, June 2 (S. 3813). Authorizing appropriations to the Atomic Energy Commission.
P.L. 91-303, July 2 (H.R. 16516). National Aeronautics and Space Administration Authorization Act, 1971.
P.L. 91-352, July 24 (S. 3430). Amending the Peace Corps Act.
P.L. 91-438, Oct. 7 (H.J. Res 589). Supporting and cooperating fully with the international biological program.
P.L. 91-439, Oct. 7 (H.R. 18127). Atomic Energy Commission appropriations, FY 1971.
P.L. 91-441, Oct. 7 (H.R. 17123). Military procurement authorization for FY 1971.
P.L. 91-447, Oct. 21 (H.R. 14685). Encouraging national efforts to increase foreign travel to the U.S.
P.L. 91-469, Oct. 21 (H.R. 15424). Merchant Marine Act of 1970.
P.L. 91-472, Oct. 21 (H.R. 17575). Departments of State, Justice, and Commerce, the Judiciary, and Related Agencies Appropriations Act, 1971.
P.L. 91-511, Oct. 26 (H.R. 17604). Military Construction Authorization Act, 1971.
P.L. 91-524, Nov. 30 (H.R. 18546). Extending the Agricultural Trade Development and Assistance Act of 1954 (P.L. 480).
P.L. 91-544, Dec. 11 (H.R. 17970). Military Construction Appropriations Act, 1971.
P.L. 91-599, Dec. 30 (H.R. 18306). Providing for increased U.S. participation in international financial institutions. (*Sec. 39*)
P.L. 91-619, Dec. 31 (H.R. 17867). Foreign Assistance and Related Programs Appropriation Act, 1971. (*Sec 39*)

P.L. 91-622, Dec. 31 (S.J. Res. 173). Authorizing an expansion grant for U.N. headquarters.
P.L. 91-652, Jan. 5, 1971 (H.R. 19911). Special Foreign Assistance Act of 1971. (*Secs. 15, 39*)
P.L. 91-668, Jan. 11, 1971 (H.R. 19590). Department of Defense Appropriation Act, 1971. (*Sec. 11*)
P.L. 91-672, Jan. 12, 1971 (H.R. 15628). Amending the Foreign Military Sales Act. (*Sec. 4*)
P.L. 91-694, Jan. 12, 1971 (H.R. 19567). Continuing the International Coffee Agreement Act of 1968 through June 30, 1971.

OTHER DEVELOPMENTS

Jan. 31. Dr. Arthur F. Burns succeeds William McChesney Martin, Jr. as Chairman of the Federal Reserve Board. (*Ch. 10*)
Feb. 18. President Nixon issues a 43,000-word message to Congress on the State of the World called *U.S. Foreign Policy for the 1970's: A New Strategy for Peace.* (*Sec. 3*)
Apr. 6. Dr. Curtis W. Tarr is sworn in as Director of Selective Service, replacing Gen. Lewis B. Hershey who resigned Feb. 16. (*Sec. 11*)
Apr. 17. Apollo 13, launched Apr. 11, reaches a safe splashdown in the Pacific following an accident which prevented the scheduled moon landing. (*Sec. 41*)
Apr. 20. President Nixon announces that the ceiling on U.S. troops in Vietnam will be reduced to 284,000 from 434,000 during the next year (*Sec. 17*)
May 4. Four Kent State University students are killed and at least 8 wounded by National Guard gunfire as a result of protests over President Nixon's announcement Apr. 30 that U.S. and South Vietnamese forces have joined operations on Cambodian soil. (*Sec. 1*)
June 24. Under Secretary of State Elliot L. Richardson succeeds Robert Finch as Secretary of the Department of Health, Education and Welfare. John N. Irwin 2nd is named Under Secretary of State Aug. 19.
July 1. Ambassador David K. E. Bruce is appointed as chief negotiator at the Paris peace talks, succeeding Philip C. Habib. (*Sec. 21*)
Nov. 3. In nationwide congressional elections, Republicans gain two seats in the Senate and the Democrats win nine additional seats in the House of Representatives. (*Sec. 1*)
Nov. 25. Secretary of the Interior Walter J. Hickel resigns and Rogers C. B. Morton, Chairman of the Republican National Committee is named to succeed him. (*Sec. 1*)
Dec. 11. Representative George H. W. Bush of Texas is appointed U.S. Permanent Representative to the U.N., succeeding Ambassador Charles W. Yost. (*Sec. 40*)
Dec. 14. Governor John B. Connally of Texas is appointed Secretary of the Treasury. He succeeds David M. Kennedy, who is named Ambassador-at-Large with Cabinet rank. (*Ch. 10*)

2. THE COMMUNIST WORLD

THE SOVIET BLOC

May 12–14. The Council for Mutual Economic Assistance (Comecon) holds its 24th session in Warsaw and charts various new steps toward economic integration. It formally establishes an International Investment Bank in Moscow on July 10, and is expected to begin operations Jan. 1, 1971. (*Sec. 7*)

June 21–22. The Foreign Ministers of the Warsaw Pact countries meet in Warsaw and approve a tentative agenda for the proposed conference on European security. (*Sec. 5*)

Aug. 20. Communist party and government leaders of the Warsaw Pact countries meet in Moscow and formally approve the West German-Soviet treaty of Aug. 12 over East Germany's objections. (*Sec. 35*)

Dec. 2. The Political Consultative Committee of the Warsaw Pact meets in East Berlin, endorses the proposed West German-Polish treaty, and reaffirms its interest in a European security conference.

U.S.S.R.

Apr. 16–Aug. 14. The second round (Phase II) of the U.S.-Soviet arms limitation talks (SALT) is held in Vienna. (*Sec. 9*)

June 14. A new Supreme Soviet is elected from party-approved lists. Aleksei N. Kosygin (first elected Oct. 15, 1964) is reelected as Chairman of the Council of Ministers on July 15. (*Sec. 6*)

June 19. Soyuz 9, a two-man, earth-orbiting spacecraft, returns safely to earth after 17 days and almost 17 hours aloft—the longest manned space flight in history.

Aug. 12. The U.S.S.R. and West Germany sign a treaty pledging to observe their current borders as inviolable. (*Secs. 5, 35*)

Sept. 12. Luna 16 is launched and effects a moon landing Sept. 21, returning to earth safely Sept. 24 with lunar rock samples.

Nov. 2–Dec. 18. Phase III of SALT is held in Helsinki. (*Sec. 9*)

Nov. 17. The Soviet Union announces that a self-propelled, 8-wheeled vehicle, Lunokhod I, is landed on the moon by Luna 17.

ALBANIA

Sept. 20. Candidates of the National Front win 100 per cent of the vote in elections to the People's Assembly.

Nov. 23. Mehmet Shehu (first elected July 20, 1954) is reelected Chairman of the Council of Ministers.

CZECHOSLOVAKIA (*Sec. 7*)

Jan. 28. Prime Minister Oldřich Cerník is replaced by Lubomír Štrougal in a shakeup of the Communist party leadership and government.

May 6. A new 20-year Treaty of Friendship, Cooperation, and Mutual Assistance is signed with the U.S.S.R.

June 26. Former party First Secretary Alexander Dubček is expelled from the party by a majority vote of the Central Committee. On July 8, the Federal Assembly unanimously votes to dismiss Dubček from his post as deputy and accepts the resignation of Cerník.

Dec. 20. Parliament approves constitutional amendments returning to the central government many of the powers given the Czech and Slovak republics under Dubček's leadership.

HUNGARY (Sec. 7)

Nov. 23–28. The Tenth Congress of the Hungarian Socialist Workers' party is held in Budapest and reelects János Kádár (first designated Oct. 25, 1956) as First Secretary of the party.

POLAND (Sec. 7)

Dec. 7. Premier Jozef Cyrankiewicz and Chancellor Willy Brandt of the Federal Republic of Germany sign a treaty calling for the normalization of relations between the two countries and the recognition of the Oder-Neisse line.

Dec. 14. Widespread rioting beginning in Gdansk and spreading to Gdynia, Sczecin, and other cities breaks out as a result of sharp increases in food prices announced Dec. 12.

Dec. 19. Calm is restored in the cities torn by riots, which reportedly caused 45 dead and 1,165 injured.

Dec. 20. Edward Gierek is appointed First Secretary of the Polish Workers' United party, replacing Wladyslaw Gomulka (elected Oct. 21, 1956).

Dec. 23. The Parliament (Sejm) elects Piotr Jaroszewicz as Chairman of the Council of Ministers, replacing Jozef Cyrankiewicz (elected Mar. 19, 1954), who in turn succeeds Marshal Marian Spychalski (elected Apr. 11, 1968), as Chairman of the Council of State.

RUMANIA ᴾ (Sec. 7)

July 7. A 20-year treaty of friendship, cooperation, and mutual assistance, drawn up in 1968, with the U.S.S.R. is signed in Bucharest.

YUGOSLAVIA ᴾ (Secs. 7, 8)

Sept. 21. President Josip Broz Tito announces a plan to establish a collective presidency with balanced representation for the nation's six republics.

3. THE WESTERN NATIONS

May 26–27. The NATO Council meets in ministerial session in Rome and proposes exploratory talks on mutual and balanced force reductions in Europe.

June 8–9. The NATO Nuclear Planning Group meets in Venice.

June 11. The Defense Planning Committee meets in ministerial session in Brussels.

Sept. 30. Manlio Brosio (Italy) resigns as Secretary-General. Joseph M.A.H. Luns (Netherlands) will succeed him, effective Oct. 1, 1971.

Oct. 1. Adm. Charles K. Duncan (U.S.) succeeds Adm. Ephraim P. Holmes (U.S.) as Supreme Allied Commander Atlantic (SACLANT).

Dec. 2. The NATO Defense Planning Committee meets in Brussels and drafts a defense plan for the 1970's.

Dec. 3–4. The NATO Council meets in ministerial session at Brussels.

ORGANIZATION FOR ECONOMIC COOPERATION AND DEVELOPMENT (O.E.C.D.)

May 20–21. The O.E.C.D. ministerial Council meets in Paris and reaches a compromise agreement on trade preferences for the developing countries. (*Sec. 39*)

Sept. 14–15. The Development Assistance Committee meets in Tokyo.

Nov. 24–25. The O.E.C.D. Committee on Environment holds its first meeting in Paris.

THE EUROPEAN COMMUNITIES

Mar. 19. A commercial agreement is signed with Yugoslavia.

May 29. The Council of Ministers appoints Franco Maria Malfatti (Italy) as President of the Commission to succeed Jean Rey (Belgium) for a two-year term beginning July 2, 1970.

June 30. Negotiations with Denmark, Ireland, Norway, and the United Kingdom for Community membership open in Luxembourg. (*Sec. 34*)

Dec. 5. Malta signs an association agreement with the E.E.C., effective Apr. 1, 1971.

Dec. 14–15. The Council of Ministers meets in Brussels and charts various steps toward full economic and monetary union. (*Sec. 34*)

EUROPEAN FREE TRADE ASSOCIATION (EFTA)

Mar. 1. Iceland is formally admitted to membership.

Nov. 5–6. The ministerial Council meets in Geneva.

WESTERN EUROPEAN UNION (W.E.U.)

June 5. France ends its 18-month boycott of the Council of Ministers.

Nov. 9. Georges Heisbourg (Luxembourg) is appointed to succeed Maurice Iweins D'Eeckhoutte (Belgium) effective Jan. 1, 1971.

AUSTRIA

Mar. 1. The Socialist party wins a plurality in elections to the National Council.
Apr. 21. A Socialist minority cabinet headed by Bruno Kreisky is sworn in.

CANADA (*Secs. 23, 30*)

Apr. 29. The Liberal party wins a large majority in the Quebec provincial elections. A new government is formed, headed by Robert A. Bourassa.
May 31. The Canadian dollar is allowed to float freely.
Oct. 13. Canada and the People's Republic of China agree to establish diplomatic relations at the ambassadorial level.

CYPRUS ˢ (*Sec. 16*)

July 5. In parliamentary elections, the majority of seats at stake are won by the moderate United party and the Progressive party of the Working People of Cyprus.

DENMARK ᴾ

FINLAND ᴾ

Mar. 15–16. Parliamentary elections show a marked swing to the right in voter sympathies.
May 14. President Urho Kekkonen appoints a new coalition government, with Teuvo Aura, a Liberal, as Prime Minister.
July 15. Another coalition, this one headed by Ahti Karjalaïnen of the Center party, takes office.
July 20. Treaty of Friendship with the U.S.S.R., in force since 1948, is extended for 20 more years. (*Sec. 5*)

FRANCE ᴾ (*Sec. 33*)

May 15. The first in a series of 8 nuclear tests is carried out at the South Pacific proving ground of Mururoa Atoll.
Nov. 9. Ex-President Charles de Gaulle dies in Colombey-les-Deux-Eglises, 13 days before his 80th birthday.

GERMAN FEDERAL REPUBLIC ᴾ (*Sec. 35*)

Mar. 19. Chancellor Willy Brandt confers with Prime Minister Willi Stoph of the German Democratic Republic in Erfurt, East Germany.
May 21. Brandt and Stoph hold a second meeting in Kasel, West Germany.
Aug. 12. The German Federal Republic and the U.S.S.R. sign a treaty renouncing the use of force in their relations and otherwise providing for greater economic and political cooperation; in Moscow.

GREECE *(Sec. 33)*

Nov. 29. Candidates for a 56-man Consultative Committee on Legislation are chosen by the regime's college of electors.

ICELAND

July 10. Premier Bjarni Benediktsson (Independence party; assumed office Nov. 1963) dies. Jóhann Hafstein (same party) is named Premier *ad interim.* Oct. 10. Jóhann Hafstein becomes Premier.

IRELAND [P] *(Sec. 33)*

ITALY [P] *(Sec. 33)*

Feb. 7. The interim all Christian Democratic cabinet headed by Mariano Rumor resigns.

Mar. 27. Rumor forms a Center-Left coalition cabinet which resigns July 6.

June 7–8. Elections to regional, provincial, and municipal assemblies register a slight setback for the Christian Democratic party.

Aug. 6. A new Center-Left coalition government is sworn in under the leadership of Emilio Colombo (Christian Democrat).

Nov. 6. Italy and the People's Republic of China announce an agreement to establish diplomatic relations and exchange ambassadors within three months.

LIECHTENSTEIN

Feb. 1. The Patriotic Union wins a majority in elections to the 15-member Parliament.

PORTUGAL [S G] *(Sec. 33)*

July 27. Former Premier Antonio de Oliveira Salazar (in office from 1928 to 1968) dies.

SPAIN [P] *(Sec. 33)*

SWEDEN *(Sec. 33)*

Sept. 20. In elections to the newly reorganized Parliament, Premier Olof Palme's Socialist party wins 163 seats in the 350-member legislature and becomes dependent on the 17 seats held by the Communist party for support on major issues.

UNITED KINGDOM ᴾ (*Sec. 34*)

June 18. In elections for a new House of Commons, the Conservative party led by Edward Heath scores an upset victory, winning 330 of 630 seats and thereby defeating the bid of Prime Minister Harold Wilson (Labor party; assumed office Oct. 1964) for another term.

June 22. Wilson resigns and Heath becomes Prime Minister.

THE VATICAN ᴾ

Aug. 14. Ambassadorial-level relations are reopened with Yugoslavia. (*Sec. 7*)

Nov. 12. Pope Paul VI receives Soviet Foreign Minister Andrei Gromyko for an audience lasting more than an hour. (*Sec. 5*)

Nov. 26–Dec. 5. Pope Paul VI undertakes a 30,000-mile journey to 9 cities in Asia and the Pacific. (*Sec. 23*)

4. THE MIDDLE EAST

THE ARAB-ISRAELI CONFLICT ˢ ᴳ

Aug. 1. Lt. Gen. Odd Bull (Norway) retires from command of the U.N. Truce Supervisory Organization and is replaced by Gen. Ensio Siilasvuo (Finland). (*Sec. 13*)

Aug. 7. A 90-day cease-fire and military standstill goes into effect along the Suez Canal. (*Sec. 13*)

Aug. 25. Representatives of Israel, Jordan, and the U.A.R. begin separate meetings with U.N. mediator Gunnar V. Jarring in New York. (*Sec. 13*)

Nov. 5. The U.A.R. extends the 90-day cease-fire for another 90 days; Israel pledges to comply on a day-to-day basis. (*Sec. 14*)

INTER-ARAB AFFAIRS

Feb. 7–9. Leaders of the U.A.R., Libya, the Sudan, Jordan, and Iraq convene in Cairo to discuss strategy against Israel.

Mar. 24–26. A meeting of 22 Islamic Foreign Ministers and two Palestinian guerrilla organizations in Jidda decides to establish a Permanent Secretariat.

Nov. 9. Libya, the Sudan, and the U.A.R. announce agreement to work toward a federation.

ISRAEL ᴾ (*Sec. 15*) (*Ch. 4*)

JORDAN ᴾ (*Sec. 15*)

June 8. A new 27-man Central Committee of Palestinian commando organizations elects Yasir Arafat over-all commander at an emergency session, as fighting erupts between Arab guerrillas and the Jordanian army.

June 9. King Hussein escapes an assassination attempt by Palestinian commandos, as fighting between commandos and the King's army spreads.
June 12. A truce is called in Jordan as commando leaders release some 60 Westerners they had been holding as hostages to their demands on King Hussein.
June 25. Premier Bahjat al-Tahouni resigns.
June 26. A new cabinet under Abdel Monem Rifai is formed.
Sept. 1. Another attempt on the life of Hussein by commandos is foiled; renewed fighting between commando groups and the army engulfs the country.
Sept. 6. The Arab League Council ends a two-day emergency session in Cairo with a plea for a halt to the fighting in Jordan. Four New York-bound airliners are hijacked over Europe by members of a Palestinian commando group; 150 passengers are held as hostages on an airstrip in Jordan; a fifth airliner is seized Sept. 9.
Sept. 12. Arab commandos release all but 40 captive passengers and blow up three hijacked airliners.
Sept. 16. King Hussein reshuffles the cabinet in a move to ease the crisis, names Brig. Gen. Mohammed Daoud Premier, and proclaims martial law.
Sept. 25. A cease-fire in Jordan's internal fighting goes into effect.
Sept. 26. A new military-civilian government is appointed with Ahmed Toukan as Premier, following the resignation of Daoud.
Sept. 27. Arab heads of state, including King Hussein and Yasir Arafat, sign a 14-point pact in Cairo, calling for an immediate cease-fire and appointing a three-man committee headed by Bahi Ladgham of Tunisia to supervise a truce.
Oct. 28. King Hussein appoints his third new government in six weeks, with Wasfi el-Tal as Premier.

LEBANON (*Sec. 15*)

Aug. 17. Suleiman Franjieh is elected President by Parliament, succeeding Charles Helou (assumed office Sept. 23, 1964).
Oct. 5. President Franjieh designates Saeb Salaam as Premier, following the resignation on Oct. 3 of Premier Karami and his cabinet.

MUSCAT AND OMAN [G] (*Sec. 16*)

July 23. Sultan Said bin Taimur is overthrown by his son, Qabus bin Said, who renames the nation "Oman" in an apparent bid for national unity.

PERSIAN GULF STATES [S] (*Sec. 16*)

Jan. 19. *Bahrain*—Shaikh Khalifa is appointed President of the Council of State.
Apr. 2. *Qatar*—A new provisional constitution is promulgated, effective July 1970.

SOUTH YEMEN (ADEN) (*Sec. 16*)

Dec. 1. A new constitution goes into effect, formally changing the name of the nation to People's Democratic Republic of Yemen and appointing a Supreme

Provisional People's Council to exercise interim legislative powers until the establishment of a permanent legislature through elections to be held before Oct. 31, 1971.

SYRIA (Sec. 15)

Oct. 19. The ruling Baath party calls an emergency session to name a successor to President and Premier Nureddin al-Atassi, who reportedly resigned on Oct. 16 and is under house arrest.

Nov. 13. Lt. Gen. Hafez al-Assad establishes himself as party and government chief and names Ahmed al-Khatib as acting Head of State.

Nov. 27. The government announces its intention of joining the tripartite alliance forming between the U.A.R., Libya, and the Sudan.

TURKEY (Sec. 16)

Feb. 14. The cabinet of Prime Minister Suleiman Demirel resigns following an adverse vote in the Grand National Assembly.

Mar. 6. Demirel's cabinet is reconstituted with the same membership as before.

UNITED ARAB REPUBLIC (Ch. 4)

Sept. 28. President Gamal Abdel Nasser dies of a heart attack at age 52; Vice-President Anwar el-Sadat becomes interim President.

Oct. 7. The National Assembly unanimously nominates Sadat as President.

Oct. 15. In a national referendum, Sadat is endorsed as President by 90.04 per cent of the voters.

Oct. 17. Sadat is sworn in for a six-year term at a Special Session of the National Assembly; Ali Sabry is sworn in as Vice-President.

Oct. 21. Mahmoud Fawzi is sworn in as Premier.

Nov. 15. Premier Fawzi resigns and is asked by President Sadat to form a new cabinet.

Nov. 17. A new cabinet is formed under Fawzi.

YEMEN (SANA)

Feb. 5. Former Premier Moshen al-Aini is appointed Prime Minister, succeeding Abdallah al-Kurshumi.

5. SOUTH ASIA

CENTRAL TREATY ORGANIZATION (CENTO)

May 14–15. The CENTO Council of Ministers holds its 17th meeting in Washington. (Sec. 16)

CEYLON (*Sec. 26*)

May 27. The Sri Lanka Freedom party wins 91 of the 157 seats in parliamentary elections.
May 28. Mrs. Sirimavo Bandaranaike becomes Prime Minister, succeeding Dudley Senanayake (appointed Mar. 25, 1960).

INDIA (*Sec. 26*)

Mar. 28. In elections to the Upper House of Parliament, the ruling New Congress party suffers a setback.
Aug. 8. India and the German Democratic Republic agree to establish diplomatic ties.
Sept. 17. Prime Minister Indira Gandhi's New Congress party registers unexpected gains in elections in the Communist-led state of Kerala.
Oct. 17. The opposition or "Old" Congress party, led by President S. Nijalingappa, installs a right-wing coalition government in Uttar Pradesh.
Dec. 20. A right-wing and socialist coalition replaces the New Congress party in control of Bihar state.
Dec. 22. Prime Minister Indira Gandhi dissolves the Lower House and calls for new parliamentary elections.

NEPAL

Apr. 13. King Mahendra II takes over the premiership following the resignation of Prime Minister Kirti Nidhi Bista.

PAKISTAN ᴾ (*Sec. 26*)

Nov. 12–13. A cyclone and tidal waves causing at least 200,000 deaths force the postponement of elections in nine East Pakistan districts for a second time.
Dec. 7. In the nation's first direct elections based on universal suffrage (originally scheduled for Oct. 5), the East Pakistani pro-autonomy Awami League led by Sheik Mujibur Rahman wins an absolute majority in the National Assembly. The Awami League makes another strong showing in elections for provincial assemblies on Dec. 17.

6. EAST ASIA AND THE PACIFIC

SOUTHEAST ASIA TREATY ORGANIZATION (SEATO)

July 2–3. The SEATO Council holds its 15th annual meeting in Manila. (*Sec. 24*)

THE ANZUS TREATY

Sept. 26. The ANZUS Council holds its 20th meeting in Washington. (*Sec. 24*)

THE ASIAN AND PACIFIC COUNCIL (ASPAC)

June 17–19. The fifth ministerial meeting of ASPAC is held in Wellington, N. Z.

ASSOCIATION OF SOUTHEAST ASIAN NATIONS (ASEAN) (*Sec. 21*)

Apr. 23. ASEAN delegates meet in Djakarta to make plans for a conference of Asian and Pacific foreign ministers to discuss the Cambodian situation.
May 16–17. An 11-nation conference of foreign ministers meets in Djakarta and calls for a broadly based conference on all of Indochina.

AUSTRALIA

Nov. 21. Partial elections to the Senate result in a sharp setback for the Liberal-Country party coalition, headed by Prime Minister John G. Gorton.

INDOCHINA CONFLICT (*Ch. 5*)

Apr. 20. President Nixon announces the scheduled reduction of the U.S. troop ceiling in Vietnam from 434,000 to 284,000 over the next 12 months.
Apr. 25–26. A summit conference of Indochinese leftist leaders, including Prince Norodom Sihanouk, is held somewhere in south China, with the participation of Chinese Premier Chou En-lai.
Apr. 29. South Vietnamese forces undertake a major offensive operation in Cambodian border areas with U.S. tactical and logistical support.
Apr. 30. President Nixon announces that U.S. combat forces have joined South Vietnamese forces in joint operations on Cambodian territory.
June 30. President Nixon announces that the last American advisers and ground troops have withdrawn from Cambodia in conformity with his deadline for a pullout.
July 5–6. Representatives of the six nations contributing troops to the anti-Communist resistance in Vietnam confer in Saigon.
Oct. 7. In a nationwide, televised address, President Nixon calls for a stand-still cease-fire throughout Indochina.

CAMBODIA [P] (*Sec. 18*)

Mar. 18. Prince Norodom Sihanouk (installed June 20, 1960) is deposed as Head of State in a bloodless coup led by Prime Minister Lon Nol and Deputy Prime Minister Prince Sisiwak Sirik Matak.
Mar. 21. Acting Head of State Cheng Heng is inducted to succeed Prince Sihanouk in an acting capacity.

May 5. From his place of exile in China, Sihanouk announces the formation of a new, left-wing political movement called the "National Front of Kampuchea [Cambodia]" (FUNK) and the formation in exile of a "Royal Government of National Union" headed by former Prime Minister Penn Nouth.
Oct. 9. Cambodia officially declares itself the "Khmer Republic."

VIETNAM, REPUBLIC OF *(Sec. 17)*

June 28. Nationwide provincial and municipal elections are successfully held despite Communist efforts at disruption.
Aug. 30. Elections are held for 30 of 60 seats in the Upper House.

CHINA, PEOPLE'S REPUBLIC OF [G]

Jan. 20. U.S. and Chinese ambassadorial representatives meet in Warsaw for the first time since Jan. 8, 1968; another meeting is scheduled for May 20. *(Secs. 2, 23)*
Apr. 24. Peking announces the launching of its first earth satellite, called "The East Is Red." *(Sec. 23)*
May 18. Peking cancels the 137th ambassadorial meeting with the United States scheduled for Warsaw on May 20. *(Secs. 2, 23)*
Aug. 23–Sept. 6. The Central Committee of the Chinese Communist party meets to approve an economic plan for 1970 and to announce that a new National People's Congress will be convened "at an appropriate time." *(Sec. 23)*

CHINA, REPUBLIC OF [P G] *(Sec. 24)*

FIJI [G S] *(Sec. 40)*

Oct. 10. The South Pacific Islands of Fiji become independent within the Commonwealth, with Sir Kamisese K. T. Mara as Prime Minister.

INDONESIA [P] *(Sec. 24)*

June 21. Former President Sukarno, a leader of Indonesia's independence movement, dies in Djakarta.

JAPAN [P] *(Secs. 25, 38)*

Jan. 14. Eisaku Sato (Liberal Democratic party; first elected Nov. 9, 1964) is reelected Prime Minister. He names an all-Liberal-Democratic cabinet with Kiichi Aichi continuing as Minister of Foreign Affairs.
Feb. 3. Japan signs the Treaty for the Non-Proliferation of Nuclear Weapons.
Mar. 14–Sept. 13. Expo '70 is held in Osaka.
June 23. The United States and Japan automatically extend their mutual security pact for another 10 years.

Dec. 21. The U.S.-Japanese Security Consultative Committee holds its 12th meeting in Tokyo.

KOREA, DEMOCRATIC PEOPLE'S REPUBLIC OF G (*Sec. 24*)

Nov. 2–13. The Korean Workers' (Communist) party holds its Fifth Congress and reelects Premier Kim Il Sung as Secretary-General.

KOREA, REPUBLIC OF G (*Sec. 24*)

Dec. 19. Paek Tu Chin is appointed Premier, succeeding Chung Il Kwon.

LAOS P (*Sec. 19*)

MALAYSIA (*Sec. 24*)

Aug. 30. Prince Abdul Rahman announces his retirement as Prime Minister, effective Sept. 21; he is succeeded by Deputy Prime Minister Abdul Razak on Sept. 22.

SINGAPORE P

Nov. 22. President Yusof bin Ishak dies.
Dec. 30. Benjamin Henry Sheares is unanimously elected President by Parliament, after being nominated for the office by Prime Minister Lee Kuan Yew.

7. AFRICA

GENERAL

Jan. 28–30. The fourth Ordinary Session of Heads of State of the Afro-Malagasy Joint Organization (OCAM) is held in Yaoundé, Cameroon; the two-year term of Falilou Kane (Senegal; appointed Feb. 24, 1968) as Secretary-General is extended for an additional year; Mauritius attends as the organization's 15th member. (*Sec. 31*)
Aug. 24–29. The Sixth Annual Meeting of the Board of Governors of the African Development Bank is held at Fort-Lamy, Chad; Abdelwahab Labidi (Tunisia) is elected to succeed Mamoun Beheiry (the Sudan) as President and Chairman of the Board of Directors.
Aug. 24–31. The Council of Ministers of the Organization of African Unity (O.A.U.) holds its 15th Ordinary Session in Addis Ababa, Ethiopia. (*Sec. 31*)
Sept. 1–3. The Seventh Session of the Assembly of Heads of State and Government of the O.A.U. meets in Addis Ababa and sharply criticizes countries

supplying arms to South Africa and Israel's continued occupation of Arab territories. (*Sec. 31*)

Dec. 9–11. An extraordinary session of the O.A.U. Council of Ministers is convened in Lagos, Nigeria to protest the invasion of Guinea by Portuguese-backed mercenaries on Nov. 22. (*Sec. 31*)

CAMEROON

Mar. 28. President Ahmadou Ahidjo (elected Mar. 20, 1965) is reelected for a five-year term in an uncontested popular election.

CONGO (BRAZZAVILLE)

Jan. 3. Commandant Marien N'Gouabi (assumed power Aug. 3, 1968) is reinaugurated as Head of State; he institutes a new constitution dissolving Parliament, whose functions are given to the ruling Congolese Labor party. (*Ch. 8*)

CONGO (KINSHASA) P

Oct. 31–Nov. 1. President Joseph D. Mobutu (assumed power Nov. 24, 1965) is reelected in an uncontested popular election; he is inaugurated Dec. 5 for a seven-year term. (*Ch. 8*)

DAHOMEY (*Ch. 8*)

Apr. 3. Presidential elections, held Mar. 9–31, are annulled in the wake of growing violence and the threat of civil war.

May 1. A three-man Presidential Council is formed, each member to serve as Chairman for two years on a rotating basis; Hubert Maga is inaugurated as the Council's first Chairman on May 7.

ETHIOPIA P (*Ch. 8*)

THE GAMBIA

Apr. 24. The Gambia is declared a republic following a national referendum held Apr. 20–23. Prime Minister Sir Dawda Kairaba Jawara is sworn in as President April 28 for a five-year term.

GHANA (*Ch. 8*)

Aug. 31. Following a decision by the National Assembly on July 30 to dissolve the three-man Presidential Commission, Edward Akufo-Addo is elected President by an Electoral College for a four-year term.

GUINEA [S]

Nov. 22. Portuguese-backed mercenaries, comprising an amphibious force of 350 men, attack the capital city of Conakry. (*Sec. 31*)

IVORY COAST

Nov. 29. President Félix Houphouët-Boigny (first elected Nov. 27, 1960) is reelected for a five-year term in presidential and parliamentary elections from a single list of candidates. He is proclaimed President Dec. 14.

KENYA

Jan. 29. President Jomo Kenyatta (reelected Dec. 6, 1969) is sworn in as President for another five-year term.

LESOTHO

Jan. 27. The first parliamentary elections since the country's independence are held. Prime Minister Leabua Jonathan suspends the constitution and annuls the election results on Jan. 30–31, following a dispute over the election returns. (*Sec. 31*)

LIBYA (*Sec. 15*)

Jan. 16. The leader of the Revolutionary Command Council, Col. Mu'ammar al-Qaddhafi (assumed power Sept. 1, 1969) becomes Prime Minister, succeeding Mahmud Suleiman al-Maghreby, and names a new cabinet including four members of the Revolutionary Command Council.

June 11. The United States formally turns over Wheelus Air Force Base to Libyan control.

MALAGASY REPUBLIC (MADAGASCAR)

Sept. 6. The Social Democratic party of President Philibert Tsiranana wins a landslide victory in elections for the National Assembly.

MALAWI (*Sec. 31*)

Nov. 26. An amendment to the constitution passed by the National Assembly makes President H. Kamuzu Banda (elected May 20, 1966) President-for-Life, effective July 6, 1971.

MOROCCO [P] (*Sec. 32*)

July 24. A new constitution providing for a limited resumption of parliamentary government is overwhelmingly approved by a national referendum.

Aug. 21, 28. In a two-stage election, a new unicameral Chamber of Representatives is chosen by popular vote, despite a boycott by opposition parties and labor groups.

NIGER

Oct. 1. President Hamani Diori (assumed office Nov. 9, 1960) is reelected, unopposed, for another five-year term.

NIGERIA (*Ch. 8*)

Jan. 12. The secessionist Biafran regime proposes an armistice in the civil war, which began July 7, 1967, following the departure of Chief of State Odumegwu Ojukwu and other Biafran leaders.
Jan. 14. The Republic of Biafra ceases to exist as its Deputy Chief of State, Philip Effiong, formally surrenders to the Federal military government of Maj. Gen. Yakubu Gowon.

SENEGAL

Feb. 26. Abdou Diouf is appointed Prime Minister.

SOUTH AFRICA ᴳ ˢ (*Secs. 31, 32*)

Apr. 22. In elections to the House of Assembly, the National party of Prime Minister Balthazar Johannes Vorster retains a reduced majority.

SOUTHERN RHODESIA ᴳ ˢ (*Secs. 31, 32*)

Mar. 2. Southern Rhodesia formally becomes a republic, cutting all ties to the British crown; Clifford W. Dupont becomes interim President, and Ian D. Smith continues as Prime Minister.
Mar. 17. Reacting to the Mar. 2 declaration, the United States closes its consulate in Salisbury.
Apr. 10. The Rhodesia Front party wins all 50 white seats at stake in elections to the House of Assembly.
Apr. 14. Acting President Dupont is appointed President and is sworn in Apr. 16.

SOUTH WEST AFRICA (NAMIBIA) ᴳ ˢ (*Secs. 31, 32*)

TANZANIA (*Sec. 32*)

Oct. 30. President Julius K. Nyerere (first elected Dec. 9, 1962) is overwhelmingly reelected for another five-year term in popular elections.

TUNISIA (*Sec. 15*)

Nov. 2. Hedi Novira (Destourian Socialist party; appointed Acting Premier Oct. 9) succeeds Bahi Ladgham (same party; appointed Nov. 6, 1969).

UPPER VOLTA

June 14. A popular referendum overwhelmingly approves a new constitution that provides for election of future presidents and legislatures through universal suffrage.

Dec. 20. In elections for a new National Assembly, the former ruling party, the Voltan Democratic Union, receives an absolute majority.

8. INTER-AMERICAN AFFAIRS

GENERAL

Apr. 2. LAFTA—Gustavo Magariños (Uruguay) is reelected Executive Secretary of the Latin American Free Trade Association for a second three-year term.

June 20. Guyana and Venezuela sign an agreement to shelve their territorial dispute for 12 years.

June 25–July 8. The first meeting of the Inter-American General Assembly, established under the revised Charter of the Organization of American States (O.A.S.) is held at the Pan American Union in Washington; the Assembly unanimously condemns terrorism, political kidnapping, and extortion as crimes against humanity on June 30. (*Sec. 27*)

Sept. 1–4. The Inter-American Committee on the Alliance for Progress (CIAP) holds its 21st meeting in Washington. (*Sec. 27*).

Oct. 13. Felipe Herrera (Chile) resigns as President of the Inter-American Development Bank (I.D.B.) effective May 1971 (first elected Feb. 1960).

Oct. 26–Dec. 4. LAFTA holds its 10th general conference in Montevideo.

Nov. 27. Ortiz Mena (Mexico) is elected to succeed Herrera as President of the I.D.B.

ARGENTINA (*Sec. 29*)

June 8. President Juan Carlos Onganía (appointed June 29, 1966) resigns on the insistence of the commanders-in-chief of the three military services.

June 13. The military junta names Gen. Roberto Marcelo Levingston as President; he is sworn in June 18.

BOLIVIA (*Sec. 28*)

Oct. 6. President Alfredo Ovando Candia (seized power Sept. 26, 1969) is overthrown by a right-wing junta led by Army chief, Gen. Rogelio Miranda.

Oct. 7. Gen. Juan José Torres, backed by leftist students and workers, takes over as President.

Oct. 9. President Torres appoints a new cabinet, half of whose members are military officers.

Dec. 23. President Torres releases French Marxist writer Régis Debray.

Dec. 31. A commission is named to draft a new constitution by June 1971.

BRAZIL (*Sec. 29*)

Nov. 15. In nationwide congressional elections, the pro-government National Renovating Alliance scores its expected victory over the legal opposition, the Brazilian Democratic Movement.

CHILE (*Sec. 28*)

Sept. 4. In presidential elections, Socialist candidate Salvador Allende Gossens of the predominantly Marxist, five-party "Popular Unity" coalition narrowly defeats the National party's Jorge Alessandri Rodríguez and Radomiro Tomic, a Christian Democrat.

Oct. 24. In congressional balloting, Allende's election to a six-year term is confirmed.

Nov. 3. Allende is sworn into office, replacing Eduardo Frei Montalva, his Christian Democratic predecessor (assumed office Nov. 3, 1964).

COLOMBIA (*Sec. 29*)

Apr. 19. In a hotly contested election, the ruling National Front candidate, Misael Pastrana Borrero, narrowly defeats Gen. Gustavo Rojas Pinilla, a "populist," for the presidency.

COSTA RICA

Feb. 1. In national presidential and legislative elections, José Figueres Ferrer of the National Liberation party is elected to a four-year term beginning May 8.

CUBA

July 26. In a speech marking the anniversary of his movement, Premier Fidel Castro announces that the effort to harvest 10 million tons of sugar in 1970 has failed; he offers to resign. (*Sec. 28*)

DOMINICAN REPUBLIC (*Sec. 29*)

Apr. 16. President Joaquín Balaguer (first elected July 1, 1966) temporarily withdraws from office as Manuel Ramon Ruiz Tajada, Chief Justice of the Supreme Court, assumes the functions of the presidency.

May 16. President Balaguer is reelected to a second four-year term beginning Aug. 16.

ECUADOR *(Sec. 29)*

June 22. President José María Velasco Ibarra (assumed office Sept. 1, 1968) assumes dictatorial powers for the remainder of his term (ending Aug. 31, 1972).

GUATEMALA *(Sec. 29)*

Mar. 1. In presidential and congressional elections, right-wing candidate Col. Carlos Arana Osorio, pledging a crackdown on urban guerrillas, wins a plurality over the ruling Revolutionary party's Mario Fuentes Pieruccini; Arana's supporters also gain control of the National Congress.
July 1. Arana is inaugurated for a four-year term.

GUYANA

Feb. 23. Guyana becomes a "Co-operative Republic" within the Commonwealth, with Arthur Chung as President and Forbes Burnham continuing as Prime Minister.

JAMAICA ᴾ *(Sec. 29)*

MEXICO ᴾ *(Sec. 29)*

July 5. In presidential and legislative elections, Lúis Echeverría Alvarez of the Ruling Institutional Revolutionary party (P.R.I.) is elected President; the P.R.I. also win a majority in the Chamber of Deputies.
Dec. 1. Echeverría takes office for a six-year term, succeeding Gustavo Díaz Ordaz (assumed office Dec. 1964).

PERU

May 31. A severe earthquake kills an estimated 50,000 people and leaves another 800,000 homeless. *(Sec. 28)*

PANAMA ᴾ

Aug. 5. The ruling Junta rejects proposals redefining the status of the Panama Canal and Canal Zone.
Dec. 1. The Atlantic-Pacific Interoceanic Study Commission conditionally recommends that a second canal be built across Panamanian territory.

VENEZUELA ᴾ *(Sec. 27)*

9. THE UNITED NATIONS

MEMBERSHIP

Oct. 13. The membership is increased from 126 to 127 by the admission of Fiji. (*Sec. 40*)

SECURITY COUNCIL

Following is a list of major Security Council actions and decisions, with resolution numbers and votes:

RES/276 (1970), Jan. 30. Condemning South Africa's illegal presence in South West Africa (Namibia) (13–0–2). (*Sec. 31*)

RES/277 (1970), Mar. 18. Demanding severance of diplomatic, consular, trade, military, and other relations with Southern Rhodesia (14–0–1). (*Sec. 31*)

RES/278 (1970), May 11. Welcoming Bahrain's wish to become fully independent (unanimous). (*Sec. 16*)

RES/279 (1970), May 12. Demanding withdrawal of Israeli forces from southern Lebanon (unanimous).

RES/280 (1970), May 19. Condemning Israeli military action against Lebanon (11–0–4) (*Sec. 12*)

RES/281 (1970), June 9. Extending the stationing of the U.N. Peace-keeping Force in Cyprus for six months ending Dec. 15 (unanimous). (*Sec. 16*)

RES/282 (1970), July 23. Opposing *apartheid* and tightening the arms embargo against South Africa (12–0–3) (*Sec. 32*)

RES/283 (1970), July 29. Reestablishing the *Ad Hoc* Subcommittee on South West Africa (13–0–2).

RES/284 (1970), July 29. Requesting the International Court of Justice for an advisory opinion on South West Africa (12–0–3). (*Sec. 32*)

RES/285 (1970), Sept. 5. Demanding complete and immediate withdrawal of all Israeli armed forces from Lebanon (14–0–1).

RES/286 (1970), Sept. 9. Appealing for immediate release of all passengers and crews held as a result of hijacking (adopted without a vote). (*Sec. 15*)

RES/287 (1970), Oct. 10. Recommending Fiji for U.N. membership (unanimous).

RES/288 (1970), Nov. 17. Reaffirming condemnation of Southern Rhodesia's illegal declaration of independence (unanimous).

RES/289 (1970), Nov. 23. Demanding immediate cessation of armed attack against the Republic of Guinea (unanimous). (*Sec. 32*)

RES/290 (1970), Dec. 8. Condemning Portugal for its invasion of Guinea (11–0–4). (*Sec. 32*)

RES/291 (1970), Dec. 10. Extending the stationing of the U.N. Peace-keeping Force in Cyprus for six months until June 15, 1971 (unanimous). (*Sec. 16*)

Other Security Council Developments:

Mar. 17. The U.S. casts its first veto to help defeat a resolution condemning the British refusal to use force in Southern Rhodesia (9–2–4). (*Sec. 40*)

Oct. 21. The Security Council holds its first periodic meeting at the Foreign Ministers' level under a decision taken by the Council on June 12. (*Sec. 40*)

Oct. 26. Burundi, Nicaragua, Poland, Sierra Leone, and Syria are elected to two-year terms on the Security Council for 1970–71, replacing Colombia, Finland, Nepal, Spain, and Zambia.

GENERAL ASSEMBLY

Sept. 15–Dec. 17. The Assembly holds its 25th Regular Session in New York under the presidency of Edvard Hambro of Norway and adopts the following resolutions, among others (with votes):

2621 (XXV), Oct. 12. Calling for full implementation of the Declaration on the Granting of Independence to Colonial Countries and Peoples (86–5–15). (*Sec. 41*)

2622 (XXV), Oct. 13. Admitting Fiji to U.N. membership (by acclamation). (*Sec. 40*)

2624 (XXV), Oct. 13. Calling on all states to implement fully the arms embargo against South Africa (98–2–9).

2625 (XXV), Oct. 24. Declaration on Principles of International Law Concerning Friendly Relations and Co-operation Among States in Accordance with the Charter of the United Nations (adopted without vote). (*Sec. 41*)

2626 (XXV), Oct. 24. International Development Strategy for the Second United Nations Development Decade (adopted without vote). (*Secs. 39, 41*)

2627 (XXV), Oct. 24. Declaration on the Occasion of the Twenty-fifth Anniversary of the United Nations (adopted without vote). (*Sec. 41*)

2628 (XXV), Nov. 4. Recommending a three-month extension of the cease-fire in the Middle East (57–16–39). (*Sec. 14*)

2632 (XXV), Nov. 9. Establishing a committee to study procedures and organization of the General Assembly (88–0–12). (*Sec. 40*)

2638 (XXV), Nov. 19. Deciding to convene in 1971 a Special International Conference of the U.N. Industrial Development Organization (adopted without objection).

2641 (XXV), Nov. 19. Requesting a review and appraisal of progress made in implementing the International Development Strategy (adopted without objection).

2642 (XXV), Nov. 20. Reaffirming that the representation of China remains an important question (66–52–7). (*Sec. 23*)

2643 (XXV), Nov. 20. Appealing for assistance to Pakistan in connection with the cyclone and tidal wave (unanimous).

2645 (XXV), Nov. 25. Condemning all acts of aerial hijacking or other interference with civil air travel (105–0–8). (*Sec. 41*)

2646 (XXV), Nov. 30. Calling for the elimination of all forms of racial discrimination (71–10–11)

2647 (XXV), Nov. 30. Urging member states to do their utmost to eliminate racial discrimination (49–33–10).

2649 (XXV), Nov. 30. Reaffirming views on colonialism (71–12–28).

2651 (XXV), Dec. 3. Commending the provisional agenda for the Fourth International Conference on the Peaceful Uses of Atomic Energy to be held in Geneva in 1971 (adopted without objection).

2652 (XXV), Dec. 3. Calling on all states to ensure the immediate interruption of all forms of transportation to and from Southern Rhodesia (79–10–14).

2656 (XXV), Dec. 7. Establishing a Working Group on ways to finance UNRWA (adopted without vote).

2657 (XXV), Dec. 7. Making further arrangements for the U.N. Conference on Human Environment to be held in 1972 (86–0–10).

2658 (XXV), Dec. 7. Calling for the promotion of science and technology in the development of nations (adopted without objection).

2659 (XXV), Dec. 7. Establishing an International Volunteer Corps (91–0–12). (*Sec. 40*)

2660 (XXV), Dec. 7. Commending the treaty prohibiting the emplacement of nuclear and mass destruction weapons on the seabed and ocean floor (104–2–2). (*Ch. 3*)

2661 (XXV), Dec. 7:
   A. Urging the U.S. and the U.S.S.R. to halt the deployment of strategic nuclear weapons systems and cease all testing (102–0–14).
   B. Requesting safeguards with respect to new techniques for uranium enrichment (107–0–7).
   C. Urging the Conference of the Committee on Disarmament to intensify its efforts to bring about a faster pace towards achieving disarmament (106–0–10).

2662 (XXV), Dec. 7. Requesting the Conference of the Committee on Disarmament to continue consideration of the problem of chemical and biological warfare (113–0–2).

2663 (XXV), Dec. 7:
   A. Requesting information on seismic data relevant to a nuclear test suspension (102–0–13).
   B. Calling for suspension of nuclear weapon tests in all environments (112–0–1).

2664 (XXV), Dec. 7. Calling for implementation of the results of the Conference of Non-Nuclear Weapon States (106–0–9).

2665 (XXV), Dec. 7. Establishing an international service for nuclear weapon explosions for peaceful purposes under I.A.E.A. auspices (109–0–5).

2666 (XXV), Dec. 7. Deploring the fact that not all nuclear-weapon states have as yet signed Additional Protocol II of the Treaty of Tlatelolco (104–0–12).

2667 (XXV), Dec. 7. Calling for a study of the economic and social consequences of the armaments race (unanimous).

2668 (XXV), Dec. 7. Reaffirming U.N. objectives in Korea (67–28–22).

2670 (XXV), Dec. 8. Requesting a comprehensive review of peace-keeping operations (unanimous). (*Sec. 40*)

2671 (XXV), Dec. 8:
   A. Expanding the membership of the Special Committee on *apartheid* (105–2–6).
   B. Requesting economic, social, and humanitarian aid in the struggle against *apartheid* (111–2–1).
   C. Requesting the widest dissemination of information on the consequences of *apartheid* (107–2–6).
   D. Requesting means of promoting concerted action against *apartheid* by trade union federations (106–2–7).
   E. Appealing for contributions to assist the victims of *apartheid* (111–2–1).
   F. Calling for further measures in opposition to South African policies (91–6–16).

2672 (XXV), Dec. 8:

A. Calling for increased support for UNRWA (111–2–1).
B. Supporting continued aid for 1967 war victims (114–1–2).
C. Supporting equal rights and self-determination for the people of Palestine (47–22–50).
D. Calling on Israel to take immediate steps for the return of displaced persons (93–5–17).

2673 (XXV), Dec. 9. Advocating protection of journalists in armed conflicts (85–0–32).

2674 (XXV), Dec. 9. Reaffirming the necessity for respect for human rights in armed conflicts (77–2–36).

2675 (XXV), Dec. 9. Reaffirming basic principles for the protection of civilians in armed conflicts (109–0–8).

2676 (XXV), Dec. 9. Calling on all parties to any armed conflict to comply with the 1949 Geneva Convention relative to the treatment of prisoners (67–30–20).

2677 (XXV), Dec. 9. Expressing the hope that a conference of government experts would be convened in 1971 to consider recommendations with respect to human rights in armed conflicts (111–0–4).

2678 (XXV), Dec. 9. Condemning South Africa for extending its policies of *apartheid* to Namibia (95–5–14).

2679 (XXV), Dec. 9. Establishing a comprehensive U.N. fund for Namibia (104–2–8).

2682 (XXV), Dec. 11. Recommending that a greater proportion of food aid be channeled through multilateral sources (101–0–9).

2683 (XXV), Dec. 11. Designating 1974 as World Population Year (71–8–31).

2702 (XXV), Dec. 14. Reaffirming the right of Oman to self-determination (70–17–22).

2707 (XXV), Dec. 14. Condemning the policy of Portugal in territories under its administration (94–6–16).

2711 (XXV), Dec. 14. Reaffirming the right of Spanish Sahara to self-determination (103–0–11).

2725 (XXV), Dec. 15. Deciding to convene the third session of UNCTAD in April 1972 (102–0–13).

2727 (XXV), Dec. 15. Calling on Israel to implement recommendations of the Special Committee investigating reputed violations of human rights in Israeli-occupied territories (52–20–43).

2729 (XXV), Dec. 16:
A. Appropriating $192,149,300 for the financial year 1971 (86–9–2).

2733 (XXV), Dec. 16:
A. Recommending international cooperation in regional satellite broadcasting services (unanimous). (*Sec. 41*)
B. Urging intensified efforts to draft a space liability convention (108–8–2). (*Sec. 41*)
C. Endorsing the work of the Committee on Peaceful Uses of Outer Space (110–0–9).

2734 (XXV), Dec. 16. Declaration on the Strengthening of International Security (120–1–1).

2749 (XXV), Dec. 17. Declaration of Principles on peaceful uses of the seabed (108–0–14). (*Sec. 41*)

2750 (XXV), Dec. 17:
C. Deciding to convene in 1973 a Conference on the Law of the Sea (108–7–6). (*Sec. 41*)

General Assembly: 25th Anniversary session (*Sec. 41*)

Oct. 14–24. The Assembly holds a commemorative session at U.N. Headquarters in celebration of the United Nations 25th anniversary. The session is attended by 42 Heads of State or Government and 44 special envoys and adopts four special documents (Resolutions 2621 (XXV), 2625 (XXV), 2626 (XXV), and 2627 (XXV), above).

Other Developments

July 9–17. A World Youth Assembly is held at United Nations Headquarters in New York. (*Sec. 42*)

Oct. 27. Nine states are elected to the Economic and Social Council for a three-year term beginning on Jan. 1, 1971.

Nov. 20. A resolution to admit the People's Republic of China to U.N. representation fails of adoption (51–29–45). (*Sec. 23*)

COMMITTEE ON DISARMAMENT (C.C.D.)

Feb. 17–Apr. 30, June 16–Nov. 3. The C.C.D. meets in Geneva and reaches a consensus on a second revised draft treaty barring nuclear and mass-destruction weapons from the seabed. (*Ch. 3, Sec. 41*)

SPECIALIZED AND RELATED AGENCIES

Food and Agriculture Organization (F.A.O.)

June 16–30. The Second World Food Congress meets at The Hague.

Nov. 16. At a meeting in Rome, the 25th anniversary of the F.A.O. is marked with a speech by Pope Paul VI.

General Agreement on Tariffs and Trade (GATT)

Feb. 17–27. The Contracting Parties meet in Geneva, with discussion focusing on the issue of non-tariff barriers to trade. (*Sec. 39*)

May 9. The accession of the U.A.R. brings the number of GATT Contracting Parties to 77.

International Atomic Energy Agency (I.A.E.A.)

Sept. 22–28. The I.A.E.A. holds its 14th General Conference in Vienna.

International Bank and Fund (I.B.R.D., I.M.F.) (Sec. 37)

Jan. 1. The International Monetary Fund allocates $3.4 billion of Special Drawing Rights to 105 of its 115 members.

Sept. 21–25. The Boards of Governors of the International Bank for Reconstruction and Development, the International Monetary Fund, and affiliated agencies hold their 25th meeting in Copenhagen.

International Civil Aviation Organization (I.C.A.O.) (Sec. 41)

June 16–30. An extraordinary session on hijacking and sabotage is convened at Montreal.

Aug. 3. Dr. Assed Kotaite (Lebanon) succeeds B. T. Twight (Netherlands) as Secretary-General.

Oct. 1. The I.C.A.O. Council, meeting in Montreal, adopts a resolution on the unlawful seizure of aircraft for blackmail purposes.

Dec. 1–16 An I.C.A.O.-sponsored, 77-nation conference on air law meets at The Hague and approves a convention on the suppression of unlawful seizures of aircraft.

International Labor Organization (I.L.O.)

Feb. 9. Director-General David A. Morse (U.S.) resigns effective May 31 (took office in 1948).

May 20. C. Wilfred Jenks (U.K.) is named to succeed Morse for a five-year term beginning June 1.

United Nations Economic, Social and Cultural Organization (UNESCO)

Oct. 12-Nov. 14. The organization's General Conference holds its 16th session in Paris.

World Health Organization (WHO)

May 5–22. The 23rd Assembly meets in Geneva.

OTHER INTERNATIONAL MEETINGS AND ORGANIZATIONS

International Telecommunications Consortium (Intelsat)

Feb. 16–Mar. 20. A third Plenipotentiary Conference on Definitive Arrangements for the organization is held in Washington.

Francophone Conference

Mar. 16–20. A conference of 21 French-speaking nations meets in Niamey, Niger and agrees to establish a permanent Agency for Cultural and Technical Cooperation.

International Tin Council

Apr. 13–15. A session in Geneva drafts the Fourth International Tin Agreement.

Diplomatic Conference on the Patent Cooperation Treaty

May 25-June 19. A treaty to simplify and standardize patent applications is drafted and signed by more than 40 participating nations in Washington.

Lusaka Conference

Sept. 8–10. The Third Conference of Nonaligned Nations meets in Lusaka, Zambia. (Sec. 40)

Notes

The following publishers and publications have kindly authorized the use of certain quotations as indicated in the notes:

Current Digest of the Soviet Press
The Economist
The New Republic
The New York Times
Newsweek
Time
The Washington Post
American Foreign Service Association (*Foreign Service Journal*)
Almqvist & Wiksell (Stockholm) and Humanities Press, Inc. (New York)
Atheneum
Doubleday & Company
The Foreign Policy Association
The International Institute for Strategic Studies
Frederick A. Praeger
The Royal Institute of International Affairs
Viking Press, Inc.

Resolutions of the U.N. General Assembly, here cited by serial number and date, are published in a supplement to the *Official Records* of each session. Preliminary texts of the more important resolutions appear in the *U.N. Monthly Chronicle.*

Official transcripts of all presidential news conferences during 1970 were published in the *Weekly Compilation of Presidential Documents,* from which the quotations in the text have invariably been taken unless otherwise noted. Other documents bearing on foreign affairs often appear in both the *Weekly Compilation* and (with minor editorial differences) in the *Department of State*

Bulletin. In such cases, the text appearing in the *Bulletin* has normally been used in the belief that it will be more readily available to users of this series.

The President's State of the World message, *U.S. Foreign Policy for the 1970's: A New Strategy for Peace—A Report to the Congress by Richard Nixon, President of the United States, February 18, 1970* (Washington: G.P.O., 1970) is referred to throughout the notes as *U.S. Foreign Policy for the 1970's.* It also appears in *Bulletin,* March 9, 1970, pp. 273–332 and in *The New York Times,* February 19, 1970.

All dates in the following notes refer to the year 1970 unless another year is specifically indicated.

1. "A New Approach . . . A New Era

1. *Documents, 1961,* p. 13.
2. Same, *1970,* No. 1; complete text in *Weekly Compilation,* Jan. 26, pp. 58–66.
3. Andrew Hacker, *The End of the American Era* (New York: Athenaeum, 1970), p. 8.
4. Same, p. 143.
5. Same, p. 6.
6. Same, p. 228.
7. Zbigniew Brzezinski, *Between Two Ages: America's Role in the Technetronic Era* (New York: Viking, 1970), p. 9.
8. Same, p. 24.
9. Same, pp. 231–2.
10. Same, p. 6.
11. Jean-François Revel, *Without Marx or Jesus,* translated by J. F. Bernard (Garden City, N.Y.: Doubleday, 1971), pp. 145–6.
12. Charles Reich, *The Greening of America* (New York: Random House, 1970).
13. *New York Times,* Mar. 13.
14. Survey cited in same, Jan. 14.
15. Same, May 16.
16. Same, Sept. 27.
17. Same, May 8.
18. Text in *Weekly Compilation,* Dec. 14, pp. 1660–3.
19. Same, Sept. 21, pp. 1227–33.
20. *New York Times,* Mar. 1.
21. Same, May 2.

22. *Documents, 1968–69,* pp. 38–43.
23. Same, *1970,* Nos. 38 and 50–51.
24. Text of agreement and State Department statement in *Bulletin,* Mar. 20, pp. 260–70.
25. *New York Times,* Dec. 12.
26. *The Economist,* Oct. 17, p. 9.
27. *U.N. Chronicle,* Nov., p. 78.
28. *Documents, 1970,* No. 2; complete text in *U.S. Foreign Policy for the 1970's.*
29. Same, *1968–69,* pp. 329–34; complete text in *Public Papers of the Presidents of the United States: Richard Nixon, 1969* (Washington: G.P.O., 1971), pp. 545–9.
30. Cf. Henry A. Kissinger, "The Vietnam Negotiations," *Foreign Affairs,* Jan. 1969, pp. 211–34.
31. Cf. Gary Wills, *Nixon Agonistes: The Crisis of the Self-Made Man* (Boston: Houghton Mifflin, 1970).
32. Same as note 28.
33. TIME-Louis Harris poll in TIME, May 2, 1969.
34. *Statement of Secretary of Defense Melvin R. Laird on the Fiscal Year 1972–76 Defense Program and the 1972 Defense Budget Before the Senate Armed Services Committee, March 15, 1971* (Washington: G.P.O., 1971), p. 131.

35. Excerpts in *Documents, 1970, No. 5*; complete text in *Statement of Secretary of Defense Melvin R. Laird Before a Joint Session of the Senate Armed Services Committee and the Senate Subcommittee on Department of Defense Appropriations on the Fiscal Year 1971 Defense Program and Budget, February 20, 1970* (Washington: G.P.O., 1970), p. 57.
36. Text in *Documents, 1963*, pp. 130–2; cf. *The United States in World Affairs, 1963*, pp. 70–2, 74–8.
37. Text in *Documents, 1968–69*, pp. 62–8.
38. Same, pp. 125–7.
39. *The Washington Post-Times Herald*, Jan. 19.
40. Hans J. Morgenthau, "Mr. Nixon's Foreign Policy," *New Republic*, Mar. 21, pp. 23–5.
41. Earl C. Ravenal, "The Nixon Doctrine and Our Asian Commitments," *Foreign Affairs*, Jan. 1971, pp. 201–17.
42. *Documents, 1950*, pp. 426–33.
43. *New York Times*, Dec. 26.
44. Text in *Documents, 1968–69*, pp. 50–1.
45. Jacob K. Javits, "The Congressional Presence in Foreign Relations," *Foreign Affairs*, Jan., p. 234.
46. *Documents, 1970*, No. 38.
47. *New York Times*, May 5.
48. Text in *Documents, 1970*, No. 39.
48a. Restrictions on troops for Cambodia were included in the Special Foreign Assistance Act of 1971 (P.L. 91–652), approved Jan. 5, 1971 and in the Department of Defense Appropriation Act, 1971 (P.L. 91–668), approved Jan. 11, 1971.
49. P.L. 91–441, approved Oct. 7.
50. *Documents, 1970*, No. 40. Text of Tonkin Gulf Resolution in same, *1964*, pp. 216–17.
51. U.S. Senate, 91st Cong., 2nd sess., *Report to the Committee on Foreign Relations by the Subcommittee on Security Agreements and Commitments Abroad* (Committee Print, Washington: G.P.O., 1970).
52. *New York Times*, Dec. 3; cf. *The United States in World Affairs, 1954*, pp. 22–4.
53. P.L. 91–652, approved Jan. 5, 1971.
54. Cf. James Reston in *New York Times*, Dec. 4.
55. Thomas P. Thornton, "The Nixon Doctrine and Beyond," *Foreign Service Journal*, Nov., p. 21.
56. *Bulletin*, Feb. 2, pp. 130–41.
57. *New York Times*, July 21. See also Rogers news conference statement, June 25, in *Bulletin*, July 13, p. 25.
58. *Documents, 1970*, No. 6; complete text in *Diplomacy for the 70's*, Department of State Publication 8551 (Washington: G.P.O., 1970).
59. *New York Times*, Jan. 1.
60. *Documents, 1970*, No. 72; cf. Sec. 42.

2. *"Where Are You Going, Russia?"*

1. Cf. Chapter 1 at note 29.
2. Address of July 10 in *Soviet News*, July 15.
3. Same, June 16.
4. For a general introduction to and critique of the revisionist viewpoint see Lloyd C. Gardner, Hans J. Morgenthau, and Arthur Schlesinger, Jr., *The Origins of the Cold War* (Waltham, Mass.: Ginn-Blaisdell, 1970).
5. For text of treaty and U.S. statements, see *Documents, 1970*, No. 22.

6. *Soviet News*, Oct. 25.
7. Same, Jan. 13.
8. *Documents, 1970*, No. 19(b).
9. *Soviet News*, June 30.
10. *Documents, 1970*, No. 21
11. Cf. Harrison E. Salisbury, *War Between Russia and China* (New York: W. W. Norton, 1969).
12. *Documents, 1970*, Nos. 49 and 50.
13. *New York Times*, May 3.
14. Same, June 11.
15. Excerpts of Brezhnev speech in same, Apr. 15.
16. *The Current Digest of the Soviet Press*, Dec. 8, p. 9.
17. Same, pp. 1-9.
18. Cf. Bernard Gwertzman in *New York Times*, May 13.
19. Same, June 10.
20. Cf. note 3.
21. *Soviet News*, June 16.
22. *New York Times*, May 15.
23. Excerpts in *Newsweek*, June 10, p. 9.
24. *The Christian Science Monitor*, Feb. 16, 1971.
25. *U.S. News & World Report*, Jan. 25, 1971; *Commerce Today*, Jan. 10, 1972, p. 12.
26. *New York Times*, Jan. 17.
27. Andrei Amalrik, *Will the Soviet Union Survive Until 1984?* (New York: Harper & Row, 1970).
28. Robert Conquest, "Stalin's Successors," *Foreign Affairs*, Apr., p. 521.
29. *Soviet News*, June 2.
30. Text of treaty in same, May 12.
31. Address of May 6 in same.
32. *New York Times*, Dec. 22.
33. Same.
34. Same.
35. Same.

36. *Soviet News*, Dec. 29.
37. *New York Times*, July 13.
38. *Weekly Compilation*, Nov. 2, pp. 1456-7, 1461-2.
39. *New York Times*, May 14; see also *Soviet News*, May 19.
40. *New York Times*, July 13.
41. Same, Oct. 30.
42. Text of joint communiqué in *Weekly Compilation*, Oct. 12, p 1237; related material in same, pp. 1322-6.
43. Same, p. 1323.
44. Cf. Sec. 7.
45. *New York Times*, Jan. 15, 1971.
46. *Documents, 1970*, No. 2; complete text in *U.S. Foreign Policy for the 1970's.*
47. *Documents, 1970*, No. 20. For complete documentation on the Nixon trip, see *Weekly Compilation*, Oct. 5, pp. 1291-1300; same, Oct. 12, pp. 1320-30.
48. *Bulletin*, Oct. 26, p. 476.
49. *Weekly Compilation*, Oct. 5, p. 1294.
50. *Documents, 1970*, No. 38.
51. James Reston in *New York Times*, May 13.
52. Cf. Sec. 1.
53. The major part of this paragraph is based on the Reston article cited in note 51.
54. Henry A. Kissinger, *A World Restored* (New York: Grosset, 1964), as cited by James Reston in *New York Times*, Jan. 29, 1969.
55. *Documents, 1970*, No. 7.
56. Same as note 50.
57. *Soviet News*, May 5.
58. *New York Times*, Oct. 10.
59. Same, Oct. 16.

3. Salt and Sufficiency: Which Way the Arms Race?

1. *Documents, 1968-69*, p. 125.
2. Cf. *The United States in World Affairs, 1967*, pp. 18-19.

3. *Weekly Compilation*, July 8, p. 1044.
4. *Documents, 1963*, pp. 115-16.

5. Same, pp. 130-2.
6. Same, *1963*, pp. 115-16.
7. Johnson remarks, July 1, 1968, in *Weekly Compilation*, July 8, 1968.
8. Text of Nixon remarks on entry into force of the nonproliferation treaty in *Documents, 1970*, No. 12.
9. Excerpts of the C.C.D. report in same, No. 8; complete text in U.N. document A/8059 (DC/233), Sept. 11. Text of U.S.-U.S.S.R. revised draft treaty in same, No. 13. For text of U.S.-U.S.S.R. draft treaty of Oct. 30, 1969, see same, *1968-69*, pp. 102-6.
10. Same, *1970*, No. 14.
11. Text in U.N. document A/7575 (S/9292), July 1, 1969; partial text in *U.N. Chronicle*, July 1969, pp. 65-7.
12. *Documents, 1968-69*, pp. 106-9.
13. Cf. same, *1970*, Nos. 16-17. Text of Geneva Protocol of 1925 in *Bulletin*, Dec. 15, 1969, pp. 541-2.
14. *Documents, 1970*, No. 15.
15. Same, No. 2; complete text in *U.S. Foreign Policy for the 1970's*.
16. Same.
17. Same.
18. See, for example, analysis by Bruce Van Voorst in *Newsweek*, Nov. 16, pp. 52-4.
19. For documentation on SALT, see *Documents, 1970*, Nos. 10-11.
20. Text of Rogers address, Nov. 13, 1969 in *Bulletin*, Dec. 1, 1969, p. 467.
21. Jeremy J. Stone, "When and How to Use 'SALT'," *Foreign Affairs*, Jan., pp. 265-6.
22. *Weekly Compilation*, Feb. 2, pp. 94-5.
23. Excerpts in *Documents, 1970*, No. 5; complete text in *Statement of Secretary of Defense Melvin R. Laird Before a Joint Session of*

the Senate Armed Services Committee and the Senate Subcommittee on Department of Defense Appropriations on the Fiscal Year 1971 Defense Program and Budget, February 20, 1970 (Washington: G.P.O., 1970), p. 2.
24. *New York Times*, Mar. 8.
25. *SIPRI Yearbook of World Armaments and Disarmament 1969/70* (Stockholm: Almqvist & Wiksell; New York: Humanities Press, Inc., 1970), pp. xviii, 57. Copyright © 1970 by Stockholm International Peace Research Institute.
26. François Duchêne, "SALT, the *Ostpolitik*, and the Post-Cold War Conflict," *The World Today*, (London: The Royal Institute of International Affairs, Dec. 1970), p. 501.
27. Michel Tatu, *The Great Power Triangle: Washington-Moscow-Peking* (Paris: The Atlantic Institute, Dec. 1970) as quoted in *New York Times*, Dec. 20 by C. L. Sulzberger.
28. *Vital Speeches*, Jan. 15, 1971, p. 194.
29. *New York Times*, Nov. 13. See also *The Military Balance 1970-71* (London: Institute of Strategic Studies, 1970), p. 9.
30. Cf. Max Beloff, "Russia's Foreign Policy: Cycle of Mistrust," *Interplay*, Feb. 1971, p. 12.
31. Laird (cited), p. 1.
32. Same, p. 51.
33. Same, p. 1.
34. Same as note 15.
35. Same as note 32.
36. See Sec. 4.
37. *Documents, 1968-69*, pp. 50-1.
38. Same, *1970*, No. 38.
39. Same, No. 9.
40. *Weekly Compilation*, Mar. 23, p. 401.
41. *New York Times*, Feb. 25.
42. Same, May 3.
43. Same, Oct. 5.
44. U.S. Senate, 91st Cong., 2nd

sess., *Report to the Committee on Foreign Relations by the Subcommittee on Security Arrangements and Commitments Abroad* (Committee Print, Washington: G.P.O., 1970), p. 13.
45. P.L. 91–668.
46. *New York Times*, Dec. 17.

47. Same, July 30.
48. Same, Sept. 29.
49. Same, Oct. 4.
50. Same, Dec. 7.
51. Excerpts in same, Feb. 22.
52. Quoted in *Newsweek*, May 4, pp. 36–7.

4. The Middle East Tinderbox

1. George Thayer, *The War Business* (New York: Simon and Schuster, 1969).
2. *Weekly Compilation*, July 6, pp. 870–1.
3. George W. Ball, "Suez Is the Front to Watch," *New York Times Magazine*, June 28.
4. *New York Times*, Apr. 29.
5. See Arnaud de Borchgrave's report from Cairo in *Newsweek*, June 1, p. 40.
6. *Documents, 1970*, No. 2; complete text in *U.S. Foreign Policy for the 1970's*.
7. Dean Acheson, *Present at the Creation: My Years in the State Department* (New York: Norton, 1969).
8. Cf. *Bulletin*, Mar. 9, p. 305; same, July 27, p. 113.
9. *Documents, 1967*, pp. 169–70.
10. *Weekly Compilation*, Feb. 2, p. 93.
11. *Documents, 1968–69*, pp. 202–5, 211–12.
12. Text of Soviet note of Dec. 23 in *New York Times*, Jan. 23. The U.S. proposal of Oct. 28 was not made public but its substance was reported in an address by Rogers on Dec. 9, 1969 (see following note).
13. *Documents, 1968–69*, pp. 212–19.
14. *New York Times*, Jan. 25.
15. The substance of the Kosygin note is summarized in *Soviet News*, Feb. 17.
16. *New York Times*, Feb. 5.

17. Same as note 10.
18. Cf. statement by Acting Secretary Richardson, Feb. 12, in *Bulletin*, Mar. 2, p. 226.
19. *Documents, 1970*, No. 28; complete text in *Bulletin*, Apr. 13, pp. 477–84.
20. *New York Times*, May 10.
21. U.N. document S/RES/280 (1970); details in *U.N. Chronicle*, June, pp. 8–37; further, *Bulletin*, June 8, pp. 726–30.
22. Same as note 19.
23. *Documents, 1970*, No. 27.
24. *New York Times*, May 24.
25. Same, May 26.
26. Same, June 2.
27. *Bulletin*, Aug. 10, p. 177.
28. Same, July 13, p. 26.
29. *Documents, 1970*, No. 29(a); complete text in *Bulletin*, July 13, pp. 25–32.
30. *New York Times*, June 18.
31. *Documents, 1970*, No. 29(b).
32. Same as note 29.
33. *New York Times*, June 26.
34. Same.
35. Same, June 30.
36. Same as note 27.
37. Communiqué summarized in *Soviet News*, July 21.
38. *New York Times*, July 30.
39. Same, June 30.
40. *Documents, 1970*, No. 29(c).
41. Same.
42. *New York Times*, Aug. 8.
43. U.N. document S/9902, Aug. 7; details in *U.N. Chronicle*, Aug.–Sept., pp. 146–7. For background of U.S. peace initiative, see

United States Foreign Policy, *1969–1970: A Report of the Secretary of State* (Department of State Publication 8575; Washington: G.P.O., 1971).

44. Israel formally accepted the terms of the U.S. peace proposal on Aug. 4. Text of Israeli reply to U.S. in *New York Times,* Aug. 5.
45. Quoted in *Newsweek,* Aug. 24, p. 29.
46. *New York Times,* Aug. 18.
47. Same.
48. Same, Aug. 19; see also *Documents, 1970,* No. 30.
49. *New York Times,* Aug. 19.
50. *Documents, 1970,* No. 31.
51. Same, No. 34.
52. Press Release, Soviet Embassy (Washington), Oct. 9.
53. Text of Yost statement and U.S. draft resolution A/L.603 in *Bulletin,* Nov. 23, pp. 656–7.
54. *Documents, 1970,* Nos. 32–33.
55. Same as note 51.
56. *Documents, 1970,* No. 99.
57. *Bulletin,* Sept. 21, p. 328.
58. Same as note 23.
59. General Assembly Resolution 2672 A (XXV), adopted by a vote of 111 in favor to 2 against, with 1 abstention; details on this and other resolutions concerning Palestine refugees in *U.N. Chronicle,* Jan. 1971, pp. 45–52; further, *Bulletin,* Jan. 18, 1971, pp. 93–8.
60. U.N. General Assembly, *Official Records: 25th Session, Supplement No. 13* (A/8013).
61. Cf. Don Peretz, "Arab Palestine: Phoenix or Phantom?" *Foreign Affairs,* Jan., pp. 322–33.
62. *New York Times,* June 14.

63. Sec. 13.
64. *New York Times,* July 26.
65. U.N. document S/RES/286 (1970); details in *U.N. Chronicle,* Oct. 1970, pp. 7–8; further, *Bulletin,* Sept. 28, p. 342. See also Sec. 41.
66. *Documents, 1970,* No. 83.
67. *New York Times,* Sept. 19.
68. Same, Oct. 8.
69. Same, Oct. 14. Excerpts of the accord in *New Middle East,* Nov. 1970, p. 49.
70. *New York Times,* Dec. 16.
71. See Rogers statement before the House Foreign Affairs Committee, Nov. 25 in *Bulletin,* Dec. 14, pp. 713–14.
72. Cf. Rogers statement, Sept. 26, in same, Oct. 12, p. 413.
73. *New York Times,* Oct. 23.
74. *Weekly Compilation,* Oct. 5, pp. 1296, 1297.
75. *New York Times,* Oct. 4.
76. Same, Nov. 13.
77. U.N. document S/RES/281 (1970); details in *U.N. Chronicle,* July, pp. 45–54; further, *Bulletin,* July 6, pp. 20–1. U.N. document S/RES/291 (1970), adopted Dec. 10; details in *U.N. Chronicle,* Jan. 1971, pp. 19–26; further, *Bulletin,* Jan. 11, 1971, pp. 70–1.
78. *Documents, 1970,* No. 36.
79. *Bulletin,* June 8, p. 711.
80. Cf. *New York Times,* Oct. 21.
81. U.N. document, S/9772; details in *U.N. Chronicle,* May, pp. 3–7.
82. *Documents, 1970,* No. 36(b). For Yost statement of May 11 to the Security Council, see same, No. 36 (a).
83. *New York Times,* May 10; July 20; Aug. 1.

5. Indochina: The War Spills Over

1. Golo Mann, *The History of Germany Since 1789* (New York: Praeger, 1968), pp. 11–12.
2. Cf. *The United States in World Affairs, 1965,* pp. 252–3.
3. Henry A. Kissinger, "The Viet-

Nam Negotiations," *Foreign Affairs*, Jan. 1969, pp. 218–19.
4. *Documents, 1968–69*, pp. 329–34. Complete text in *Public Papers of the Presidents of the United States: Richard Nixon, 1969* (Washington: G.P.O., 1971), pp. 545–9.
5. *Documents, 1968–69*, pp. 276–88.
6. Television interview of Dec. 23, 1969 in *Bulletin*, Jan. 19, 1970, p. 58.
7. *New York Times*, Feb. 2.
8. *Weekly Compilation*, Feb. 2, pp. 92–6.
9. Department of State estimates as reported in *New York Times*, Jan. 7.
10. Same, Jan. 9.
11. Same, Feb. 22.
12. Same, Feb. 12.
13. Same, June 14.
14. Same, Feb. 2.
15. *Documents, 1970*, No. 42.
16. Same, *1968–69*, pp. 261–7.
17. Same, pp. 275–6.
18. Same, p. 290.
19. *New York Times*, Feb. 7
20. Same, Mar. 13.
21. Same, Mar. 17.
22. Same, Mar. 21.
23. Same, Mar. 20.
24. *Weekly Compilation*, Mar. 23, p. 399.
25. Same as note 15.
26. *New York Times*, Mar. 20.
27. Same, Apr. 22.
28. Same, Apr. 23. For a detailed analysis of events surrounding the President's decision, see Hedrick Smith in same, June 30; further, U.S. Senate, 91st Cong., 2nd sess., *Cambodia: May 1970* (Committee Print, Washington: G.P.O., 1970), pp. 1–15.
29. Hedrick Smith in *New York Times*, June 30.
30. Same.
31. Sec. 21, below. For discussion of the 1954 Geneva Conference see *The United States in World Affairs, 1954*, pp. 238–49.
32. Sec. 21.
33. *New York Times*, Apr. 28 and Apr. 29.
34. Same as note 29.
35. *New York Times*, Apr. 23.
36. Same, Apr. 28.
37. *Documents, 1970*, No. 38.
38. *New York Times*, May 1.
39. Sec. 1.
40. *Cambodia: May 1970* (cited), pp. 7–8.
41. *New York Times*, May 3 and May 4.
42. *Documents, 1970*, No. 2; complete text in *U.S. Foreign Policy for the 1970's*.
43. Same as note 6.
44. *New York Times*, Mar. 17.
45. *Bulletin*, May 25, pp. 646 and 649.
46. *Weekly Compilation*, May 11, p. 618.
47. *New York Times*, May 11 and June 14.
48. Sec. 21.
49. *New York Times*, May 28.
50. Same.
51. *Documents, 1970*, No. 39.
52. Cf. *New York Times*, July 4.
53. Sec. 21.
54. *Soviet News*, May 5.
55. For details, see same, June 16.
55a.Cf. *Documents, 1970*, Nos. 50–51.
56. *New York Times*, June 17.
57. Same, June 26; June 29; and July 3.
58. Same, Aug. 6.
59. Same, July 6 and Oct. 10.
60. Text of U.S. note to Cambodia in *Bulletin*, Oct. 5, pp. 387–8.
61. Same, p. 386. For details on Agnew's Asian trip see same, pp. 379–87.
62. P.L. 91–652, approved Jan. 5, 1971. For text of Nixon message, Nov. 18, requesting supplemental assistance funds, see *Documents, 1970*, No. 99.
63. Cf. *Cambodia: December 1970* (cited), pp. 4–5.

64. Same, *May 1970*, p. 15.
65. *Bulletin*, Feb. 2, pp. 127–9.
66. *New York Times*, Jan. 16.
67. Same, Jan. 12.
68. *Bulletin*, Feb. 2, p. 129.
69. *New York Times*, Feb. 12.
70. Hedrick Smith in same, June 30.
71. *New York Times*, May 17 and May 18. For U.S. reaction, see *Bulletin*, June 8, pp. 710–11.
72. *U.N. Chronicle*, June, pp. 44–5.
73. *Bulletin*, May 25, p. 653.
74. *New York Times*, June 14.
75. Cf. note 77, below.
76. Cf. *The United States in World Affairs, 1962*, pp. 198–9.
77. *Documents, 1970*, No. 37; complete text in *Weekly Compilation*, Mar. 9, pp. 322–8.
78. *New York Times*, Mar. 8 and Mar. 9.
79. Same, Mar. 10 and Mar. 11.
80. Same, Mar. 15.
81. Same, Mar. 29.
82. Same.
83. Same, Oct, 21.
84. *Documents, 1970*, No. 39.
85. *Weekly Compilation*, July 6, p. 861.
86. *Documents, 1970*, No. 44.
87. Same, *1968–69*, pp. 249–52.
88. Same as note 86.
89. *Weekly Compilation*, Aug. 3, p. 1000.
90. *New York Times*, Sept. 18.
91. *Bulletin*, Oct. 12, p. 408.
92. *Documents, 1970*, No. 45.
93. Same, *1968–69*, pp. 252–60.
94. *Bulletin*, Oct. 26, p. 468.
95. *New York Times*, Oct. 8. Cf. Nixon remarks, Oct. 8, in *Weekly Compilation*, Oct. 12, pp. 1353–5.
96. *New York Times*, Oct. 9.
97. *Bulletin*, Oct. 26, p. 471.

98. *New York Times*, Oct. 9 and Oct. 11.
99. Same, Oct. 23.
100. For statement by Ambassador Bruce, see *Bulletin*, Nov. 23, pp. 652–3.
101. *Weekly Compilation*, Dec. 14, pp. 1650–1.
102. *New York Times*, Nov. 1.
103. Same as note 17.
104. All figures cited are from *U.S. Foreign Policy for the 1970's*, pp. 59–60.
105. Same, pp. 76–7.
106. *New York Times*, Nov. 8.
107. Same, Mar. 14.
108. Same, Aug. 2.
109. Same, June 26.
110. *Weekly Compilation*, Aug. 10, pp. 1030–1.
111. *Bulletin*, Oct. 12, pp. 405–8.
112. *New York Times*, Nov. 22. See also Nixon remarks, Dec. 10, in *Weekly Compilation*, Dec. 14, pp. 1650–1.
113. Same, Nov. 30, p. 1599.
114. U.S. Senate, Committee on Foreign Relations, 91st Cong., 2nd sess., *Bombing Operations and the Prisoner-of-War Rescue Mission in North Vietnam: Hearings . . . with Secretary Laird, November 24, 1970* (Washington: G.P.O., 1971), p. 6.
115. *New York Times*, Dec. 11. For Bruce statement, see *Bulletin*, Dec. 28, p. 773.
116. General Assembly Resolution 2676 (XXV); details in *U.N. Chronicle*, Jan. 1971, pp. 82–3; further, *Bulletin*, Jan. 4, 1971, pp. 8–13. For U.S. statement, see *Documents, 1970*, No. 46.
117. *Weekly Compilation*, Dec. 28, pp. 1728–9.

6. China and the Rim of Asia

1. For a detailed analysis of U.S. trade policies toward China, see *Commerce Today*, May 3, 1971, pp. 4–9.

2. *Documents, 1970,* No. 2; complete text in *U.S. Foreign Policy for the 1970's.*
3. *Peking Review,* Jan. 2, p. 7.
4. Same, Mar. 20, pp. 6–8; *New York Times,* Mar. 8.
5. Text of communiqué in *Peking Review,* Sept. 11, pp. 5–7.
6. *New York Times,* Nov. 6.
7. Michel Oksenberg, "China: The Convulsive Society," *Headline Series,* No. 203 (New York: Foreign Policy Association, Dec. 1970), pp. 44–5.
8. Sec. 19.
9. Text in *Peking Review,* Apr. 10, p. 4.
10. *New York Times,* June 30; cf. *Peking Review,* June 19, p. 9.
11. Sec. 5.
12. *New York Times,* Oct. 14. See also joint Canadian-Chinese communiqué in *Peking Review,* Oct. 16, p. 12.
13. *New York Times,* Nov. 7.
14. Same, Dec. 5.
14a. General Assembly Resolution 2642 (XXV); details in *U.N. Chronicle,* Dec., pp. 27–40; further, *Bulletin,* Dec. 14, pp. 733–5.
15. U.N. document A/L. 605. Cf. note 14a.
16. Statement of Nov. 12 in *Bulletin,* Dec. 14, pp. 733–5.
17. *Peking Review* (Special Issue), May 23, pp. 8–9.
18. *Documents, 1970,* Nos. 50–51.
19. *Bulletin,* Aug. 3, p. 145.
20. Cf. Department of State announcement, Mar. 15, 1971, in *Bulletin,* Apr. 12, 1971.
21. Same as note 1.
22. *Weekly Compilation,* Dec. 14, p. 1655.
23. *Documents, 1968–69,* pp. 329–34; complete text in *Public Paper of the Presidents of the United States: Richard Nixon, 1969* (Washington: G.P.O., 1971), pp. 545–9.
24. Remarks of Jan. 2 in *Bulletin,* Feb. 23, p. 192.

25. Remarks of Jan. 16, in same, p. 200.
26. *Weekly Compilation,* Jan. 24, p. 53.
27. *New York Times,* July 29.
28. Same, Feb. 26.
29. Same, Apr. 22. For State Department statement of Apr. 24 on Chiang visit, see *Bulletin,* May 18, p. 622.
30. *New York Times,* July 9.
31. *Documents, 1970,* No. 47(a).
32. Same, No. 47 (b).
33. *New York Times,* July 4.
34. Statement of July 15 in *Bulletin,* Aug. 3, pp. 125–6.
35. *New York Times,* July 9. Cf. Rogers news conference of July 15 in *Bulletin,* Aug. 3, p. 130.
36. *New York Times,* July 25.
37. Quoted in *Newsweek,* Sept. 7, p. 15.
38. Same. See also *New York Times,* Aug. 25.
39. *Bulletin,* Oct. 5, p. 382; related material in same, pp. 380–2.
40. *New York Times,* Aug. 30.
41. Same. See also *Newsweek,* Sept. 7, p. 16.
42. *Bulletin,* Oct. 5, pp. 384–5.
43. *Documents, 1970,* No. 48.
44. *Weekly Compilation,* June 1, p. 691.
45. Same, p. 697.
46. Same as note 2.
47. *Documents, 1968–69,* pp. 336–41.
48. *Bulletin,* Aug. 3, p. 149.
49. Robert Guillain, *The Japanese Challenge,* translated from the French by Patrick O'Brian (Philadelphia: Lippincott, 1970).
50. Herman Kahn, *The Emerging Japanese Superstate: Challenge and Response* (New Jersey: Prentice-Hall, 1970).
51. *New York Times,* Apr. 11.
52. Same, Jan. 7.
53. *Bulletin,* Mar. 2, pp. 228–9.
54. *Peking Review,* Nov. 6, pp. 12–13.
55. *Documents, 1970,* No. 52.

56. *New York Times,* Jan. 25.
57. Same, Feb. 14.
58. *Peking Review,* Nov. 6, p. 12.
59. *Bulletin,* Apr. 27, pp. 537–42.
60. *New York Times,* Apr. 14. For additional details see Sec. 38.
61. Same as note 2.

62. *New York Times,* Feb. 24 and May 18.
63. Same, Oct. 24.
64. Same, Oct. 9 and Oct. 11.
65. Same, Oct. 23 and Oct. 25.
66. Same, Oct. 11.

7. The Americas: Left and Right Take Center Stage

1. *New York Times,* Nov. 8.
2. Same, June 1 and June 6.
3. Excerpts in *Survival,* Mar. 1971 (London: Institute for Strategic Studies), pp. 95–100.
4. *Documents, 1970,* No. 2; complete text in *U.S. Foreign Policy for the 1970's.*
5. Same.
6. Same.
7. Same.
8. Text of report entitled "Quality of Life in the Americas," together with letter of transmittal, dated Aug. 30, 1969 in *Bulletin,* Dec. 8, 1969, pp. 495–540; text of Nixon statement on release of report Nov. 10, 1969 in *Documents, 1968–69,* pp. 439–41.
9. Cf. statement by Under Secretary Richardson to the Senate Subcommittee on Western Hemisphere Affairs in *Bulletin,* Apr. 13, pp. 498–9.
10. Cf. *Documents, 1968–69,* p. 436.
11. Same as note 4.
12. Same.
13. *Documents, 1968–69,* pp. 429–38.
14. *New York Times,* Feb. 7. Cf. *Documents, 1970,* No. 67.
15. *New York Times,* Oct. 22.
16. *Documents, 1968–69,* pp. 399–405.
17. Same, *1970,* No. 67(a).
18. Same, No. 68.
19. *Weekly Compilation,* Jan. 4, 1971, p. 10.
20. *New York Times,* Apr. 11.

21. Same, Nov. 1.
22. Same, Oct. 30.
23. *Bulletin,* June 29, pp. 796–9.
24. Same as note 4.
25. For background, see George W. Grayson, Jr., "Peru's Military Populism," *Current History,* Feb. 1971, pp. 71–7, 116.
26. *New York Times,* June 15.
27. Same, July 29.
28. Grayson (cited), p. 72.
29. Same as note 4.
30. Amendment to the Foreign Assistance Act of 1962 (P.L. 87–565, approved Aug. 1, 1962). Excerpts in *Documents, 1962,* pp. 513–15.
31. *New York Times,* Mar. 16 and May 17.
32. Details on Mrs. Nixon's visit, June 25–30, in *Weekly Compilation,* July 6, pp. 860–1.
33. Cf. Thomas G. Sanders, "Allende's First Months," v. xviii, no. 2 (American Universities Field Staff, 1971).
34. *New York Times,* Nov. 6.
35. For background, see Alan Angell, "Chile: From Christian Democracy to Marxism?" *Current History,* Feb. 1971, pp. 84–9, 117.
36. Same.
37. *New York Times,* Nov. 13.
38. Major provisions of draft investment code summarized in *Commerce Today,* Apr. 5, 1971, pp. 53–4.
39. *Weekly Compilation,* Jan. 11, 1971, p. 37.

40. Sanders (cited), p. 8; see also *New York Times*, Nov. 14.
41. Same, July 13.
42. Cf. David Burks, "Cuba Today," *Current History*, Feb. 1971, pp. 108–11, 118.
43. Same, p. 118.
44. *Bulletin*, July 27, p. 117.
45. Text in U.S. Arms Control and Disarmament Agency, *Documents on Disarmament, 1967*, pp. 69–83.
46. Text of Additional Protocol II and related material in *Documents, 1968–69*, pp. 392–9.
47. Same, *1970*, No. 70.
48. Text of Jova statement in *Bulletin*, May 25, p. 662.
49. Same, Aug. 31, p. 270.
50. Text of resolution, June 30, in *Documents, 1970*, No. 66(b).
51. *New York Times*, July 23.
52. *Newsweek*, Mar. 16, p. 56.
53. Sanders (cited), p. 2.
54. *New York Times*, Aug. 8.
55. Same, Aug. 17.

56. *Bulletin*, May 25, p. 655.
57. Text of treaty and related material in same, Aug. 17, 206–9.
58. Cf. same, p. 206.
59. Text of State Department announcement in same, Dec. 21, pp. 765–6; background in same, Sept. 14, pp. 296–300.
60. Same, Dec. 14, p. 717. See also Nixon-Díaz communiqué, Aug. 21, in *Documents, 1970*, No. 71.
61. *New York Times*, Apr. 5.
62. Same, Mar. 21.
63. Same, June 1.
64. Cf. Sec. 23.
65. Text of Nixon announcement in *Weekly Compilation*, Mar. 16, pp. 347–8; for Canadian reaction, see *New York Times*, Mar. 11.
66. Same, June 25.
67. Cf. *Documents, 1970*, No. 72.
68. Text of joint communiqué in *Bulletin*, Dec. 14, pp. 730–2.
69. Same, p. 730.

8. Africa: The Second Decade

1. Cf. *Swiss Review of World Affairs*, Dec., pp. 14–15.
2. *New York Times*, Dec. 17. For background, cf. Taye Geremaw, "Rebellion in Eritrea—Who Is Behind It? What Are Its Aims?" *New Middle East*, Apr. 1971, pp. 24–8.
3. *New York Times*, May 17.
4. Same, Jan. 16; cf. Richardson statement in *Documents, 1970*, No. 57.
5. Same, Jan. 14 and Jan. 15; cf. Newsom statement in *Documents, 1970*, No. 58.
6. Cf. *U.N. Chronicle*, Feb., pp. 19–20. For details on Thant's trip to West Africa, see same, pp. 16–19.
7. *New York Times*, Oct. 2.

8. Same, Oct. 11.
9. Same, Sept. 2.
10. *Documents, 1970*, No. 61; details in *U.N. Chronicle*, Aug.–Sept., pp. 3–27; further, *Bulletin*, Aug. 17, pp. 203–205.
11. *New York Times*, Sept. 30.
12. Same, Oct. 17.
13. Same, Nov. 6.
14. See especially J. E. Spence, *The Strategic Significance of Southern Africa* (London: Royal United Service Institution, 1970).
15. *New York Times*, Oct. 13.
16. Cf. Christian P. Potholm, "The Future of Africa South," *Current History*, March 1971, p. 147.
17. *Documents, 1970*, No. 64; details in *U.N. Chronicle*, Dec., pp. 11–16.

18. U.N. document S/1009 and Add. 1.
19. Text in *Documents, 1970,* No. 65; details in *U.N. Chronicle,* Jan. 1971, pp. 3–19; further, *Bulletin,* Jan. 18, 1971, pp. 98–101.
20. *New York Times,* Dec. 12.
21. Same, Mar. 2.
22. Rogers statement, released Mar. 9, in *Bulletin,* Mar. 30, p. 412.
23. U.N. document S/9696/Corr. 1 and 2; details in *U.N. Chronicle,* Apr., pp. 3–35; further, *Bulletin,* Apr. 13, pp. 501–10.
24. *Documents, 1970,* No. 59.
25. Same, No. 60.
26. Same, No. 2; complete text in *U.S. Foreign Policy for the 1970's.*
27. Statement of Feb. 7 in *Bulletin,* Mar. 23, p. 365.
28. Statement of Feb. 11 in same, p. 370.
29. Statement, Feb. 18, in same, p. 376.
30. *Documents, 1970,* No. 55.
31. *Bulletin,* June 8, p. 718.

32. *Documents, 1970,* No. 62; details in *U.N. Chronicle,* Aug.–Sept., pp. 27–39; further, *Bulletin,* Sept. 7, pp. 284–6.
33. *Documents, 1970,* No. 63; details in *U.N. Chronicle,* Aug.–Sept., pp. 27–39; further, *Bulletin,* Sept. 7, pp. 284–6.
34. U.N. document S/RES/276, adopted Jan. 30 by a vote of 13 (U.S.) to 0, with 2 abstentions; details in *U.N. Chronicle,* Feb., pp. 3–13; further, *Bulletin,* Mar. 16, pp. 359–61.
35. Cf. George F. Kennan, "Hazardous Courses in Southern Africa," *Foreign Affairs,* Jan. 1971, pp. 218–36.
36. Waldemar A. Nielsen, *The Great Powers and Africa* (New York: Praeger for the Council on Foreign Relations, 1970).
37. The project was officially inaugurated Oct. 26; see *New York Times,* Oct. 27.
38. Same, May 31.
39. Same, July 22.

9. Western Europe: A Rebirth of Diplomacy

1. *Documents, 1970,* No. 2; complete text in *U.S. Foreign Policy for the 1970's.*
2. *New York Times,* Jan. 22.
3. *Documents, 1970,* Nos. 38, 45.
4. Sec. 5.
5. *Documents, 1970,* No. 23.
6. Same, Nos. 9–11.
7. *New York Times,* May 26.
8. Same, June 8.
9. Same, June 9; see also Arrigo Levi, "Italy: The Crisis of Governing," *Foreign Affairs,* Oct., pp. 147–60.
10. *New York Times,* Oct. 10.
11. Zbigniew Brzezinski, "America and Europe," *Foreign Affairs,* Oct., p. 19.
12. Secs. 8, 15.

13. *Weekly Compilation,* Oct. 5, p. 1292.
14. *Documents, 1970,* No. 21.
15. Complete documentation on Nixon visit to Spain in *Weekly Compilation,* Oct. 12, pp. 1328–30 and 1359.
16. Cf. *Bulletin,* Apr. 6, p. 446.
17. Same, May 4, p. 578.
18. Rogers remarks, May 28, and text of joint U.S.-Spanish communiqué, May 29, in same, June 22, pp. 776–7.
19. *Documents, 1970,* Nos. 24(a) and 24(c); complete documentation in *Bulletin,* Aug. 31, pp. 237–43.
20. *New York Times,* May 30.
21. Cf. statement in *Congressional*

336 NOTES

Record (Daily Edition), July 31.
22. U.S. Senate, Committee on Foreign Relations, 91st Cong., 2nd sess., *Hearings on the Spanish Base Agreement, August 26* (Washington: G.P.O., 1970), p. 20.
23. Same, p. 55.
24. Same, p. 14.
25. Same, pp. 31 and 37.
26. *New York Times,* June 21.
27. Same, Apr. 16.
28. Same, Apr. 11.
29. Same, Apr. 17.
30. *Documents, 1970,* No. 25.
31. *New York Times,* Oct. 3.
32. *Bulletin,* June 22, p. 777; see also *New York Times,* May 31.
33. Same, Dec. 3.
34. Same, Oct. 9.
35. *Weekly Compilation,* Mar. 2; related material in same, pp. 263–4, 269–70 and 276–8.
36. Same, Mar. 9, p. 303.
37. *New York Times,* Jan. 28.
38. Same, Feb. 16.
39. Same, Feb. 11.
40. Notes 35–36. Text of address, Feb. 25, in *Bulletin,* Mar. 30, pp. 415–17.
41. *New York Times,* Jan. 3.
42. Same, Mar. 5.
43. Same, Mar. 6.
44. Sec. 31.
45. *New York Times,* Oct. 28.
46. For background, see *Britain and the European Communities* (London: Central Office of Information, Feb. 1971).
47. *New York Times,* Feb. 9.
48. Same, Mar. 7.
49. Same, Dec. 16.
50. Same, June 6 and June 10.
51. Same, Feb. 11.
52. Same, Oct. 1.
53. Text in Great Britain, Foreign Office, *Miscellaneous No. 12 (1970): The United Kingdom and the European Communities, June 30, 1970* (Cmnd. 4401;

London: H.M.S.O., 1970).
54. *New York Times,* Feb. 14.
55. Same, Oct. 7.
56. Sec. 34 at note 46.
57. Cf. Fred Luchsinger, "Disenchanted *Ostpolitik,*" *Swiss Review of World Affairs,* July 1971, pp. 2–3.
58. *New York Times,* June 17.
59. Same.
60. Sec. 5.
61. *New York Times,* Aug. 13.
62. *Documents, 1970,* No. 23.
63. *New York Times,* Dec. 8.
64. For a general review of the 4-power Berlin negotiations cf. same, Sept. 24, 1971.
65. Sec. 9.
66. Same as note 1.
67. Documentation on Brandt's U.S. visit in *Weekly Compilation,* Apr. 13, pp. 507–10.
68. *Bulletin,* May 4, p. 566.
69. *Documents, 1970,* No. 22 (c).
70. Same, No. 22 (a).
71. *Bulletin,* May 18, pp. 633–4.
72. *Documents, 1967,* pp. 110–14.
73. Cf. *NATO Letter,* Dec., pp. 4–5.
74. *Documents, 1968–69,* pp. 166–73.
75. *New York Times,* May 27.
76. Cf. *Bulletin,* June 22, p. 776.
77. *Documents, 1970,* No. 19 (b).
78. Same, No. 19 (a).
79. *New York Times,* Feb. 4.
80. Text of final communiqué in *NATO Letter,* July–Aug., p. 20.
81. Cf. *New York Times,* Oct. 8.
82. Same, Oct. 1 and Oct. 8.
83. *Documents, 1970,* No. 21 (b).
84. *New York Times,* Dec. 3.
85. *Bulletin,* Jan. 4, 1971, p. 7.
86. Same, p. 2.
87. S. Res. 300, 89th Cong., 2nd sess., Aug. 31, 1966. Background in *The United States in World Affairs, 1966,* pp. 175, 176; same, *1967,* 198–9.
88. *New York Times,* Apr. 21.
89. Same as note 1.

10. Dollars, Trade, and Aid

1. Nixon message on economic report for 1970 in *Documents, 1970*, No. 88; complete text in *Weekly Compilation*, Feb. 9, pp. 119–23. Cf. also Nixon budget message, Feb. 2, in same, pp. 106–19.
2. Cf. *The United States in World Affairs, 1966*, pp. 12–16.
3. *Weekly Compilation*, Feb. 9, p. 108.
4. Report by the Secretary-General of the O.E.C.D., *Inflation: The Present Problem*, Dec., p. 7.
5. *New York Times*, Feb. 1.
6. Same, June 22.
7. *Weekly Compilation*, July 27, p. 969.
8. *Annual Report of the Council of Economic Advisers*, transmitted to the President Jan. 30 (Washington: G.P.O., 1970), p. 26.
9. *New York Times*, Jan. 4.
10. Same, May 19.
11. Same, May 27.
12. Same, June 11.
13. *Weekly Compilation*, June 22, p. 777.
14. Cf. same, Aug. 10, pp. 1031–2; same, Dec. 7, p. 1630.
15. Same, Dec. 21, p. 1687.
16. *Documents, 1970*, No. 2; complete text in *U.S. Foreign Policy for the 1970's.*
17. Same as note 16.
18. Cf. *Documents, 1968–69*, pp. 509–15.
19. Same as note 16.
20. International Monetary Fund, *Annual Report of the Executive Directors for the Fiscal Year Ended April 30, 1970* (Washington: I.M.F., 1970), pp. 177–84.
21. Same, *April 30, 1971*, pp. 42–3 and 157.
22. International Monetary Fund, *The Role of Exchange Rates in the Adjustment of International Payments: A Report by the Executive Directors* (Sept. 1970).
23. Cf. Statement by Secretary of the Treasury Kennedy, Sept. 22, in *Documents, 1970*, No. 89; complete text in *Bulletin*, Oct. 12, pp. 431–5.
24. Cf. "Daylight Ahead for U.S. Balance of Payments," *International Economic Letter* (First National City Bank, Jan. 1971), p. 6.
25. *New York Times*, Sept. 22.
26. *Economic Report of the President, Transmitted to the Congress February 1971, Together with the Annual Report of the Council of Economic Advisers* (Washington: G.P.O., 1971), p. 151.
27. *Commerce Today*, Feb. 22, 1971, pp. 10–14.
28. Same, Jan. 12, pp. 6–7.
29. Cf. *Documents, 1970*, No. 92.
30. Cf. *New York Times*, Nov. 5.
31. Same, Oct. 10.
32. *Documents, 1968–69*, pp. 522–30.
33. *New York Times*, Jan. 23.
34. Same, Feb. 3.
35. Same, Feb. 19.
36. Same, Apr. 14.
37. Same, July 2.
38. Same, July 15.
39. *Commerce Today*, Nov. 2, pp. 40–1.
40. *Documents, 1970*, No. 92.
41. *New York Times*, July 15.
42. Same, June 19.
43. Cf. Tom Wicker in same, Nov. 17.
44. Joint U.S.-Japanese statement, June 24, in *Documents, 1970*, No. 53. For Nixon announcement on aid to shoe industry, see *Weekly Compilation*, June 29, pp. 811–13.
45. *New York Times*, Oct. 13. For Rogers statement before the Senate Finance Committee, Oct. 12,

see *Bulletin*, Nov. 2, pp. 556–7.
46. *New York Times*, Oct. 13.
47. *Documents, 1970*, No. 90.
48. *New York Times*, Feb. 22.
49. Same as note 43.
50. Cf. *The United States in World Affairs, 1961*, pp. 358, 377.
51. *Documents, 1970*, No. 78; complete text in *U.N. Chronicle*, Nov., pp. 105–20; details in *Bulletin*, Nov. 16, pp. 607–22.
52. *World Economic Survey, 1969–70* (U.N. Publication, Sales No.: E.71.II.C.1; New York, 1971), pp. 11–12.
53. Same, p. 34.
54. *The OECD Observer*, Aug. 1971, pp. 10–11.
55. *Weekly Compilation*, Feb. 9, p. 114.
56. *New York Times*, June 2.
57. Same, Apr. 11.
58. P.L. 91–599, approved Dec. 30. For Nixon signature statement,

Dec. 31, see *Weekly Compilation*, Jan. 4, 1971, p. 10.
59. *Documents, 1970*, No. 99.
60. P.L. 91–652, approved Jan. 5, 1971. For Nixon signature statement, Jan. 6, see *Weekly Compilation*, Jan. 11, 1971, p. 45.
61. Excerpts in *New York Times*, Sept. 29.
62. *Bulletin*, Nov. 30, p. 676.
63. *Documents, 1970*, No. 77.
64. Same as note 51.
65. *Documents, 1970*, No. 93.
66. *New York Times*, Oct. 13 and Oct. 19.
67. *Documents, 1970*, No. 95; complete text in *Bulletin*, Apr. 6, pp. 447–67.
68. *New York Times*, Mar. 8.
69. Same as note 67.
70. *Documents, 1970*, No. 97.
71. *New York Times*, Mar. 10.
72. Same as note 70.

11. The World Takes Stock

1. *U.N. Chronicle*, Oct., p. ii.
2. Same, July 1969, p. ii.
3. Same, Nov., 82–3.
4. *New York Times*, May 26.
5. Same, Feb. 8.
6. Same, Oct. 22.
7. *Documents, 1970*, No. 59; see also Secs. 31, 32.
8. Same, No. 2; complete text in *U.S. Foreign Policy for the 1970's*.
9. *Documents, 1970*, No. 75.
10. Same, *1968–69*, pp. 466–76.
11. Same, *1970*, No. 63; Sec. 31.
12. R.G.A. Jackson, *A Study of the Capacity of the United Nations Development System* (U.N. Publication DP/5) (2 vols., Geneva, 1969). Cf. Markus Timmler, "Pearson-Bericht und Jackson-Studie für D D 2," *Aussenpolitik*, Apr., pp. 225–37.

13. *Bulletin*, Aug. 10, p. 181.
14. Same, Oct. 5, pp. 390–3.
15. S. Res. 192, 78th Cong., 1st sess., Nov. 5, 1943; text and related material in *Documents, 1943–1944*, pp. 316–23.
16. *Bulletin*, Mar. 30, p. 433.
17. Same as note 9.
18. *Bulletin*, Jan. 18, 1971, p. 89.
19. Same, p. 91.
20. General Assembly Resolution 2670 (XXV); details in *U.N. Chronicle*, Dec., pp. 52–5; same, Jan. 1971, p. 42; further, *Bulletin*, Jan. 18, 1971, pp. 89–92.
21. Same as note 19.
22. Text in *Bulletin*, June 8, p. 733.
23. U.N. document, S/9824, June 5.
24. *U.N. Chronicle*, Nov., pp. 124–5.
25. *Bulletin*, Oct. 19, pp. 444–5.
26. General Assembly Resolution 2622 (XXV), adopted by accla-

mation; details in *U.N. Chronicle*, Nov., p. 126.
27. Same as note 12.
28. *Introduction to the Report of the Secretary-General on the Work of the Organization, September 1970* (U.N. General Assembly, *Official Records: Twenty-Fifth Session, Supplement No. 1A* [A/8001/Add.l]).
29. *Documents, 1970*, No. 76.
30. Sec. 39.
31. *Bulletin*, Aug. 11, p. 106.
32. For a statement on U.S. population policy, see address by Philander P. Claxton, Aug. 21, in same, Sept. 21, pp. 317–26; see also Yost statement to U.N., Sept. 30, in same, Oct. 19, pp. 442–3.
33. Cf. *Documents, 1968–69*, p. 474.
34. General Assembly Resolution 2659 (XXV); details in *U.N. Chronicle*, Jan. 1971, p. 70.
35. Economic and Social Council Resolutions 1532 (XLIX), July 24 and 1559 (XLIX), Nov. 11.
36. General Assembly Resolution 2719 (XXV); details in *U.N. Chronicle*, Jan. 1971, p. 72.
37. General Assembly Resolution 2720 (XXV); details in *U.N. Chronicle*, Jan. 1971, p. 72.
38. General Assembly Resolution 2657 (XXV), Dec. 3; details in *U.N. Chronicle*, Jan. 1971, p. 69.
39. *New York Times*, Oct. 16.
40. General Assembly Resolution 2627 (XXV); details on commemorative session in *U.N. Chronicle*, Nov., 3–123.
41. General Assembly Resolutions 2621 (XXV), Oct. 13 and 2707 (XXV), Dec. 14; details in *U.N. Chronicle*, Nov., pp. 96–8; same Jan. 1971, pp. 54–5.
42. General Assembly Resolutions 2624 (XXV), Oct. 13 and 2671 A-F (XXV), Dec. 8; details in *U.N. Chronicle*, Nov., pp. 141–4; same, Jan. 1971, pp. 42–5.

43. General Assembly Resolution 2625 (XXV), Oct. 24; details in *U.N. Chronicle*, Nov., pp. 99–105.
44. *Documents, 1970*, Nos. 77–78; details in *U.N. Chronicle*, Nov., pp. 105–20.
45. Sec. 39.
46. Same as note 45.
47. Report of C.C.D. in *Documents, 1970*, No. 7; complete text in U.N. document A/8059 (DC/233), Sept. 11. Text of Resolution 2660 (XXV) in *Documents, 1970*, No. 14; details in *U.N. Chronicle*, Dec., pp. 47–8; same, Jan. 1971, pp. 29–31; further, *Bulletin*, Dec. 28, pp. 803–7.
48. *Documents, 1968–69*, pp. 102–6.
49. Same, *1970*. No. 13.
50. Same, No. 79.
51. Same, No. 80. For discussion of the second session of the Seabeds Committee, see *U.N. Chronicle*, Aug.-Sept., pp. 40–3.
52. Resolution 2749 (XXV); details in *U.N. Chronicle*, Jan. 1971, pp. 37–8.
53. Resolution 2750 A-C (XXV); details in *U.N. Chronicle*, Jan. 1971, pp. 38–42.
54. *Documents, 1968–69*, p. 474.
55. *Bulletin*, Oct. 5, pp. 398–402.
56. Resolutions 2733 A-D (XXV); details in *U.N. Chronicle*, Jan. 1971, pp. 35–7.
57. Sec. 14.
58. *Documents, 1970*, No. 83.
59. S/RES/286 (1970); details in *U.N. Chronicle*, Oct., pp. 7–8; further, *Bulletin*, Sept. 28, 342–3
60. Same, Oct. 19, pp. 449–53.
61. Same, p. 453.
62. *Documents, 1970*, No. 84.
63. Same, No. 85.
64. *Bulletin*, Jan. 11, 1971, pp. 53–5.
65. *Documents, 1970*, No. 73.
66. Details in *U.N. Chronicle*, Aug.-Sept., pp. 109–38; Nixon statement in *Bulletin*, Oct. 5, p. 393.

Index

Abrams, Creighton W., 133
Acheson, Dean, 33, 87, 247
Africa, 208–222; *apartheid,* 213–16, 220–21, 286; Chinese presence in, 221; and EEC, 238; pan-Africanism, 212; Soviet presence in, 221; U.S. policy toward, 218–22; "White" strongholds, 212–18; *see also* East African Community; South Africa; individual country entries
African Development Bank, 220
African Party for the Independence of Guinea and Cape Verde, 217
Afro-Malagasy Joint Organization (OCAM), 212, 213
Agency for International Development (AID), 37, 268; and Latin America, 185, 189; scrapping of (proposed), 272, 273, 274; *see also* Foreign aid
Agnew, Spiro T., 19–20; Asian tours, 144, 165, 168–69; on Nixon Doctrine, 168
Agriculture, 178, 264
Ahomadegbe, Justin, 210
Airborne Warning Control System (AWACS), 79
Air piracy, *see* Hijackings

Akuko-Addo, Edward, 209
Albania, 60
Allessandri Rodríguez, Jorge, 195
Allende Gossens, Salvador, 23, 47, 183, 194–97 *passim*
Algeria, 222
Allen, Ward P., 290
Alliance for Progress, 28, 183, 195; Inter-American Committee for (CIAP), 186, 187
Almeyda, Clodomiro, 195
Amalrik, Andrei, 52
American Civil Liberties Union (ACLU), 82
American Selling Price (A.S.P.), 261, 262, 264
American Smelting and Refining, 192
Andean Group, 197
Angola, 212, 213, 217
Anti-ballistic missiles (A.B.M.), 70–82 *passim*
ANZUS, 169
Apartheid, 213–16, 220–21, 286
Apithy, Sourou-Migan, 210
Arafat, Yasir, 106, 111, 113
Aramburu, Pedro Eugenio, 24, 200
Arana Osorio, Carlos, 201

341

International Security Assistance Program, 273
International Volunteer Service Corps (proposed), 285
Iran, 115–19 *passim*, 285
Iraq, 108, 111, 117–18, 119
Ireland, 236, 237, 238
al-Iryani, Abdul Rahman, 119
Israel, and E.E.C., 238; and France, 234; and nonproliferation treaty, 69; on Rogers cease-fire plan, 95–96, 98, 102; Soviet support for, 84; U.S. military aid to, 90–91, 94, 103, 104, 269; U.S. policy toward, 86–88; *see also* Middle East
Italy, 43, 224, 226–28; recognition of China, 162
Ivory Coast, 210, 211, 212, 213

Jackson, Robert, 279, 282
Jamaica, 203
Japan, 28, 30, 43, 167, 171–77; aid programs, 174, 266; balance-of-payments position, 176; and China, 174; economic strength, 172–73, 174; "Expo '70," 172; defense policies, 173–74, 175; and Middle East oil, 83, 86; Nixon-Sato agreement, 171–72; and nonproliferation treaty, 69, 173; Okinawa issue, 171–72; Self-Defense Force, 173; trade policies, 175–77, 261, 263, 264; and U.S.S.R., 161; U.S.-Japanese Security Treaty, 172, 174
Jaroszewicz, Piotr, 58
Jarring, Gunnar V., 21, 88, 89
Jarring mission, 95, 100, 101–102, 103–104
Javits, Jacob K., 33, 269–70
Jewish Defense League, 49
Johnson, Lyndon B., 21, 34; and China, 158; and Eastern Europe, 63; and nonproliferation treaty, 69; and SALT talks, 69
Johnson, U. Alexis, 174–75, 231

Jonathan, Leabua, 209
Jordan, 92; anti-Americanism, 94; Army, 105, 107, 111; civil war, 105, 107, 109–13; Palestinian commandos, *see* Palestinian commandos; and Rogers cease-fire plan, 97–98, 100; U.S. aid to, 112, 269
Jova, Joseph J., 199

Kádár, János, 59
Kahn, Herman, 172
Kansas State University, 19
Karami, Rashid, 113
Kaunda, Kenneth, 212–13
Kennedy, David M., 188, 254
Kennedy, Edward M., 80, 154
Kennedy, John F., 13, 14
Kennedy, Robert F., 14
Kennedy Round, 260; *see also* GATT
Kent State University, 18, 20, 65, 136
Kenya, 209
Khan, Ayub, 179
Khan, Yahya, 179
al-Khatib, Ahmed, 113
Khrushchev, Nikita S., 25
Kim Il Sung, 161
King, Martin Luther, Jr., 14
Kissinger, Henry A., 25–26, 36, 38; and Cambodia, 134; on foreign policy, 66; and "strategic parity," 74, 79; on Vietnam, 121
Kittikachorn, Thanom, 169
Korea, Democratic People's Republic, 161, 170
Korea, Republic of, 33, 35, 158, 166, 267; economic growth, 169–70; North Korean attacks on, 170; and Okinawa, 172; U.S. military aid to, 269; U.S. troop reductions, 167–69
Korry, Edward M., 272
Kosygin, Aleksei N., 45, 53, 244; on Laos, 147, 148; on Middle East conflict, 90; on Nasser's death, 114; on Nixon's foreign policy, 67; and

U.N. Fund for Population Activities, 284

U.N. Peace-keeping Force in Cyprus (UNFICYP), 116, 283

U.N. Relief and Works Agency (UNRWA), 105

U.N. Special Committee on Peace-keeping Operations, 281–82

U.N. Truce Supervision Organization, 100

United Nations Volunteers, 285

U.N. World Youth Assembly, 293–94

United States, Army surveillance, 82; antiballistic missiles, 73–74; balance-of-payments position, 255, 256–57, 258–59, 264–65; campus unrest, 18–19; census (1970), 13; Congress, *see above;* Council of Economic Advisors, 253, 254; Defense Department, 73–78, 79–82; Defense Appropriations Act, 80; defense spending, 29–30, 78, 79–82; dollar, role of, 255–60; economic problems, 23, 252–55; Federal Reserve Board, 254; Food for Peace program, 268; foreign aid, *see* Foreign aid, Congress and foreign aid; foreign policy decision-making, 35, 36–38; inflation, 252–55, 258, 265; "low profile" of, 24–39, *see also* Nixon Doctrine; missile build-up, 73–78; mood of, 14–16; Mutual Security Program, 266; National Security Council (N.S.C.), 36, 37, 134; Peace Corps, 180, 197, 268; People-to-People program, 197; polarization of, 16–21; Presidential Task Force on International Development, 272–73; President's Commission on an All Volunteer Armed Force, 81–82; President's Commission on Campus Unrest, 18, 19; press, 151; revolutionary movements, 14, 16–17, *see also* Terrorism; State Department reform proposals, 37–38; Sixth Fleet, 41, 78, 110; unemployment, 252, 253, 265; and U.S.S.R.,

United States (*cont.*)
see U.S.-Soviet relations, *below;* wage-price controls, 254, 265; Washington Special Action Group (WASG), 36, 134

U.S. Arms Control and Disarmament Agency (ACDA), 71

U.S. International Development Bank (proposed), 272

U.S. International Development Corporation (proposed), 273

U.S. International Development Council (proposed), 272

U.S. International Development Institute (proposed), 272

U.S.-Japanese Security Treaty (1960), 172, 174

U.S. Tariff Commission, 260, 263

U.S.-Soviet relations, 26, 30–31, 48, 49, 65–67; Brezhnev on, 41–42, 48; cultural exchange agreement, 22; deterioration in, 47–49, 50; and "hot line," 69; Kennedy-Khrushchev agreement on strategic weapons (1962), 48; "linkage theory," 65; and Middle East, 88, 90, 93–101 *passim;* and missile build-up, 73–78; mutual force reductions, 44, 45; Nixon on, 38–39

Uruguay, "Tupamaros," 23, 24, 191, 200

Velasco Alvarado, Juan, 191–94 *passim*

Velasco Ibarra, José María, 202

Venezuela, 190, 200

Vietnam, Democratic Republic of, 125–26; Soviet aid to, 126, 142

Vietnam, Republic of, 122–27, 152, 153; anti-Americanism in, 154; and Cambodia, 139, 140, 142; C.O.S.V.N., 128, 137; Provisional Revolutionary Government (P.R.G.), 126

Vietnam War, 14, 19, 153–56; and

COUNCIL ON FOREIGN RELATIONS

Recent Publications

FOREIGN AFFAIRS (quarterly), edited by Hamilton Fish Armstrong.

THE UNITED STATES IN WORLD AFFAIRS (annual), by Richard P. Stebbins.

THE CARIBBEAN COMMUNITY by Robert D. Crassweller (1972).

INDIA, PAKISTAN AND THE GREAT POWERS, by William J. Barnds (1972).

DOCUMENTS ON AMERICAN FOREIGN RELATIONS (annual), by Richard P. Stebbins and Elaine P. Adam.

CONGRESS, THE EXECUTIVE, AND FOREIGN POLICY by Francis O. Wilcox (1971).

THE REALITY OF FOREIGN AID, by Willard L. Thorp (1971).

POLITICAL HANDBOOK AND ATLAS OF THE WORLD, 1970, edited by Richard P. Stebbins and Alba Amoia (1970).

JAPAN IN POSTWAR ASIA, by Lawrence Olson (1970).

THE CRISIS OF DEVELOPMENT, by Lester B. Pearson (1970).

THE GREAT POWERS AND AFRICA, by Waldemar A. Nielsen (1969).

A NEW FOREIGN POLICY FOR THE UNITED STATES, by Hans J. Morgenthau (1969).

MIDDLE EAST POLITICS: THE MILITARY DIMENSION, by J. C. Hurewitz (1969).

THE ECONOMICS OF INTERDEPENDENCE: Economic Policy in the Atlantic Community, by Richard N. Cooper (1968).

HOW NATIONS BEHAVE: Law and Foreign Policy, by Louis Henkin (1968).

THE INSECURITY OF NATIONS, by Charles W. Yost (1968).

PROSPECTS FOR SOVIET SOCIETY, edited by Allen Kassof (1968).

THE AMERICAN APPROACH TO THE ARAB WORLD, by John S. Badeau (1968).

U.S. POLICY AND THE SECURITY OF ASIA, by Fred Greene (1968).

NEGOTIATING WITH THE CHINESE COMMUNISTS: The U.S. Experience, by Kennetn T. Young (1968).

FROM ATLANTIC TO PACIFIC: A New Interocean Canal, by Immanuel J. Klette (1967).

TITO'S SEPARATE ROAD: America and Yugoslavia in World Politics, by John C. Campbell (1967).

U.S. TRADE POLICY: New Legislation for the Next Round, by John W. Evans (1967).

TRADE LIBERALIZATION AMONG INDUSTRIAL COUNTRIES: Objectives and Alternatives, by Bela Balassa (1967).

THE CHINESE PEOPLE'S LIBERATION ARMY, by Brig. General Samuel B. Griffith II U.S.M.C. (ret.) (1967).

THE ARTILLERY OF THE PRESS: Its Influence on American Foreign Policy, by James Reston (1967).

TRADE, AID AND DEVELOPMENT: The Rich and Poor Nations, by John Pincus (1967).

BETWEEN TWO WORLDS: Policy, Press and Public Opinion on Asian-American Relations, by John Hohenberg (1967).

THE CONFLICTED RELATIONSHIP: The West and the Transformation of Asia, Africa and Latin America, by Theodore Geiger (1966).

THE ATLANTIC IDEA AND ITS EUROPEAN RIVALS, by H. van B. Cleveland (1966).

EUROPEAN UNIFICATION IN THE SIXTIES: From the Veto to the Crisis, by Miriam Camps (1966).

THE UNITED STATES AND CHINA IN WORLD AFFAIRS, by Robert Blum, edited by A. Doak Barnett (1966).

THE FUTURE OF THE OVERSEAS CHINESE IN SOUTHEAST ASIA, by Lea A. Williams (1966).

ATLANTIC AGRICULTURAL UNITY: Is it Possible?, by John O. Coppock (1966).

TEST BAN AND DISARMAMENT: The Path of Negotiation, by Arthur H. Dean (1966).

COMMUNIST CHINA'S ECONOMIC GROWTH AND FOREIGN TRADE, by Alexander Eckstein (1966).

POLICIES TOWARD CHINA: Views from Six Continents, edited by A. M. Halpern (1966).

THE AMERICAN PEOPLE AND CHINA, by A. T. Steele (1966).

INTERNATIONAL POLITICAL COMMUNICATION, by W. Phillips Davison (1965).

ALTERNATIVE TO PARTITION: For a Broader Conception of America's Role in Europe, by Zbigniew Brzezinski (1965).

THE TROUBLED PARTNERSHIP: A Re-Appraisal of the Atlantic Alliance, by Henry A. Kissinger (1965).